Women and Management

Women and Management

GLOBAL ISSUES AND PROMISING SOLUTIONS

VOLUME 2: SIGNS OF SOLUTIONS

Michele A. Paludi, Editor

Women and Careers in Management
Michele A. Paludi, Series Editor

 PRAEGER

AN IMPRINT OF ABC-CLIO, LLC
Santa Barbara, California • Denver, Colorado • Oxford, England

Copyright 2013 by ABC-CLIO, LLC

Library of Congress Cataloging-in-Publication Data

Women and management : global issues and promising solutions /
Michele A. Paludi, editor.

    v. cm. — (Women and careers in management)

    Includes index.

    Contents: v. 1. Degrees of challenge — v. 2. Signs of solutions.

    ISBN 978-0-313-39941-1 (hbk. : alk. paper) — ISBN 978-0-313-39942-8 (ebook)

1. Women executives.   2. Leadership in women.   3. Management.

I. Paludi, Michele Antoinette.

    HD6054.3.W6346   2013

    658.0082—dc23   2012029053

ISBN: 978-0-313-39941-1
EISBN: 978-0-313-39942-8

17   16   15   14   2   3   4   5

This book is also available on the World Wide Web as an eBook.
Visit www.abc-clio.com for details.

Praeger
An Imprint of ABC-CLIO, LLC

ABC-CLIO, LLC
130 Cremona Drive, P.O. Box 1911
Santa Barbara, California 93116-1911

This book is printed on acid-free paper ∞

Manufactured in the United States of America

The greatest gift we can give to our children is to raise them in a culture of peace.
Louise Diamond

I dedicate "Women and Management: Global Issues and Promising Solutions" to
Andrea Nguyen
and
Andrew Nguyen
For giving me hope for a culture of peace
And to their parents,
Huy Quang and Tram Anh Nguyen
For giving me the opportunity to have their children in my life.

Contents

Series Foreword

Michele A. Paludi, Series Editor

> *Ma muaka kite a muri*
> *Ma muri ka ora a mua*
> *(Those who lead give sight to those who follow,*
> *Those who follow give life to those who lead)*
>
> —Pauline Tangiora

Welcome to the Women and Careers in Management Series at Praeger. This series examines the status of women in management and leadership and offers discussions of issues which women managers and leaders face, including:

Differences in leadership styles

Traditional gender roles reinforcing women's subordinate status in the workplace

Obstacles to advancement and pay

Benefit and resource inequity

Discrimination and harassment

Work–life imbalance

This series acknowledges that gender is one of the fundamental factors influencing the ethics, values, and policies of workplaces and that the discrimination against women managers and leaders explains the pervasiveness of institutionalized inequality. This series also discusses interconnections among equality issues: sex, race, class, age, sexual orientation, religion, and disability. Thus, this series brings together a multidisciplinary and multicultural discussion of women, management, and leadership.

Women and Careers in Management encourages all of us to think critically about women managers and leaders, to place value on cultural experiences and integrate empirical research and theoretical formulations with experiences of our family, friends, colleagues, and ourselves. It is my hope that the books in this series will serve as a "life raft" (Klonis, Endo, Crosby, & Worrell, 1997), especially for the millennial and subsequent generations.

I am honored to have *Women and Management: Global Issues and Promising Solutions* published in the Women and Careers in Management Series. These volumes share Pauline Tangiora's sentiment:

> Those who lead give sight to those who follow,
> Those who follow give life to those who lead.

The contributors to these volumes have addressed important issues women managers and leaders face: glass ceilings, sex discrimination, pay inequity, men's perceptions of women leaders, sexual harassment, and gender mainstreaming. An overview of biases toward women leaders in several countries is also offered: Turkey, Puerto Rico, Australia, Japan, Great Britain, Israel, Czech Republic, Dominican Republic, India, Nepal, Korea, Sri Lanka, and Indonesia.

These issues addressed in these volumes are those that many women managers and leaders face, supporting Hanisch's (1969) conclusion: "the personal is political." The personal problems faced by women managers and leaders throughout the world today are political problems, the result of systematic oppression. I hope readers of these volumes will see the information contained in them as a continuing catalyst for individual, organizational, and societal change.

References

Hanisch, C. (1969). The personal is political. In K. Sarachild (Ed.), *Feminist revolution: Redstockings of the women's liberation movement* (pp. 24–25). New York: Random House.

Klonis, S., Endo, J., Crosby, F., & Worrell, J. (1997). Feminism as life raft. *Psychology of Women Quarterly, 21,* 333–345.

Acknowledgments

Fill your paper with the breathings of your heart.

—William Wordsworth

My work on this two-volume set was accomplished during the 2011–2012 academic year, when I was the Elihu Root Peace Fund Visiting Professor of Women's Studies at Hamilton College. I would like to acknowledge students who participated in my course, "Gender, Violence, Power and Culture," at Hamilton College in fall 2011. You have all increased my understanding of the issues and make me want to work harder for educational equity and students' safety: Stephanie Lang, Anthony Mathieu, Marta Pisera, Leah Sorenson, and Lindsay Shankman.

I would also like to thank especially students in my "Psychology of Women" course at Hamilton College during fall 2001. You have increased my understanding of what research needs to be conducted in order to make psychology truly the scientific study of *all* people: Cynthia Batista, Hailey Bobin, Foxfire Buck, Megan Calabrese, Sarah Dempsey, Sarah Dreyer-Oren, Emily Evans, Jennifer Kim, Thea Moore, Kerry Nieman, Sarah Ohanesian, Olusade Oyalowo, Krisen Pallen, Lucas Sadoff, Ashley Sutton, Morolake Thompson, Melissa Zorilla, Elizabeth Chapin, Woodger Faugas, Kimberly Goidell, Mahima Karki, Eva Kramer, Lindsey Luker, Jonice Mendoza, and Elizabeth Siff.

I wish to acknowledge my colleagues at Hamilton who have greatly influenced my thinking about feminism, women's studies programs, and women's lives and realities:

Joan Stewart

Amy Gowans

Shelley Haley

Meredith Bonham

Barbara Gold

Carl Rubino

Amit Taneja

Esther Kanipe

Marianne Janack

Nancy Thompson

Steven Orvis

Francis Manfredo

Angel Nieves

I also thank my sisters, Rosalie Paludi and Lucille Paludi, for their support of my writing and editing this set.

Friends and family also deserve my appreciation: Florence L. Denmark, Steven Earle, Brad Fowler, Tony Deliberti, and Tony LoFrumento. Thank you for reading earlier drafts of my writing.

I also acknowledge Brian Romer and his colleagues at Praeger for always supporting my ideas, offering sage advice, and understanding my love of writing and editing books. Preparing this current set reminded me of Sharon O'Brien's sentiment: "Writing became such a process of discovery that I couldn't wait to get to work in the morning: I wanted to know what I was going to say."

Introduction

Michele A. Paludi

> *We have to start looking at the world through women's eyes, how are human rights, peace and development defined from the perspective of the lives of women? It's also important to look at the world from the perspective of the lives of diverse women, because there is not a single women's view, any more than there is a single men's view.*
>
> —Charlotte Bunch

During the course of preparing this book set, the 2011 Nobel Peace Prize was awarded to Tawakkul Karman, Leymah Gbowee, and Ellen Johnson Sirleaf. Karman is a journalist and a member of Islah. She also directs Women Journalists without Chains, a human rights organization. Gbowee is the director of Women Peace and Security Network Africa. Sirleaf is president of Liberia. In announcing these awards, Thorbjorn Jagland, chair of the Nobel committee stated:

> We cannot achieve democracy and lasting peace in the world unless women obtain the same opportunities as men to influence developments at all levels of society. (cited in Cowell, Kasinof, & Nossiter, 2011, p. 2)

Secretary of State Hillary Rodham Clinton noted:

> The unflinching courage, strength and leadership of these women to build peace, advance reconciliation and defend the rights of fellow citizens in their own countries provide inspiration for women's rights and human progress everywhere. (quoted in Cowell et al., 2011, p. 4)

Karman, Gbowee, and Sirleaf join 12 women who have been awarded this prize since 1901: Baroness Bertha von Suttner, Jane Addams, Emily Green Balch, Betty Williams, Mairead Corrigan, Mother Teresa, Alva Myrdal, Aung

San Suu Kyi, Rigoberta Menchu Tum, Jody Williams, Shirin Ebadi, and Wangari Maathai. Like these laureates, Karman, Gbowee, and Sirleaf were recognized for promoting peace, democracy, and gender equality: "for their non-violent struggle for the safety of women and for women's rights to full participation in peace building work" (Nobel Peace Prize, 2011).

Aung San Suu Kyi was described as follows when accepting her prize:

> She uses deep commitment and tenacity with a vision in which the end and the means form a single unit. Its most important elements are: democracy, respect for human rights, reconciliation between groups, non-violence, and personal and collective discipline.

Leymah Gbowee was praised by the Nobel Committee for mobilizing women "across ethnic and religious dividing lines to bring an end to the long war" (in Liberia) (Cowell, et al., 2011, p. 6).

Each of the Nobel laureates experienced great adversity for their leadership work in human rights. For example, Aung San Suu Kyi was unable to attend the Nobel ceremonies as she was being held in detention by the military dictatorship in Myanmar. Women Nobel laureates also persevered in the face of adversity. Aarvik once noted:

> I have, despite all disillusionment, never, never allowed myself to feel like giving up. This is my message today; it is not worthy of a human being to give up. (Aarvik, quoted in Abrams, 1997, p. 7)

Women as Transformational Leaders

The awarding of the Nobel Peace Prize to Tawakkul Karman, Leymah Gbowee, and Ellen Johnson Sirleaf once again stimulated discussion regarding women's leadership and managerial styles. These Nobel laureates share the characteristics identified in research concerning women's leadership (Caliper, 2005): Women:

Are more persuasive than their male counterparts.

Learn from adversity and carry on with an "I'll show you" attitude.

Demonstrate an inclusive, team-building leadership style of problem solving and decision making.

Are likely to ignore rules and take risks.

In addition, Rodgers-Healey (2003) reported women defined leadership in terms of listening, empowering others, being collaborative, facilitating change, mentoring others, and being effective communicators. In addition, most of the women indicated that encouragement, equality, and the presence of role models are necessary in order to achieve their visions of being good leaders.

Chin (2008, p. 714) also noted that feminist women leaders' objectives include empowering others in the following ways: Creating the vision, social advocacy and change, stewardship of an organization's resources, changing organizational cultures to create gender-equitable environments, and promoting feminist policies and agendas.

Eagly, Johannesen-Schmidt, and van Engen (2003), Fine (2007), and Paludi and Coates (2011) noted that for women, an effective managerial and leadership style is *transformational*, a style that incorporates empowerment, ethics, inclusiveness, nurturance, encouraging innovation and social justice; characteristics associated with the 2011 Nobel laureates. Thus, transformational leadership describes leaders who "motivate subordinates to transcend their own self-interests for the good of the group or organization" (Powell, Butterfield, & Bartol, 2008, p. 159).

A transformational style is in contrast to a *transactional style,* in which leaders form exchange relationships through using rewards and punishment as incentives for employee performance (Paludi & Coates, 2011). Transactional leadership rewards competition, aggression, and an authoritarian managerial style (Eagly & Johannesen-Schmidt, 2001).

Gatekeepers to Women's Leadership

This research on a transformational leadership style would predict that women should not encounter any barriers to becoming leaders and managers; that individuals would prefer to work with transformational leaders as opposed to transactional ones. In fact, Jandeska and Kraimer (2005) noted that collective organizational cultures exist that reward more transformational leadership and managerial styles. These collectivistic cultures focus on cooperation and empowerment and are conducive to women being more satisfied with their careers and more engaged to the success of the organization (Paludi & Coates, 2011).

However, most women do not work in a collective organizational culture. Jandeska and Kraimer (2005) found that most organizations are structured by traditional and stereotypical masculine cultures that value and reward men who exhibit these stereotypical traits more so than women. Women struggle to find their place within these organizations. According to Jandeska and Kraimer (2005):

> This "code of conduct" in masculine cultures, while recognizable to males, can be completely alien to females and thus would be considered less hospitable towards women's careers. For example, an "old-boy network" excludes women from centers of influence and valuable sources of information, often trivializing or ignoring their contributions. (p. 465)

Women experience barriers, including dealing with gatekeepers, pay inequity, lack of work/life integration, sexual harassment, and discrimination (because of age, disability, religion, race, national origin), which keep them from reaching their full potential as leaders (Martin, 2011; Paludi & Coates, 2011; Paludi, Paludi, & DeSouza, 2010). In addition, Davison and Burke (2000) and Eagly and Karau (2002) noted that there is an incongruity between agentic leadership and femininity. Women may be perceived as ineffective leaders no matter what leadership style they use. When women engage in managerial or leadership behaviors (considered "counternormative"; Heilman, Wallen, Fuchs, & Tamkins, 2004), they may not be perceived similarly to men and often are evaluated more negatively than when conforming to stereotypes of women (Doyle & Paludi, 1998). Thus, as Rosener (1990) concluded, with respect to women and leadership: "When attributes or behaviors associated with women are considered negative or of little value, gender is seen as relevant. When attributes or behaviors associated with women are considered positive or valuable, gender is seen as irrelevant" (p. 170).

Pew Social and Demographic Trends (2008) reported that its survey of 2,250 adults indicated that women leaders, compared to men, are more compassionate, creative, and outgoing. In addition, individuals judged women leaders as being better than men in dealing with social issues, for example, health care and education while men leaders are better than women in dealing with crime, public safety, defense, and national security. However, only 6% of the respondents indicated that women make better political leaders than men. When asked why the United States still hasn't reached gender parity in top political position, respondents offered three major explanations: (1) Americans aren't ready for a woman in high office, (2) women are held back by men, and (3) women are discriminated against in society, and thus in politics.

Furthermore, the Global Gender Gap Index (2011) reported that of the countries studied, only 50–55% narrowed the gender gap in economic participation, health, educational attainment and political empowerment. In addition,

TABLE I

Country	Wage Differentials Between Women and Men in Member States of the European Union
Austria	67%
Belgium	79.4% for blue-collar workers
	70.1% for white-collar workers
Denmark	82%
Finland	82%
France	75.8%
Germany	75.8% for blue-collar workers
	70.4% for white-collar workers
Greece	80%
Ireland	84.5%
Italy	81.7%
Luxembourg	85%
Netherlands	77%
Portugal	76.5%
Spain	76.9%
Sweden	82%
United Kingdom	80.6%

wage differentials still exist between men and women in the Member States of the European Union (Paludi et al., 2010). For example, women's average pay as a percentage of men's is the following for some of the member states of the European Union.

Pay inequities tend to be more pronounced in Asia than Europe. In a 2008 study of eight countries in East Asia (i.e., China and the Hong Kong Special Administrative Region, Japan, the Republic of Korea, Malaysia, the Philippines, Singapore, Thailand, and Vietnam) researchers found a pronounced gender pay gap. The researchers found that women earned less than or just half of men's rates of pay in Japan, Malaysia, the Republic of Korea, and Singapore; approximately 60% in Hong Kong SAR, the Philippines, and Thailand; and about two-thirds in China and Vietnam. The level of pay inequity was found to be unrelated to the country's level of economic development, but was tied to age—specifically, the pay gap was wider between older women and their male peers (Haspels & Majurin, 2008).

As another example of discriminatory treatment of women in managerial and leadership positions, at the 66th session of the United National General

Assembly, it was recognized that women make up less than 10% of the world's leaders. Women hold presidencies or prime minister positions in the following countries: Ireland, Finland, Germany, Liberia, India, Argentina, Bangladesh, Iceland, Croatia, Lithuania, Kyrgyzstan, Costa Rica, Trinidad and Tobago, Australia, Slovakia, Brazil, Switzerland, Peru, Kosovo, and Thailand. Countries with reigning queens include United Kingdom, Denmark, Netherlands, Saint Lucia, Antigua and Barbuda, and Australia.

Catalyst published the percentage of women legislators, managers and senior officials throughout the world in 2008. Its results indicated the following:

TABLE 2

Country	Percentage of women legislators, senior officials, and managers
Philippines	53.3
Russian Federation	38.7
Thailand	23.7
Japan	9.3
Chile	23.2
Panama	48.7
Barbados	44.9
Brazil	36.1
Costa Rica	30.9
Peru	5.6
Argentina	23.2
Hungary	36.7
Poland	36.2
Czech Republic	28.3
Croatia	26.3
France	38.5
Germany	37.8
United Kingdom	34.7
Spain	32.4
Sweden	32.3
Norway	31.3
Switzerland	30.2

(Continued)

TABLE 2
(Continued)

Country	Percentage of women legislators, senior officials, and managers
Israel	26.1
Ethiopia	20.1
West Bank and Gaza Strip	9.9
Egypt	11.1
United Arab Emirates	9.9
United States	42.8
Canada	36.0
Mexico	30.7
New Zealand	40.0
Australia	36.8

As Jandeska and Kraimer (2005) noted:

> Even women in senior roles in large corporations find themselves "on the outside looking in" when it comes to information sharing and access to the inner circle, where decisions are made. . . . Women characterize such a culture as exclusionary and claim that upper management often lacks awareness of the barriers it creates to women's assimilation and advancement. (p. 465)

Women and Global Management and Leadership: To the Future

According to Chin (2008):

> We need to view leadership as contextual, value driven, diversity inclusive, and collaborative. We look to transform models of leadership—to identify diverse leadership styles across diverse groups, to embrace core values that motivate those in leadership roles, and to identify effective leadership styles for men and women to achieve the outcomes they envision for the organizations and institutions they lead. . . . Women can and should be effective leaders without needing to change their essence or adopting values that are not syntonic with their gender or culture. (pp. 713–714)

This two-volume set on women and management worldwide features scholarly research and practical applications about challenges women leaders and managers have faced in meeting their career aspirations and career goals. In Volume 1, *Degrees of Challenge,* contributors address overt and subtle biases concerning women leaders, including women facing the glass ceiling, sex discrimination, pay inequity, incivility, and microaggressions and sexual harassment. These biases and forms of discrimination are discussed in several countries, including Turkey, Israel, Great Britain, China, Czech Republic, and Nepal.

In Volume 2, *Signs of Solutions,* contributors address strategies for organizational change, including ways to overcome barriers to advancing women into leadership positions, gender mainstreaming and legal and policy analyses regarding bullying and sexual harassment. These empowering strategies are discussed from several perspectives, including ways the following countries are eliminating the gender bias in managerial and leadership positions: Australia, Puerto Rico, and Japan. We also include a discussion of women in management in the next century.

In both volumes, contributors address the intersectionalities of gender and race, national origin, and sexual orientation. We also discuss generational differences in individuals' perceptions of women leaders and managers. Lists of global organizations concerned with women managers and leaders are also provided. I also feature brief biographies of and quotations from prominent women leaders and managers.

Contributors to these volumes have noted that while change in advancing women into leadership and managerial positions has been slow to occur, change has occurred and is still progressing (Morgan, Gilrane, McCausland, & King, 2011). For example, in September 2011, Melbourne Australia's Federal Minister for the Status of Women, Kate Ellis, published a report that examined the hidden biases against women in the workplace, including women in leadership and managerial positions. According to Martin (cited in CEDA, 2011): "Hosting a combination of public and private sessions with both men and women enabled the identification of subtle hidden barriers that sit below the surface. These are not always readily available for scrutiny, but can see women excluded from leadership" (p. 1).

Michelle Bachelet, Under-Secretary-General and Executive Director of UN Women, stated:

> We are bound by a common goal—to open the way for women to participate in all decisions affecting not only their own lives, but the development of our world, at the global, regional, national and local levels. By making full use of the half of the world's intelligence—the intelligence of women—we improve our chances of finding real and lasting solutions to the challenges that confront us.

Each of the contributors to these two volumes works toward fulfilling Michelle Bachelet's goal.

References

Abrams, I. (1997). *Heroines of Peace—The Nine Nobel Women.* Retrieved from http://www.nobelprize.org/nobel_prizes/peace/articls/heroines/index.html?print=1

Caliper (2005). *Women Leaders Study: The Qualities that Distinguish Women Leaders.* Retrieved from http://www.caliperonline.com/brochures/Women LeaderWhitePaper.pdf

Chin, J. (2008). Women and leadership. In F. Denmark & M. Paludi (Eds.), *Psychology of women: A handbook of issues and theories* (pp. 701–716). Westport, CT: Praeger.

Cowell, A., Kasinof, L., & Nossiter, A. (2011). Nobel Peace Prize awarded to three activist women. *New York Times.* Retrieved from http://www.nytimes.com/2011/10/08/world/nobel-peace-prize-johnson-sirleaf-gbowee-karman.html?scp=1&sq=nobel%20peace%20prize%20awarded%20to%20three%20activist%20women&st=cse

Davison, H., & Burke, M. (2000). Sex discrimination in simulated employment contexts: A meta-analytic investigation. *Journal of Vocational Behavior, 56,* 225–248.

Doyle, J., & Paludi, M. (1998). *Sex and gender.* New York: McGraw-Hill.

Eagly, A., & Johannesen-Schmidt, M. (2001). The leadership styles of women and men. *Journal of Social Issues, 57,* 781–797.

Eagly, A., Johannesen-Schmidt, M., & van Engen, M. (2003). Transformation, transactional and laissez-faire leadership styles: A meta-analysis comparing women and men. *Psychological Bulletin, 108,* 233–256.

Eagly, A., & Karau, S. (2002). Role congruity: Theory of prejudice toward female leaders. *Psychological Review, 109,* 573–598.

Fine, M. (2007). Women, collaboration and social change: An ethics-based model of leadership. In J. Chin, B. Lott, J. Rice & J. Sanchez Hucles (Eds.), *Women and leadership: Transforming visions and diverse voices* (pp. 177–191). London: Blackwell.

Haspels, N. & Majurin, E. (2008). Work, income and gender equality in east Asia: Action guide. Bangkok: ILO.

Heilman, M., Wallen, A., Fuchs, D., & Tamkins, M. (2004). Penalties for success: Reactions to women who succeed at male gender-typed tasks. *Journal of Applied Psychology, 74,* 935–942.

Jandeska, K., & Kraimer, M. (2005). Women's perceptions of organizational culture, work attitudes, and role-modeling behaviors. *Journal of Managerial Issues, 18,* 461–478.

Martin, J. (2011). Straddling the line: Leadership roles for women in the private sector. In M. Paludi & B. Coates (Eds.), *Women as transformational leaders:*

From grassroots to global interests. Vol. 2: Organizational obstacles and solutions (pp. 1–23). Westport, CT: Praeger.

Morgan, W., Gilrane, V., McCausland, T., & King, E. (2011). Social stigma faced by female leaders in the workplace. In M. Paludi & B. Coates (Eds.), *Women as transformational leaders: From grassroots to global interests. Vol. 1: Cultural and organizational stereotypes, prejudice and discrimination* (pp. 27–50). Westport, CT: Praeger.

Nobel Peace Prize. (2011). *The Nobel Peace Prize 2011.* Retrieved from http://www.nobelprize.org/nobel_prizes/peace/laureates/2011/

Paludi, M., & Coates, B. (Eds.). (2011). *Women as transformational leaders: From grassroots to global interests.* Westport, CT: Praeger.

Paludi, M., Martin, J., Paludi, C., Boggess, S., Hicks, S., & Speach, L. (2010). Pay equity as justice: United States and international perspectives. In M. Paludi (Ed.), *Feminism and women's rights worldwide* (pp. 147–176). Westport, CT: Praeger.

Paludi, M., Paludi, C., & DeSouza, E. (2010). *Praeger handbook on understanding and preventing workplace discrimination.* Westport, CT: Praeger.

Pew Social and Demographic Trends. (2008). *Men or women: Who's the better leader: A paradox in public attitudes.* Retrieved from http://www.pewsocial trends.org/2008/08/25/men-or-women-whos-the-better-leader/

Powell, G., Butterfield, D., & Bartol, K. (2008). Leader evaluations: A new female advantage? *Gender in Management: An International Journal, 23,* 156–174.

Rodgers-Healey, D. (2003). *12 Insights into leadership for women.* Retrieved from www.leadershipforwomen.com.au.

Rosener, J. (1990). Ways women lead. *Harvard Business Review, 68,* 119–225.

Part One

Pushing for Change

The one thing I have learned as a CEO is that leadership at various levels is vastly different. When I was leading a function or a business, there were certain demands and requirements to be a leader. As you move up the organization, the requirements for leading that organization don't grow vertically; they grow exponentially.

—Indra Nooyi
CEO, PepsiCo

I

Burnout of Women Managers and Leaders Subsequent to Recurrent Stress in the Workplace[1]

Wesley S. Parks, Paula K. Lundberg-Love, Jeanine M. Galusha, and Sara Deitrick

Understanding the Constructs

To understand any problem, we first need an operationalized understanding of the phenomena that we are studying. With respect to stress and burnout, however, the waters are more than a little murky. Since there is no precise model for either condition, or a good across-the-board transition model, it is difficult to understand how stress leads to burnout. Even though there are numerous inventories and checklists, each condition is unique to the person manifesting the "symptoms." What is stressful to one person may simply be challenging or invigorating to another. Similarly, not each person who experiences stressors eventually experiences burnout. Perhaps, given the variability inherent in persons and manifestations, it is better to have a global understanding of the stress and burnout constructs and how stress can progress to burnout.

Operationalization—Stress

There is no succinct, readily agreed upon definition of stress. There are as many definitions of the concept as there are authors trying to describe it. Applying this to a specific arena, in this case the workplace, becomes even more difficult. Colligan and Higgins (2005) have suggested that stress in the workplace must be conceptualized as a function of the parent concept of stress. They essentially recapitulated Selye's (1980) categorizations of good stress

3

(eustress) and bad stress (distress). Noting that stress is inherently a reaction to stimuli, most people forego eustress and focus on distress (Selye, 1980). Interestingly, their examples of eustress (birth of a child, marriage, new friends, buying a home, workplace promotion) can actually be examples of distress depending on the circumstance.

Pop culture definitions are equally lacking in descriptive prowess. Bookstores have entire sections of self-help tomes dedicated to stress reduction. A quick perusal of these and one again sees an operational problem. Authors of these books, from celebrity mental health professionals to laypersons capitalizing on their own experiences, each have a unique interpretation regarding what stress is and how it affects us. A popular television drama once suggested that stress was a Madison Avenue word that could be cured with flavored coffee and bubble bath (Sorkin & Misiano, 2002). Even radio and television call-in shows offer de facto definitions based on a description of stressful events. In all, it appears that for most people, a good definition of stress remains elusive.

In this chapter, we will examine stress primarily as it relates to the workplace for women managers and leaders and not generalized life stressors unless there is a clear-cut work–life interaction. To that end, we will consider Noblet and LaMontagne's (2006) explanation that stress for most individuals includes physical, social, organizational, and economic conditions that are overlaid with any number of work variables (workload, decision making, community styles, interpersonal conflict, compensation).

As with so many mental health problems that lie on a continuum, job stressors can be broad or specific, and there are no set criteria for what constitutes stress. That is, there are no diagnostic criteria wherein an individual needs to meet three of the five stressors, or two in group A and two in group B, for stress to be problematic. As such, there are no clear diagnostic criteria for understanding stress, even as it relates to the specific area of the workplace. Over 20 years ago, Murphy (1995) noted that there was not one standardized model for understanding workplace stress. In a review of models and the existent research at that point in time, Murphy (1995) identified five broad categories of job stressors:

- Factors intrinsic to the job. These included workload (overload and underload), workplace, autonomy, shiftwork, and characteristics of physical environment characteristics.
- Role in the organization. This included role conflict, role ambiguity and level of responsibility.
- Level of career development. This included over/under promotion, job security and career development opportunities.

- Relationships at work. These included relationships with supervisors, coworkers and subordinates.
- Organizational structure/climate. This included participation in decision-making, management style and communication patterns.

Murphy's "model," was by no means comprehensive or all-inclusive. Rather, he acknowledged that it was merely a representation of prior work intended to facilitate further study. However, it was a good starting point in that he took lists of stressors and categorized them for specificity.

According to Caplan (1987), the person-environment fit model put forth by French, Rodgers, and Cobb (1974) is probably the most studied model when it comes to understanding occupational stress. Caplan (1987) summarized the model quite succinctly as the need to examine the nexus between a person and their chosen environment. In this case, to understand stress in the workplace, it is important to look at the interconnection between the employees, their work, and their work environment. Simply put, does the job meet the needs of an employee, and does the employee meet the needs of the company? It is a duality in that a good fit requires both parties to be satisfied. Edwards and Van Harrison (1993) elaborated that the central issue of occupational stress occurs when there is a mismatch between the person and the environment, and this leads to psychological, physiological, and behavioral strains on the psyche and the physical being. In fact, Edwards and Van Harrison (1993) opined that the deleterious effects of such strains ultimately increase mortality. Thus, any significant misfit can have drastic consequences on the worker.

In Caplan's (1987) review of this model in terms of operationalization, he put forth numerous questions about what to change, the person or the environment? Obviously, the answer depends upon whether you are the worker or the company. Caplan (1987) noted that businesses believed that the person should make the change, and workers felt that their environment should be changed. In determining how to make the change, to say nothing of who was ultimately responsible for said change, Caplan (1987) noted numerous problems with this model, not the least of which was the lack of an objective measure of the person or the environment.

There are numerous other models of occupational stress that have been well-researched, such as the transactional model of stress and coping, job strain model, and the job demand-control model to name a few (LaMontagne, Keegel, Louie, & Ostry, 2010; Murphy, 1995). Summarizing the models of stress, which are vastly more complicated than a few paragraphs would imply, is quite difficult and not practical for the purposes of a single book chapter. Rather, the models presented above provide a basic theoretical framework that highlights the most primary cause of job stress, namely a mismatch between the expectations of the worker and what is afforded them. When this mismatch reaches a certain threshold, burnout can occur.

Operationalization—Burnout

As with stress, there is also no readily agreed upon definition of burnout. As a metaphor (Schaufeli, Leiter, & Maslach, 2009), burnout refers to the smothering of a fire when there is a lack of sufficient resources to keep the flame burning. Over time, employees lose the capacity to provide meaningful contributions and accomplish less and less. To complete the metaphor, it is an exhaustion of an employee's capacity to maintain productivity (flickering of the candle) and eventual lack of positive or productive impact in the workplace (the flame dies out). Maslach, Schaufeli and Leiter (2001) note that the concept of "burnout," which they identified as being brought to the collective conscious with that very term in the novel, *A Burn-Out Case* (Maslach et al., 2001), has been a well-known, though relatively undocumented social construct for years. Though initially thought of as a pop psychology book, they stated that the term entered our vernacular thanks to its remarkably descriptive account of the workplace experience.

To understand the current lack of commitment to addressing burnout in today's workplace, it helps to understand the evolution of the construct. Schaufeli et al. (2009) writes that the origins of burnout began in the 1960s, when once lofty positions of the cultural revolution, teachers, doctors, social workers, law enforcement, and nurses, began to lose their prestige and people relying on these professions began to demand more than most workers were capable of delivering. In turn, there emerged a discrepancy between the professionals' efforts and the reward for those efforts. Maslach et al. (2001) wrote that research in this field began with a mental health professional describing a loss of motivation and commitment to work by himself and his associates. A psychiatrist at a substance abuse facility by the name of Herbert Freudenberger (1974) authored a paper based on his own observations. Given the lack of research on the subject at that time, he referenced only three articles, and they all were his own. He included physical symptoms (headaches, fatigue, exhaustion, sleeplessness, gastrointestinal disturbances, and shortness of breath), as well as behavioral symptoms including irritation, frustration, paranoia, anger, hostility, overconfidence, risk-taking, and excessive use of substances to manage these symptoms. He believed this burgeoning problem would only worsen over time without sufficient intervention.

From the outset, burnout was viewed from a sociological perspective in terms of understanding the stressors implicit in various relationships (Maslach et al., 2001). In the 1980s, the empirical phase of burnout research commenced, and burnout was viewed as a form of job stress. As empirical study continued through the 1990s, research was broadened beyond the helping professions into all manner of work. Schaufeli, Bakker, Hoogduin, Schaap, and Kladler (2001) noted that burnout is now a well-established concept that has been described in over 6,000 books, chapters, dissertations and journal articles. In fact, Schaufeli et al. (2009) suggested that as burnout became a global phenomenon, research shifted from viewing burnout as a social problem to conceptualizing it as more of a medical problem.

What does burnout look like? How would one identify it in the workplace? That is the limit to operationalizing burnout. There is no readily agreed-up definition or checklist. In addition to what was observed by Freudenberger (1974), Domeyer (2004) listed classic burnout symptoms. His list included: flat affect (lack of enthusiasm, excitement or pleasure about work), constant late hours and/or missed breaks, chronic irritability, significant drop in work quality or performance, repeated tardiness, missed deadlines or forgotten tasks, inability to manage workload, and the reluctance to volunteer for new assignments. For the sake of this text, we will consider these to be some of the possible behavioral manifestations of burnout.

Model of Burnout

Probably the most widely studied model of burnout in the workplace was put forth by Maslach and Leiter (1997). Their model identified three dimensions of burnout: exhaustion, depersonalization, and inefficacy. Exhaustion is the most widely reported aspect of burnout. The authors go beyond the lay definition of being tired or worn out, and describe exhaustion also as distancing oneself from ones work cognitively or emotionally. Depersonalization (often also called cynicism) is an attempt to distance oneself from others by actively ignoring the qualities that make others unique and engaging. Inefficacy is defined as a reduction in personal accomplishment. The authors note that there have been arguments that depersonalization and inefficacy are merely byproducts of exhaustion, but they disagree. They do concede that the relationship between inefficacy and the other two dimensions is difficult to categorize, and at times inefficacy may actually be a byproduct of combined exhaustion and depersonalization. In general, though, they feel that exhaustion and depersonalization emerge from work overload and interpersonal dysfunction, and inefficacy emerges from a lack of resources (Maslach & Leiter, 1997). In summarizing the model, Maslach et al. (2001) state that a job-person fit model, such as that proposed by French et al. (1974) in the person-environment fit model, appears to be the appropriate framework for understanding burnout. They also stated that the same mismatches that led to job stress can lead to burnout at a later point in the process, when the mismatches become chronic.

Summarizing the 1997 theory in terms of the person-environment fit model, the authors identified six areas of worklife that encompass the central relationships with burnout (Maslach et al., 2001):

- **Workload**—Workload is most directly related to exhaustion. Mismatch can be a function of the wrong person for the job, too much work, or not having enough information to complete the job successfully.
- **Control**—Mismatch in control is generally related to inefficacy. People have insufficient control over the resources needed to work, or have insufficient authority to work in the manner they think is most effective.
- **Reward**—Lack of reward is also related to inefficacy. The most obvious lack of reward is not receiving the salary or benefits commensurate with achievements or workload. Lack of reward can also take the form of a lack of praise or appreciation by others. In addition, lack of intrinsic reinforcement (pride) regarding ones position can lead to mismatch.
- **Community**—Mismatch also occurs when people lose a sense of positive connection with others in the workplace. Social support reaffirms membership in a group with shared values. Jobs with isolation exacerbate this potential mismatch. Unresolved conflict is the biggest threat to community.
- **Fairness**—Fairness communicates respect and confirms self-worth. Mismatch occurs when there is no perceived fairness or there is a perceived unfairness (e.g., unequal compensation). This exacerbates burnout in two ways: unfair treatment is emotionally upsetting and exhausting and it fuels a deep sense of cynicism (depersonalization).
- **Values**—A conflict in values can arise when workers feel they have to participate in unethical work practices (e.g., falsifying records), when they work for a company with values different from their own or when there are conflicting values within the workplace (highest quality services versus stringent cost containment) (Maslach et al., 2001).

The totality of this model lies in the relationship between the six worklife areas, as well as their overlap with the three dimensions of burnout. In demonstrating that any understanding of stress or burnout depends upon the individual, research by Maslach et al. (2001) suggests that there are several potential mediating interactions. The area of values may play a mediating role for the other five areas. The authors further note that it is conceivable that any area, or combination of areas, could prove to be mediators due to the differences among individuals. It is also unclear how much mismatch people are willing to tolerate. To that end, this model provides a framework for understanding the person-environment fit in specific worklife domains.

The Maslach Burnout Inventory (MBI) was developed in 1981 to measure the three dimensions of burnout. Subsequent editions of the MBI have employed the same three basic constructs, but with slightly modified terms depending upon the field of study. For example, the General Survey version categorizes the phenomena as exhaustion, cynicism, and reduced personal efficiency (Maslach et al., 2001). Regardless of the version used and terminology employed, all versions of the MBI are in essence measuring exhaustion, detachment, and lowered productivity.

Irrespective of which version of the MBI was employed or what the dimension and domains were termed, there was no definitive progression that led to eventual burnout. Maslach et al. (2001) found that in longitudinal studies in general, the sequence was from exhaustion to cynicism. The link to lowered productivity was less clear. The authors readily conceded that there were numerous sequential combinations that were observed. Thus, there does not seem to be one type of progression from happily employed to burned out and looking for change.

Using the MBI constructs of exhaustion, depersonalization, and inefficacy to measure burnout, it is all a matter of degree and personality states. Lacking clinically validated cutoffs and having only arbitrary cutoffs in the MBI manual, Schaufeli et al. (2001) sought to provide clinical validation of the measure. In their study, they applied the MBI to a group of patients diagnosed with neurasthenia. The authors used the following criteria for neurasthenia from the International Classification of Diseases (Schaufeli et al., 2001):

- Either persistent or distressing complaints of bodily weakness and exhaustion after minimal mental effort.
- At least two of the following: feelings of muscular aches and pains, dizziness, tension headaches, sleep disturbance, inability to relax, irritability, and dyspepsia.
- Any autonomic or depressive symptoms present that are not sufficiently persistent and severe to fulfill the criteria for any of the more specific disorders in the ICD-10 classification.

The authors noted these criteria were more or less similar to Maslach's burnout dimensions, and by requiring the symptoms to be work related, they opined that job-related neurasthenia was the ICD-10 equivalent of burnout. When comparing individuals with job-related neurasthenia to MBI surveys, the authors found a superior fit to the MBI dimensional model. Thus, their results suggest that the MBI can be used for diagnostic purposes.

Prevalence of Burnout

According to the American Psychological Association report on Stress in America (American Psychological Association, 2009), the last year wherein workplace stress was surveyed as a separate variable, 51% of employees surveyed reported lost productivity due to stress. Younger workers were more likely than older workers to report lost productivity. For the first time in this survey, more respondents agreed than disagreed that they typically feel tense or stressed out during the workday. However, one of the most interesting aspects of these findings was that even with the levels of reported stress, 65% indicated that they were satisfied with their jobs, which was an increase over the prior year. As the workplace across America has variable demographics, it may be helpful to view prevalence rates as a function of specific demographic categories.

Age

In reviewing 25 years of burnout research, Maslach et al. (2001) noted that age was the demographic most strongly correlated to burnout. Younger employees had higher rates of burnout. Since age is confounded with work experiences, it has been surmised that those able to progress up the job ladder have more satisfaction and less burnout. Note that this assumption may be fallacious for a number of reasons. For one thing, when unhappy people leave a job, they often leave behind happier people. This is similar to weeding a garden in that flowers usually bloom when the crabgrass is removed. Furthermore, this association does not take into account the number of people who change careers for reasons not related to burnout. While advancing age may mean greater maturity and better adapted skills in general, there needs to be more study focused on career changers to eliminate some confounds before accepting age as the most correlated demographic variable, and a potentially predictive variable.

Gender

Swanson (2000) noted that nearly half of the American work force is female. In addition, many of these women are in male-dominated careers and face greater job-related stress because of gender role stereotypes, sex discrimination, sexual harassment, and the need to balance work and family demands (see volume 1 of this book set). Piotrkowski (1998) found that gender harassment, that is harassment of the female gender without a specific sexualized component, occurred in 70% of his sample. Particularly noteworthy was his finding that women who reported any type of gender harassment, even as little as one instance, reported significantly more distress in the workplace than those who reported no harassment. Portello and Long (2001) studied woman managers and leader, and found that people who behave in a way dissonant to their basic world view or self-view are more likely to experience psychological distress. This is consistent with other models, such as Maslach's (Maslach et al., 2001), that a conflict in values, that is a conflict between the values of the individual and the values of the company as translated into role responsibility for this particular group, generates stressful reactions.

Maslach et al. (2001) noted that gender has not been a strong predictor of burnout. Some studies show higher rates for men, and some for women. They note the possibility that gender role stereotypes may be a confounding variable. For example, men often score higher on cynicism and women often score higher on exhaustion. These confounds could include career choice, as well as the social milieu outside of work (women, who receive little assistance from their partners, come home and still have to cook and clean and rear children; Peeters, Montgomery, Bakker, & Schaufeli, 2005).

In a contrasting meta-analysis of 183 prior studies on burnout, Purvanova and Muros (2010) found that women were more likely to report burnout than men. However, they cautioned against viewing this on face value alone, and suggested that a more nuanced interpretation of the numbers painted a more accurate picture of reality. Specifically, they found that women were more likely to report emotional exhaustion, and men were more likely to report depersonalization. So while women overall reported higher rates of burnout, the core component reported by each gender was different. They noted that the effect size was actually close to zero, suggesting little research utility. However, they wisely proposed viewing the data in terms of percent overlap statistics. That is, apply it to the real world on a larger basis. Assuming that one million workers of each gender were tested/interviewed, their finding suggests that 80,000 more women than men will report emotional exhaustion, and 140,000 more men than women will report depersonalization. If one expands this observation to the actual working population in this country, the numbers grow. Hence, these data do have practical implications for the workforce.

Education

According to Maslach et al. (2001), some studies show that higher education correlates with higher rates of burnout. The authors were unsure how to interpret this finding, as education has confounds with other variables such as occupation, gender, and socioeconomic status. They hypothesized that those with higher levels of education took positions with inherently more stress, that also had higher job performance expectations, which led to a mismatch among the six worklife areas (workload, control, reward, community, fairness, and values). It is also conceivable that those with higher levels of education are more able to recognize mistreatment, or see the proverbial "writing on the wall" when analyzing growth opportunities within a company or industry.

Occupation

Measuring burnout with respect to a specific occupation is difficult. Maslach et al. (2001) discussed research that included five occupational sectors that were studied in the United States and in Holland. They included teaching, social services, medicine, mental health, and law enforcement. There were no conclusive data to suggest that any one of those fields was more prone to burnout. In fact, when the authors reviewed the study in terms of the MBI three-dimensional model, levels of burnout in all three dimensions varied among occupations and between the two countries. For example, the medical field in both countries was characterized by higher levels of inefficacy, but lower levels of exhaustion and depersonalization. Law enforcement had high levels of depersonalization and inefficacy, but low levels of exhaustion. Mental health varied on all three dimensions between the two countries. In short, their review of this study against a dimensional model of burnout demonstrated the complexities of adequately categorizing the causes and effects of job stress and burnout.

Personality

Individuals will have cognitive, behavioral, emotional, and physical responses to both good and bad stress. The quality of these responses is governed largely by personality traits (Colligan & Higgins, 2005). If one is well prepared, the responses to stress can be mitigated and thus will have limited effects. Those who are ill prepared can have chronic emotional, psychological, and even physical reactions.

Maslach et al. (2001) noted numerous personality factors associated with increased job stress and burnout. Higher rates of burnout were reported by those with an external locus of control, those with poor coping skills or individuals who coped in a passive way, and people with low self-esteem. Burnout was related to neuroticism as well as trait anxiety, hostility, depression, self-consciousness, and vulnerability. Those who were emotionally unstable were more prone to burnout. In less scientific terms, higher rates of burnouts were reported by those who described themselves as Type A personalities (people who feel driven and are competitive) as well as those who categorized themselves as "feeling" rather than "thinking" types. Not surprisingly, higher rates of burnout were reported by those who had higher expectations of work and life in general.

In reviewing the work of other leaders in the field, Vlăduţ and Kállay (2010) also identified personal characteristics that were associated with burnout. They found higher rates of burnout among those with lower self-esteem, an external locus of control, Type A behaviors, alexithymia (difficulty recognizing emotional states as they occur or adequately being able to describe feelings), low sense of coherence (lack of interest in meeting challenges, with or without the necessary resources), and high levels of neuroticism, which are results similar to those of Maslach's (Maslach et al., 2001). Vlăduţ and Kállay (2010) note that some of the characteristics associated with burnout may be the result of the workplace, while others are brought into the workplace in their current manifestations. That is, some people come into the workplace with personality traits that are generally associated with burnout, similar to a powder keg needing only a spark to ignite an explosion. Others without such a predisposition develop such traits as a result of job stress and eventual burnout. Whatever the reality, these are vulnerabilities that increase the likelihood of burnout.

Noblet and La Montagne (2006) noted that there is considerable variation in how people perceive stressful events based on personality and situational variables. What one person may find debilitatingly stressful, another may find challenging and stimulating. Thus, correlating burnout with personality characteristics has been fraught with challenges and confounds.

Cultural Effects

Maslach et al. (2001) found that there had not been sufficient study of burnout as related to ethnicity to know if there was, indeed, any correlation. Clearly this issue requires further study. Purvanova and Muros's meta-analysis (2010) found that American workers reported higher rates of burnout than workers in the European Union (EU). American workers also reported the same gender-specific findings previously mentioned (women with higher rates of emotional exhaustion and men with higher rates of depersonalization) at higher rates than EU workers. Thus, burnout is a global phenomenon, but workers in the United States reports higher rates of burnout. Xiaobing, Xianming and Xin (2002) noted that job burnout for women in China is reaching epidemic proportions.

Bullying

Much research and public policy is focusing on bullying. According to a study commissioned by the Workplace Bullying Institute (2010), nearly 35% of respondents ($N = 4,210$) reported being bullied in the workplace either at the time of the study or at some point prior to the study. This result was consistent with a similar study by the same organization in 2007 with a sample of more than 7,700 working adults. (Workplace Bullying Institute, 2007). Thus, the WBI concluded that the prevalence rate of nearly one-third of the country was stable and consistent across surveys. When the stratified demographics were examined, it was found that men were more often the perpetrators and the recipients of the bullying. However the numbers of women bullying other women were quickly increasing in number. Most bullying occurred at the mid-career stage. There was not much difference with respect to educational level attained. Most respondents reported that their employers were unengaged in preventing or addressing bullying (42.6%). Though the survey did not collect data on the effects of bullying, it is not hard to imagine that for the one-third of those being bullied in the workplace, the effects are deleterious at best and potentially toxic at worse. There is no doubt that bullying contributes to stress and burnout in the workplace.

In fact, Hood (2004) discussed anecdotal data regarding workplace bullying and its resulting stress to both the worker and the economy. He noted that such behaviors destroy the mental and physical health of the victims. Edwards and Van Harrison (1993) also noted that workplace misfit had deleterious psychological and physical health effects. Hood (2004) opines that aside from compassionate grounds, executives should be concerned about bullying because by disrupting teamwork, efficiency, and productivity, bullying ultimately costs money. In his view, employers have a fiduciary interest in reigning in workplace bullying in order to have an impetus for change.

Effects of Job Stress

Mental Health Factors

It was noted by LaMontagne et al. (2010) that there have been few published studies regarding job stress-attributable mental disorders. In their review of the literature, they cite several studies in various nationalities that make that link. In a Finnish study cited by LaMontagne et al., depressive suicides were related to job strain in over 14% of male and over 9% of female suicide victims. The authors also reported that a New Zealand birth cohort study found that 45% of incident cases of depression and anxiety were attributable to job stress. In a study of Canadian worker's compensation claims, LaMontagne et al. (2010) noted that while overall claims were decreasing, there was an 83% increase in mental health-related claims in an 8-year period. In a review of published studies and dissertations, Mazzola, Schonfeld, and Spector (2011) found that across the globe psychological reactions to job stress included anger, annoyance, tension, anxiety, sadness, depression, disappointment and psychological strains. Citing numerous studies, Vlăduț and Kállay (2010) reported that the most frequent emotional complaints associated with burnout were depression, anxiety, substance abuse, sleep disturbance, anger, and frustration. Depression is one of the more prevalent mental health concerns in the workplace and has become a major occupational health issue. Fifty-five percent of British nurses who were on long-term disability for depression cited work stress as a major contributing factor to their depressed mood (DeVries & Wilkerson, 2003).

Of current interest in research circles is the relationship between occupational stressors in the military and subsequent mental health. Campbell and Nobel (2009) distinguished between types of deployment when considering the nature and level of stressors facing enlisted personnel. Stressors encountered in deployment were similar to stressors encountered in extraordinary settings such as catastrophic events, accidents, and disasters. Humanitarian missions fared better, with lower levels of stress. At first glance, this would appear to be more related to the potential for posttraumatic stress disorder (PTSD). However, it is important to note that enlisted personnel may be in combat zones for months or years at a time, and in this light many of their stressors become chronic and can be conceptualized in the person-environment fit model. For example, soldiers working long stints without furlough may experience a mismatch on the workload factor. Alternatively, with news reports of military vehicles being destroyed because of a lack of sufficient armor protection, soldiers may experience a mismatch on the control factor. Clearly with soldiers, and likely with private sector employees given time employed, there can be the development of PTSD following stressors. But what is important to note is that the everyday stressors of a war zone that do not necessarily lead to a traumatic event, still exact a heavy psychological toll. Indeed, Hourani, Williams, and Kress (2006) estimated that 13% of military personnel met the diagnostic criteria for depression as a result of job stress. They note this is very likely an underestimate, given that much of their data were collected before the current combat operations in Afghanistan and Iraq.

Substance Abuse

A two-stage survey by Rospenda, Fujishiro, Shannon, and Richman (2008) found that as little as one or more instances of generalized workplace harassment (harassment other than sexual harassment) led to a 17% increase in heavy episodic drinking in men. The same increase was not observed in women. However, there was a greater than 40% increase in heavy episodic drinking for women when high general life stress was perceived. This study did not identify any individual stressors that could be categorized as general life stress, but it is conceivable that for at least some of the respondents work stress contributed to life stress.

Health Functioning

Changes in the workplace have long been known to cause distress. In studying uncertainly in the workplace, Pollard (2001) cited numerous articles and book chapters establishing a strong correlation between employment stressors and cardiovascular health. Blood pressure can be affected via the sympathetic nervous system and hypothalamic-pituitary-adrenal axis. Glucose and lipid metabolism are also negatively impacted. Pollard's (2001) research showed that when employees' cardiovascular functioning was assessed shortly before and after a business reorganization, an elevation in blood pressure was observed that directly correlated to self-reported psychological distress. This finding is consistent with known biological feedback models of stressors and clearly is applicable to the workplace. In citing prior studies linking job strain and risk of a first coronary heart disease event, Aboa-Éboulé et al. (2007), posited a positive relationship between continued job strain and additional coronary heart events. While following 972 men and women who returned to work after a first coronary heart event, 21% had a second coronary event within the 9-year study period. They concluded that job strain after an initial cardiovascular event was associated with recurrent events.

Schreurs, van Emmerik, Notelaers, and De Witte (2010) examined job insecurity and self-efficacy in terms of recovery need and impaired general health. Recovery need was conceptualized nicely in the simple terms of needing a brief respite to replenish resources or recharge ones battery. Impaired general health was conceptualized as how long-term stressors impacted medical and mental health conditions over time. They reported positive correlations between job insecurity (fear of losing a job) and both short-term and long-term health outcomes. Not surprisingly, they found that having a sense of control over one's job (job control) and having confidence in one's ability to exercise that control (self-efficacy) both mitigated the negative effects of job insecurity.

Citing numerous studies, Vlăduț and Kállay (2010) reported that the most frequent physical complaints associated with burnout were headaches, muscular pain, gastrointestinal problems, hyperventilation, chronic fatigue, sexual problems, sleep disorders, and cardiovascular problems.

Occupational Factors

It is certainly not a stretch of the imagination to understand how job stress can, in turn, impact current and future job performance. Maslach et al. (2001) found that workers who reported high levels of job stress were prone to absenteeism, intention to leave their current position, lowered productivity, ineffectiveness, decreased job satisfaction, and reduced commitment to the employer. They also found that employees who perceived themselves under significant stress had a negative impact on their colleagues via dysfunctional personal contact or disrupted job tasks. The authors described this as "contagious" and self-perpetuating through repeated interpersonal interactions.

Economic Factors

Adams (2009) describes the cost of stress to the workplace in terms of invisible overhead, which was his term for all for the costs a company incurs due to direct reimbursements for medical coverage, absenteeism, poor decisions, bad judgments, turnover and attrition, and recruitment and training of replacement employees. Taken together, these represent a significant annual overhead charge.

Nicholson et al. (2006) attempted to find a numerical factor to determine the true cost of missed work as a function of job stress. Using data from 800 managers in twelve different industries, they found that the cost of missed work varied based upon whether a perfect replacement could be found (i.e., an exact match of skills to the absent employee), whether the person was part of a team, and the time constraints of that person's work product. Across their study, they determined the cost of missed work, for whatever reason, to be 1.28 times the worker's wage. Thus, mental health clearly impacts the bottom line for all businesses, and worldwide employers are starting to recognize the need for interventions from a cost-benefit perspective (DeVries & Wilkerson, 2003). Still, DeVries and Wilkerson (2003) also noted that many employers remain either unaware or unconcerned about the overall impact of good mental health on profitability.

Citing data from a 2003 national health study, the United States Occupational Safety and Health Administration estimated that the total rates and costs of lost work and lost productivity due to illness and injury were $63 billion

(High Cost of Missed Work Days, 2007). This total figure did not include separate demographics for injury versus illness. Retrieving such statistics from the United States Department of Labor Bureau of Labor Statistics (United States Department of Labor, 2011) is a daunting challenge, as raw data are not coded in the same manner year by year.

Attempts at procuring data based on mental-health related illness in the workplace for a better understanding of both the prevalence rates of such illness and the costs for employers were all but impossible to download and conceptualize given the thousands of codes per year and the variations year by year. Clearly, this would be a major challenge for any researcher, and may explain why such data are not readily available.

Burnout

Per Maslach et al. (2001), the link from burnout to mental health consequences remains unclear. The common assumption is that burnout causes dysfunction via anxiety, depression, lowered self-esteem, and other variables. Put another way, burnout is believed to impact mental health in the same way generalized job stress does, but presumably to a higher degree because burnout is the end result of recurrent job stress. Without a clear definition of what constitutes burnout, determining just how many people are affected and exactly how they are affected becomes a research quagmire. Whatever the reality, and even in the absence of a clear diagnostic model, burnout is clearly one of the effects of significant job stress.

Intervention

As early as 1974, with the initial foray into burnout research, Freudenberger (1974) realized that merely describing the phenomenon was useless without considering possible interventions. At that time, he listed some preventive measures that seem common sensical now, but at the time were likely groundbreaking, since they were included in a peer-reviewed article. His suggestions included using volunteers for an extra labor pool, providing training, avoiding overly repetitive work, limiting hours worked, scheduling flexible working times, enhancing team cohesiveness, sharing experiences and frustrations, and engaging in physical exercise. Many of these practices are used in corporate America to this day. In fact, workplaces are littered with pamphlets and memoranda about the warning signs of burnout. Career-oriented journals and magazines, and even mainstream magazines and e-zines, routinely run articles with checklists of warning signs of job stress and burnout, and helpful suggestions upon ways to be more productive. It was argued by Maslach et al.

(2001) that people who were psychological healthier at the outset of employment were better able to cope with job stress and showed greater levels of job satisfaction. Hence, interventions aimed at maintaining psychological health are easily justified. But in considering what constitutes appropriate and effective interventions, the problem often remains a function of where to target limited financial resources.

Individual Approach

From early on, Maslach et al. (2001) believed that in a person-environment fit model, preventing burnout required addressing both sides of the equation. Helping a person develop coping strategies can be somewhat effective via educational interventions (Maslach et al., 2001). Research shows that people can learn new ways to cope with stress. Unfortunately, they cannot always apply it to the workplace because work behaviors are stipulated by employers. People are hired for job function, not personality. Research by Maslach et al. (2001) showed that using an individual approach to intervention resulted in mixed findings with respect to burnout. Reduction in exhaustion was reported in some cases, but not all. Rarely were reductions in cynicism or inefficacy reported (Maslach et al., 2001).

Vlăduţ and Kállay (2010) also found that individual-oriented interventions can be effective. They reviewed 25 studies using individual interventions such as cognitive-behavioral training, counseling, psychosocial skills, and communication training and anxiety management techniques such as relaxation and autogenic training. Their review of these studies suggests that individual intervention is effective, in that 80% of the studies reviewed showed positive effects. However, they caution that as a whole the effect sizes were small. Still, if generalized to the larger workforce, they believe individual-based techniques can be quite effective in reducing burnout (Vlăduţ & Kállay, 2010).

Angerer (2003) wrote that workers can find ways of coping with job stress, and that efforts at individual-based interventions tend to focus on the exhaustion component of burnout. However, with that being only one component, individual focus is not always effective. In addition, without inventions aimed at the workplace itself, any techniques targeting cynicism or inefficiency are not likely to be effective because workers themselves cannot change the constraints placed upon them in the workplace by their companies. Hence, for methods taught in self-help books such as *Seven Habits of Highly Effective People* (Covey, 2004) and other commercially successful titles, to make a real impact on burnout will require the combined efforts of workers and management. Maslach (2003), undoubtedly the expert in this field, opined that addressing burnout solely by aiming interventions at the employee was paradoxical, given that research has shown situational and organizational factors play a larger role in burnout than individual factors. In addition, as with Angerer (2003), Maslach (2003) contends that individual interventions were doomed to fail because people have little control over stress in the work domain. That is why, after all, they are feeling stressed and suffering burnout. Maslach and a colleague (Maslach & Leiter, 2008) had authored a text on implementing strategies at the organizational level based on their own 3-year study. At the end of the 3 years, they still did not have enough data to evaluate the effectiveness of the interventions they studied. In fact, Maslach and Leiter (2008) noted that a challenge to implementing organizational strategies difficult to prove effectiveness, given that one needs longitudinal follow-up studies to validate the impact of the interventions. This may be cost prohibitive for companies who answer to stringent shareholders. In reality, the corporate mindset may be that it is cheaper to replace employees who are burned out than repair the system that led to the burnout.

Collective Approach
In balancing the equation, Maslach's research (Maslach, 2003; Maslach & Goldberg, 1998; Maslach et al., 2001) found that the most effective strategy for mitigating burnout was to change the environment while changing the person. Though Vlăduţ and Kállay (2010) noted significant improvement through individual intervention alone, they also noted that organization-based interventions in addition to individual-based ones may have the strongest and most lasting impact on mitigating workplace stress. In a review of 25 primary intervention studies, Awa, Plaumann, and Walter (2010) found that both individual- and organization-based interventions showed some positive effect, as did the combination of both approaches. They found that individual approaches were 82% effective at reducing burnout, with the effects lasting up to 6 months. The organization-based approaches also were successful, though there were far fewer of those to study. In both cases, refresher courses resulted in longer lasting positive effects.

Regardless of what specific strategies are employed, be it stress management, individual therapy, wellness initiatives, support groups, or organizational reviews, there are specific factors to consider for successful intervention (Adams, 2009; Flaxman & Bond, 2010; Jimmieson, McKimmie, Hannam & Gallagher, 2010; Murphy, 1995; Noblet & LaMontagne, 2006):

- Programs should be multifaceted, with a wide variety of solutions for the wide variety of problems facing individual workers.
- Interventions should be based on the idea that preventing stress and health problems requires changing the habits of the person and the company.

- Employee involvement should be as extensive as possible, so that lasting change will involve individuals at many levels within the organization.
- Individual-level interventions should focus on knowledge, skills and resources to cope with stress. The goal would be to implement these resources prior the employees feeling/reporting stressed.
- Interface-level (direct employee-employer interaction) interventions should target the connection between employee and employer in terms of role ambiguity, work relationships, person-environment fit, decision-making, and support groups as well as role clarification.
- Environmental-level interventions should focus on the physical, organizational, and social environments that produce stress. Interventions could include providing family-friendly policies (e.g., Peeters et al., 2005), on-site child care, bus pass vouchers, and companywide initiatives like wellness programs offering yoga, sick banks, and food banks. Additional resources may be found in Paludi and Neidermeyer (2007).
- The program must be fully accepted and actively supported by the company's leadership in order to be effective.
- Effective evaluation of return on investment must be evaluated in order to monitor the cost effectiveness of the program.

In conclusion, for such programs to be effective, all three areas must be addressed, or long-term success will not be achieved. Addressing any one of the three areas may show a short-term and significant gain, but not one with enduring effects.

Cost-Benefit Analysis

Maslach and Leiter's research (2008) based on longitudinal studies suggests it is relatively easy to predict burnout. Their results also indicate that inconsistent scores on the MBI-GS and high job-person incongruence are strong predictors of burnout. Furthermore, they assert that these are easy-to-measure variables in the workplace if assessments are utilized on a regular (annual) basis. The take away message from their research seems to be the integration of burnout screening tools into yearly performance appraisals that would be administered on an annual basis. Such a process could be designed to foster communication between employee and supervisor about opportunities for improvement.

Baicker (Baicker, Cutler, & Zirui 2010) suggested that it has been difficult to estimate the long-term savings of employee wellness plans because there has been no standardized nomenclature in the field or systematic data collection. Her meta-analysis demonstrated an average savings of $3.27 for every dollar spent in wellness care. Admittedly, this total is for general medical expenses and not psychological expenses, but given the number of physiological symptoms that present with psychological conditions, it is conceivable that there was some overlap in the conditions studied. At the very least, addressing medical concerns can allay anxiety and depression in some workers whose symptoms are, indeed, tied to medical conditions. Return on investment (ROI) is a formal business term for the more simplified concept of a cost-benefit analysis. Within any workplace, the ROI is a critical measure of the benefit of any program or wellness benefit. In considering absenteeism, Baicker's study (Baicker et al., 2010) found an ROI of $2.73 for every dollar spent in wellness care. All but one of the 22 studies analyzed showed a reduction in absentee days. Adams (2009) believes these costs of what he termed "invisible overhead" due to job stress are recoverable through the promotion of organizationally supported work/life balance programs. He cites several corporate examples where the ROI was quite high for such programs.

Conclusions

To date, research regarding the prevalence of burnout and the impact of interventions for its remediation remain unclear due to confounds in the current research and the potential for missed data (non-reporting, underreporting, absence of screening, and nonrecognition of burnout). While it is unlikely that one model will be found that can be applied to all corporate organizational flowcharts and performance manuals, we still need to focus upon how we can prevent employee burnout. But we also need to find methods for the rehabilitation of employees who do experience burnout. Maslach and Goldberg (1998) argue that the "meta-message" from the emerging research on burnout is that we cannot address burnout with attempts to "fix" broken employees. Rather, the only way to truly mitigate workplace stress and lessen the prevalence rates for burnout is to tie prevention and rehabilitation efforts to the workplace itself, which includes the building, the people, the managers, the corporate culture, the shareholders, and the individual employee's position within that context. Indeed, without making the investment in truly understanding individual employees with a social context and person-situation interactions, we will continue to rely on generalizations likened to cogs in wheels or viewing employees as numbers rather than people. From a business perspective, it is understandable that no one company can create wellness packages or prevention strategies to accommodate every conceivable job stressor and its potential to lead to burnout. However, research shows that not enough is being done by most companies to address the basic job stressors that over time have a cumulative effect that lead to increased burnout. There is no obvious or easy solution, but companies that have focused on addressing this problem have reaped financial benefit in the long run.

Note

1. Portions of this chapter were published in M. Paludi and B. Coates (Eds.), *Women as Transformational Leaders* (Westport, CT: Praeger, 2011). This chapter is reprinted here with permission from Praeger, Westport, CT.

References

Aboa-Éboulé, C., Brisson, C., Manusell, E., Mâsse, B., Bourbonnais, R. Vézina, M., . . . Dagenais, G. (2007). Job strain and risk of acute recurrent coronary heart disease events. *Journal of the American Medical Association, 298,* 1652–1660.

Adams, J. (2009). Cost savings from health promotion and stress management interventions. *OD Practitioner, 41,* 31–37.

American Psychological Association. (2009). *Stress in America 2009.* Washington, DC: Author.

Angerer, J. M. (2003). Job burnout. *Journal of Employment Counseling, 40,* 98–107.

Awa, W. L., Plaumann, M., & Walter, U. (2010). Burnout prevention: A review of intervention programs. *Patient Education & Counseling, 78,* 184–190.

Baicker, K., Cutler, D., & Zirui, S. (2010). Workplace wellness programs can generate savings. *Health Affairs, 29,* 1–8.

Campbell, D. J., & Nobel, O. (2009). Occupational stressors in military service: A review and framework. *Military Psychology, 21,* 47–67.

Caplan, R. D. (1987). Person-environment fit theory and organizations: Commensurate dimensions, time perspectives, and mechanisms. *Journal of Vocational Behavior, 31,* 248–267.

Colligan, T. W., & Higgins, E. M. (2005). Workplace stress: Etiology and consequences. *Journal of Workplace Behavioral Health, 21,* 89–97.

Covey, S. R. (2004). *The 7 habits of highly effective people: Restoring the character ethic.* New York: Free Press.

deVries, M., & Wilkerson, B. (2003). Stress, work and mental health: A global perspective. *Acta Neuropsychiatrica, 15,* 44–53.

Domeyer, D. (2004). How to deal with burnout before it's too late. *Women in Business, 56,* 10.

Edwards, J. R., & Van Harrison, R. R. (1993). Job demands and worker health: Three-dimensional reexamination of the relationship between person-environment fit and strain. *Journal of Applied Psychology, 78,* 628–648.

Flaxman, P. E., & Bond, F. W. (2010). Worksite stress management training: Moderated effects and clinical significance. *Journal of Occupational Health Psychology, 15,* 347–358.

French, J. R, Rodgers, W., & Cobb, S. (1974). Adjustment as person-environment fit. In C. V. Coelho, D. A. Hamburg & J. E. Adams (Eds.), *Coping and adaptation,* 316-333. New York: Basic Books.

Freudenberger, H. J. (1974). Staff burn-out. *Journal of Social Issues, 30,* 159–165.

High cost of missed work days. (2007). *Industrial Engineer, 39,* 18.

Hood, S. B. (2004). Workplace bullying. *Canadian Business, 77,* 87–90.

Hourani, L. L., Williams, T. V., & Kress, A. M. (2006). Stress, mental health, and job performance among active duty military personnel: Findings from the 2002 department of defense health-related behaviors survey. *Military Medicine, 171,* 849–856.

Jimmieson, N. L., McKimmie, B. M., Hannam, R. L., & Gallagher, J. (2010). An investigation of the stress-buffering effects of social support in the occupational stress process as a function of team identification. *Group Dynamics: Theory, Research, and Practice, 14,* 350–367.

LaMontagne, A. D., Keegel, T., Louie, A. M., & Ostry, A., (2010). Job stress as a preventable upstream determinant of common mental disorders: A review for practitioners and policy-makers. *Advances in Mental Health, 9,* 17–35.

Maslach, C. (2003). Job burnout: New directions in research and intervention. *Current Directions in Psychological Science, 12,* 189.

Maslach, C., & Goldberg, J. (1998). Prevention of burnout: New perspectives. *Applied & Preventive Psychology, 7,* 63–74.

Maslach, C., & Leiter, M. P. (1997). *The truth about burnout.* San Francisco, CA: Jossey-Bass.

Maslach, C., & Leiter, M. P. (2008). Early predictors of job burnout and engagement. *Journal of Applied Psychology, 93,* 498–512.

Maslach, C., Schaufeli, W., & Leiter, M. (2001). Job burnout. *Annual Review of Psychology, 52,* 397–422.

Mazzola, J. J., Schonfeld, I., & Spector, P. E. (2011). What qualitative research has taught us about occupational stress. *Stress & Health: Journal of the International Society for the Investigation of Stress, 27,* 93–110.

Murphy, L. R. (1995). Occupational stress management: Current status and future directions. In C. L. Cooper & D. M. Rousseau, (Eds.), *Trends in organizational behavior* (Vol. 2, pp. 1–14). West Sussex: John Wiley.

Nicholson, S., Pauly, M. V., Polsky, D., Sharda, C., Szrek, H., & Berger, M. L. (2006). Measuring the effects of work loss on productivity with team production. *Health Economics, 15,* 111–123.

Noblet, A., & LaMontagne, A. D. (2006). The role of workplace health promotion in addressing job stress. *Health Promotion International, 21,* 346–353.

Peeters, M., Montgomery, A., Bakker, A., & Schaufeli, W. (2005). Balancing work and home: How job and home demands are related to burnout. *International Journal of Stress Management, 12,* 43–61.

Piotrkowski, C. S. (1998). Gender harassment, job satisfaction, and distress among employed white and minority women. *Journal of Occupational Health Psychology, 3,* 33–43.

Pollard, T. M. (2001). Changes in mental well-being, blood pressure and total cholesterol levels during workplace reorganization: The impact of uncertainty. *Work & Stress, 15,* 14–28.

Portello, J. Y., & Long, B. C. (2001). Appraisals and coping with workplace interpersonal stress: A model for women managers. *Journal of Counseling Psychology, 48,* 144–156.

Purvanova, R. K., & Muros, J. P. (2010). Gender differences in burnout: A meta-analysis. *Journal of Vocational Behavior, 77,* 168–185.

Rospenda, K. M., Fujishiro, K., Shannon, C. A., & Richman, J. A. (2008). Workplace harassment, stress, and drinking behavior over time: Gender differences in a national sample. *Addictive Behaviors, 33,* 964–967.

Schaufeli, W. B., Bakker, A. B., Hoogduin, K., Schaap, C., & Kladler, A. (2001). On the clinical validity of the maslach burnout inventory and the burnout measure. *Psychology & Health, 16,* 565.

Schaufeli, W. B., Leiter, M. P., & Maslach, C. (2009). Burnout: 35 years of research and practice. *Career Development International, 14,* 204–220.

Schreurs, B., van Emmerik, H., Notelaers, G., & De Witte, H. (2010). Job insecurity and employee health: The buffering potential of job control and job self-efficacy. *Work & Stress, 24,* 56–72.

Selye, H. (1980). The stress concept today. In. I. L. Kutash and L. B. Schlesinger (Eds.), *Handbook on stress and anxiety* (127–143). San Francisco, CA: Jossey-Bass.

Sorkin, A. (writer), & Misiano, C. (director). (2002). Night five [Television series episode]. In A. Sorkin (producer), *The West Wing.* Burbank, CA: Warner Bros Entertainment.

Swanson, N. (2000). Working women and stress. *Journal of the American Medical Women's Association, 55,* 76–79.

United States Department of Labor. (2011). *Various data files.* Retrieved from http://www.bls.gov

Vlăduț, C., & Kállay, É. (2010). Work stress, personal life, and burnout. Causes, consequences, possible remedies—A theoretical review. *Cognition, Brain, Behavior: An Interdisciplinary Journal, 14,* 261–280.

Workplace Bullying Institute. (2007). *The WBI U.S. workplace bullying survey conducted by Zogby International.* Bellingham, WA: Gary Namie.

Workplace Bullying Institute. (2010). *The WBI U.S. workplace bullying survey conducted by Zogby International.* Bellingham.

Xiaobing, Z., Xianming, Z., & Xin, Z. (2009). Reasons and countermeasures for job burnout of female employees: An explorative case study of female employees in Shanghai. *E-Business and Information System Security,* 1–5.

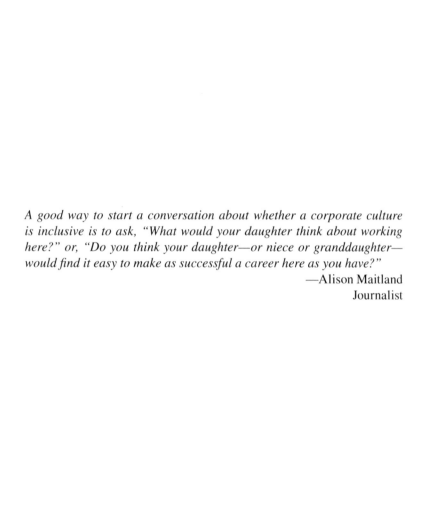

A good way to start a conversation about whether a corporate culture is inclusive is to ask, "What would your daughter think about working here?" or, "Do you think your daughter—or niece or granddaughter— would find it easy to make as successful a career here as you have?"

—Alison Maitland
Journalist

2

Bullying and Harassment in Schools: Analysis of Legislation and Policy

Jennifer L. Martin, Holly Kearl, and Wendy J. Murphy

According to Gruber and Fineran (2008), 79% of LGBTQ students experience bullying, and 71% of LGBTQ students experience sexual harassment. Eighty-five percent of LGBTQ students report being verbally harassed, 40% report being physically harassed, and 19% report physical assault (GLSEN, 2007). Sixty percent of these students failed to report these incidents to school staff members because they felt that nothing would be done about it. Thirty-one percent of students who did report their incidents of harassment indicated that nothing was done in response (GLSEN, 2007). This comports with other data showing a general reluctance on the part of students to report bullying to authorities (Mishna, Pepler, & Wiener, 2006).

Students who are harassed and bullied report feeling greater levels of alienation, helplessness, hopelessness, loneliness, and worthlessness than their heterosexual peers. As a result, suicide is a leading cause of death for harassed and bullied students—particularly for LGBTQ youth (Robinson & Espalage, 2011). Human Rights Watch found that LGBTQ youth are more than four times as likely as heterosexual students to attempt suicide (Robinson & Espalage, 2011).

Recent high-profile suicides of bullied and harassed students have provoked the popular media to highlight the problem of bullying in schools (Hampson, 2010). Celebrities like Dan Savage and Lady Gaga have made bullying, especially the bullying of LGBTQ youth, their activist issue. Despite increased public awareness, many schools do not specifically include the category of LGBTQ status in policies and procedures prohibiting bullying or harassment (Martin, 2010).

While the definitions of harassment and bullying cover similar kinds of behavior, and both types of harm occur in similar ways and locations, for example, on school grounds, on school buses, at school activities, and via social media and other "off-campus" technology such as cell phones, harassment and bullying usually have different definitions and the legal protections for victims vary based on which definition is applied. In this chapter, we will discuss current laws prohibiting harassment and bullying, their effectiveness, and suggestions for improved legislation to better protect all students from both types of harm.

Definitions

Harassment

Harassment includes unwanted harmful behaviors that affect an individual or a group and are based on factors such as sex, gender, race, sexual orientation, religion, ethnicity, or disability. Sexual harassment, for example, is defined as unwanted sexual behavior including sexual assault, verbal and written comments, requests for sexual favors, unwelcome sexual advances, spreading sexual rumors, gestures, pictures or images, and/or physical coercion. Sexual harassment can occur directly or indirectly, or through the use of technology (U.S. Department of Education Office for Civil Rights, 2010). According to Steineger (2001) harassment is "about intimidation, control, misuse of power, and the attempt to deny the victim equality" (p. 14). Behaviors that constitute harassment can include: name calling; slurs based on stereotypes; graffiti; the dissemination of offensive materials or drawings (such as racist or sexist literature); vandalism; comments about personal appearance; sexual innuendoes; sexual leering; unwanted touching; inappropriate gestures; unwanted contact via phone, Internet, and e-mail; unwanted gifts and attention; repeated and unwanted requests for dates; pressure for sexual favors; sexual rumors; and sexual assault (actual, attempted, simulated, or threatened) (Steineger, 2001).

Bullying

Bullying is typically defined as repeated unwanted behavior used to intentionally ridicule, humiliate, or intimidate another person, but it is not necessarily based upon the individual's membership in a protected class or the target's group identity (Espelage & Swearer, 2010; Meyer, 2009). Bullying and harassment are related concepts and their definitions overlap in terms of the behaviors they prohibit, but there are at least two important differences. For bullying, some state laws require proof that the perpetrator intended the harm. For harassment, the intention of the perpetrator is almost always irrelevant and the victim's perception of the behavior is largely determinative (McGrath, 2006). Another important difference is that bullying laws are not aimed at redressing offensive environmental conditions in schools where bullying has occurred, while one strand of antiharassment law deals specifically with repairing the harm caused by behavior that created a "hostile educational environment" (U.S. Department of Education Office for Civil Rights, 2010).

Another important difference is that the definition of harassment is fairly uniform among all 50 states while bullying laws vary widely. For example, although in most jurisdictions, more than one harmful act is required to constitute bullying, a wide variety of terms is used to define the amount of activity required such as, "systematic and chronic,"[1] "severe or pervasive,"[2] "repeated,"[3] "pattern,"[4] "repeatedly and over time,"[5] "continuous pattern."[6] In many jurisdictions, a single act is enough to constitute bullying, which is also the case for harassment, so long as the act is "severe" (Murphy, 2011). For example, Alaska requires "an intentional act,"[7] and "a single significant incident" will suffice in New Hampshire.[8] Some jurisdictions require the act to be "intentional" but many, such as Hawaii, define bullying as "any act" that causes an enumerated harm, irrespective of the intentions of the bully.[9]

States also vary widely on whether bullying must "interfere" with the victimized student's access to education. Some states include such a requirement but many have enacted laws that make no mention of a requirement that the conduct has a negative impact on the victim's educational experience. For a list of the various definitions, see http://www.nsba.org /SchoolLaw/Issues/Safety/Definitions.pdf.

Another important difference between anti-bullying and antiharassment laws is that schools almost invariably have no liability exposure for violations of bullying laws, (Murphy, 2011) while they face multiple pathways of potential liability if they fail to abide antiharassment laws.

To be held liable for the harassment of students by other students, school officials must have actual knowledge of the harassment and act with deliberate indifference in response thereto (Martin, 2010). While this liability standard has been criticized as too weak (Murphy, 2011), it offers at least the possibility of a lawsuit. Schools can also be held accountable (though not for money damages) by the Department of Education's Office for Civil Rights (and similar state agencies vested with similar responsibilities) under a less strict standard if their handling of a harassment complaint and/or their policies and procedures related to the redress of harassment are not "prompt and equitable" (U.S. Department of Education Office for Civil Rights, 2010).

Without effective oversight, bullied students and their parents will be incentivized to utilize antiharassment laws to redress bullying as they provide more opportunities for effective legal redress in the event a school's response is inadequate.

Racial Harassment

The bullying of racial minorities can constitute racial harassment. Racial harassment is prohibited by Title VI of the Civil Rights Act of 1964, which protects students from discrimination based on race, color, and national origin in schools and colleges receiving federal funds. Under Title VI, the discrimination may include racial epithets and slurs and racially motivated attacks. It also may include a racially hostile environment that can be created through verbal, written, or physical conduct that interferes with, or limits the ability of an individual to participate in, or benefit from school programs and activities (U.S. Department of Education Office for Civil Rights, 2005).

Disability Harassment

Likewise, the bullying of students with disabilities can constitute prohibited harassment under both Section 504 of the Rehabilitation Act of 1973 and Title II of the Americans with Disabilities Act of 1990. Disability harassment under Section 504 and Title II is defined as intimidation or abusive behavior toward a student based on disability that creates a hostile environment. The harassment may include verbal acts and name-calling, as well as nonverbal behavior, such as graphic and written statements, or physical harassment (U.S. Department of Education Office for Civil Rights, 2000).

Sexual Harassment

Bullying of females and LGBTQ students can amount to sexual harassment, a form of sex discrimination under Title IX of the Education Amendments of 1972 (Murphy, 2011). (See Appendix for more information on Title IX.) Although Title IX by its express terms covers only harassment "based on sex," it has been interpreted to include LGBTQ students since 1997 when the Department of Education's Office for Civil Rights issued a policy statement declaring that Title IX covered sexual harassment of gay students. More recently, a 2010 Dear Colleague Letter from the Office for Civil Rights made it clear to schools that any harassment motivated by a student's gender is also considered unlawful under Title IX and that this includes real or perceived sexual orientation, gender identification, and expression. Other federal laws that are sometimes used to redress harassment of LGBTQ students based on sexual orientation or gender expression include: the First Amendment and the Equal Protection Clause of the Fourteenth Amendment.

Sexual harassment typically takes the form of verbal acts and name-calling, as well as nonverbal behavior, such as graphic and written statements, but sexual assault, rape, and other forms of sexual violence are also considered sexual harassment under Title IX.

Harassment that targets students who fit in none of these categories is covered by the Tinker doctrine, a decision of the United States Supreme Court that determined the circumstances under which a school can discipline a student for generic verbal harassment. The Court upheld the right of a school to impose discipline, even if the conduct at issue would be protected speech under the First Amendment were it to occur in ordinary society rather than the special environment of a school, but only if the words cause a substantial disruption (*Tinker v. Des Moines Independent Community School District,* 1969).

Both bullying and harassment often involve conduct that also constitutes criminal activity, which means in addition to school-based sanctions, perpetrators can also face criminal prosecution.

State Laws

At the time of this writing, most states had some form of antiharassment law applicable to schools and 47 states had enacted anti-bullying laws. Anti-bullying laws became popularized by the 1999 Columbine High School massacre in Colorado. Several states passed anti-bullying laws in the hope of preventing future school shootings (*Bully Police USA,* 2011).

In general, state anti-bullying laws require schools to create, publicize, and enforce anti-bullying policies. State antiharassment laws tend to mirror the federal laws discussed above. As of 2008, seven states and the District of Columbia had enacted legislation protecting students from harassment based upon sexual orientation and gender expression: California, Iowa, Maine, Maryland, Minnesota, New Jersey, and Vermont. California includes gender identity as well.

Irrespective of whether a state has enacted effective laws to redress all forms of bullying and harassment, and no matter how a school responds under state law, federal laws always applies and can be enforced separately from state law.

This section provides a critical look at anti-bullying laws in North Dakota, Michigan, Oregon, New Jersey, and Massachusetts. We have organized this discussion by examining examples of enumerated and nonenumerated laws:

laws that define bullying as applying broadly to all students, versus applying to categories of students based on characteristics such as race, religion, national origin, sex, sexual orientation, gender identity or expression, disability, or other distinguished or perceived characteristic (Olweus, 2009). We follow with a discussion of the strengths and weaknesses of anti-bullying laws in two states: Massachusetts and New Jersey.

Examples of Nonenumerated Anti-Bullying Laws

Among the states that have passed anti-bullying laws, 34 have nonenumerated laws which generally offer fewer protections to LGBQT students. North Dakota is one of the last states to pass an anti-bullying law (HB1465 in April, 2011). In part, the law states:

> "Bullying" means: a. Conduct[10] that occurs in a public school, on school district premises, in a district owned or leased school bus or school vehicle, or at any public school or school district sanctioned or sponsored activity or event and which: (1) Is so severe, pervasive, or objectively offensive that it substantially interferes with the student's educational opportunities; (2) Places the student in actual and reasonable fear of harm; (3) Places the student in actual and reasonable fear of damage to property of the student; or (4) Substantially disrupts the orderly operation of the public school; or b. Conduct that is received by a student while the student is in a public school, on school district premises, in a district owned or leased school bus or school vehicle, or at any public school or school district sanctioned or sponsored activity or event and which: (1) Is so severe, pervasive, or objectively offensive that it substantially interferes with the student's educational opportunities; (2) Places the student in actual and reasonable fear of harm;
>
> Places the student in actual and reasonable fear of damage to property of the student; or
>
> Substantially disrupts the orderly operation of the public school.

States that enacted nonenumerated laws did so in part because many people feel that using generalities will prevent the inadvertent exclusion of any person or group. However, many activist organizations, such as the National Organization for Women Michigan, argue that enumerated laws are more effective, especially when it comes to the pervasive bullying students face if they are gender nonconforming or identify as something other than heterosexual (GLSEN, 2005).

A 2005 National School Climate Survey found that many school officials do not recognize the bullying motivated by someone's actual or perceived sexual orientation or gender expression to be unacceptable behavior; thus, they do not respond to the problem unless there is a specific law or policy stating that they must, such as an enumerated bullying policy (GLSEN, 2005). This occurs despite federal guidelines that require a response either way. The report also found that students from schools with enumerated policies report less bullying than students at schools with nonenumerated policies for factors such as physical appearance (36% vs. 52%), sexual orientation (32% vs. 43%), and gender expression (26% vs. 37%) (GLSEN, 2005).

For many years, the Michigan legislature has attempted to pass anti-bullying legislation. The issue holding up passage is enumeration. The types of bill introduced are split based primarily on party lines. In general, Democrats advocate for enumerated legislation that mandates school policies to include protected categories such as race, color, religion, ancestry, national origin, gender, sexual orientation, gender identity and expression; or a mental, physical, or sensory disability or impairment; or by any other distinguishing characteristic. In general, Republicans advocate for nonenumerated legislation. Rick Jones, Republican and author of the latest nonenumerated bill (SB 137), has indicated that to include protected categories is shortsighted, for the legislature will then have to revise the law to include newly developed categories year after year. Michigan advocacy organizations, such as Equality Michigan and the National Organization of Women Michigan, advocate only for enumerated anti-bullying and harassment legislation. They argue that enumeration is necessary to protect vulnerable groups.

For years, Michigan has received an "F" by *Bully Police USA*[11] because the legislature has failed to pass an anti-bullying and harassment law. In his Special Message on Education Reform on April 27, 2011, Michigan's Governor Rick Snyder called for a comprehensive anti-bullying law to be in place for the 2011–2012 school year. That did not happen. However, Governor Snyder, perhaps unknowingly, called for enumeration by advocating the use of the Michigan State Board of Education (2006) model policy which recommends enumeration and includes the following actual or perceived characteristics: "race, color, religion, ancestry, national origin, gender, sexual orientation, gender identity and expression; or a mental, physical, or sensory disability or impairment; or by any other distinguishing characteristic."

In a letter to Snyder, the National Organization for Women Michigan advised the governor to promote the creation of state law in line with federal laws and guidelines and advised him to heed the "Letter to Colleague" guidance on bullying and harassment issued on October 26, 2010 by Russlynn Ali, Assistant Secretary for Civil Rights at the Department of Education.

This guidance was used most recently in Michigan in a case of LGBTQ harassment. In a recent settlement with the West Branch-Rose City Area Schools, the U.S. Department of Justice directed the district to provide staff training on Title IX, sexual harassment, and anti-gay harassment when a student left school after experiencing systematic anti-gay harassment. Students in the district are also to receive antiharassment (including anti-gay harassment) education.

At the time of this writing, the National Organization for Women Michigan and Equality Michigan, among other organizations, are advocating for Senate Bill 137 to be amended to include specific protections for the following: race, color, religion, ancestry, national origin, gender, sexual orientation, gender identity and expression; or a mental, physical, or sensory disability or impairment; or by any other distinguishing characteristic. If this enumeration is included, the bill will be in line with federal civil rights protections. School officials then must include the recommended enumeration in their anti-bullying and harassment policies, which will necessarily increase awareness of their responsibilities under the law. The hope is that they will then inform and train teachers on their responsibilities to protect all students from harassment, with an emphasis on the fact that certain students are targeted based on characteristics described in the enumerated list.

Examples of Enumerated Anti-Bullying Laws

Thirteen states have passed enumerated anti-bullying laws with language that protects LGBTQ students: Arkansas, California, Colorado, Connecticut, Iowa, Illinois, Maryland, New Jersey, New York, North Carolina, Oregon, Rhode Island, Vermont, and Washington (GLSEN, n.d.).

Oregon has been wrestling with the question of enumeration. Oregon passed an anti-bullying law in 2001 and a 2009 study found that rates of bullying had not decreased as a result. The 2009 study found that more than 40% of eighth-graders had experienced bullying, with the highest rates among students of color, girls, and LGBTQ students (Oregon Healthy Teens Survey, 2009). To better address the most targeted groups, Oregon added protected categories to the law: "Harassment, intimidation or bullying may be based on, but not be limited to, the protected class status of a person. 'Protected class' means a group of persons distinguished, or perceived to be distinguished, by race, color, religion, sex, sexual orientation, national origin, marital status, familial status, source of income, or disability" (Oregon, HB 2599). More research is necessary to determine whether enumeration will favorably impact bullying rates in Oregon.

The story of Rutgers student Tyler Clementi, who committed suicide after being tormented because of his sexual orientation, inspired the New Jersey legislature to enact an Anti-Bullying Bill of Rights, which became effective on September 1, 2011. The state's previous anti-bullying law did not significantly reduce incidents of school bullying; thus, a stronger law was crafted and has been described by some as the toughest state anti-bullying legislation to date.

The legislation is 22 pages in length and includes cyber-bullying, incidents of bullying that occur outside of school, and the requirement of appointing and training anti-bullying specialists at the school level and anti-bullying coordinators at the district level. Each school must also appoint safety teams that include parents, teachers, and staff responsible for various aspects of bullying prevention, including dealing with complaints of bullying, harassment, and intimidation, strengthening school climate, educating the community, and training staff. The law requires that public school teaching staff complete at least two hours of suicide prevention training, including how suicide is related to incidents of bullying, harassment, and intimidation. New Jersey defines harassment, bullying, and intimidation as follows:

> "Harassment, intimidation or bullying" means any gesture, any written or physical act, or any electronic communication whether it be a single incident or a series of incidents, that is reasonably perceived as being motivated either by any actual or perceived characteristic, such as race, color, religion, ancestry, national origin, gender, sexual orientation, gender identity and expression, or a mental, physical or sensory disability, or by any other distinguishing characteristic that takes place on school property, at any school-sponsored function, on a school bus, or off school grounds . . . that substantially disrupts or interferes with the orderly operation of the school or the rights of other students.

The law does not provide guidance on the differences between bullying, harassment, and intimidation, although it provides enumerated categories as described above.

Anti-Bullying Laws: Massachusetts and New Jersey

Massachusetts and New Jersey passed anti-bullying laws, in 2009 and 2011, respectively. This section will compare and contrast these two state laws for their strengths and weaknesses.

In April 2009, 11-year-old Carl Walker-Hoover of Springfield, Massachusetts, committed suicide after schoolmates bullied him for weeks. Nine months later, 15-year-old Phoebe Prince of South Hadley, Massachusetts, committed suicide after months of verbal, physical, and sexual harassment by classmates. In both cases, victims' parents reported these incidents to school officials, but the behavior persisted. Ultimately, public outrage led to the creation of the first anti-bullying statute in Massachusetts in May, 2010.

The Massachusetts law defines "bullying" as:

> [T]he repeated use by one or more students of a written, verbal or electronic expression or a physical act or gesture or any combination thereof, directed at [another student] that: (i) causes physical or emotional harm to the [other student] or damage to the [other student's] property; (ii) places the [other student] in reasonable fear of harm to himself or of damage to his property; (iii) creates a hostile environment at school for the [other student]; (iv) infringes on the rights of the [other student] at school; or (v) materially and substantially disrupts the education process or the orderly operation of a school.

Strengths. The Massachusetts law provides a separate definition for the term "cyber-bullying" as involving "bullying through the use of technology or any electronic communication." A hostile environment is defined in this legislation as "a situation in which bullying causes the school environment to be permeated with intimidation, ridicule or insult that is sufficiently severe or pervasive to alter the conditions of the student's education." The statute also provides that bullying is prohibited "on school grounds" or in connection with school activities, and in off-campus locations when the incidents create a hostile educational environment which "infringes on the rights of the victim at school or materially and substantially disrupts the education process or the orderly operation of a school." This fairly unusual provision may actually provide protection superior to the protection afforded by harassment laws because it regulates off-campus conduct based not on where the behavior originated but on where the harmful effects land.

Under the New Jersey law, district policies to prevent bullying, harassment, and intimidation must be linked to the homepage of the district's website, and the name, school, phone number, school address, school email address of the school anti-bullying specialist and the district anti-bullying coordinator must be listed. Policies must include consequences and remedial actions for persons who report false allegations as a means of retaliation or to bully, harass, or intimate. In addition, schools and districts are required to implement, document, and assess bullying prevention programs. Incidents of bullying, harassment, and intimidation must be reported to the school principal on the same day as school personnel either witnessed or learned of them, and in writing within two days. Investigations of reported incidents of bullying, harassment, and intimidation must begin within one day, the results of which must be reported to the school superintendent within two days of the completion of the investigation.

The report cards must identify the number and nature of reports of bullying, harassment, and intimidation.

Other strengths of the New Jersey law include that the definition of bullying is quite broad and includes a *single act or series of incidents*. It also covers behavior that occurs off school grounds, but causes harm on campus and includes a requirement that schools produce annual report cards showing how many incidents were reported and how they were resolved. It also imposes a short 10-day period for resolving complaints. The law also requires a teacher certification programs to ensure that all teachers are effectively trained in handling reports of bullying, harassment, and intimidation.

Weaknesses. The Massachusetts law includes a provision for students who knowingly make false accusations to "be subject to disciplinary action." This suggests a greater need to address false reports of bullying than to address bullying itself given that false reporting carries mandatory punishment whereas sanctions for bullying are only discretionary. The threat of mandatory punishment for false reporting will likely quell reporting; some victims will fear being disbelieved and disrespected.

More importantly, the Massachusetts anti-bullying law prohibits private rights of action and conflicts with antiharassment laws in several ways. First, it does not require a school's response to be "equitable," which is mandatory under harassment laws and ensures, for example, that the same policies and procedures used to redress race-based bullying should be used to redress sex-based bullying, so forth. Second, the *resolution* of a bullying complaint is not subject to a "promptness" requirement as is mandatory under harassment laws. This is problematic because a swift investigation affords little benefit or protection to the victim if the matter is if not also resolved promptly. Although schools are required to ensure that no further acts of "bullying or retaliation" occur, harassment laws require more because they also obligate schools to "eliminate the hostile environment created by the harassment" and "address its effects" (United States Department of Education Office for Civil Rights, 2010). Addressing the effects of a hostile environment may include providing specific support and restitution to the victim such as counseling, reassigned classes, repeating courses at no cost, tuition adjustments, and private tutoring.

The Massachusetts law fails to mention that "bullying" may also violate a victim's civil rights, if, for example, the behavior constitutes "sexual harassment." Some scholars have warned against enacting legislation that fails to articulate the relationship between bullying laws and harassment laws including that if a school fails to include sexual harassment in its anti-bullying policy, this may be seen as an attempt to minimize or mask the problem (Martin, 2010; Meyer, 2009; Murphy, 2011; Stein, 2003). Others argue that the "misframing" of sexual harassment as "bullying" diminishes attention to the problem of sexual harassment in education which could undermine effective enforcement of antidiscrimination laws (Murphy, 2011). In response to this problem, the United States Department of Education issued an advisory in October 2010 directing states and school officials to be mindful of their responsibility to respond to incidents based on the nature of the conduct reported, irrespective of how the behavior is labeled (see United States Department of Education Office for Civil Rights, 2010).

Perhaps most importantly, the Massachusetts law lacks meaningful enforcement provisions. It requires school officials to take certain steps when incidents of bullying are reported, but there are no sanctions if the required steps are not taken. School officials thus possess no incentive to respond effectively to bullying. As Murphy (2011) states:

> Put simply, if lawmakers see fit to mandate or forbid conduct, such laws should be enforceable lest they be perceived as a meaningless tease or ploy to subvert the democratic process by which social values are expressed in codified rules of behavior. Enacting a law that forbids bullying, while explicitly disallowing enforcement, may well incentivize the very conduct the law seeks to deter because doing nothing becomes an expressly tolerated legal option. (p. 16)

School officials may have legitimate concerns about liability, but without meaningful enforcement, schools can safely opt to do little or nothing in response to reports of bullying behavior. In turn, students may become reluctant to report bullying because they perceive that adults will do little or nothing to help. If a situation escalates, a victim may be even further deterred from reporting and choose more desperate measures. If such circumstances occurred before the new Massachusetts law had been enacted, school officials who discouraged the victim from reporting might have been vulnerable to liability for playing a role in "originally causing" the victim's harm by intentionally discouraging her from reporting (Murphy, 2011). Under the new law, the same school official will enjoy complete immunity, even for "original causation," because the statute forbids *all* private rights of action

At the same time, nothing in Massachusetts law forbids bullies from filing suit against school officials for wrongful discipline. In short, *all* relevant laws in Massachusetts forbid the filing of legal actions against school officials for their wrongful failure to protect victims from harm but *no* laws forbid bullies from suing schools for wrongful discipline. From a risk-management perspective, this means school officials are incentivized to side with the bully every time. And because desperation is often a by-product of inadequate legal protection, the relatively unprotected victim is at greater risk, ironically due to the enactment of a law ostensibly designed to protect her from harm.

There are also numerous problems with the New Jersey law. First, the law requires that each district adopt a policy prohibiting bullying, harassment, and intimidation; however, it also indicates that districts may do so according to local control (the adoption of which must include representation by parents, school employees, volunteers, students, administrators, and community representatives). Policy decisions, such as whether to enumerate a list of protected categories of students who may be targeted for bullying, are left up to individual districts. This is a potential weakness in the legislation as the interests of the most vulnerable populations may not be represented in policy decisions. Second, these new requirements do not include allocating funds to schools that are obligated to pay for training on bullying, harassment, and intimidation for school staff.

Third, the New Jersey law requires the development of a grievance process for resolving complaints, which sounds good but in practice may limit the oversight value of potential litigation by the victimized student. This is because schools are effectively immunized from liability if they do *anything* in response to a report of bullying, such as convening a grievance hearing, even if the hearing itself is ineffective and unfair to the victim. This gives schools an escape in terms of lawsuits by victims even under Title IX where schools are protected from liability so long as they are not "deliberately indifferent" to a report of bullying. This is one of the reasons why students are often better off addressing a school's unfair handling of a bullying complaint, where the behavior also constitutes harassment, with the Office for Civil Rights at the Department of Education. OCR can hold schools accountable irrespective of the deliberate indifference standard, whenever the school fails to provide a "prompt and equitable" response. While OCR does not pay out damages, they wield significant authority over schools and have the capacity to coerce officials to change policies and/or reconsider decisions that were inadequately responsive to a victim's complaint.

A fourth problem can be seen in New Jersey's description of the amount of conduct necessary to establish that bullying has occurred. Bullying is forbidden only if it "severely or pervasively causes physical or emotional harm" which is a much higher standard than that which defines harassment under federal law. Title IX, for example, defines harassment as "severe or pervasive" conduct, irrespective of harm. New Jersey also adopted an unusually high standard for the definition of "hostile environment" bullying in that it must "substantially disrupt or interfere with the orderly operation of a school or interfering with a student's education." Under Title IX, hostile environment need only "interfere" with a student's access to equal education.

A fifth problem, that should also be seen as a strength, deals with the consequences for school officials who ignore bullying. The maximum punishment for a school official who fails to investigate or who should have known but fails to take action is the possibility of "discipline." This provision is a strength because most laws are silent as to whether a school official can even be subject to sanctions, but it is also a weakness in that discipline is not mandatory. The statute says only that officials will be "subject to" discipline, which means even a blatant violation may never actually be disciplined.

A sixth problem is that there is no mention of sexual assault as a form of bullying under this new law. In a list of behaviors for which a student can be expelled, physical, but not sexual, assault is included. This leads to a seventh problem with the law: the omission of the word "sex" altogether from the definition of bullying. Bullying is qualified by the phrase "motivated by" and a list of characteristics is provided but the word "sex" is excluded. This is curious and a cause for concern because while "gender" is included, the exclusion of "sex" means that sexualized bullying is not covered.

The word "sex" is a term of art in this context and is the sole word used to define harassment under Title IX. Without the word "sex" in the New Jersey definition, the law arguably excludes all bullying that involves sexual assault unless it can be shown that the assault was driven by gender animus. It is unclear why New Jersey would have chosen a less inclusive word than that which has been codified in federal law since 1972. The word "sex" has been construed in federal law to include both sex and gender, but the word "gender" does not necessarily include "sex." Making things more confusing, the New Jersey law makes reference to existing laws against discrimination, which use the word "sex" not "gender," which means lawmakers knew that by using the word "gender" they would be excluding a large category of sexualized bullying. The result of this terminology choice means that if a student is bullied and it is sexualized in nature but not necessarily "based on gender" the student has no choice but to rely on Title IX because the behavior is not forbidden under New Jersey's anti-bullying law. This is a perplexing aspect of New Jersey's law given that most bullying of girls is sexual—even if not driven by gender animus.

Finally, the New Jersey law includes an annual "report card" requirement that obligates schools to publicly reveal data on bullying. This is a positive feature of the law, but it has built-in weaknesses in that schools face no sanctions for not reporting, or for reporting numbers that may not reflect the actual number of reported incidents. It would have been better for lawmakers to include a sanction for noncompliance, as is required under an analogous federal law that mandates annual disclosures of crimes on campus in higher education. The Clery Act originally carried no sanctions for schools that filed no annual report cards or reported false information. When Congress added a sanction of $25,000 per violation, compliance rates skyrocketed. In short, reporting standards (report cards) are a good idea, but are less valuable without sanctions for noncompliance.

Conclusions. With both of these relatively new state anti-bullying laws in Massachusetts and New Jersey, the weaknesses may outweigh the strengths. Tougher standards and lack of meaningful enforcement suggest that federal antiharassment laws provide superior protection and redress for victims.

Pending Federal Laws

Since state laws and their effectiveness vary greatly, numerous organizations like the American Federation of Teachers, the American School Health Association, the National Education Association, and the National Parent Teacher Association are advocating for a federal anti-bullying law. In 2011, Congress introduced legislation for the creation of a federal anti-bullying law and to provide funding for schools to create bullying prevention programming.

In April 2011 the Safe Schools Improvement Act (SSIA) was introduced in both the House (H.R. 1648) and Senate (S. 506). SSIA would amend the Elementary and Secondary Education Act to require schools receiving federal funds to adopt codes of conduct specifically prohibiting bullying and harassment, including on the basis of sexual orientation and gender identity. States would have to report data on bullying and harassment to the Department of Education and then the Department of Education would have to provide Congress with a data-driven report every two years. In addition, the proposed law would allow schools to use funding under the Safe and Drug-Free Schools and Communities Act to provide professional development for staff to learn prevention strategies and how to effectively intervene when incidents of bullying or harassment occur and to implement student education programs.

Organizations that champion rights for LGBTQ individuals, like Human Rights Campaign and GLSEN, support SSIA because it would help prevent and address the harassment of LGBTQ students nationwide, something that is long overdue. As previously stated LGBTQ students experience harassment and bullying at higher rates than their non-LGBTQ peers (Human Rights Campaign, 2011).

The American Association of University Women (AAUW) also supports the bill. One of the leading organizations in documenting sexual harassment in schools through research reports and advocating for change through public policy and community programming, AAUW recognizes that bullying adversely impacts students' education. Further, AAUW supports legislation that clearly enumerates categories of students that are protected for this research indicates that children who attend schools with antiharassment policies containing clearly enumerated student categories report that they feel safer (54% vs. 36%) and are less likely to skip a class because they feel uncomfortable or unsafe (5% vs. 16%) (AAUW, 2009).

In her 2011 testimony at the U.S. Commission on Civil Rights hearing on "Peer-to-Peer Violence and Bullying: Examining the Federal Response," Lisa Maatz, AAUW's Director of Public Policy and Government Relations argued:

> AAUW strongly believes that our country should provide an excellent education for all children, yet the prevalence of bullying and harassment prevents many children from accessing these opportunities. Whether based on race, color, national origin, sex disability, sexual orientation, religion, gender identity or any other characteristic, bullying and harassment interfere with both students' safety and ability to learn. Therefore, AAUW supports the adoption and enforcement of a federal law to deter and address bullying and harassment, which will help ensure a safe learning environment for all students. (AAUW, 2011)

Critics of the proposed federal law argue that educators should focus on improving their school climate and on prevention programming than on a law that may or may not be enforced (Trump, 2011). It is a valid point and fortunately, a month after the introduction of SSIA, a second bill was introduced into the Senate, the Successful, Safe, and Healthy Students Act (SSHSA) of 2011 (S.919), to address the prevention side.

SSHSA aims to improve student achievement by promoting student health and wellness, preventing bullying, harassment, violence, and drug use, and fostering a positive school climate. SSHSA will authorize $1 billion in grants to states so they can develop comprehensive, data-driven and evidence-based programs that promote student health and wellness, prevent bullying, violence and drug use, and foster a positive school climate. Education agencies will have to establish policies to prohibit and prevent bullying and harassment of all students, including LGBTQ students, in order to be eligible for the funding. This bill also has wide support from activist and educational organizations.

The proposed federal legislation resembles early versions of the campus-based Clery Act in terms of requiring data to be gathered and reported to public. The benefits of this legislation include the requirement of public report cards regarding harassment and the inclusion of all forms of protected classes, especially since some states do not cover all protected categories. Defining harassment to include all categories creates baseline protection for all students equally.

One area of concern regarding the proposed law is the standard for determining whether harassment or bullying has occurred. Bullying need not be severe or pervasive, as is required under federal antiharassment laws, but it must place students in *reasonable* fear of physical harm. This is not only a disturbingly high standard, it also conflicts with the definition of harassment which *must* be severe or pervasive, yet need not place students in fear of physical safety. This confusion between the standards may expose some students who are not members of protected classes to more bullying and harm while also inhibiting redress of bullying that does not create a reasonable fear of physical harm. For example, a child may be terrified of a bully but the school could still find his fear of physical harm to be "unreasonable."

Another problem is that violations carry no sanctions; thus, a school can refuse to provide data, or produce false data, yet face no consequences. Congress should learn from its experience with the Clery Act. Schools generally refused to comply until Congress amended the law to provide for sanctions. A similar sanction provision should be added to this bill.

A third problem involves the proposed grievance procedures. While the new law allows for grievance procedures, which is a good thing, they are not required to be "prompt" or "equitable" as is required under antiharassment laws. These requirements should be added to the bill to ensure that bullying complaints are resolved swiftly and fairly

Conclusions

Bullying and harassment are too often misconceived as normal parts of growing up: behaviors we all experience at some time in our lives that may be unpleasant, but eventually make us stronger. But research shows that bullying and harassment are not normal. To the contrary, bullying, harassment, and intimidation are often criminal in nature and implicate the fundamental civil rights of victims to achieve and equal education.

Misframing and downplaying the nature of the harm leaves many victims unaware of their rights and may inhibit their access to legal redress. The word "bullying" alone creates confusion through distortion because it evokes no understanding of the harm as an offensive act committed against a person based on who they are in society. Indeed, at the time of this writing, the United States Department of Education's Office for Civil Rights is investigating at least two Connecticut school districts for mishandling Title IX violations as bullying.

Labeling behavior as "bullying" changes nothing about a school's legal responsibilities to redress harassment as a civil rights violation. Yet the failure of officials to use the word "harassment" may well prevent victims from exercising their rights in a timely fashion, if at all, simply because they may never come to appreciate the harm they suffered as subject to redress under federal civil rights legislation. Schools benefit from framing offensive behavior as "bullying" for many reasons, including that erroneous labeling can create false data. For example, if criminal sexual assault or sexual harassment is labeled "bullying," a school can publicly claim to have little or no issues with criminal activity or discrimination. Thus, the bullying label keeps liability costs down.

- To protect against the risk that anti-bullying laws will inhibit victims' understanding of the harm as civil rights harassment, and to ensure that victims will have a full opportunity to pursue all available means of legal redress, state lawmakers should codify a clear cross-reference to federal and state antiharassment and civil rights laws in anti-bullying statutes. This would make the public acutely aware that bullying behavior may *also* violate antiharassment/discrimination laws. Anti-bullying laws should also require that schools adopt policies and procedures that provide for a "prompt and equitable" response and resolution to reports of bullying as this is the standard schools must apply when responding to reports of harassment. It is also the standard applied by the United States Department of Education Office for Civil Rights when victims file complaints against schools for their mishandling of harassment complaints. An ideal statute should also state that a school is mandated to take "immediate" action to "eliminate" any hostile environment caused by bullying, prevent its recurrence and address its effects with "effective correction action," including disciplinary action against the bully because, again, these things are mandatory under antiharassment laws.

- Legislators should also add language that allows for damages lawsuits in state court when a school official is "deliberately indifferent" to bullying as this roughly mirrors the antiharassment liability standard applicable in federal court when a school official fails to respond to reports of sexual harassment. Legislators should eliminate the economic pressure schools now function under that incentivizes officials to ignore certain behaviors, side with bullies, and misframe the problem of harassment, particularly sexual harassment, so as to render it effectively invisible.

- As stated previously, the most vulnerable populations are not greatly helped by non-enumerated anti-bullying laws and policies. Although policy alone cannot solve the problem, it can help shape our understanding of the harm, and influence out expectations of how we are treated and how we treat others. Responsible policy design can do much to change how we think about ourselves, others, and the world in general. Legislation that guides anti-bullying policy can do much to protect student populations currently targeted by bullying and harassment, yet underserved in existing disciplinary codes.

The problems of both bullying and harassment are serious and they threaten the ability of many students to achieve an education. Simple legislative remedies can be adopted to ensure that all forms of bullying are properly named and effectively redressed. Without effective policies for meaningful enforcement, student suicides will continue because desperation is a by-product of inadequate legal protection.

Finally, even the best laws are meaningless if the people they are designed to protect are unaware of their existence or have no means by which to seek enforcement. Thus, it is imperative that schools take effective steps to ensure that both students and parents are aware of their rights, and understand all the laws that protect students from harassment and bullying in school. Parents and advocates should also be proactive about understanding not only school policies but also state and federal laws that address bullying and harassment, and they should take steps to inform school boards and community leaders of the need for improvements in awareness and enforcement of anti-bullying and antiharassment laws.

Notes

1. Fla. Stat. Ann. § 1006.147.
2. 105 Ill. Comp. Stat. Ann., 5/27–23.7.
3. Ind. Code Ann. § 20–33–8–0.2.
4. Miss. Code Ann. § 37–11–67.
5. Nev. Rev. Stat. Ann. §§ 388.122 388.125.
6. Ala. Code § 16–28B-3.
7. Alaska Stat. Ann. §14.33.250.
8. N.H. Rev. Stat. Ann. § 193-F:3.
9. Haw. Admin. Code § 8–19–2.
10. "Conduct" includes the use of technology or other electronic media.
11. Bully Police USA is an advocacy organization for bullied children, which reports on state antibullying laws.

References

American Association of University Women. (2009). *Written testimony of the American Association of University Women before the U.S. House Committee on Education and Labor, Early Childhood, Elementary and Secondary*

Education Subcommittee and Healthy Families and Communities Subcommittee Hearing on Strengthening School Safety through Prevention of Bullying. Retrieved from http://www.aauw.org/act/issue_advocacy /actionpages/upload/ SchoolSafety_070809.pdf

American Association of University Women. (2011). *Crossing the line: Sexual harassment in schools.* Washington, DC.

Bully Police USA. (2011). Retrieved from http://www.bullypolice.org/

Espelage, D., & Swearer, S. (2010). *Bullying in north American schools.* New York: Taylor & Francis.

GLSEN. (2005). *From teasing to torment: School climate in America, a survey of students and teachers.* Retrieved from http://www.glsen.org/cgi-bin/iowa/all/ news /record /1859.html

GLSEN. (2007). *The 2007 national school climate survey: Key findings on the experiences of lesbian, gay, bisexual and transgender youth in our nation's schools.* Executive Summary. Retrieved from http://www.glsen.org/binary-data/GLSEN_ATTACHMENTS/file/000/001/1306–1.pdf

GLSEN. (n.d.). *States with safe school laws.* Retrieved from http://www.glsen.org/ cgi-n/iowa/all/library/record/2344.html?state=media

Gruber, J. E., & Fineran, S. (2008). Comparing the impact of bullying and sexual harassment victimization on the mental and physical health of adolescents. *Sex Roles, 59,* 1–13.

Hampson, R. (2010, April). A "watershed" case in school bullying? *USA Today.* Retrieved from http://www.usatoday.com/news/nation/2010–04–04-bullying_N.htm

Human Rights Campaign. (2011). *Safe schools improvement act.* Retrieved from http://www.hrc.org/issues/12142.htm

Martin, J. L. (2010). Bullying and sexual harassment of peers. In M. Paludi & F. Denmark (Eds.), *Victims of sexual assault and abuse: Resources and responses for individuals and families,* Vol. 1: *Incidence of psychological dimensions* (pp. 89–109). Westport, CT: Praeger.

McGrath, M. J. (2006). *School bullying: Tools for avoiding harm and liability.* Thousand Oaks, CA: Corwin Press.

Meyer, E. (2009). *Gender, bullying, and harassment: Strategies to end sexism and homophobia in schools.* New York: Teachers College Press.

Michigan State Board of Education. (2006). *Model anti-bullying policy.* Retrieved from http://www.michigan.gov/documents/mde/SBE_Model_AntiBullying_ Policy_Revised_9.8_172355_7.pdf

Mishna, F., Pepler, D., & Wiener, J. (2006). Factors associated with perceptions and responses to bullying situations by children, parents, teachers, and principals. *Victims & Offenders, 1,* 255–288.

Murphy, W. (2011). Sexual harassment and Title IX: What's bullying got to do with it? *New England Journal on Criminal and Civil Confinement, 37,* 11–24.

Olweus Bullying Prevention Program. State and Federal Bullying Information. (2009). Retrieved from http://www.olweus.org/public/bullying_laws.page

Oregon Healthy Teens Survey. (2009). Retrieved from http://public.health.oregon. gov BirthDeathCertificates/Surveys/OregonHealthyTeens/Pages/index.aspx

Robinson, J. P., & Espelage, D. L. (2011). Inequities in educational and psychological outcomes between LGBTQ and straight students in middle and high school. *Educational Researcher, 40,* 315–330.

Stein, N. (2003) Bullying or sexual harassment: The missing discourse of rights in an era of zero tolerance. *Arizona Law Review, 45,* 783–799.

Steineger, M. (2001). *Preventing and countering school-based harassment: A resource guide for K-12 educators.* Portland, OR: Northwest Regional Educational Laboratory.

Successful, Safe, and Healthy Students Act of 2011. (2011). S. 919, Retrieved from http://www.opencongress.org/bill/112-s919/show

Tinker v. Des Moines Independent Community School District, 393 U.S. 503 (1969).

Trump, K. (2011). *Proactive school security and emergency preparedness planning.* Thousand Oaks, CA: Corwin Press.

United States Department of Education Office for Civil Rights. (2000, July). *Reminder of responsibilities under section 504 of the Rehabilitation Act of 1973 and Title II of the Americans with Disabilities Act.* Retrieved from http://ed.gov/ about/offices/list/ocr /docs/disabharassltr.html

United States Department of Education Office for Civil Rights. (2005, March). *Frequently asked questions about racial harassment.* Retrieved from http:// ed.gov/about/offices/list/ocr/qa-raceharass.html

United States Department of Education Office for Civil Rights. (2010, October). *Dear colleague letter.* Retrieved from http://www2.ed.gov/about/offices/list / ocr/letters/colleague-201010.pdf

Appendix

Title IX Fact Sheet for K-12 Students and Parents

Developed by Jennifer L. Martin, PhD, with help from Wendy Murphy, New England Law, Boston

Title IX of the Education Amendments of 1972 states: *No person in the United States shall, on the basis of sex, be excluded from participation in, be denied the benefits of, or be subjected to discrimination under any education program or activity receiving federal financial assistance.*

Title IX was named the Patsy T. Mink Equal Opportunity in Education Act on October 9, 2002.

Your Rights under Title IX

Title IX protects students of all genders and sexual orientations from sex discrimination in schools. Students in federally funded institutions, public schools, colleges, and universities[1] have a right to an education free from discrimination on the basis of sex, including equitable access to all academic programs, activities, athletics, course offerings, admissions, recruitment, scholarships, and be free from harassment (including assault) based upon sex, gender, gender identity and expression (real and perceived), and sexual orientation (real and perceived).[2] Title IX protects students in academic and nonacademic activities because of pregnancy, birth, miscarriage, and abortion. Title IX also protects faculty, staff, and whistle-blowers from sexual harassment, sex discrimination, and retaliation.[3]

School policies must provide for prompt and equitable investigation and resolution, including time frames for resolution and an antiretaliation statement (Title IX prohibits retaliation against those who file complaints). School policies must specifically indicate that sexual assault, even a single incident, is covered under Title IX. Students have the right to file a complaint with the school if their rights under Title IX are violated. Victims may also file a complaint with the Department of Education's Office for Civil Rights if a school's policies or handling of a complaint are not compliant with Title IX. Victims may also recover monetary damages under Title IX if the school shows *deliberate indifference* in dealing with the discrimination or related retaliation.

Each federally funded institution (school district) must designate a Title IX Coordinator to oversee compliance and grievance procedures. The identity and contact information of the Title IX Coordinator must be made public and be readily available to students, staff, and parents.

What You Can Do

1. Investigate whether your school (your child's school) is equitable in terms of sports scheduling and facilities.
2. If you are experiencing sexual harassment, keep a log of times, dates, and specific experiences.
3. Tell your parents, as well as school personnel, what is happening.
4. Find your district's antiharassment policy and become familiar with the policies and procedures for reporting, investigation, and resolution. If the policy does not enumerate protected categories (such as sex; gender; sexual orientation and gender identity, real and perceived), ask responsible school officials to include them. Advocate for the inclusion of all other policies to ensure that a school is compliant with Title IX's prompt and equity mandate.

5. Find out who your Title IX Coordinator is. This information should be made public. If your district does not have a Title IX Coordinator, advocate for the designation and training of one.
6. See the Department of Education's Office for Civil Rights "Letter to Colleagues" (October 26, 2010) for more information about your rights to be free from harassment in school under Title IX and other antidiscrimination laws: http://www2.ed.gov/about/offices/list/ocr/letters/colleague-201010.pdf
7. See the Department of Education's Office for Civil Rights "Letter to Colleagues" (April 4, 2011) for more information about the responsibility of schools to prohibit sexual violence: http://www.whitehouse.gov/sites/default/files/dear_colleague_sexual_violence.pdf

Notes

1. Most private institutions are subject to Title IX regulation for their acceptance of federal funds.
2. Bullying, sexual harassment, and sexual assault are often conflated or used interchangeably. Such mislabeling does not alleviate schools from responding properly and enforcing Title IX provisions.
3. Schools may have the authority and responsibility to address sexual harassment even if the behavior occurs off campus, and/or in social media and other cyber venues.

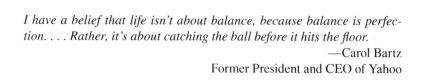

I have a belief that life isn't about balance, because balance is perfection. . . . Rather, it's about catching the ball before it hits the floor.

—Carol Bartz
Former President and CEO of Yahoo

3

Advancing Women into Leadership: A Global Perspective on Overcoming Barriers

Janet L. Kottke and Kathie L. Pelletier[1]

College student interchange, circa 1976, in a world history class:

Student (exclaiming excitedly): The majority of the physicians in the Soviet Union are women!

Another student who had visited the Soviet Union: Yes, and they are treated as second-class citizens, and paid low wages.

Both students were correct. In 1976, 77% of medical professionals were women; 52% of "head doctors" were women, indicating that though women constituted more than three-fourths of the profession, they were less likely to be appointed to the more prestigious head doctor post; and finally, female physicians earned, on average, two-thirds of men's salaries (Buckley, 1981). The situation of female physicians in the Soviet Union in 1976 illustrates a prevalent theme for women: despite high levels of skill, knowledge, and education, even in a society that paid lip service to the value of both men and women's work, women were less likely to be promoted to the higher ranks of a profession valued in societies worldwide.

Succeeding in a Man's World

Few would argue that the auto industry is not dominated heavily by men. Of the millions of autoworkers worldwide (Automobile Industry, 2008), few are women (Catalyst, 2011a), with the top spots nearly an exclusive men's club (Adams, Gupta, Haughton, & Leeth, 2007; Catalyst, 2011a). Yet, in the Philippines, four women have achieved top leader status in four different automobile companies: Elizabeth H. Lee, Chief Operating Officer of Universal Motors Corp/Nissan; Fe Perez-Agudo, President and Chief Operating Officer of Hyundai Asia Resources Inc.; Ginia Domingo, President of Columbian Auto Car, Philippine owner of Kia; and Maricar Cristobal Parco, President of Columbian Auto Car, an exclusive distributor of BMW. It is no accident that the Philippines is where we find women who have achieved top executive status, even in as tough a nut to crack as the auto industry (Salazar, 2011). In the Philippines, 50% of senior management positions are held by women, the largest proportion in the world (Grant Thornton, 2009; McIndoe, 2007). Further, in 2009, women comprised 47% of the membership of private firms' boards of directors in the Philippines, again the highest percentage across the globe for that year (Grant Thornton, 2009). How did the United States and the United Kingdom compare on this latter demographic of boardroom membership, a high point of organizational power? 20% and 21%, respectively (Grant Thornton, 2009).[2] Why such a difference? Women in the Philippines historically have held strong roles in the home and at work; men are used to having a woman as a boss, women have more education than their male counterparts, and affordable child care is readily available (McIndoe, 2007). Nevertheless, gender discrimination lingers in the Philippines: women make, on average, about 75% of men's salaries, although this disparity (surprisingly) narrows at the very top organizational rungs (McIndoe, 2007) such that the disparity averages 5% across all jobs; yet, women are disproportionately represented in undervalued jobs such as nursing (Dejardin, 2009). Although success at attaining leadership positions for the women of the Philippines provides inspiration for women around the world, occupational disparity for women in the Philippines and the comparatively fewer female top executives in the two Anglo countries demonstrates that leadership gender equality has not been achieved.

Women Are Working, But Not Often at the Top

The number of women in top leadership positions, though growing, remains remarkably small across almost all industries in most countries. That fewer women than men are in the boardroom or at the helms of *Fortune* 500 or *Financial Times* Stock Exchange (FTSE) 100 companies is not in dispute (Catalyst, 2007, 2011b; Singh, Terjesen, & Vinnicombe, 2008). For example, when Hansen, Ibarra, and Peyer (2010) selected the best-performing CEOs worldwide, only 29 (1.5%) of the 2,000 firms they reviewed were headed by women. In the United Kingdom in 2010, 12.5% of the top 100 firms were headed by women (Vinnicombe, Sealy, Graham, & Doldor, 2010). In the United States at the time of this writing, just 3.2% of the *Fortune* 500 have women at their helms (Catalyst, 2011b)—and that included the newly appointed Meg Whitman to computer giant Hewlett-Packard.

Identifiable Barriers

As considerable data exist to address the firewalls (Bendl & Schmidt, 2010) that block women's advancement in business organizations, we are focusing our chapter on the status of women in organizational leadership positions. First, we will provide illustrative statistics, across regions, of the proportions of women in the workforce, their educational levels, professional occupational attainment, and proportions of top leadership spots held by women, which will demonstrate a number of disparities. We will then turn to the possible causes for these disparities, using as our framework, the barriers to women in leadership as outlined by Yukl (2010). These barriers include:

- Initial placement in dead-end jobs
- Lack of mentoring and/or sponsorship
- Little or no access to critical development assignments
- Differential standards on performance appraisals
- Little or no access to informal networks of communication
- Counterproductive behavior and harassment by coworkers (e.g., sabotage, undermining, threats, hostile work environments)

In this chapter, we focus our attention on placement of women in (1) dead-end jobs, (2) lack of or inadequate mentoring, and (3) differential performance standards. Although our focus is mainly on these three barriers, it is important to note that all of these barriers are interrelated, with all operating in a cycle that limits the movement of women up the corporate ladder. For example, when women are placed in dead-end jobs, their access to meaningful mentoring experiences and/or sponsorships is limited. Moreover, the mentors might not be in a position to influence positively their protégés' mobility. Further, when women are in lower level positions, they are not typically given critical or "push" assignments that develop their skills. In fact, when women are on the periphery, they have little to no access to informal networks where critical information is shared, thus they lack important feedback as to their performance. Consequently, they are not likely to be afforded opportunities to showcase their talents and contributions to the upper echelon. The implications of these dynamics are that women tend to be underrepresented in the highest levels of the hierarchy. The sixth barrier, counterproductive behavior and coworker harassment, is a behavioral dynamic that not only disenfranchises women who seek leadership positions but also works to penalize women as they make upward strides. In addition, undermining and harassing actions tend to operate covertly in the occupational environment. Thus, there is limited data on this barrier in global, organizational contexts.

Finally, we will conclude by summarizing the positive actions that women, men, and organizations can take to ensure that both women and men are provided equal opportunities. In a nutshell, we are going to look at why women are more often in dead-end jobs, and when they are able to achieve a career path toward a top leadership spot, women are less sponsored and differentially evaluated.

There is considerable theorizing, research, and anecdotal data regarding the reasons for why so few women advance to the top tiers of the corporate ladder. By necessity, there will be some overlap in discussion of the barriers. For example, differential performance standards are likely to play a role in why women are less often mentored or more often placed in dead-end jobs.

Dead-End Jobs Leading to Underrepresentation of Women in Leadership Positions

Though the number of women working outside the home is substantial (International Labour Office [ILO], 2010; see Table 3.1 for employment rates of women for 20 developed and developing countries), the vast majority of these women are working in jobs that are occupationally segregated, often poorly paid, and frequently not in the pipeline to the top executive jobs (Carter, & Silva, 2010). Some women may be making conscious choices to work in what are essentially dead-end jobs (Hakim, 2002), but it is as likely that women have been limited by past discrimination (Lyness & Heilman, 2006)—including the nearly universal expectation that women will take primary responsibility for child care and household—obligations that makes comprehensive options not as available for women as they are for men (Catalyst, 2006). That women are far more likely to bear the responsibility for child care is a common explanation for why women are more likely to be in temporary and informal work arrangements. Furthermore, this explanation is also often cited for the disparity in men and women's salaries (ILO, 2010). Although men have picked up some of the household and child care duties, their share of such work remains less than that of women's (Hook, 2010). Given trends across both traditional (e.g., Poland) and egalitarian countries (e.g., Norway), the results of cross-country

TABLE 3.1
Education and Employment Status of Women in 20 Countries

Countries	% Tertiary education (1)	% Working (2)	% Women/men in part-time jobs(3)	% in Professional and technical jobs(4)	% Women legislators, senior officials, managers (4)	% on Corporate Boards (5,6)
Australia	53	70.1	39/12	53.7	36.8	2.5
Austria	51	68.4	32/5	46.5	28.4	7.5
Brazil	56	64.3	*	52.2	36.1	5.1
Canada	53	75.2	26/11	56.5	36.0	10.3
China	49	74.4	*	*	*	8.5
Finland	64	73.6	16/8	55.3	29.6	24.5
Germany	53†	71.2	39/8	50.3	37.8	11.2
Italy	57	51.8	30/5	47.1	33.2	3.7
Japan	42	61.8	33/9	46.6	9.3	.9
Mexico	49	46.3	22/8	41.3	30.7	6.8
Netherlands	51	73.7	60/16	49.8	27.4	14.0
Norway	59	75.7	32/11	51.4	31.3	39.5
Philippines	51	50.7	*	62.1	53.3	23.0
Poland	59	56.2	15/6	60.3	36.2	10.8
Russia (CIS)	56	68.8	*	64.0	38.7	5.8

(Continued)

TABLE 3.1
(Continued)

Countries	% Tertiary education (1)	% Working (2)	% Women/ men in part-time jobs(3)	% in Professional and tech- nical jobs(4)	% Women legislators, senior officials, managers (4)	% on Corporate Boards (5,6)
South Korea	35[7]	54.9	13/6	39.9	8.8	1.9
Spain	51	63.1	21/4	50.2	32.4	9.3
Thailand	53	70.4	*	55.6	23.7	8.7
UK	54	69.4	39/10	47.2	33.9	12.5
US	55	68.1	18/8	56.7	42.8	15.7

*no data available

[1]ILO, 2004, *Breaking through the glass ceiling*, except for Germany obtained from: http://epp.eurostat.ec.europa.eu/statistics_explained/index.php/
Tertiary_education_statistics

[2]Labor participation rate, age 15 to 64, World Bank database, based on ILO data, 2009

[3]Department of Economic and Social Affairs of the UN, The World's Women 2010: Trends and Statistics, Table 4.9

[4]ILO Labour Statistics, 2008 most recent year available, laborsta.ilo.org, retrieved and compiled October 25, 2011

[5]Catalyst, 2011, http://www.catalyst.org/publication/433/women-on-boards

[6]http://www.bis.gov.uk/policies/business-law/corporate-governance/women-on-boards

[7]Other sources suggest higher percentages, e.g., 58%, from http://wikigender.org/index.php/Gender_Equality_in_South_Korea

studies (Geist & Cohen, 2011; Hook, 2010) would caution us not to be overly optimistic for housework to be shared equally by men and women in the near future. Thus, to accommodate both child care responsibilities and economic needs, many women work part-time. As can be seen in Table 3.1, women are noticeably more likely than men to be working part-time in all countries listed. Part-time work is often contingent work and, by its very definition, dead-end work. In addition to part-time work, women are more likely to be found in the segments of the workforce that, though within professional and technical skill areas, are balkanized as "women's work." Women often work in highly segregated work spheres, which interestingly also often limits their rise to top positions. As illustrative, women from the heavily female human resources realm are rarely, if ever, named CEOs (Adams et al., 2007).

Occupational Segregation, Vertical and Horizontal

Horizontal segregation refers to the fact that women and men tend to work in different industries. In the developed countries, women are more likely to work in clerical work, service and retail (Reeves, 2010). If we look at the participation rates of women at work, we find that across the globe, they are more likely to be in service occupations than in manufacturing, with the exception of Asian economies where women compose 47% of the manufacturing workforce. When women work in the male-dominated industrial sectors within Europe and Latin American, however, they are more likely to be working within specific categories (e.g., clerical) at lower paying jobs than men (ILO, 2010). This latter type of occupational segregation, vertical, typifies again the view that women are working in jobs that are not in the pipeline to the top, but rather are assistants to the real workers, men. Assistants rarely rise to become CEOs.

The strong occupational segregation in the developed countries surprises many, especially in light of various initiatives to encourage more women into less traditional fields (e.g., science, technology education in the U.K., U.S., Europe, and Australia; Bøe, Henriksen, Lyons, & Schreiner, 2011; Charles, 2011; Phipps, 2008). After examining occupational segregation in 44 countries, Charles and Bradley (2009) offered two intersecting explanations that may undergird the continuation of, and in some cases, encourage, greater occupational segregation in developed societies. Charles and Bradley make the argument that developed countries have "gender essentialist ideologies" that are deeply embedded within their cultures. Gender essentialist ideology refers to the notion that men and women are seen as innately different, not just biologically, but as inherently different in interests and skills. In addition, "doing gender" (i.e., enacting out societal norms for one's own gender; West and Zimmerman, (1987) is well rewarded throughout these cultures, including within the curricula of primary, secondary and tertiary schooling (Bradley & Charles, 2004; Charles & Bradley, 2002). In other words, men and women choose different occupational paths fairly early in life (Eccles, 2007) that correspond to gender expectations. Thus, despite the large percentages of women (see Table 3.1) enrolled in tertiary education around the world, they are more likely to be in traditionally female dominated majors such as education, health, and humanities, and underrepresented in engineering and math (Charles & Bradley, 2002). That these gendered selves correspond to stereotypes makes it all the harder for women who cross gender boundaries to be selected for jobs in the pipeline. As will be demonstrated with data later, gender stereotyping is extremely resistant to modification. One of these persistent stereotypes that prevents women from acquiring pipeline jobs is the international "think manager, think male" bias.

Think Manager (or Leader) and Think Male

One likely source of difficulty for women to be hired into or promoted into managerial jobs is that there is consistent evidence, worldwide, that people think of the prototypical manager as male. Schein (1973, 1975) and others (Schein, Mueller, Lituchy, & Liu, 1996; Sczesny, Bosak, Neff, & Schyns, 2004), in studies spanning decades, find regularly that adjectives rated as descriptive of the genderless "manager" significantly overlap ratings of "male managers." Happily, over the nearly 40 years since Schein's (1973) first study, female ratings of the prototypical "female manager" and "manager" have grown much closer. In contrast, male ratings have not. Men continue to rate the female manager target as different from the genderless, but presumably male, manager (Duehr & Bono, 2006). These effects are remarkably consistent across developed countries (e.g., the United States, Australia, Germany, Japan) from markedly different cultures and economic systems (Sczesny et al., 2004). These findings are descriptive and not explanatory, but illustrate that such perceptions are resistant to change and contribute to the perceptual barriers that women face in being hired into, or promoted to, line positions that lead to leadership spots. The best explanation for these findings may be "doing gender" is deeply ingrained in virtually all cultures.

We note here that dead-end jobs are a complaint that male employees also give when frustrated with their lack of progress to the top (Carter & Galinsky, 2008). We recognize that dead-end jobs are barriers to career advancement for both men and women; we suggest, however, that women face additional constraints that men do not: disproportionate responsibility for child care and housework and negative stereotyping of their qualifications for leadership. Another barrier that appears to affect women's career advancement disproportionately is a lack of mentoring and sponsorship, which we discuss next.

In sum, evidence that women are hired into dead-end jobs comes from the large number of part-time positions women accept, often as a result of their primary caregiver role, that they work in largely segregated workforces, and that prevailing gender stereotypes make their access to the jobs that lead to the top echelon more challenging. After we have commented on the other two barriers, we will suggest mechanisms for improving on women's disproportionate share of dead-end jobs.

Lack of Mentoring, Sponsorship, and Networks

Research is clear that achieving professional success is made more possible via mentors and sponsors, as well as networking with peers (Reeves, 2010). The importance of mentorship was evident in the experience of one of the Philippine women who became a top automobile industry executive. Before she achieved the presidency of Columbian Auto Car, Ginia Domingo "was introduced to a guy who saw the potential in me. He believed I had the self-confidence to represent Toyota." Thus, she started her auto career in sales, learning from her male peers during "drinking sessions and client calls" (Salazar, 2011).

Mentoring relationships are usually differentiated as informal and formal. Formal mentoring programs assign seasoned executives to prospective protégés, whereas informal mentoring relationships form voluntarily and on the basis of mutual attraction (Ragins, Cotton, & Miller, 2000). Informal mentoring relationships are typically associated with stronger career outcomes for the protégé (Blake-Beard, 2001; Chao, Walz, & Gardner, 1992; Ragins, & Cotton, 1999; Scandura, & Williams, 2001), with that success attributed to the more intimate quality of the informal mentor-protégé relationship (Wanberg, Welsh, & Hezlett, 2003).

As there are more men at the highest levels of organizational management, it stands to reason that there will be more opportunities for men to mentor and to be mentored, particularly with regard to informal mentoring. That informal mentoring appears to be more available to men and is more influential in career outcomes, including salary, shifts our attention to networks (or "social capital"; Hezlett & Gibson, 2007). Analyses of networks at work indicate that women often have a similar number of contacts as men within their individual networks, but the nature of those contacts differ in ways that are more likely to advantage men, with cross cultural data supporting that these differences hold beyond the United States (Bu & Roy, 2005; Carter & Galinsky, 2008). In particular, the majority of men's networks consist of other men and of these, men who are likely to hold powerful positions within the organization. Further, within these hemophilic networks, men are more likely than women to receive help from their male contacts (McGuire, 2002). In other words, men have more status, more powerful contacts, and are more likely to be sponsored by men from positions higher in the hierarchy. Women, thus, receive less network help, even when they are at comparable levels of the organizations, simply because they have fewer powerful men in their networks (Reeves, 2010).

Unlike dead-end jobs, the solution to a lack of mentoring, sponsorship, and networking is reasonably straightforward: provide equivalent opportunities for sponsorship to women. In Table 3.2, we highlight nine large companies that have instituted mentoring and sponsorship programs for women. Here, we highlight briefly three of the most noteworthy efforts sponsored by multinational companies. Intel, the largest producer of computer micro processing chips, has a two-pronged approach to supporting women, the first of which is a Women's Leadership Council that has as its primary objective the development and promotion of women; further, Intel has a sponsorship program that is designed to make female talent, especially in technology, visible within the company. Since 2004, the percentage of women holding jobs at Intel has increased 25% with about 20% of senior management held by women. KPMG, which is one of the largest consulting firms worldwide, has explicitly made mentoring an expectation for employees within the partner track at its U.S. firm. As a result, about 60% of the employees are mentors and/or protégés. At a high rate, KPMG employees agree that management encourages mentoring (in 2008, 77% agreement). In 2010, nearly a quarter of the new partner class was female; that year, 41% of the promotions were to women achieving senior manager, director, or managing director positions. At Sodexo, a large food service and facilities management company, there are several programs that support women seeking paths toward management positions. First, there is BRIDGE, a computerized social networking tool in which potential mentors offer their expertise; protégés create a profile and connect with these mentors. Peer2Peer is part of the ongoing affinity networks within Sodexo that provides opportunity for informal mentoring matches to be made. Finally, IMPACT is a formal mentoring program that links mid-level managers and above to protégés. The value of IMPACT is weighed by its return on investment (ROI) in terms of productivity and employee retention. In 2009, the ROI for the IMPACT program was a 2 to 1 return on investment. Sodexo's experience proves that companies that choose to establish programs to support and sponsor women are likely to realize financial returns beyond the cost of the investment.

TABLE 3.2

Best Practices: Sponsorship for Women by Firms Operating Globally

Company	Brief company overview	Countries	Program	Best practices	Outcomes
American Express	Headquarters: New York City, US World's largest card issuer by sales volume Operates in more than 130 countries, Employees: est. 58,000	United States, United Kingdom, India	WIN—Women's Interest Network	Senior leadership actively seeks out employees to sponsor Development Plans Each employee prepares a development plan, which includes a description of the support needed to accomplish the plan.	Women compose 65% of its workforce 25% of top 500 positions globally are filled by women. Rated as one of the top 100 companies for women to work for by CNN, Diversity, Inc.
Nestlé	Headquarters: Vevey, Switzerland Largest food company in the world. Employees: over 280,000	Operates in more than 80 countries	Corporate Mentoring Programs	Pairs employees with senior level mentors. Gives employees opportunities to learn and develop; mentors promote protégés' talent and encourage advancement.	27.3% of leadership positions across their global operations are held by women.
Alcoa (Aluminum Company of America)	Headquarters: Pittsburgh, US World's third largest producer of aluminum Employees: 59,000	Europe Africa Asia Australia North and South America	Alcoa Women's Network (AWN)	Prioritizes the development, advancement and promotion of women leaders throughout the company. Mentoring emphasized through the Alcoa Women's Network as well as in the communities in which the company operates.	40% of board of directors are women.

(Continued)

65

TABLE 3.2
(Continued)

Company	Brief company overview	Countries	Program	Best practices	Outcomes
Intel	Headquarters: Santa Clara, US World's largest semiconductor chip maker based on revenue Operates in five continents Employees: 96,500	North and South America Europe Africa Asia	Intel Women's Leadership Council (IWLC) and Intel Sponsorship Programs	The IWLC consists of female vice presidents and fellows. Primary goal is to champion existing and newly formed internal efforts around the development and retention of women. Goal of the Intel Sponsorship Programs is to identify, sponsor and showcase talent, especially that of female technologists.	About 20% of senior management is occupied by women. Female positions have increased by around 25% since 2004. The company is widely recognized as one of the best places for women to work.
Johnson & Johnson	Headquarters: New Brunswick, US Produces pharmaceuticals, medical devices, and consumer packaged goods Employees: 114,000	Over 60 countries	Mentoring Program	Specifically targets career development for women. Organization sets several program goals around the mentoring program. Goals are to increase the number of women leaders in the organization.	Women represent 22% of the highest management and director positions.
KPMG	Swiss Collective Organization with member firms self-governing KPMG is one of the Big Four global auditors	146 countries and 87 U.S. cities	KNOW (KPMG's Network of Women)	Provides venue for women to connect with peers, meet mentors Partner-track employees expected to specify mentoring as a formal career goal.	Women account for: 18.8% of the firm's partners; was 12.9% in 2003 24% of the firm's 2010 new partner class

	Employees: 138,000	Mentoring at KPMG LLP (US)	Nearly 60% of KPMG's workforce participate (9,862 protégés and 5,990 mentors); there are 1.6 protégés per mentor. 2008 KPMG survey reported 77% of employees agreed that management actively supports and encourages mentoring.	41% of all 2010 promotions were into senior manager, director, and managing director positions
Sodexo, Inc.	80 countries Headquarters: Issy-les-Moulineaux, France One of the world's largest food services and facilities management companies Employees: 380,000	BRIDGE Peer2Peer Informal Mentoring Programs IMPACT (formal mentoring program)	BRIDGE: Social networks within business lines; protégés create a profile and specify development needs—mentors create profiles showing their areas of expertise. Peer2Peer: Affinity network groups launched in 2005 based on strong empirical evidence that linked mentoring to positive ROI. IMPACT is linked to ROI results (job satisfaction, organizational commitment, diversity awareness, and teamwork). Structured, year-long initiative for mid-level managers and above. Program chaired by director of diversity and inclusion, who monitors the program and distributes companywide survey of employees to determine ROI.	Listed in Top 50 Companies for Diversity. ROI is calculated as the ratio of the cost to run IMPACT to the human capital financial gains based on IMPACT. In 2009, the program received an ROI of 2 to 1, attributed to increases in productivity and employee retention.

(Continued)

TABLE 3.2
(Continued)

Company	Brief company overview	Countries	Program	Best practices	Outcomes
			Cross-cultural and Cross-gender Mentoring Partnerships	In 2008, 70% of pairs were composed of individuals from different cultures of different genders, exceeding Sodexo's goal of 60%.	90% of pairs were employees from different operational and administrative business areas. 40–50% of participants were women, aligned with Sodexo's employee gender composition.
Abbott	Headquarters: Chicago, US Produces pharmaceuticals, medical devices, nutritional health products Employees: 90,000	100 countries	Executive Inclusion Council	Led by chair and CEO, who monitor the hiring of women and their advancement into management. In the United States, the representation by women has been a focus area for the past decade.	One of the "50 Best Companies for Diversity" for eight consecutive years. 50% increase in women in managerial ranks; For the past 4 years, Abbott has exceeded goals for U.S. hiring and promoting women.
General Mills	Minneapolis, US Among the world's largest food companies	100 countries	Corporate Mentoring Program (CMP)	CMP focuses on career and professional development. Matches newly hired employees of color with more senior mentors. Pairs set goals and receive training to ensure productive experiences.	DiversityInc "Top 50 Best Company's for Diversity" seven times In 2009, women made up 47.6% of the U.S. salaried workforce, 36% in management positions.

| Employees 33,000 | Senior Co-Mentoring Program | Pairs female director-level and above employees with the top management.

Designed to promote a cross-functional, two-way learning exchange and dialogue between the two partners. | 52% of promotions were awarded to women. |

American Express
1. http://about.americanexpress.com/news/pr/2011/intlwd.aspx
2. http://careers.americanexpress.com/working/diversity/employee-networks.html
3. http://careers.americanexpress.com/occupation/training-development.html
4. http://economictimes.indiatimes.com/quickiearticleshow/9123953.cms

Nestlé
1. http://www.nestle.com/CSV/OurPeople/GenderBalance/Pages/GenderBalance.aspx
2. http://www.nestle.com/CSV/OurPeople/TrainingLearning/Pages/EmployeeMentoring.aspx

Alcoa
1. http://www.alcoa.com/sustainability/en/info_page/operations_soc_people.asp
2. http://www.theresourcechannel.com.au/blog/alcoa-employer-choice-women
3. http://www.alcoa.com/global/en/news/news_detail.asp?pageID=20110406006259en&newsYear=2011

Intel
1. http://www.intel.com/about/corporateresponsibility/education/programs/iccn/index.htm
2. http://www.simply-communicate.com/case-studies/company-profile/how-intel-empowers-their-female-work-force
3. http://diversity-executive.com/article.php?article_id=1064&start=7755&page=2

Johnson and Johnson
1. http://www.jnj.com/connect/about-jnj/diversity/programs

KPMG International

1. http://www.catalyst.org/publication/365/making-mentoring-work
2. www.kpmgcampus.com

Sodexo

1. http://www.catalyst.org/publication/365/making-mentoring-work
2. www.nrn.com/article/sodexo-mentor-program-focuses-diversity
3. http://pt.sodexo.com/ptpt/Images/Sodexo_Diversity_Inclusion_Report_tcm241-284660.pdf

Abbott

1. http://www.abbott.com/citizenship/programs/workplace/diverse-inclusive.htm
2. http://www.abbott.com/global/url/content/en_US/50.30.10.10:10/general_content/General_Content_00466.htm
3. http://www.abbott.com/global/url/content/en_US/60.30.60:60/general_content/General_Content_00094.htm

General Mills

1. http://www.veteranstoday.com/2011/02/15/general-mills-enters-second-year-with-hireveterans-com/
2. https://careers.generalmills.com/WorkingHere
3. http://www.generalmills.com/en/Media/NewsReleases/Library/2011/March/DiversityInc.aspx

Differential Performance Standards: Equivalent Human Capital, Different Expectations for Men and Women in Leadership

We have covered the barriers of dead-end jobs and lack of sponsorship. Here, we turn to the differential expectations and resulting standards that are applied to women in leadership roles. What is the evidence that there are different standards for men and women? One could make the case that women and men are evaluated by the same standards and that women simply lack the requisite human capital to become leaders. There is, however, little evidence to support this idea. For example, Singh et al. (2008) analyzed U.K. corporate board appointments, a common pathway to CEO status (Daily, Certo, & Dalton, 1999), and found that the human capital of women was comparable to that of men, with women having an edge in educational credentials and international diversity. Nevertheless, beliefs persist that it is hard to find qualified women for boards of directors (e.g., Russell Reynolds, 2002; Helfat, Harris, & Wolfson, 2006). Why? Several interlocking explanations exist for this perception, with one likely framework emphasizing the appropriate societal roles for women and men.

In particular, women who aspire to leadership roles are swimming against the current of societal opinion that will, in most cultures, consider women unfit for leadership, as performing in such roles would be seen as inappropriate for women. One theory that is especially relevant to the evaluation of female leaders in the global context is role congruity theory (Eagly & Karau, 2002). The propositions of role congruity theory include less desirable evaluations of women's potential for leadership because leadership ability is perceived as prototypical of men and not of women (i.e., the already discussed "think manager, think male" phenomenon). Further, there tends to be a devaluation of women's actual behavior when in a leadership role. When women exhibit stereotypical agentic (i.e., masculine-like) behaviors, there tends to be a substantial disapproval of women because they are acting in ways that are incongruent with society's beliefs about how women should behave (Ridgeway, 2009).

According to role congruity theory, there are prejudices toward women in leadership roles based on the inherent incongruity between the expected gender roles of women and the role of leaders. This prejudice is based on two forms of sexism: Hostile and benevolent. Hostile sexism is the devaluation of women when they are in roles that are incongruent with societal expectations of the roles women should occupy "as women." In the "think manager, think male" paradigm already mentioned, women who deviate from expected gender norms are punished in various ways. They are rated lower on performance, are less likely to be promoted, and are often sabotaged or undermined. Benevolent sexism is equally harmful to women as women are rewarded vis-à-vis societal approval for "knowing their place" and refraining from seeking opportunities to advance (Eagly & Karau, 2002; Glick & Fiske, 2001). Further, there is evidence from large cross sectional studies that both benevolent and hostile sexism operate across cultures, with both types of sexism related to the level of gender inequality within a culture (Glick et al., 2000).

Because role congruity theory relies on context, we have a reasonable framework with which to assess why there could be different proportions of women in leadership positions in the Philippines, the United States, and the United Kingdom. In other words, different settings may correspond to different expectations about role congruity. These contexts might be useful to explain how it is that there seems to be more movement into top jobs in some countries that we might not expect, whereas there is slow movement in countries in which we would expect more women in leadership. Paradoxically, using role congruity theory as a lens may also help to explain a number of consistent findings in female promotion rates into executive suites as well as other reactions to women as leaders.

Considering the Pipeline to the Top

Before we turn to expectations for women in leadership, we will review briefly the promotion rates for men and women. Differential promotion rates by gender matter because even small discrepancies in promotion rates can be magnified, given the tournament nature of most organizational hierarchical structures. Just a fraction fewer women being promoted at lower levels can lead to gross discrepancies at the executive ranks (Martell, Lane, & Emrich, 1996).

Promotion rates for women relative to men in the United States and the United Kingdom appear largely to depend on the study although some consistencies emerge. In most cases (e.g., Ransom & Oaxaca, 2005), women are promoted less often than men; in some cases, no difference is found (e.g., Giulano, Levine, & Leonard, 2005); and in a few studies, women are promoted proportionately more frequently than men (e.g., Barnett, Baron, & Stuart, 2000).

In an effort to clarify the inconsistency in U.S. numbers, Blau and Devaro (2007) controlled for performance and ability, and found that across all types of jobs and industries in a large cross sectional sample, women were promoted less often than men. Blau and Devaro's U.S. results echo international findings. Research from Canada, the U.K., Australia, Sweden, Norway, Japan (Wright,

Baxter, & Gunn, 1995), Austria (Winter-Ebmer & Zweimuller, 1997), Finland (Pekkarinen & Vartiainen, 2004), France (Sabatier, 2010), and Israel (Bamberger, Admati-Dvir, & Harel, 1995) indicates that on average, within developed countries, women are promoted less frequently than men. We cannot say if these promotion differences hold in other regions of the world, but ILO (2010) data indicate that the lower paying jobs tend to be those held by women, which would certainly suggest that women are not promoted relative to their proportions in the workforce across the globe. Further, given the economic gender inequality-sexism link that Glick et al. (2000) found across a range of developed and developing countries, the promotion rates are likely connected to the role congruity thesis proposed by Eagly and Karau (2002). Bottom line: For the most part, women are less likely to be promoted, even with comparable levels of education, experience, and ability. Thus, as have many others (Carter & Silva, 2010), we make the basic case that the pipeline to the C-suite is more congested for women than it is for men. We now turn to a brief discussion of leadership qualities, which will permit us to consider if there are differences by gender as well as by culture.

What Makes for a Good Leader?

Given our focus on women's ascendancy to the executive ranks around the world, we ask two questions: What are the personal characteristics of effective leaders? Are the same characteristics valued equally across cultures? When we ask people about the characteristics of good leaders, the characteristics that are considered important include planning, participative behaviors, empowering followers, delegating tasks, and providing vision (Eagly, 2007; Paris, Howell, Dorfman, & Hanges, 2009; Prime, Jonsen, Carter, & Maznevski, 2008). Interestingly, several of these characteristics have traditionally been labeled as "feminine," and thus more likely to be associated with women. In fact, some have suggested that in terms of perceived skill sets, women may have an "advantage" for leadership (i.e., Eagly, 2007; Eagly, Johannesen-Schmidt, & Van Engen, 2003). Yet, as already noted, women do not sit at the top of companies or on boards of directors in proportion to their representation in the workforce (see Table 3.1). Could cultural differences be relevant to the scarcity of women at the top?

As with regard to the research on the distribution of labor within families (Geist & Cohen, 2011; Hook, 2010), there are differences across cultures in expectations for leadership (Ashkanasy, 2002). Researchers of cross-country differences in leadership have created clusters of nations on the basis of cultural consistencies such as individualism, humane orientation, or power distance. In addition, researchers working in the GLOBE project (Chhokar, Brodbeck, & House, 2007) have distinguished leadership styles into dimensions such as participative and autonomous. Managers in Anglo cultures (e.g., United Kingdom, Australia), for example, tend to value participative styles, consistent with individual employees expecting to have a voice. In contrast, in Asian cultures, especially those with Confucian origins (e.g., China, Japan), the leader is expected to speak on behalf of his or her followers, keeping to a collectivist mindset that values harmony, but is not expected to consult them, given that status differentials are also respected. As Confucian cultures value power differentials on the basis of familial relationships such as husband-wife, supervisor-employee, and tend to endorse traditional gender roles (Chia, Moore, Lam, Chuang, & Cheng, 1994), we would anticipate that women would be less likely to be accepted in executive positions. Accordingly, we might expect that there would be more movement of women into leadership roles in the Anglo (Australia, Canada, United Kingdom, United States) and Nordic (Finland, Norway) countries than in the Confucian Asian countries (China, Japan, Korea). As we can see in Table 3.1, there *are* greater percentages of female leaders in the Nordic and Anglo countries, with few in the Confucian Asian countries. The noticeably lower percentages of women in leadership positions may be attributed in part to the strong infusion of Confucian ideals within those cultures, which correspond neatly to role congruity theory predictions. In the absence of quotas for managerial and professional jobs in state-owned entities, there would probably be even fewer women in management in China; a survey of Chinese employees found that none of the 75 men in the sample supported women as managers (Jones & Lin, 2001).

We now review men and women's views of the importance of specific leadership attributes cross-culturally. The same data from which we referenced cultural leadership differences earlier, when further analyzed, indicate that gender stereotypes appear to be strong even within cultures that have relatively robust "gender egalitarian" values. In fact, the differences that emerged from cross-cultural studies reveal expected gender role stereotypes more reliably than differences based on national culture. In their study of 10 European, Scandinavian, and North American countries, Prime et al. (2008) surveyed 1,165 alumni of a European-based executive training program, asking these executives to rate their perceptions of men and women as possessing 14 leadership behaviors (e.g., delegating, planning). Although differences were found based on nationality (i.e., the four culture clusters, Anglo, Germanic, Latin, and Nordic), the resulting patterns of stereotyping were more strongly linked to respondent gender than to culture. Men in Nordic and Anglo cultures, presumably more gender egalitarian cultures, devalued women relative to men on several of the leadership behaviors (influencing upward, problem-solving, providing intellectual stimulation, and role-modeling). These behaviors were those that were rated by men as being more effective for leaders but also that men did not believe women possess. What men think matters because it is predominantly men in the hierarchy who are in the positions to sponsor women for leadership jobs, and evaluate those women, once they have achieved the executive ranks.

Firm Performance and Investor Reactions

Another avenue of research that addresses the perceptions of important constituents and suggests differential evaluations for men and women is that which has explored the performance of firms with women on the boards of directors and investor reactions to the appointment of women to CEO or director positions. Several diversity researchers have made the case that the bottom line can be improved with more diversity, including gender diversity (Robinson & Dechant, 1997). This line of reasoning follows that if companies can be convinced it is in their financial interest to hire and promote women, companies will have a vested material interest in opening up the executive suite. The Sodexo ROI data noted earlier support this strategy. Further, there is correlative support as applied to women in management. Francoeur, Labelle, and Sinclair-Desgagne (2008) found with Canadian firms that more women on boards of directors was positively related to company stock values. Similarly, Kang, Ding, and Charoenwong (2010) found that the appointment of women to the CEO and the board of directors in Singapore was related positively to stock prices. However, there are also some contradictory findings, suggesting that women are viewed as less capable or as appropriate leaders under specific situations. Lee and James (2007) found that stock returns for U.S. firms were more negative after a firm named a female CEO to its helm. Reviewing U.K.'s FTSE firms, Ryan and Haslam (2005) found that women were more likely to be appointed CEO when the firm was in precarious financial shape, thus the "glass cliff" effect for women. In a follow up multi-study paper, Haslam and Ryan (2008) replicated the glass ceiling effect experimentally, finding that women were seen as suitable for top management jobs particularly when companies were in financial trouble. Using data from the U.S. Standard & Poor's database, Adams, Gupta, and Leeth (2009) did not find a glass cliff effect, with firm data that suggested either no difference in the health of the firm prior to the appointment of a male or female leader, or a bias toward women such that the firm had more positive valuation at the time of the appointment of a female leader.

In an effort to reconcile these puzzling and inconsistent results, de Luis-Carnicer, Martínez-Sánchez, Pérez-Pérez, and Vela-Jiménez (2008) proposed that the relationship between firm performance and gender on the board of directors and within top management is curvilinear—that is, that homogeneity is counterproductive. The thesis proposed by de Luis et al. (2008) is completely consistent with the suggestion of Konrad, Kramer, and Erkut (2008) that *three* women on the board of directors is the critical mass that can make a difference. At least three women are needed on a board for them to ascend beyond token status and the onus to "represent their sex." Once there are three women on a board, they can operate as board directors. They are then less likely to be marginalized, and will be more likely to influence policies that relate to the firm's responsibilities, fiduciary and ethically (Torchia, Calabro, & Huse, 2011). Women are seen as more suitable for crisis level situations in organizations, which on the surface, could be considered a positive view of women's skills to solve serious and pressing problems, On the other hand, such thinking could condition employers to overlook women except when times are bad, thus plunging women into precarious leadership positions. If the woman fails, the failure is then attributed to her leadership, not the very precarious situation in which she was thrust.

The broad question, in essence is, are men and women held to different standards of performance, behaviors, and leadership styles? The short answer appears to be a qualified yes. If we consider experimental research, there is ample evidence that women (and men) are expected to behave in ways that are congruent with societally appropriate masculine and feminine roles. Stepping outside of those roles has negative ramifications for both men and women. But with that said, for leadership roles, women are simply perceived as not having the requisite characteristics to lead, even when they do!

Practices and Policies That Support Gender Equality in Business Leadership

If gauging the success of working women solely by their percentages in the workforce, women have made considerable strides. Women in the United States and the European Union constitute a large percentage of the workforce. In Asia, Africa, and Latin America, the numbers of working women vary considerably but on the whole are greater than 20 years ago (ILO, 2010). If we look at percentages of women in executive level jobs, there has been progress, though very uneven and not necessarily in the countries we might expect (i.e., the developed economies). How *have* women gotten to the top? What practices have been the most instrumental for women to achieve top job status?

Table 3.3 shows recommendations at multi levels, based on the research and the differences in geographical regions where diversity initiatives have brought about positive results in the number of women in top positions. In our critical analyses, we identify strategies countries have employed that have been instrumental in the elevation of women.

At the macro level in developed economies, we suggest that key factors include governmental intervention in the form of anti-discrimination legislation and court action. In the United States, United Kingdom, and Canada, as examples, affirmative action has helped women more than ethnic minorities in achieving managerial positions (Kalev, Dobbin, & Kelly, 2006). In Norway, the federal government passed a law that required all publicly held companies to have a minimum of 40% women on their boards by 2007 (Hoel, 2008). At

TABLE 3.3
Overview of Recommendations

Governmental, Societal, and National Levels

- Provide materials that display relevant role models in nontraditional fields
- Celebrate the value of female leaders in fields held traditionally by women (i.e., place value on what is considered "women's work")
- Implement diversity initiatives that are championed by legislative bodies
- Foster advocacy groups that promote equal pay for equal work, as well as monitor women's promotion rates

Institutional Strategies

- Articulate gender equality as a key organizational value; embed the value within the organizational culture through reward systems, mission statements, and ceremonies.
- Assess progress toward the stated goals by collecting and evaluating key indicators.
- Appoint qualified women to the boards of directors and achieve "critical mass."
- Showcase accomplishments of females in company materials (print and electronic).
- Monitor the proportions of women in entry-level jobs and part-time work.
- Assess the feasibility of providing more flexible schedules for full-time workers.
- Provide mentoring and networking programs, see Table 3.2 for excellent examples.
- Assess whether different standards are being applied to promotion criteria.
- Evaluate performance appraisals for adverse impact and train raters on subjectivity bias.

Individual Actions

- Set goals and promote yourself.
- Actively seek feedback from your supervisors.
- Monitor your progress relative to others in the organization.
- Network with men as well as with women.
- Find male allies who will support you and make your contributions visible.
- Mentor other women.

Suggested Reading

Baumgartner, M. S., & Schneider, D. E. (2010). Perceptions of women in management: A thematic analysis of razing the glass ceiling. *Journal of Career Development, 37,* 559–576.

Hopkins, M. M., O'Neil, D. A., Passarelli, & Bilimoria, D. (2008). Women's leadership development: Strategic practices for women and organizations. *Consulting Psychology Journal: Practice and Research, 60,* 348–365.

Kilian, C. M., Hukai, D., & McCarty, C. E. (2005). Building diversity in the pipeline to corporate leadership. *Journal of Management Development, 24,* 155–168.

Singh, V. (2008). Diversity management practices in leading edge firms. In R. J. Burke & C. L. Cooper (Eds.), *Building more effective organizations: HR management and performance in practice* (pp. 252–277). Cambridge: Cambridge University Press.

the institutional level, corporate practices such as diversity programs have had considerably less effect on advancement for women, probably because these practices are more likely to be unfocused and not tied to specific outcomes as is affirmative action (Kalev et al., 2006).

Ending the dead-end job syndrome for women requires intervention at all levels. The solution to dead-end jobs is not simply the case of telling women (or men) to study for college degrees that lead to lucrative careers; rather, is a societal obligation to treat men and women fairly in the systems. As is clear from Table 3.1, women in developed countries already have studied for and entered professional and technical jobs; the issue is that even with those college degrees, women are not as likely as men to be placed into positions that lead to top management. From the very beginning of the career choice pipeline, girls need role models that show it is "cool" to be in science and math and at the top levels of management as company presidents. Gender stereotypes, compounded with differential occupational interests, will no doubt persist (Correll, 2004), but providing evidence of female role models at all levels of education and in the work setting (cf. Bosak & Sczesny, 2008) certainly would help to make women feel more welcome in the executive suite. Of course, simply providing photographs of women with recruiting materials or on company web sites will not change the potential for dead-end jobs. Kalev et al. (2006) reviewed U.S. promotion rates for men and women across a wide range of firms for a 30-year period. They compared the effects of mandatory affirmative action with softer corporate interventions such as mentoring and diversity programs. Affirmative action proved to be the most effective in raising women to management positions with mentoring programs, by themselves, showing modest effects. Mentoring that accompanied affirmative action provided additional increases in women into management beyond that of affirmative action alone. These effects for the U.S. are echoed in the mandatory actions taken by

Nordic governments in the last decade. The substantial numbers of women on corporate boards in Norway are a direct result of the Norwegian Parliament passing a law requiring that women constitute 40% of those boards by 2007. Although there was initial resistance to the law by business leaders, echoing the complaints of affirmative action foes in the United States that the women appointed as a result of the quotas would be unqualified and the companies' financial situations would suffer, the actual situation turned out to be quite different. Women who were appointed to the boards were highly qualified, with greater education levels than existing board members, and had demonstrated professional proficiency in their careers (Hoel, 2008).

Mentoring, sponsorship, and networking of women will take place predominantly at the organizational and individual level. As noted in Table 3.2, there are excellent programs under way at many multinational companies. The key is to provide sponsorship for promising leadership talent. We also encourage women to seek out mentors and form networks across the organizational hierarchy.

Equalizing differential standards will require multi-level efforts. At the governmental level, enforcement of the existing laws that prohibit discrimination on the basis of sex would be a good start. At the institutional level, concerted efforts on the part of organizational members to reflect on pending decisions can make a difference. As noted in Kottke and Agars (2005), simply examining promotion decisions for differential standards by gender can surface unrecognized stereotypes in decision making. Organizations can also, as part of ongoing diversity monitoring, compare the progress of women and examine if there are apparent lags for women relative to men. Further, examination of exit interviews could also provide clues if there are differential numbers of female managers leaving and the reasons for their exit.

Conclusion

In this chapter, we have identified and discussed the common barriers women face when seeking to advance into top leadership positions. We examined these barriers cross-culturally and described the role of gender stereotypes and gender role expectations in hindering upward progress of women. We also highlighted numerous organizations that have implemented successful diversity initiatives that are reaping the rewards of these strategies. Women who are placed into dead-end jobs, or who self-select into these occupations based on cultural and societal gender role expectations are at a disadvantage when promotion decisions are made. Further, the lack of effective mentoring and sponsorship of women also works in tandem with dead-end assignments to slow the progress of women into high levels leadership positions. It is our hope that our readers will implement the suggestions we offer, and that other companies have already implemented, to begin changing the composition of the top tiers of organizations to give women equal opportunities to showcase their talents.

Notes

1. The authors thank Rakel Engles and Janet Bent, who provided valuable insights and assistance in preparing the tables for this chapter.
2. The astute reader will note a difference in the percentages reported in the text, attributed to Grant Thornton, and those in Table 3.1 for the Philippines, the United Kingdom, and the United States. These differences appear to be a function of the type of sampling done by the different agencies that collect such data. The data in Table 3.1 are based on Governance Metrics International (March 2009), which examines data from industry sources. Grant Thornton conducts a quarterly survey of senior executives in privately held businesses in 39 countries. Because the relative differences in the Philippines, the United Kingdom, and the United States are comparable in both sets of data, we left the Grant Thornton data intact in the text. In either case, the Philippines outpaces both the United Kingdom and the United States in the proportions of women sitting on boards of directors. Only Nordic Europe has proportionately more women on boards of directors than the Philippines in either set of data.

References

Adams, S. M., Gupta, A., & Leeth, J. D. (2009). Are female executives overrepresented in precarious leadership positions? *British Journal of Management, 20,* 1–12. doi: 10.1 111/j.14 67–8551.200 7.00549. x

Adams, S. M., Gupta, A., Haughton, D. M., & Leeth, J. D. (2007). Gender differences in CEO compensation: Evidence from the USA. *Women in Management Review, 22,* 208–224.

Ashkanasy, N. M. (2002). Leadership in the Asian century: Lessons from GLOBE. *International Journal of Organisational Behaviour, 5,* 150–163.

Automobile Industry. (2008). *International encyclopedia of the social sciences.* 2008. Retrieved from http:/www.encyclopedia.com/doc/1G2–3045300143. html

Bamberger, P., Admati-Dvir, M., & Harel, G. (1995). Gender-based promotion discrimination in Israeli high-technology firms: Do unions make a difference? *Academy of Management Journal, 38,* 1744–1761.

Barnett, W. P., Baron, J. N., & Stuart, T. E. (2000). Avenues of attainment: Occupational demography and organizational careers in the California Civil Service. *American Journal of Sociology, 106,* 88–144.

Bendl, R., & Schmidt, A. (2010). From "glass ceilings" to "firewalls"—Different metaphors for describing discrimination gender. *Work and Organization, 17,* 612–634.

Blake-Beard, S. D. (2001). Taking a hard look at formal mentoring programs: A consideration of potential challenges facing women. *Journal of Management Development, 20,* 331–345.

Blau, F. D., & Devaro, J. (2007). New evidence on gender differences in promotion rates: An empirical analysis of a sample of new hires. *Industrial Relations, 46,* 511–550.

Bøe, M. V., Henriksen, E. K., Lyons, T., & Schreiner, C. (2011). Participation in science and technology: Young people's achievement-related choices in late modern societies. *Studies in Science and Education, 47,* 37–72.

Bosak, J., & Sczesny, S. (2008). Am I the right candidate? Self-ascribed fit of women and men to a leadership position. *Sex Roles, 58,* 682–688.

Bradley, K., & Charles, M. (2004). Uneven inroads. Understanding women's status in higher education. *Research in the Sociology of Education, 134,* 247–274.

Bu, N., & Roy, J. P. (2005). Career success networks in China: Sex differences in network composition and social exchange processes. *Asia Pacific Journal of Management, 22,* 381–403.

Buckley, M. (1981). Women in the Soviet Union. *Feminist Review, 8,* 79–106. doi: 10.1057/fr.1981.13

Carter, N. M., & Galinsky, E. (2008). *Leaders in a global economy: Talent management in European cultures.* New York: Catalyst.

Carter, N. M., & Silva, C. (2010). *Pipeline's broken promise.* New York: Catalyst.

Catalyst. (2006). *Women "take care," men "take charge:" Stereotyping of U.S. business leaders exposed.* New York: Author.

Catalyst. (2007). *The double-bind dilemma for women in leadership: Damned if you do, doomed if you don't.* New York: Author.

Catalyst. (2011a). *Women in the automotive industry* (Quick Takes). New York: Author.

Catalyst. (2011b). *Women CEOs of the Fortune 1000.* Retrieved from http://www.catalyst.org/publication/271/women-ceos-of-the-fortune-1000

Chao, G. T., Walz, P., & Gardner, P. D. (1992). Formal and informal mentorships: A comparison on mentoring functions and contrast with nonmentored counterparts. *Personnel Psychology, 45,* 619–636. doi: 10.1111/j.1744–6570.1992.tb00863.x

Charles, M. (2011). A world of difference: International trends in women's economic status. *Annual Review of Sociology, 37,* 355–371.

Charles, M., & Bradley, K. (2002). Equal but separate: A cross-national study of sex segregation in higher education. *American Sociological Review, 67,* 573–599.

Charles, M., & Bradley, K. (2009). Indulging our gendered selves? Sex segregation by field of study in 44 countries. *American Journal of Sociology, 14,* 924–976.

Chhokar, J. S., Brodbeck, F. C., & House, R. J. (2007). *Culture and leadership, across the world: The GLOBE book of n-depth studies of 25 societies.* Mahwah, NJ: Erlbaum.

Chia, R. C., Moore, J. L., Lam, K. N., Chuang, C. J., & Cheng, B. S. (1994). Cultural differences in gender role attitudes between Chinese and American students. *Sex Roles, 31,* 23–30.

Correll, S. J. (2004). Constraints into preferences: Gender, status, and emerging career aspirations. *American Sociological Review, 69,* 93–113.

Daily, C., Certo, T., & Dalton, D. (1999). A decade of corporate women: Some progress in the boardroom, none in the executive suite. *Strategic Management Journal, 20,* 93–99.

de Luis-Carnicer, P., Martínez-Sánchez, A., Pérez-Pérez, M., & Vela-Jiménez, M. J. (2008). Gender diversity in management: Curvilinear relationships to reconcile findings. *Gender in Management: An International Journal, 23,* 583–597.

Dejardin, A. K. (2009). *Gender (in)equality, globalization and governance* (Working Paper No. 92, Policy Integration and Statistics Department, International Labour Office). Geneva: ILO. Retrieved from http://www.ilo.org/integration/resources/papers/WCMS_108648/

Duehr, E. E., & Bono, J. E. (2006). Men, women, and mangers: Are stereotypes final changing? *Personnel Psychology, 59,* 815–846.

Eagly, A. H. (2007). Female leadership advantage and disadvantage: Resolving the contradictions. *Psychology of Women Quarterly, 31,* 1–12.

Eagly, A. H., & Karau, S. J. (2002). Role congruity theory of prejudice toward female leaders. *Psychological Review, 109,* 573–598.

Eagly, A. H., Johannesen-Schmidt, J., & Van Engen, M. L. (2003). Transformational, transactional, and laissez-faire leadership styles: A meta analysis. *Psychological Bulletin, 129,* 569–591.

Eccles, J. S. (2007). Where are all the women? Gender differences in participation in physical science and engineering. In S. J. Ceci & W. M. Williams (Eds.), *Why aren't more women in science? Top researchers debate the evidence.* Washington, DC: APA.

Francoeur, C., Labelle, R., & Sinclair-Desgagne, B. (2008). Gender diversity in corporate governance and top management. *Journal of Business Ethics, 81,* 83–95.

Geist, C., & Cohen, P. N. (2011) Headed toward equality? Housework change in comparative perspective. *Journal of Marriage and Family, 73,* 832–844. doi: 10.1111/j.1741-3737.2011.00850.x

Giulano, L., Levine, D. I., & Leonard, J. (2005). *Do race, gender, and age differences affect manager-employee relations? An analysis of quits, dismissals, and promotions at a large retail firm.* Paper 18. Center for Responsible Business, University of California, Berkeley.

Glick, P., & Fiske, S. T. (2001). An ambivalent alliance: Hostile and benevolent sexism as complementary justifications for gender inequality. *American Psychologist, 56,* 109–118.

Glick, P., Fiske, S. T. Mladinic, A., Saiz, J. L. Abrams, D., & Lopez, W. L. (2000). Beyond prejudice as simple antipathy: Hostile and benevolent sexism across cultures. *Journal of Personality and Social Psychology, 79,* 763–775.

Grant Thornton. (2009). Retrieved from http://grant-thornton.sq1sch.co.uk/infographics/women-in-the-boardroom/women_infographic.jpg

Hakim, C. (2002). Lifestyle preferences as determinants of women's differentiated labor market careers. *Work and Occupations, 29,* 428–459.

Hansen, M. T., Ibarra, H., & Peyer, U. (2010). The best-performing CEOs in the world. *Harvard Business Review, 88,* 104–113.

Haslam, S. A., & Ryan, M. K. (2008). The road to the glass cliff: Differences in the perceived suitability of men and the road to the glass cliff. *Leadership Quarterly, 19,* 530–546.

Helfat, C. E., Harris, D., & Wolfson, P. J. (2006). The pipeline to the top: Women and men in the top executive ranks of U.S. corporations. *Academy of Management Perspectives, 20,* 42–64. doi: 10.5465/AMP.2006.23270306

Hezlett, S. A., & Gibson, S. K. (2007). Linking mentoring and social capital: Implications for career and organization development. *Advances in Developing Human Resources and Organization Development, 9,* 384–412. doi: 10.1177/1523422307304102

Hoel, M. (2008). The quota story: Five years of change in Norway. In S. Vinnicombe, V. Singh, R. J. Burke, D. Bilimoria, & M. Huse (Eds.), *Women on corporate boards of directors International research and practice* (pp. 79–87). Northampton, MA: Edward Elgar.

Hook, J. L. (2010). Gender inequality in the welfare state: Sex segregation in housework, 1965–2003. *American Journal of Sociology, 115,* 1480–1523.

International Labour Office (ILO). (2004). *Breaking through the glass ceiling: Women in management. Update 2004.* Geneva: Author.

International Labour Office. (2010, March). *Women in labour markets: Measuring progress and identifying challenges.* Geneva: Author.

Jones, C. L., & Lin, L. (2001). *A comparison of attitudes toward women as managers in China and in the U.S.* Pomona, CA: California State Polytechnic University. Retrieved from http://www.csupomona.edu/~jis/2001/Jones_Lin.pdf

Kalev, A., Dobbin, F., & Kelly, E. (2006). Best practices or best guesses? Assessing the efficacy of corporate affirmative action and diversity policies. *American Sociological Review, 71,* 589–617. doi: 10.1177/000312240607100404

Kang, E., Ding, D. K., & Charoenwong, C. (2008). Investor reaction to women directors. *Journal of Business Research, 63,* 888–894.

Konrad, A. M., Kramer, V. W., & Erkut, S. (2008). Critical mass: The impact of three or more women on corporate boards. *Organizational Dynamics, 37,* 145–164.

Kottke, J. L., & Agars, M. D. (2005). Understanding the processes that facilitate and hinder efforts to advance women in organizations. *Career Development International, 10,* 190–202.

Lee, P. M., & James, E. H. (2007). She'-e-os: Gender effects and investor reactions to the announcements of top executive appointments. *Strategic Management Journal, 28,* 227–241. doi: 10.1002/smj.575

Lyness, K. S., & Heilman, M. E. (2006). When fit is fundamental: Performance evaluations and promotions of upper-level female and male managers. *Journal of Applied Psychology, 91,* 777–785. doi: 10.1037/0021–9010.91.4.777

Martell, R., Lane, D., & Emrich, C. (1996). Male-female differences: A computer simulation. *American Psychologist, 51,* 157–158,

McGuire, G. (2002). Gender, race and the shadow structure: A study of informal network and inequality in work organizations. *Gender & Society, 16,* 303–322.

McIndoe, A. (2007, October 15). *In the Philippines, women bosses rule. AsiaOne.* Retrieved from asiaone.com.sg

Paris, L. D., Howell, J. P., Dorfman, P. W., & Hanges, P. J. (2009). Preferred leadership prototypes of male and female leaders in 27 countries. *Journal of International Business Studies, 40,* 1396–1405. doi: 10.1057/jibs.2008.114

Pekkarinen, T., & Vartiainen, J. (2004). *Gender differences in job assignment and promotion on a complexity ladder of jobs.* IZA Discussion paper no. 1184 (June). Retrieved from http://papers.ssrn.com/sol3/papers.cfm?abstract_id= 562451

Phipps, A. (2008). *Women in science, engineering and technology: Three decades of UK initiatives.* Staffordshire: Trentham Books.

Prime, J., Jonsen, K., Carter, N., & Maznevski, M. L. (2008). Mangers' perceptions of women and men leaders: A cross cultural comparison. *International Journal of Cross Cultural Management, 8,* 171–210.

Ragins, B. R., & Cotton, J. L. (1999). Mentor functions and outcomes: A comparison of men and women in formal and informal mentoring relationships. *Journal of Applied Psychology, 84,* 529–550. doi: 10.1037/0021–9010.84.4.529

Ragins, B. R., Cotton, J. L., & Miller, J. S. (2000). Marginal mentoring: The effects of type of mentor, quality of relationship, and program design on work and career attitudes. *Academy of Management Journal, 43,* 1177–1194.

Ransom, M., & Oaxaca, R. L. (2005). Intrafirm mobility and sex differences in pay. *Industrial and Labor Relations Review, 58,* 219–237.

Reeves, M.E. (2010). *Women in business: Theory, case studies and legal challenges.* New York: Taylor & Francis.

Ridgeway, C. L. (2009). Framed before we know it: How gender shapes social relations. *Gender & Society, 23,* 145–160.

Robinson, G., & Dechant, K. (1997). Building a business case for diversity. *Academy of Management Executive, 11,* 21–31.

Russell Reynolds and Associates. (2002). *What makes an effective board? Views from FTSE 100 chairmen.* London: Author.

Ryan, M. K., & Haslam, S. A. (2005). The glass cliff: Evidence that women are over-represented in precarious leadership positions. *British Journal of Management, 16,* 81–90.

Sabatier, M. (2010). Do female researchers face a glass ceiling in France? A hazard model of promotions. *Applied Economics, 42,* 2053–2062.

Salazar, T. (2011, August 3). March is their month: Women hold the wheel. *Philippine Daily Inquirer.* Retrieved from http://business.inquirer.net/money/features/view/20110308-324274/March-is-their-month

Scandura, T. A., & Williams, E. A. (2001). An investigation of the moderating effects of gender on the relationships between mentorship initiation and protégé perceptions of mentoring functions, *Journal of Vocational Behavior, 59,* 342–363. doi: 10.1006/jvbe.2001.1809

Schein, V. E. (1973). The relationship between sex role stereotypes and requisite management characteristics. *Journal of Applied Psychology, 57,* 95–100.

Schein, V. E. (1975). The relationship between sex role stereotypes and requisite management characteristics among female managers. *Journal of Applied Psychology, 60,* 340–344.

Schein, V. E., Mueller, R., Lituchy, T., & Liu, J. (1996). Think manager–think male: A global phenomenon? *Journal of Organizational Behavior, 17,* 33–41.

Sczesny, S., Bosak, J., Neff, D., & Schyns, B. (2004). Gender stereotypes and the attribution of leadership traits: A cross-cultural comparison. *Sex Roles, 51,* 631–645. doi: 10.1007/s11199–004–0715–0

Singh, V., Terjesen, S., & Vinnicombe, S. (2008). Newly appointed directors in the boardroom: How do women and men differ? *European Management Journal, 26,* 48–58.

Torchia, M., Calabro, A., & Huse, M. (2011). Women directors on corporate boards: From tokenism to critical mass. *Journal of Business Ethics, 102,* 299–317.

Vinnicombe, S., Sealy, R., Graham, J., & Doldor, E. (2010). *Female FTSE Index and Report 2010.* Cranfield: Cranfield School of Management.

Wanberg, C. R., Welsh, E. T., & Hezlett, S. A. (2003). Mentoring research: A review and dynamic process model. *Research in Personnel and Human Resources Management, 22,* 39–124.

West, C., & Zimmerman, D. (1987). Doing gender. *Gender & Society, 1,* 125–151.

Winter-Ebmer, R., & Zweimuller, J. (1997). Unequal assignment and unequal promotion in job ladders. *Journal of Labor Economics, 15,* 43–71.

Wright, E. O., Baxter, J., & Gunn, E. B. (1995). The gender gap in workplace authority: A cross-national study. *American Sociological Review, 60,* 407–435.

Yukl, G. (2010). *Leadership in organizations* (7th ed.). Upper Saddle River, NJ: Prentice Hall.

In Their Own Voice

Katie Halpin

> *Example is not the main thing in influencing others, it is the only thing.*
> —Albert Schweitzer

An effective leader is one who would never ask you to do something that they wouldn't do themselves. They don't just tell you their expectations; they show you. An effective leader is one who strikes a balance between strategy and detail. They have an understanding and appreciation for what goes on day-to-day, but they recognize that preparation and development are imperative for the future. An effective leader exudes integrity. They do what they say and deliver what they promise. An effective leader is one who says thank you, when thank you is deserved. They recognize that teamwork and transparent communication are at the core of success.

Ambition is not a four-letter word.

—Moya Greene
CEO, Royal Mail
United Kingdom

4

The Challenges and Opportunities in Developing an Organizational Approach to Managing Workforce Diversity

Erica L. French, Glenda Strachan, and John Burgess

For the past two decades, the concept of managing individual difference in the workforce has been popular in many Western organizations with calls to manage this "diversity" for the greater good of the organization and the individuals in it (Kossek, Lobel, & Brown, 2006). Paradoxically, there is no agreed definition for the concept and its description remains unclear, and often contested (Jonsen, Maznevski, & Schneider, 2011). Indeed, there are a range of terms used which include the word "diversity": diversity at work, managing diversity, diversity management, workplace diversity; productive diversity, and others. The foundation of the concept of managing diversity rests on the idea that an organization's workforce displays a range of "diverse" characteristics. The characteristics that are included under the heading of "diversity" vary.

According to Drucker (2007), diversity encompasses many demographic and socioeconomic aspects of society including the ageing population; the greater reliance on knowledge workers; increases in immigration; the changing role of women in the workplace; and the increasing cultural and gender differences in organizations. Kirton and Greene (2005) suggest that gender and race can be regarded as the major organizing principles of diversity in the labor market, with disability, age and sexual orientation being other features of workforce diversity. But many interpretations of diversity go further than these labor market demographic groups. For example, Heery and Noon (2001, p. 215), in the Oxford *Dictionary of Human Resource Management*, describe diversity as "the concept of recognizing the wide variety of qualities possessed by people within an organization." The concept "emphasizes the individuality of people, and the importance of valuing each person for his or her unique combination of skills, competences, attributes, knowledge, personality traits, etc." "Managing diversity" or having an organizational diversity program is "the concept of recognizing the wide variety of qualities possessed by people within an organization" (Heery & Noon, 2001, p. 215). Other writers take this notion further to include the idea of changing the way the organization operates and terms such as "productive diversity," "valuing diversity" and others are used (Cope & Kalantzis, 1997). Diversity, therefore, can be understood as contextually specific and linked to the demographic and sociopolitical features of a particular population and its workforce.

This chapter begins by discussing what diversity and managing diversity is and then proceeds to examine the relationship between managing diversity and business goals. Managing diversity programs are then examined, and the relationship between these policies and current practices in human resource management (HRM) is evaluated. The chapter concludes by looking to the future of managing diversity discussing strategies and policies and research to support new directions in diversity management.

What Is Managing Diversity?

The term "managing diversity" is now broadly used to include a range of legislated and nonlegislated processes for managing difference in the workplace. Thomas (1990) identified "managing diversity" as a process by which organizations could create an environment that encourages all employees to reach their full potential in pursuing company objectives. He called the process "managing diversity" to reflect the importance of "management" in creating such an environment. Thomas (1991, 1996) suggested the process of managing diversity offers a means of developing the full potential of every individual in the organization. Kossek, Lobel, and Brown (2006, p. 8) advocate a definition of diversity that "emphasizes intergroup interaction and is inclusive of power differences, rather than focusing on individual differences."

One reason for the promotion of managing diversity programs was to overcome the failure of legislated affirmative action in the United States which, Thomas (1990) argued, had not achieved equity goals, largely because it did not deal with the root causes of prejudice and inequality. Researchers in the United Kingdom (Wilson & Iles, 1999) echo these views for their country. While there is debate about exactly what constitutes policies and programs variously labeled "diversity" and "managing diversity" (Bacchi, 2000; Kirton

& Greene, 2005), a universal factor includes the incorporation of elements of organizational and culture change.

A major complexity when discussing managing diversity is that it is often intertwined with the compliance of national legislation covering nondiscrimination and equal opportunity in employment. As managing diversity is a product of the 1990s, in many countries it comes after such legislation and today lies alongside a continuing expansion of legislation encouraging a mix of approaches utilized by organizations to manage inequality, discrimination, individual difference and exclusion. This presents a dichotomy and a challenge for organizational policies and practices as legislation usually follows a social group-based approach to achieving equality of opportunity while a managing diversity approach frequently emphasizes a range of differences possessed by an individual. Hence questions of difference and sameness between legislated and managing diversity approaches are in essence, country specific.

Much of the literature has categorized the managing diversity approach as a higher or better level of organizational program when compared to antidiscrimination, affirmative action or equal opportunity (e.g., Maxwell, Blair, & McDougall, 2001, p. 469). Implicit in these arguments is the idea that managing diversity programs will achieve improved equity and inclusion outcomes (see e.g., Wilson & Iles, 1999). Wilson and Iles (1999) argue that the paradigm of managing diversity is internally driven and based on organizational objectives (compared to equal opportunities based on legal and moral arguments); and, the managing diversity agenda is an investment in organizational goals (compared to equal opportunities which is formal and minimalist with organizations only needing to reach set targets). Others support the view that the managing diversity approach offers an extension of other approaches (Liff, 1999; Thomas, 1990, 1991, 1996). But again there is a lack of agreement among scholars on this point. Still further researchers argue that managing diversity is radically different from earlier organizational approaches such as affirmative action (Kandola & Fullerton, 1994; Thomas & Ely, 1996) because managing diversity offers an alternative individually based approach, set against the group and collective approaches of affirmative action or equal opportunity.

The managing diversity approach is also not without its critiques. Bacchi (2000) suggests the change from legislated equal opportunity to "managing diversity," with an emphasis on individual values and individual manager responsibilities, has weakened any obligations to legislative equal opportunity. Replacing collective goals with responsibilities for reporting and setting targets through a voluntarist process that may or may not include equity targets can result in outcomes that are very conditional on the individual organizational programs and managerial discretion. Thomas (1996) also suggests that the managing diversity approach implemented through substantive culture and organizational change may take up to 25 years, so speed is not one of its virtues.

A prominent feature of the diversity discourse is that it fails to recognize the past disadvantage or discrimination against identifiable groups in the labor market. Yet these remain a feature of most labor markets, where ongoing division, inequality and exclusion are recurring features. There is a history of division in the labor market based on race, gender, and ethnicity, among other attributes, with immigrants, for example, often located in precarious and clandestine jobs (Dyer, 2010), and indigenous populations among the most marginalized groups in the labor market (Dyer, 2010). Women have traditionally been segregated into service and caring occupations that are frequently low-paid and often associated with irregular forms of employment (Whitehouse & Frino, 2003). The International Labour Organization (ILO, 2011) has highlighted these divisions and forms of exclusion through its Decent Work Agenda which seeks to highlight that millions of workers worldwide are employed under conditions that exclude them from fundamental rights and conditions (such as equal pay, antidiscrimination legislation, and the right to bargain) Many of these issues of labor market inequalities have been variously addressed through national legislation which attempts to remove current discrimination and historical disadvantage, and, to a lesser extent, promote organizational programs with equity aims (Burgess et al. in Strachan, French, & Burgess, 2010, p. 18).

Managing Diversity and Business Goals

The business case for managing diversity identifies the need for organizations to increase and respond to various aspects of employee differences to enable the better harnessing of talents and abilities of all employees in response to an increasingly complex and dynamic environment (O'Leary & Weathington, 2006). The business interest in workplace diversity had its origins in three basic arguments (Konrad, 2003). First, a diverse labor force requires businesses to attract, retain and recruit from a diverse labor pool as the traditional white male share of the labor force declines. Second, changes in the business environment such as globalization and social reporting (including diversity management) requires organizations to be able to respond to a more diverse customer base, meet more extensive reporting requirements, and satisfy a more diverse group of stakeholders. Third, recognition that possessing a workforce that is representative of the population can have advantages in terms of problem-solving, marketing, and creativity tasks because diverse groups contain a greater variety of information, experience, perspectives, and cognition. However, there is conflicting evidence regarding the extent to which diversity can deliver that competitive advantage in business. Some scholars advocate that managing diversity can assist with competitiveness as businesses deal with "an increasingly diverse workforce, a multicultural customer base, and a growing challenge for market share from international competitors" (Kreitz, 2008, p. 106). In contrast, advocates of social identity theory (see Bassett-Jones, 2005) argue that diversity damages cohesiveness, reduces communication, and produces in-groups and out-groups, resulting in discord, distrust, poor service quality, and a lack of customer focus and market orientation. These mixed arguments of the effects of diversity provoked Milliken and Martins (1996) to identify diversity in the organization as a "doubled edged sword" (see O'Leary & Weathington, 2006, p. 285).

While scholars debate the effectiveness of managing diversity programs to deliver business and competition outcomes, some question the very foundation of managing diversity and its reliance on the business case. They argue that the business case is not sufficient to deliver the social goals of equity and justice (Dickens, 1994, 1999; Noon, 2007; Syed & Kramar, 2009). Regardless of the arguments for and against the business case, organizations are generally driven by a business imperative and the need to maximize stakeholder returns. Addressing diversity as a key strategic requirement, through HR strategy and policy "signals that diversity is a core part of the organization and is unequivocally, unconditionally valued" (Richard & Johnson, 2001 in Oyler & Pryor, 2009, p. 436).

Managing Diversity Programs

Given that there is a general lack of definition as to exactly what constitutes diversity and its management, and the fact that national labor market demographics and legislation differ between countries, it is hard to say exactly what should be included in diversity programs. Arrendondo (1996, in Jonsen et al. 2011, p. 38) describes these programs as "a strategic organizational approach to workforce diversity development, organizational culture change and empowerment of the workforce." Organizations operate within national legislation which usually enforces no discrimination and promotes equal opportunities in employment. Konrad and Yang (2011) believe that the best diversity management practices incorporate these aspects by accomplishing three goals: (a) promote perceptions of organizational justice and inclusion, (b) reduce discrimination, and (c) improve financial competitiveness. Thus, programs come in a variety of forms, the critical components of which include initiatives to recruit, promote, and retain a diverse group of employees (Jayne & Dipboye, 2004).

Diversity initiatives in the United States, the United Kingdom, and Australia have emerged against changes operating at both societal and organizational levels. Their populations are increasingly diverse and enhancing diversity at work is the logical response to changing demographics and good social policy. There is no doubt that versions of managing diversity have been adopted by both the public and private sector in these countries, but there has been an uneven spread in the uptake across countries and organizations. In many countries, public organizations are rapidly implementing diversity programs, but there appears to be confusion as to what needs to be undertaken. In a survey of HRM managers in the United States, Kellough and Naff (2004) found that 90% of federal agencies adopted formal diversity management programs with an inconsistent approach taken to the implementation of initiatives. This suggests managers are unclear how to approach and utilize diversity programs. Pitts and Wise (2010) investigated the link between workforce diversity and organizational performance in the public sector through a review of 89 research articles that appeared from 2000 to 2008 focusing on the dimensions of diversity and research methodology. Their findings indicate that scholars provided little practical assistance to HRM practitioners about how their organizations might leverage diversity for greater efficiency or effectiveness.

Some national studies allow further insights into the nature of these programs, how they work and how far they have spread. In the United Kingdom, the 2004 Workplace Employment Relations Survey identified only 18% of British workplaces as having procedures to encourage applications from groups such as women, ethnic minority employees, older and disabled employees, or the unemployed (Walsh, 2007). The first comprehensive diversity management survey conducted nationally in the United Kingdom in 2006–2007 identified that only 10% of the private sector and 51.7% of the public sector conducted impact assessment to measure diversity (Klarsfeld, 2010). Further, the majority of organizations in the United Kingdom do not collect data on the business benefits of diversity, nor set diversity objectives. Yet recent decades have seen substantial immigration of different ethnic groups into the United Kingdom which has created a society so diverse that the term "super-diversity" has been coined in an attempt to convey the diversification of diversity (Vertovec, 2007).

The business case for diversity was enthusiastically adopted by the previous Labour Government in the United Kingdom (Guerrier & Wilson, 2011), but it is unclear what diversity policies are currently being implemented. A study undertaken by Greene and Kirton (2011) of a U.K. public service organization with well-established diversity management identified that the implementation of diversity management policies depended on the individual manager. The outcome indicates that through a lack of understanding or due to competing pressures, many choose to ignore or not prioritize diversity issues, resulting in disparities between practices in different sections of the organization (Greene & Kirton, 2011).

The inconsistency and uncertainty of practice in the implementation of diversity initiatives is a constant finding in the literature. For example, Kandola and Fullerton (2005) conducted in-depth interviews with managers, HR specialists, and employees across three distinct business units of a long-established U.K. major high-street retailer. Their findings identified difficulties experienced by these managers in the operationalizing of diversity management based on a conceptual confusion about how it differs from equal opportunities and the demands of other work priorities.

In Australia the legislation requires larger private-sector companies to institute organizational programs that promote equity for women and, in the public sector for women and indigenous people, those from non-English speaking backgrounds, and people with a disability (Strachan, Burgess, & Sullivan, 2004; Strachan et al., 2010). In the public sector, managing diversity is influenced by a government (nonlegally) binding policy known as "Productive Diversity," which seeks to align diversity management with the national economic reform agenda (Bakalis, Levenson, & Joyner, 2009). The Public Service Act 1999 requires the Australian Public Service (APS) to develop and establish workplace diversity programs that focus on the links between diversity and organizational effectiveness and the elimination of discrimination on the grounds of gender, race, or ethnicity (Syed & Kramar, 2010). The key indicators of diversity management used in the APS include informing staff of their rights and responsibilities under antidiscrimination provisions and legislation; the promotion of fairness in employment and helping employees to establish a work life balance; establishment of recruitment and selection processes that are sensitive to the diverse backgrounds of prospective applications; and the use of feedback mechanisms such as staff surveys to identify staff satisfaction. Syed and Kramar (2010) conclude that this approach to diversity management is a narrow one, focusing on individuality rather than addressing the inclusion of ethnic/racial and religious minority groups and individuals.

In the Australian private sector, diversity management represents a voluntary corporate strategy, and research has identified a limited application or integrated approach to diversity management. Bakalis et al. (2009) found that of 1,500 Australian companies surveyed in 2001 more than 51% did not have a written diversity management policy. Organizations that do implement such programs utilized four approaches in equity and diversity management to meet legislative requirements, with a range of outcomes (French, 2001). Many Australian organizations have only implemented diversity initiatives to respond to a tight labor market (Burgess, French, & Strachan, 2009), due in part to a lack of appreciation or application of the productive potential of diversity within organizational operations (Pyke, 2005). This may be problematic as diversity is recognized as a key feature of Australia's national identity continuing to influence sociocultural and economic potential (Syed & Kramar, 2010).

There is also a lack of systematic and convincing evidence about the overall impact of diversity initiatives (Gonzalez & DeNisi, 2009). In 1998, a not-for-profit group of business leaders in the United States set up the Business Opportunities for Leadership Diversity initiative, which established a collaborative study into the effects of workplace diversity on corporate performance (Jehn & Kochan, 2001). This study incorporated a 5-year large-scale field research project to examine the relationships between diversity and business performance (Kochan et al., 2003). The findings were unable to identify any direct effects (either positive or negative) of diversity on performance arguing that HRM practitioners pay little analytical attention to diversity issues in organizations. The study identified a need for strategies to better measure the impact of managing a diverse workforce, in support of a business case for its implementation and management. The business case for managing diversity effectively, it was determined, requires a sustained, systemic approach and long-term organizational commitment. Similar findings in relation to outcomes were reported in a study by Holmes (2005) facilitated by the Society for Human Resource Management and *Fortune* magazine. This research identified that although more than 75% of the surveyed organizations had engaged in some type of diversity activity or initiative such as diversity recruitment, training and education, community outreach, or diversity-related career development there were little identifiable outcomes.

While more organizations than ever emphasize diversity as a core element in their business, there is a lack of empirical research investigating any relationship between managing diversity programs and organizational outcomes. Relatively few of these initiatives have been seen to make a substantial impact on overall performance. One reason attributed to the lack of success is the failure to connect diversity programs to organizational performance systems and processes such as strategic planning, performance management, compensation, and human resource development (Cox, 2001; Holmes, 2005). Other writers reflect on the complexity of organizational activities. Choi (2010) attempts to explain inconsistent research results regarding the effects of diversity on organizational outcomes as being indicative of a more complex relationship which may be moderated by effects of contextual factors, such as organizational culture and demographic characteristics of group members and supervisors. Herdman and McMillan-Capehart (2010) argue that it is a lack of understanding of the intermediary process mechanisms, such as senior management attitudinal and perceptual views, that affect the efficiency of organizational diversity programs.

Managing Diversity through Human Resources Structures

In understanding where diversity management fits within human resource management, it is possible to see diversity management and diversity goals operating at a number of levels and in concert with human resource management structures. In the short term, diversity management is used to satisfy legislative and reporting requirements, and to attract and retain staff; in the long term, to develop human resources and to align the workforce to the realization of organizational goals. HRM had its foundation in two U.S.-based models. The Harvard Model, developed by Beer and colleagues (1985) (Prowse & Prowse, 2010), emphasizes communication, teamwork, and the utilization of individual talents, advocating a "soft" HRM approach. In contrast, the Michigan model, by Fombrun, Tichy, and Devanna (1984), presents a "hard" approach to HRM and introduces the concept of strategic human resource management (Prowse & Prowse, 2010). Essentially, soft HRM draws on the Human Relations School and emphasizes the long term maximization of human potential and intellectual capital requiring a sensitive and complex management approach. Conversely, hard HRM focuses on the short-term control of labor resources and emphasizes the quantitative, calculative, and strategic aspects of managing human resources as another economic factor of production (Davidson, McPhail, & Barry, 2011). A key element in this perspective is the requirement that the functions of an organization's HRM practice "fit" with one another in supporting its strategy (Schuler, 1989). Keenoy (1997 in Watson, 2004, p. 454) argues that a "dominant conceptual–analytical interpretive scheme" within the HRM field identifies that managers need to adopt one of these dimensions. However, as noted by Kane, Crawford, and Grant (1999) the "soft" and "hard" views of HRM are embedded at the theoretical level, but they have not, with the exception of a few organizations, been translated into practice, suggesting a gap between the espoused theory and theory in practice.

The 21st century has brought a greater a focus on high-performance workplaces, talent management, and the reexamination of what strategic HRM means in terms of structure, while human capital and knowledge management are becoming key themes for organizations (Baird, 2008). A change in the approach to HRM theory and practice has occurred in response to changes in the broader social, legal, and political climate as well as organizational demands for efficiency (Van Buren, Greenwood, & Sheehan, 2011). A significant trend in HRM theory and practice has been toward making the function more supportive of organizational strategies transforming HRM into strategic human resource management (SHRM). While the origins of SHRM can be traced back more than a century (Moore & Gardner, 2004), the trend in the modern era was first posited by Schuler and Jackson (1987). The authors built upon the work of Miles and Snow (1984), who argued that different strategy types (cost reduction, quality improvement, and innovation) require different types of employee role behaviors to fit the strategy, and that HR practices should be used to ensure those behaviors take place. The exact definition and nature of SHRM have been debated in the literature, and a number of different frameworks and competing theoretical approaches to SHRM are apparent (Lengnick-Hall, Lengnick-Hall, Andrade, & Drake, 2009).

Despite conceptual differences, the general consensus is that SHRM involves the recognition of organizations' human resources as essential to the achievement of organization goals, the acceptance and coordination of human resource practices at all organizational levels, and the strategic integration of human resource policies into organizational planning and decision making (Moore & Gardner, 2004). In developing a strategic approach to managing diversity, Kossek and Lobel (1996) suggest organizations can view increasing diversity as an end in itself; to meet legal requirements or to address the changing demographics in the market place.

Designing Structures, Strategies and Policies to Support Diversity

Incorporating diversity management into HRM structures has resulted in the development of different categories of formalized HRM structures, strategies, and policies, with questions and limitations regarding their effectiveness identified through the indicators of the employment status of specific groups. The majority of the research cited here relates to so-called equity programs and to the position of women or those from different cultural backgrounds within organizations, and this is reflective of where most of the research has been undertaken. In investigating whether the effects of equity legislation (including antidiscrimination and equal opportunity legislation mentioned earlier) focused on the employment status of protected groups or formalized HRM structures, Konrad and Linnehan (1995) identified two HR structures: those that explicitly and formally include demographic group identity into human resource decisions and those that do not. Identity-blind structures are those designed to ensure that the HR decision-making process is the same for each individual regardless of any identity differences. Identity conscious structures include the demographic group identity in the decision-making process (Konrad & Linnehan, 1995). Results show that the use of identity conscious HR structures were found to be significantly and positively associated with some of the indicators of employment status of women and for people of color. In contrast, identity-blind HR decision structures were not associated with indicators of employment status of women or people of color. Research also indicates that identity-conscious structures are less prevalent in organizations than identity-blind structures. In a similar study of almost 2,000 Australian organizations over 100 persons in size, French (2001) found that approximately one quarter of Australian organizations ($n = 618$) implemented identity-conscious strategies and that these strategies were significantly linked to increased numbers of women in management and across all management tiers in these organizations. In addition, it was noted that more organizations utilized identity-blind structures ($n = 699$) with limited or no links to any of the measures of increased status of women. While 244 organizations did not implement any equity strategies subscribing to the view that market pressures were driving their strategies, and 401 organizations reported their implementation of identity-neutral rather than identity-blind decision structures. Identity-neutral decision structures involved more than the nonrecognition of gender in the decision process but the recognition of the need to change organizational culture to suit the needs of people of both genders equally. However, neither the identity-neutral structures nor the market-driven HR structures were significantly linked to any indicators of increased numbers of women at work or women in management.

In a study of equity and diversity policy implementation across two industries in Australia (the female-dominated finance industry and the male-dominated transport industry), 300 "equity" program reports were reviewed (French & Strachan, 2007). Results indicate that organizations take a range of approaches to implementing equity and diversity policies with various outcomes. Over 50% of all organizations in the finance and transport industries did not address equity or diversity in their HR employment practices. This failure was noted across all major HR policy areas, including recruitment and selection, promotion and transfer, training and development, and work organization and conditions of service. Relatively few organizations in either industry implemented identity-conscious strategies in recruitment and selection; promotion and transfer, and training and development. Those organizations that implemented identity-neutral strategies utilized them in the HR areas of work organization and conditions of service. French and Strachan

(2009) speculate that the increasing recognition of parents' needs to combine work and family responsibilities may drive organizations to rely on these HR areas to deliver on equity and diversity. However, substantive equity outcomes are unlikely to result from single policy types (French & Maconachie, 2004; Kanter, 1977; Sheridan, 1998). Indeed, this study examined the relationship between the equity and diversity policies implemented and the numbers of women in management. Organizational size was the only contributing factor to increased numbers of women in management in those finance and transport organizations. None of the strategic activities across of the HR policy areas was a significant indicator of increased status of women in employment or women in management (French, 2001).

Other studies of the effectiveness of different organizational approaches to managing equity and diversity have produced mixed results. In a study of women in the banking industry in Australia, Metz (2003) found that women were advancing into management chiefly on their own merits—their knowledge and their skills, indeed their human capital—supporting Ragins and Sundstrom's (1989) model that women's managerial advancement is related principally to factors in the individual environment, including education levels, years of work experience and access to appropriate child care, rather than to any organizational factors. However, in a small study ($n = 98$) of early career women in Australia (Burke, Burgess, & Fallon, 2006), 5 years of organizational practices aimed at supporting and developing professional and managerial women were examined and different results emerged. All five areas—management, policy, administration, training and development, and recruitment and external relations—were significantly and positively correlated, indicating performance at high (or low) levels in one area predicted the same performance (high or low) in the other areas. That is, organizations in this study that had policies in one area also had policies in the other areas to provide a broad support base for addressing equity and diversity. The women who experienced these supportive organizational practices also acknowledged greater job and career satisfaction and higher levels of psychological well-being.

HR structures are influential in addressing equity and diversity, but so too is policy type. Kanter (1977) identified three different policy types used in equity management: social structural policies related to changes in structure and culture with organizations to accommodate difference; role-related policies designed to address specific difference between women's and men's roles at work and home; and so-called temperamental policies aimed at overcoming the often identified deficiencies in women's knowledge skills and abilities at work. Sheridan (1998) found that in addition to the three policy types Kanter (1977) identified, specific "opportunity policies" defined as programs used to enhance women's career opportunities at work were being implemented. French and Maconachie (2004) identified the further policy of "support policies" defined as programs offering support and inclusivity opportunities for specific employees, particularly those working in areas lacking substantial numbers of women such as nontraditional areas of work and management.

Findings indicate that identity-conscious decision making in the social structural policy areas that support women and men and their careers needs—namely recruitment and selection, promotion and transfer, and training and development—promote both well-being and the entry of more women into management roles. While the better integration of work and family responsibilities and better conditions of service continue to facilitate women's entry into the workforce, it is the soft option in equity and diversity management, as it does not address the hard fact of the lack of opportunities for women to access management positions. Without explicit support by top management for structural and cultural change, the numbers of women in management remain low.

The issue of gender equity is but one important challenge in designing and implementing diversity management strategies, and it affects structures, policies, and outcomes within workplaces. But it is not the only challenge. As Kirton and Greene (2005) suggested, gender and race are two major organizing principles of diversity, but developing an inclusive environment where all members can flourish is an important function of managing diversity (Kossek & Lobel, 1996). Mor Barak (2011, p. 323) asserts that "The goal of diversity management is not to assimilate people of diverse characteristics into the dominate culture but to create a social, legislative, and organizational environment that respects and values individual differences."

Few systematic studies examine the dynamics of diversity management practices within the HR structures of organizations. Drawing on in-depth interviews with recruitment specialists from employment agencies, one Australian study interrogated the front stage and backstage talk which shapes organizational structures and practice to discover its culturally laden construct (Wong, in Strachan et al., 2010). Although skills and qualifications are formally touted as essential meritorious benchmarks in recruitment, these markers are subsumed and subordinated to a particularistic workplace culture that privileges and normalizes a rather specific mainstream (in this case, white Australian) discourse. In this study, recruiters' judgments from five focus group sessions were summarized. They fell into four distinctive analytic categories, covering intelligibility, body language, technical expertise, and workplace values. What was different about this study is that unlike numerous studies that investigate the critical gate keeping role of the interview in an intercultural context, this study investigated the hidden process of the appointment that follows the interview where interviewees are talked about in an informal and relatively uncensored process where benchmarks and authoritative evaluative judgments and decisions are arrived at. Recruiters demonstrated certain expectations of how candidates would conduct themselves, and these expectations were revealed in the informal comments made after the initial judgments backstage. The dominant ideal candidate who speaks slowly, makes eye contact, seems friendly, and might joke about sport listens to and answers questions by responding methodically, looks trustworthy, and conforms to a "colorless," bland environment where differences remain invisible in the name of "cultural fit" for the organization. If the goal of managing diversity is to celebrate difference as a positive influence on organizational creativity and innovation, the reality appears to be poles apart.

Implementing Diversity Programs

The results of diversity management strategies and structures remains imprecise and patchy as some organizations are better than others in turning their intentions into practice. The following three studies provide an example across three continents and indicate that organizations are implementing practices to manage diversity informed by their changing demographics, influenced by EEO legislation and controlled by top management viewpoints. Approaches taken are wide ranging, including an application through both hard and soft structures of human resources with policies to address aspects of equity and inclusivity. Individual and group applications are evident. Managing diversity in practice continues to maintain a link with EEO and organizational size remains a significant indicator of managing diversity applications.

In the United Kingdom, a longitudinal research project of managing diversity at the BBC Scotland office corroborates the theory that the managing diversity definition centers on the individual with organizational outcomes for managing diversity in recruitment, creativity, competitive advantage and corporate image (Maxwell, 2004). Analysis indicates that managing diversity is enabled by, and to some extent bounded by, the equal opportunities law. The BBC Scotland case also underlines the importance of top management support and organizational culture as an important dimension in the implementation of diversity initiatives.

In Australia, analysis of 15 equity reports across a range of industries, including retail, mining, transport, IT, engineering, charity, legal services, and manufacturing, submitted to the Equal Opportunity for Women in the Workplace Agency (a government agency administering EEO legislation) and identified as exemplars in terms of their EEO programs were examined. EEO programs were often conflated with managing diversity (Burgess et al., 2009). Many of the organizations discussed EEO and managing diversity as though the terms were interchangeable—classifying their programs under the label of diversity management or equating them with EEO programs for women employees with diversity management for all. The organizations judged as "best practice" tended to integrate managing diversity with standard human resource management functions such as recruitment and selection procedures, and particularly the instigation or expansion of flexible work arrangements. The large organizations (those with more than 4,000 employees) specifically linked managing diversity strategies with their overall business goals. Most of the smaller organizations also made the link with their organizational strategy. All the organizations framed their programs within an organizational business case. Most quantified savings to the organization in some way, citing more female recruitment, increased retention, and higher return rates from maternity leave. At one level, managing diversity and EEO were observed to represent a form of public relations and also placed within the context of good corporate citizenship. At another level, managing diversity reflected the realities of a changing workforce composition. The reality is that the workforce is becoming more feminized, older, and with growing numbers of immigrant workers from non-European origins (Sappey, Burgess, Lyons, & Buultjens, 2006, ch.3). At another level, the rise of managing diversity and the formal EEO program requirement is also linked to the rise of human resource management programs and strategic HRM within large organizations. This gives a strategic edge to managing diversity programs and links managing diversity to organizational performance. However, the HRM driver is not without its limitations, especially if the HR programs are of the "hard" variety, where cost and efficiency goals take precedence over "softer" equity objectives (Kirton & Greene, 2005).

In a study of 58 municipalities in North Carolina, United States, and their managing diversity practices, findings indicate that most cities in North Carolina did not seem to take diversity and its related issues seriously (Hur, Strickland, & Stefanovic, 2010). More cities identified as adopting diversity practices such as empowerment, diversity training, implementing diversity outreach programs, promoting senior management involvement in diversity planning, and affirmative action planning. These practices equate with the "soft" approach to managing diversity. Those cities that recognized diversity and its related issues as more serious used the "hard" approach linking diversity management practices to mission, planning, policy, training, and involvement. The least popular practices among cities were mentoring, internships, resourcing, advocating, and establishing a diversity committee. Findings also indicate that population size, heterogeneity of population, and urbanization affect the emphasis that the cities place on diversity and its management. In general, managers' backgrounds were not related with diversity management practice. Only the manager's age was determined to have a significant relationship with the diversity management practice. Municipal governments with older managers in were more likely to have higher numbers of diversity management practices.

Limitations, Conclusions, and the Future

The findings of the diversity management initiatives across the three jurisdictions of the United Kingdom, Australia, and the United States suggest a lack of effective and consistent assistance provided in the literature for HR managers charged with balancing demands of equity and performance. Curtis and Dreachslin (2008) identified that specific diversity interventions undertaken to improve organizational performance were not well researched in the laboratory, classroom, or field. A major concern raised suggests the studies analyzed showed a lack of deliberate gathering and analysis of data to evaluate the outcomes of diversity interventions. Pitts (2006) explains the problem as one of collecting research, suggesting that organizations do not allow access to relevant information as they do not wish researchers to discover that their diversity programs are not working. It is also argued that this field of research lacks ties to comprehensive theoretical models for understanding organizational diversity, which leads to confusion over causal influences and makes any research on the issue exploratory and the generalizing of the findings problematic (Pitts, 2006). Research continues to focus on individual initiatives rather than on diversity strategies and does little to identify solutions to challenges encountered in the implementation of programs with practices described in the abstract without any practical advice or specific methods of implementation to address HRM practice or the interests of the HRM practitioner (Kossek, Lobel, & Brown, 2006; Rynes, Giluk, & Brown, 2007).

Informational diversity is seen as lacking in the postgraduate educational background of authors of the most influential diversity articles (defined as those with more than 100 citations). Sixty-six percent of authors hold degrees in psychology (including social and organizational psychology); 62% held degrees in management (including organizational behavior and theory); noting that anthropology, history, sociology, and biology were predominately absent (Jonsen et al., 2011).

Further, the education of new HRM practitioners is also called into question. The design and delivery of diversity courses tends to be based on prevailing business norms (Stewart, Crary, & Humberd, 2008) and tends to focus on the business case (Kulik & Roberson, 2008), where diversity management is characterized as a function of human resource management (Pitts, 2006). Yet HRM theory and practice is underpinned by a unitarist ideology. The "unitarist approach" toward HRM, according to Moore and Gardner (2004, in Geare, Edgar, & McAndrew, 2006), is one "in which the common interests between employers and employees are assumed." Proponents of the unitarist perspective argue that conflict is a result of poor management! This creates a paradox for HRM practitioners in planning diversity programs as conflict is recognized as inherent within a diverse workforce (Jayne & Dipboye, 2004). This contradiction for the practitioner may be exacerbated by other factors such as resentment and defensiveness. In a review of the diversity literature and pedagogy, Stewart et al. (2008) suggest that while academics may espouse teaching inclusion associated with diversity, they may (unknowingly) teach exclusion by making distinctions between groups. The approach of highlighting nondominant group perspectives can evoke feelings of resentment and defensiveness among students, which can minimize the likelihood of substantive learning or an attitude change (Stewart et al., 2008).

Diversity management has emerged as a major challenge for organizations across the globe. While there are mandatory programs that address workforce discrimination and equal employment opportunity, diversity management is more holistic in terms of its view of the workforce and it is voluntarist. At the same time it is layered on top of existing legislative programs that address workforce discrimination and exclusion. The business case supports diversity management programs as a means of achieving competitive advantage through strategic human resource management involving the developing and nurturing the people resources of organizations to realize corporate goals. However, when it comes to practice, it is clear that many different types of diversity management programs are in place, acknowledging different drivers of the programs, and different goals to which they are aligned. Mir, Mir, and Wong (2006) identify the strategic issues of viewing the global movement of labor through postcolonial theoretical lens and the global movement of money which seeks to recreate "the local" in the image of "the dominant global"; the changing nature of work; and the everyday resistances to these changes in the workplace as the current challenges in managing diversity. The challenge for employers to reap the benefits of a diverse workforce is the adoption of a broad vision of inclusivity encompassing four levels, the organization, its community, and its national and international environments (Mor Barak, 2011).

Facilitating individual employees into the decision structures and information networks of the organization has its own barriers. Mor Barak (2011) identifies discrimination, prejudice, and the perception of a lack of job security, at the micro level of the organization, as barriers to the inclusive organization. The challenge for researchers remains the need to better track diversity programs, and importantly to interpret and evaluate their effectiveness not only in realizing organizational goals but in also realizing the broader societal and the individual aspirations linked to them.

References

Arrendondo, P. (1996). *Successful diversity management initiatives: A blueprint for planning and implementation.* Thousand Oaks, CA: Sage.

Bacchi, C. (2000). The seesaw effect: Down goes affirmative action, up comes managing diversity. *Journal of Interdisciplinary Gender Studies, 5,* 64–83.

Baird, M. (2008). *Human resource management—Strategies and processes.* South Melbourne, Australia: Thomson.

Bakalis, S., Levenson, L., & Joyner, T. A. (2009). Managing cultural diversity and perceived organizational support Evidence from Australia. *International Journal of Manpower, 30,* 377–392.

Bassett-Jones, N. (2005). The paradox of diversity management, creativity and innovation. *Diversity Management, Creativity and Innovation, 14,* 169–175.

Burgess, J., French, E., & Strachan, G. (2009). The diversity management approach to equal employment opportunity in Australian organizations. *Economic and Labour Relations Review, 2,* 77–92.

Burke, R. J., Burgess, Z., & Fallon, B. (2006). Benefits of mentoring to Australian early career women managers and professionals. *Equal Opportunities International, 25,* 71–79.

Choi, S. (2010). Managing diversity in U.S. federal agencies: Effects of diversity and diversity management on employee perceptions of organizational performance. *Public Administration Review, 70,* 109–121.

Connell, J., & Burgess, J. (2009) Migrant workers, migrant work, public policy and human resource management. *International Journal of Manpower, 30,* 412–421.

Cope, B., & Kalantzis, M. (1997). *Productive diversity: Management lessons from Australian companies.* Occasional Paper no. 20, Sydney: Centre for Workplace Communication and Culture.

Cox, T. (2001). *Creating the multicultural organization.* San Francisco, CA: Jossey-Bass.

Curtis, E. F., & Dreachslin, J. L. (2008). Integrative literature review: Diversity management interventions and organizational performance: A synthesis of current literature. *Human Resource Development Review, 7,* 107–134.

Davidson, M.C.G., McPhail, R., & Barry, S. (2011). Hospitality HRM: Past, present and the future. *International Journal of Contemporary Hospitality Management, 23,* 498–516.

Dickens, L. (1994). The business case for women's equality: Is the carrot better than the stick? *Employee Relations, 16,* 5–19.

Dickens, L. (1999). Beyond the business case: A three-pronged approach to equality action, *Human Resource Management Journal, 9,* 9–19.

Drucker, P. (2007). *Managing in the next society.* Oxford: Butterworth Heinemann.

Dyer, S. (2010). Employing indigenous Australians. In G. Strachan, E. French, & J. Burgess (Eds.), *Managing diversity in Australia* (pp. 137–153). Sydney: McGraw-Hill.

Fombrun, C. J., Tichy, N. M., & Devanna, M. A. (1984). *Strategic human resource management.* New York: Wiley.

French, E. (2001). Approaches to equity management and their relationship to women in management. *British Journal of Management, 12,* 267–285.

French, E., & Maconachie, G., (2004). Managing equity: Structure, policy and justice influences. *Women in Management Review, 19,* 98–108.

French, E., & Strachan, G., (2009). Evaluating equal employment opportunity and its impact on the increased participation of men and women in the transport industry in Australia. *Transport Research Part A: Policy and Practice, 43,* 78–89.

Geare, A., Edgar, F. & McAndrew, I. (2006). Employment relationships: Ideology and HRM practice. *International Journal of Human Resource Management, 17,* 1190-1208.

Gonzalez, J. A., & DeNisi, A. S. (2009). Cross-level effects of demography and diversity climate on organizational attachment and firm effectiveness. *Journal of Organizational Behavior, 30,* 21–40.

Greene, A., & Kirton, G. (2011). Diversity management meets downsizing: The case of a government department. *Employee Relations, 33,* 22–39.

Guerrier, Y., & Wilson, C. (2011). Representing diversity on UK company web sites. *Equal Opportunities International, 30,* 183–185.

Heery, E., & Noon, M. (2001). *A dictionary of human resource management.* Oxford: Oxford University Press.

Herdman, A. O., & McMillan-Capehart, A. (2010). Establishing a diversity program is not enough: Exploring the determinants of diversity climate. *Journal of Business and Psychology, 25,* 39–53.

Holmes, T. A. (2005). How to connect diversity to performance. *International Society for Performance Improvement, 44,* 13–17.

Hur, Y., Strickland, R. A., & Stefanovic, D. (2010). Managing diversity: Does it matter to municipal governments? *International Journal of Public Sector Management, 23,* 500–515.

International Labour Organization (ILO). (2011). *Decent work agenda.* Retrieved from http://www.ilo.org/global/about-the-ilo/decent-work-agenda/lang—en/index.htm

Jayne, M. E., & Dipboye, R. L. (2004). Leveraging diversity to improve business performance: Research findings and recommendations for organizations. *Human Resource Management, 43,* 409–424.

Jonsen, K., Maznevski, M. L., & Schneider, S. C. (2011). Diversity and it's not so diverse literature: An international perspective. *International Journal of Cross Cultural Management, 11,* 35–62.

Kandola, R., & Fullerton, J. (1994). Diversity: More than just an empty slogan. *Personnel Management, 26,* 46–50.

Kane, B., Crawford, J., & Grant, D. (1999). Barriers to effective HRM. *International Journal of Manpower, 20,* 494–515.

Kanter, R. M. (1977). *Men and women of the corporation.* New York: Basic Books.

Kellough, J., & Naff, K. (2004). Responding to a wake-up call: An examination of federal agency diversity management programs. *Administration and Society, 36,* 62–90.

Kirton, G., & Greene, A. M. (2005). *The dynamics of managing diversity: A critical approach* (2nd ed.). Oxford: Elsevier.

Klarsfeld, A. (2010). *International handbook on diversity management at work: Country perspectives on diversity and equal treatment.* New York: Edward Elgar.

Kochan, T., Bezrukova, K., Ely, R., Jackson, S., Joshi, A., Jehn, K., . . . Thomas, D. (2003). The effects of diversity on business performance: Report of the diversity research network. *Human Resource Management, 42,* 3–21.

Konrad, A. M. (2003). Defining the domain of workplace diversity scholarship. *Group & Organization Management, 28,* 4–17.

Konrad, A. M., & Linnehan, F. (1995). Formalize HRM structures: Coordinating equal employment opportunity or concealing organizational practices? *Academy of Management Journal, 36,* 787–820.

Kossek, E. E., Lobel, S. A., & Brown, J. (2006). Human resource strategies to manage workforce diversity: Examining the business case. In A. Konrad, P. Prasad, & J. Pringle (Eds.), *Handbook of workplace diversity* (pp. 53–74). London: Sage.

Kreitz, P. A. (2008). Best practices for managing organizational diversity. *Journal of Academic Librarianship, 34,* 101–120.

Kulik, C. & Roberson, L. (2008). Common goals and golden opportunities: Evaluations of diversity education in academic and organizational settings. *Academy of Management Learning and Education, 7,* 309-331.

Lengnick-Hall, M. L., Lengnick-Hall, C. A., Andrade, L. S., & Drake, B. (2009). Strategic human resource management: The evolution of the field. *Human Resource Management Review, 19,* 64–85.

Liff, S. (1999). Diversity and equal opportunities: Room for a constructive compromise? *Human Resource Management Journal, 9,* 65–75.

Maxwell, G. A. (2004). Minority report: Taking the initiative in managing diversity at BBC Scotland. *Employee Relations,26,* 182–202.

Maxwell, G., Blair, S., & McDougall, M. (2001). Edging towards managing diversity in practice. *Employee Relations, 23,* 468–482.

Miles, R. E., & Snow, C. C. (1984). Designing strategic human resources systems. *Organizational Dynamics, 13,* 36–52.

Milliken, F. J., & Martins, L. L. (1996). Searching for common threads: Understanding the multiple effects of diversity in organizational groups. *Academy of Management Review, 21,* 402–433.

Mir, R., Mir, A. & Wong, D. (2006). Diversity: The cultural logic of global capital? In A. Konrad, P. Prasad & J. Pringle (Eds.), *Handbook of workplace diversity* (pp. 167–188). Thousand Oaks, CA: Sage.

Moore, B., & Gardner, S. (2004). HR managers, SHRM and the Australian metals mining sector: Embracing the unitarist vision. *Asia Pacific Journal of Human Resources, 42,* 274–299.

Mor Barak. M. E. (2011). *Managing diversity: Toward a globally inclusive workplace* (2nd ed.). Los Angeles: Sage.

Noon, M. (2007). The fatal flaws of diversity and the business case for ethnic minorities. *Work, Employment and Society, 21,* 773–784.

O'Leary, B. J., & Weathington, B. L. (2006). Beyond the business case for diversity in organizations, *Employee Responsibilities and Rights Journal, 18,* 283–292.

Oyler, J. D., & Pryor, M. G. (2009). Workplace diversity in the United States: The perspective of Peter Drucker. *Journal of Management History, 15,* 420–451.

Pitts, D. W. (2006). Modelling the impact of diversity management. *Review of Public Personnel Administration, 26,* 245–268.

Pitts, D. W., & Wise, L. R. (2010). Workforce diversity in the new millennium: Prospects for Research. *Review of Public Personnel Administration, 30,* 44–69.

Prowse, P., & Prowse, J. (2010). Whatever happened to human resource management performance? *International Journal of Productivity and Performance Management, 59,* 145–161.

Pyke, J. (2005, July). *Productive diversity: Which companies are active and why.* Paper presented at Australian Social Policy Conference, University of New South Wales, Sydney.

Ragins, B. R., & Sundstrom, E. (1989). Gender and power in organizations: A longitudinal perspective. *Psychological Bulletin, 105,* 51–88.

Richard, O. C., & Johnson, N. B. (2001).Understanding the impact of human resource diversity practice on firm performance. *Journal of Managerial Issues, 13,* 177–196.

Rynes, S. L., Giluk, T. L., & Brown, K. G. (2007). The very separate worlds of academic and practitioner periodicals in human resource management: Implications for evidence-based management. *Academy of Management Journal, 50,* 987–1008.

Sappey, R., Burgess, J., Lyons, M., & Buultjens, J. (2006). *The new federal workplace relations system.* Sydney: Pearson Education.

Schuler, R. S. (1989). Strategic human resource management. *Human Relations, 42,* 157–184.

Schuler, R. S., & Jackson, S. E. (1987). Linking competitive strategies with human resource management practices. *Academy of Management Executive, 1,* 207–219.

Scott, L. M., Harrell, M. C., & Kavanagh, J. (2007). *Managing diversity in corporate America: An exploratory analysis.* Santa Monica, CA: RAND Corporation.

Sheridan, A. (1998). Patterns in the policies: Affirmative action in Australia. *Women in Management, 13,* 243–252.

Stewart, M, Crary, L. & Humberd, B. (2008). Teaching diversity: On the folly of espousing inclusion while practicing exclusion. *Academy of Management Training and Education, 7,* 374-386.

Strachan, G., Burgess, J., & Sullivan, A. (2004). Affirmative action or managing diversity: What is the future of equal opportunity policies in organizations. *Women in Management Review, 19,* 196–204

Strachan, G., French, E., & Burgess, J. (2010). *Managing diversity in Australia theory and practice.* Australia: McGraw-Hill.

Syed, J., & Kramar, R. (2009). Socially responsible diversity management. *Journal of Management & Organization, 15,* 639–651.

Syed, J., & Kramar, R. (2010). What is the Australian model for managing cultural diversity? *Personnel Review, 39,* 96–116.

Thomas, D. A., & Ely, R. J. (1996). Making differences matter: A new paradigm for managing diversity. *Harvard Business Review*, September--October, 79–90.

Thomas, R. R. (1990). From affirmative action to affirming diversity. *Harvard Business Review, 68,* 107–118.

Thomas, R. R. (1991). *Beyond race and gender: Unleashing the power of your total work force by managing diversity.* New York: American Management Association.

Thomas, R. R. (1996). *Redefining diversity.* New York: American Management Association.

Van Buren, H. J., Greenwood, M. M., & Sheehan, C. (2011). Strategic human resource management and the decline of employee focus. *Human Resource Management Review, 21,* 209–219.

Vertovec, S. (2007). Super-diversity and its implications. *Ethnic and Racial Studies, 30,* 1024–1054.

Walsh, J. (2007). Equality and diversity in British workplaces: The 2004 Workplace Employment Relations Survey. *Industrial Relations Journal, 38,* 303–319.

Watson, T. J. (2004). HRM and critical social science analysis. *Journal of Management Studies, 41,* 447–467.

Whitehouse, G., & Frino, B. (2003). Women, wages and industrial agreements. *Australian Journal of Labour Economics, 6,* 579–596.

Wilson, E. M., & Iles, P. A., (1999). Managing diversity—an employment and service delivery challenge. *International Journal of Public Sector Management, 12,* 27–49.

I feel very strongly that change is good because it stirs up the system.
—Ann Richards
Governor of Texas
1991–1995

5

Introducing Intersectionality to the Field of Academic Leadership

Meredith Harper Bonham

Conventional categorical analyses do not broaden our understanding of academic leadership, even when studies focus on gender and leadership, or race and leadership. In fact, I contend that "special" case studies dealing with one particular identity category such as women, African American women, or African American leaders do not inherently challenge or change the universal male/female binary framework that predominates in the field. Moreover, the subject of gender enters the study only when women are involved because gender is assumed to be only about women. Thus, the role of gender in leadership styles is assumed to be a female rather than a male issue, and theories incorporating gender and leadership are focused solely on women leaders—usually white women leaders. Likewise, an examination of the role of race in leadership identity tends to be centered on African American men with African American women relegated to either special, separate mention or an entirely separate study. Whiteness as a racialized identity is not considered, nor is the question of how whiteness intersects when gender, race, and class are taken up.

A large body of work about academic leadership, beginning with seminal leadership texts, provides context, advice, and recommendations on how to lead colleges and universities. More recently, leadership theorists have focused on women leaders in particular, noting the different ways in which women lead. Comparative research on American college and university presidents remains typically focused on either male or female identities with generalized conclusions made about the leadership styles of one group versus another, thereby contributing to a false homogeneity/universality within leadership frames.

Unfortunately, this has the effect of focusing on between-group differences, essentially eliminating anyone who may identify with multiple groups, including race, sexuality, and nationality. Furthermore, white male leadership is established as the norm with (white) women as the comparison group. Of course, these homogenized binary gender categories inadequate and tend to reinforce traditional (and usually sexist) assumptions made regarding leadership traits, for example, that women presidents are more nurturing and that male presidents are more aggressive. Just as feminist theorists have abandoned pursuit of women's essential traits (Baca Zinn & Thornton Dill, 1996), we need to abandon universalizing notions of how presidents lead based on gender. In particular, our operative definitions of gender and of leadership tend to rely on stereotypically *white* notions of gender within the United States.

The Benefits of an Intersectional Approach

The fact that most academic leadership studies rely on a white, male norm may not be terribly surprising since until recently, most American college presidents were white, heterosexual men. But the demographics are changing. From 1986 to 2006, the percentage of women college and university leaders jumped from 9.5% to 23%. During the same period, presidents who were members of minority groups (presumably both men and women) grew at a slower pace from 8.1% to 13.6% (Hassen, 2007). The stereotype of the white, male president in a suit and tie is increasingly being challenged as more women and especially women of color ascend to the presidency. And although they remain in the minority at the presidential level, the data trend compels us to create fissures in our operative frameworks and theories of leadership because women and women of color represent multiple identities, just as men do. The growth in numbers of nonwhite male leaders virtually demands that intersectionality be employed as a means of understanding leadership styles within institutions and across higher education.

Instead of promoting the existing bifurcation of the field according to two genders and two homogeneous leadership styles, the "both/and" intersectional approach provides a means of achieving greater insight into academic leadership. Like anyone, academic leaders are far from unidimensional beings acting in isolation. But the nature of their position and the opportunity for better understanding make the application of intersectionality especially compelling. American college and university presidents lead highly complex organizations serving a diversity of constituencies including faculty, students, boards, employees, and community members. How they choose to lead, and what leadership styles they adopt, are greatly informed by their own multilayered identities. Comparing leadership styles using a single-axis analysis is a disservice not only to the field of leadership study but also to the leaders themselves. Without intersectionality, studies on leadership (especially those which focus primarily on between-group difference) fail to account for the complexity of experience and the societal implications of gender and race, thereby limiting the possibility of understanding the experiences of these leaders and the institutions they serve. Encouraging scholars to reconsider how categories are employed contributes significantly to our insights into leadership experiences.

One mode in incorporating identity categories to leadership study incorporates them as an "add on" or subcategory. For example, a study of women college presidents will mention briefly, as an aside, that there are a certain number of African American women presidents included in the research. But the predominant approach for incorporating race and gender into leadership study analyzes only one facet of identity in isolation from all others. This additive approach doesn't explore how their complex subjectivities and multiple identities overlap and contribute, as a whole, to leadership. To provide a theoretical framework, Leslie McCall defines intersectionality as "the relationships among multiple dimensions and modalities of social relations and subject formations" (McCall, 2005, p. 1770). As subject formations, gender and race provide useful starting points but they do not incorporate the totality of experience and intersecting ways of knowing. The separate treatment of identities as applied to leadership is in effect an extrapolation of what feminist theorist Elizabeth Spelman calls "tootsie roll" or "pop-bead" metaphysics whereby each component of an individual's identity seems as if it may be separated out (Spelman, 1988). Applying intersectionality as a theoretical paradigm to the study of leadership requires examining what is not categorized, or what has been flattened and oversimplified through the use of pop-bead analytic categories. And there is a great deal of meaning in what is *not* presented in leadership studies, especially when race and gender are presented comparatively to a white male ideal for instance. To further illustrate this point, I will later describe several recent leadership studies which delve into issues of gender and race but do so without the benefit of intersectional analysis. Since studies that incorporate race *and* gender tend to focus on African American (as opposed to Latino/a or Asian Americans) leaders, I will concentrate on this body of research for the purpose of examination.

In questioning the adequacy of the traditional, dual gender modes of comparison and language evident in the field of leadership study, disrupting universal theories of gendered leadership styles permits a deeper examination of who these leaders are as individuals and of how their identities inform their leadership. Given the changing, albeit slow, demographic of college and university presidents, it is imperative that leadership studies incorporate feminist theory and in particular intersectionality. Doing so will account for a more diverse array of experiences and thus a more complete understanding of multiple identities—as well as expanding opportunities for potential leaders and the institutions they may serve. Intersectionality expands our knowledge of leadership because it (1) promotes a more complex view of leadership identities; (2) rejects having white male leadership as the norm against which other leaders are compared; (3) avoids theoretical comparisons based on separate and homogenized categories of gender and race; and (4) takes into account the critical role of institutional context in how leadership styles are accepted.

When within-group differences remain unaccounted for, we risk, according to scholar Kimberlé Crenshaw, reinforcing the marginalization of those with multiple identities and further obscuring claims "that cannot be understood as resulting from discrete sources of discrimination" (Crenshaw, 2000, p. 209). Therefore, the risk occurs when one identity category is assumed as providing equal privilege for everyone within that group—such as all women—without accounting for oppression in other areas. Identity categories furthermore run the risk of privileging one identity category *over* another. Incorporating multiple, overlapping ways of being and knowing illuminates our understanding of academic leaders and in particular of women leaders and others who challenge the prevailing stereotype of the white, male heterosexual mold.

Claims based on a white, male norm lose applicability when considering the experiences of anyone who does not fit that mold. Leadership theories therefore are extremely limiting not only about those who have different identities but even for those white heterosexual men who, although they enjoy a certain privilege for being at the traditional center of analysis, should not be judged according to a white male heteronormative standard. To paraphrase theorists Maxine Baca Zinn and Bonnie Thornton Dill, race and gender must matter for everyone (Baca Zinn & Thornton Dill, 1996) in an effort to better understand leadership as a whole and leadership styles as mutually constitutive—instead of from a simplistic, unitary standpoint. White male leaders should not have greater authority about their ability to lead simply because they are men, nor should they be evaluated in an overly simplistic and singularly categorical manner that ignores or flattens out the role that race and gender privileges play in grasping their leadership styles.

A Reconceptualization of Previous Studies

Recent leadership studies have sought to address identity is to separate out identity groups into discrete categories for study and analysis. Three examples in this vein include "African American Female College and University Presidents: Experiences and Perceptions of Barriers to the Presidency" (Jackson, 2007), "An Overview of African American College Presidents: A Game of Two Steps Forward, One Step Backward, and Standing Still" (Holmes, 2004), and "Female Leadership Advantage and Disadvantage: Resolving the Contradictions" (Eagly, 2007). These three studies were selected because they are helpful in illuminating the experiences of a specific group of women leaders, and because they all have been published in the last seven years. They illustrate how the methodology employed and the lack of intersectional analysis limit the findings and, consequently, a more multidimensional understanding of women leaders' experiences.

The Jackson study employs quantitative analysis to compare various barriers that 43 African American women leaders experienced leading up to the presidency. One barrier cited is "gender discrimination" while another is "ethnicity." Why the split? And how did they measure the effects of each barrier versus multiple barriers? The study concludes that "female stereotyping" and "preconceptions of women" were the top experiences cited by the participants, but it is difficult to understand fully the meaning behind these categories given the reliance on a male/female binary. The problem is that other identity categories, and most obviously race, remain unaccounted for when the sole focus is on gender. Jackson suggests that future African American women leaders "can become university presidents, but they must recognize the barriers before them, work hard, and develop strong mentoring relationships" (Jackson, 2007, p. 133), thereby professing that the traditional American work ethic is all it takes to manifest a desired goal. Interestingly, there is no acknowledgment of how power, privilege and oppression are unquestionable factors in the ascension of African American women leaders to presidencies. The lack of any in-depth analysis of overlapping, multiple experience and systems limits considerably the reader's ability to comprehend what hurdles have been overcome over the course of their lives and careers. A systemic analysis, or even an acknowledgment of systemic factors, would provide greater understanding of individual circumstances given that we do not act in isolation but instead we are impacted by systems and organizations beyond our individual control.

The Holmes study, which examined the experiences of six African American university presidents, is equally problematic. At the outset Holmes accepts that "the categories presented do not reflect the experiences of each president who participated in this study because no two people will have the exact experience; nor does a 'prototypical case' of the African American president exist" (Holmes, 2004, p. 26). She thereby presents an encouraging nod to intersectionality, since treatment of gender roles—especially with respect to family obligations—provide a particular impediment to women leaders. But while race is a frequent theme throughout the article, gender is mentioned when the experiences of *women* African American are described compared to their male counterparts. On several occasions the author quotes the experience of "one president" (gender is ambiguous, but assumed to be male) and then of "one female president." In conclusion, Holmes recommends that "women desiring senior-level career advancement opportunities must consider the impact of these positions on their roles as wives and mothers. Most women will have to make decisions related to child-bearing and other family responsibilities if spousal support is not available" (Holmes, 2004, p. 35). The author accepts that child-bearing and family responsibilities are only issues of concern for women, and assumes that all women are in fact wives and mothers. There is no questioning of sexist or heteronormative assumptions or systems, thereby representing a troubling limitation in the article's analysis.

In posing the research question "How can women enjoy a leadership advantage but still suffer from disadvantage?" (which is why the article was chosen for critique), Eagly lays out an encouraging nod to the simultaneous privilege and oppression faced by women leaders in all types of organizations. She addresses the standards by which "good" leaders are judged, acknowledging that often those standards have been crafted according to a masculine ideal (Eagly, 2007). While Eagly's research is important in disrupting the masculine ideal, it is limited to strict gender categories. There is no mention of race or for that matter any other identity category until a passing reference at the end, which states, "Women continue to encounter impediments to leadership within organizations, but many of these impediments can be removed or weakened by organizational changes designed to improve women's (and minorities') access to and success in leadership roles" (Eagly, 2007, p. 9). Although the research and findings hold a great deal of promise in terms of revealing perceptive bias towards women leaders, the study fails to take into account impediments that nonwhite women face and fails to acknowledge at all the multiplicity of experiences across a broad spectrum of women's leaders, much less explain how these experiences shape shape perceptions of leadership.

In all three cases an intersectional approach would allow us to understand leadership styles and institutional barriers to leadership more fully. For example, acknowledging how race and gender overlap would make the Jackson study more complex and relevant to our conceptions of identity. Similarly, the incorporation of systemic analysis would contextualize the experiences of leaders in both the Holmes and the Eagly studies. One might argue that the use of quantitative method, in the case of the Jackson and Eagly studies, limits the applicability of intersectional analysis. However, as McCall stipulates, methodology cannot be an excuse for why intersectionality cannot be applied to studies of leadership and identity, since we "must overcome the disciplinary boundaries based on the use of different methods in order to embrace multiple approaches to the study of intersectionailty" (McCall, 2005, p. 1795). Likewise, Stephanie Shields acknowledges the difficulty of going from *"acknowledging* linkages among social identities to *explaining* those linkages or the processes through which intersecting identities define and shape one another" (Shields, 2008, p. 304). The methodology may be more complicated than comparing one group versus another, but it is necessary in order to achieving greater understanding of the interlocking systems at work.

Recent Application of Intersectionality

Intersectionality disrupts prevailing notions of false universals as related to identity categories, and rejects a hierarchy of identity/oppression. By acknowledging a more complex view of individuals, it also promotes the inclusion of context and environment to further our understanding of oppressive systems and how leaders operate within them. As a relatively new theoretical construct as applied to leadership and identity, it poses a particular challenge when evaluating how leaders are perceived by their constituencies. While on the one hand a unidimensional approach is understandable given the relatively small numbers of nonwhite, heterosexual presidents, and given the unidimensional frames for the field of study, a shift away from the pop-bead approach is increasingly necessary so we may better understand individual leadership identity. Even leadership studies that profess to use intersectional analysis fail to achieve their goal.

A recent article entitled "Intersectionality and Leadership," with its promising title, begins with the gender-primary question, "are there differences between how males and females lead?" (Richardson & Loubier, 2008). While the study provides a first step in examining how leadership styles are defined and evaluated, its comparative stance analyzing the perceptions of two leaders—one male and one female within the same university—misses the mark. Despite the references to feminist theorists, the phenomenological study relies on strict binary categories and on gender as an isolatable category in addressing perceptions of leadership styles, even suggesting that "gender-congruent trait descriptors and gender-neutral terms participants used to describe outcomes were consistent" thereby supporting "previous research that people tend to use language perceived as culturally correct for each gender" (Richardson & Loubier, 2008, pp. 154–155). The flattening of gender is troubling because the study fails to account fully for within-group differences and multiple identities such as race and class, and relies on the norms of appropriate gender style and language. The questions one might ask are: why only gender when the authors profess an intersectional approach? Where are the disruptions of prevailing notions of gender and gender-specific language? What are the contexts for these assumptions? A more complete picture would emerge if these questions are considered.

A more recent article adopts an intersectional paradigm approach with greater success. In "Women and Women of Color in Leadership: Complexity, Identity, and Intersectionality" (Sanchez-Hucles & Davis, 2010), the authors discuss how acknowledging multiple, interlocking identities can assist in understanding the unique challenges faced by women and women of color in leadership positions and those who aspire to them. They further describe how women of color "are required to display leadership competence while simultaneously conforming to European American prototypes representing traditional ethnic, racial, and gender behavior" (Sanchez-Hucles & Davis, 2010, p. 174) and that "to ignore aspects of identity is to ignore the unequal manner in which hierarchies and systems of power provide opportunities for leadership" (Sanchez-Hucles & Davis, 2010, p. 178). The authors convincingly maintain that ignoring race and ethnicity when studing women leaders provides an incomplete anaylysis and inaccurately limits the frame through which leadership identity may be studied, and that future research must incorporate complex and diverse lived experiences. I agree. Their observations provide great promise for the future of the field and demonstrate the value of applying intersectionality to leadership studies.

Given that leaders are judged and assessed every day by boards, faculty, and students, the field of leadership studies is ripe for further examination and analysis using intersectionality. But how best to go about it? Rather than setting up a study *comparing* perceptions of gendered or racialized leadership styles, as previous studies have done, a more enlightened approach would be to conduct interviews of constituencies and then find common themes through qualitative data analysis. Finding those themes, and incorporating feminist theory and in particular intersectionality will provide context for our understanding. How the study is set up is equally important for, as McCall states, "different methodologies produce different kinds of substantive knowledge" and "a wider range of methodologies is needed to fully engage with the set of issues and topics falling broadly under the rubric of intersectionality" (McCall, 2005, p. 1774). For instance, what questions are asked by the researchers, and what language is employed to describe the leadership styles would be just as illuminating as what the leaders themselves have to say.

Why Intersectionality?

The purpose of this chapter essentially is to answer the question "why apply intersectionality to academic leadership study?" The use of a strict male/female or black/white binary in attempting to categorize and assess leadership styles limits the field but also undermines our ability to see leaders for the complex individuals they are. When leaders are assessed by boards and faculty, and even the public, they are judged based on prevailing assumptions about their social location in terms of how they should act or what they should know and therefore what sort of authority they have (Anderson, 2010). This is dangerous because they are held to an unfair standard that (1) incorporates inaccurate stereotypes about how they should act/lead because of their race, gender, and so on and (2) assumes one right way of leading when in fact leadership styles are just as complex and multidimensional as the leaders who employ them. Assuming that all women are alike in their leadership styles obscures any within group differences and runs the risk of privileging white women in particular by placing *them* (as opposed to white men) at the center. To conceptualize this argument, I suggest a twist on an argument set forth by theorist Elizabeth Spelman by inserting the word "leader":

> This ought to tell us that rather than first finding out what is true of some women [leaders] as women and then inferring that this is true of all women [leaders] and thus is common to all women [leaders], we have to investigate different women's lives and see what they have in common other than being female and being called "women." Only then (if at all) can we talk about what is true of any and all of them as women [leaders]. (Spelman, 1988, p. 137)

The application of intersectional analysis to leadership therefore disrupts the false universals employed when we assume that what is true for some women leaders is therefore true for all women leaders regardless of their background and institutional context. With the potential for greater diversity at the highest leadership level in colleges and universities, enlarging the spaces to allow for enhanced ways of knowing will encourage future researchers to resist narrow modalities and will permit members of underrepresented groups to recognize themselves when the categories are not so narrowly defined. But we must take care to acknowledge that simply having leaders represent different identities does not equate intersectionality (Bowleg, 2008). Future studies should examine the complexity of identities and how they intersect, and also acknowledge the impact of other factors such to institutional context.

In studying leadership, accounting for institutional culture and history are key to providing context around experience. For example, leading a predominantly white Research I university will be very different from the experience of leading a historically black women's liberal arts college. Since the contexts might be as different as the individuals being studied, they in turn shape the leadership experience and impact on the institution. This further complicates many studies formulated around leadership. Including organizational context disrupts homogeneous tendencies used in most research to date—and the incredible diversity of institutional type within American higher education complicates this task further. But intersectionality demands that the research attends to environment so that the individual is not viewed in isolation. Even the possibility of leading the college or university has a great deal to do with the organization's culture and history since some will be more receptive than others to hiring and welcoming someone who looks and acts differently than previous leaders. When analyses of leadership identity fail to account for the lived contextual experience of the leader, we miss a significant aspect of who they are as presidents and what types of opportunities they have to be successful. This, in turn, will affect not only how they are perceived by their constituents but also how they view themselves.

The notion of "simultaneous privilege/oppression" also has direct applicability to the use of intersectionality in leadership theory. Once a leadership position is actually achieved, despite any educational, perceptive, and experiential barriers that are encountered along the way, presidents inherently enjoy particular privilege by virtue of their position (which also is linked with higher socioeconomic benefits). Yet they may also be members of a particular oppressed category or of multiply oppressed categories. The fact that they have achieved positions of power does not mean that they are immune from sex and race discrimination. As stated above, they are often judged by faculty, students and boards using unfair, traditionalist standards. And since presidents are assessed by boards of trustees who nationally remain predominantly white and male (Fain, 2010), there is great potential for racism, sexism, and so on to seep into the evaluative process. It is important to acknowledge that these biases against leaders still exist and that perceptions of leadership are greatly affected by their identities.

There is still danger—as evidenced by several recent studies—of falling into the "add and stir" approach to research whereby leaders are successively and distinctly categorized based on their identities or even what category of institutions they lead. While some scholars may adopt this atomized approach in order to establish neat and distinct claims, the categorization falsely homogenizes leaders. As outlined in the examples provided, comparative studies have been done of women presidents and of African American presidents, and then others of specifically African American women presidents. The desire to group individuals in an effort to formulate a cohesive argument remains prevalent throughout the literature, as is an analysis of how they differ from the white, male, heterosexual norm. The latter category is maintained at the center against which all leaders are described and assessed, thereby marginalizing all others. It becomes essential, therefore, to resist the trap of defined categories within which generalizations are made and instead acknowledge the capacity for understanding complex identities and leadership styles using situated knowledge and experience. In so doing, we can better understand the experiences of leaders in all their complexity and acknowledge their numerous and varied contributions to the field.

Practical Implications

In addition to the impact on leadership study, homogenizing leaders can have the practical impact of impeding the advancement of those from underrepresented groups. An obvious example is the common assumption that women are incapable of meeting the relentless demands of a college presidency because of the demands of motherhood. But of course many women do not have children, either by choice or circumstance, to say nothing of the potential for a spouse or partner to be the primary caregiver. Similarly, women leaders often are expected to be more caring than men, thereby creating unfair expectations and/or assessments about how women lead. An intersectional perspective offers the benefit of resisting these assumptions and disregarding the stereotypes that have characterized so many studies (see Holmes, 2004; Madsen, 2008)—and likely so many presidential searches—since the opportunity for women to achieve leadership positions is at risk from the start. Intersectionality provides the opportunity to disturb the prevailing stereotypes that prevent qualified persons from underrepresented groups to achieve leadership positions.

Institutions and especially board members must embrace the possibility of leaders from a variety of backgrounds rather than reject qualified candidates who might be considered "other" if they do not fit the white/male/straight norm. Opening up the possibility of women leaders and their diversity of experience will only broaden the pool of talent from which colleges and universities can draw (Sanchez-Hucles & Davis, 2010). This will in turn have the ripple effect of encouraging potential leaders to consider a presidency once they see the possibility of advancement based on others' experiences. Furthermore, institutions cannot assume that a member of a particular category will behave a particular way or exhibit particular sympathies—as opposed to merely being the *best* leader to meet the needs and chart a future, innovative path for that college or university. There are larger structural, systemic issues at play that get in the way of trustees hiring presidents who do not fit the traditional ideal—and who don't look like the people sitting around the board table. Yet there is reason for optimism. Although the numbers of nonwhite, male presidents are relatively small, they will continue to grow as the pool of potential leaders grows in diversity and complexity, thereby necessitating the exploration of experience within difference as opposed to categorical decisions influenced by gender and race. Broadening our notions and analysis will expand our ability to accept leaders for who they are and for the promise of their leadership to have an effective and positive impact on the institutions they serve.

Future Directions

Most academic leadership research has been constructed based on male/female distinctions or the use of a separate study for a particular group. Thus there is potential to achieve greater understanding of how people lead as individuals and as situated knowers rather than relying on generalized assumptions of how people lead according to single group identities. The implications of neatly bound, distinct categories, and the qualities that are believed to be inherent in those categories, can no longer be assumed to be valid or adequate. In particular, the use of gender-only lenses as situated knowledge becomes highly problematic because of the lack of complexity. Basing analysis strictly on gender, especially using binary comparisons and without the benefit of contextual factors, is entirely too limiting. Disrupting these assumptions will challenge the use of false universals as descriptors or modes of explanation about leaders, and will promote the agency of leaders from underrepresented groups (Wilkinson & Blackmore, 2008).

The use of intersectionality promises to disturb prevailing, traditional notions of a leadership modality based on an outdated perception of who should be in charge of an institution of higher learning in the United States. It should be noted, however, that the study of intersectionality and academic leadership may be applied to any culture in which a more diverse leadership is emerging from women and ethnic minority groups (for a study of women's identity formation and leadership in Australian universities, see Wilkinson & Blackmore, 2008). Introducing an inclusive set of experiences will broaden the scope of study and welcome a plethora of voices who can offer substantial contributions to the field. But it must be more than simply "adding value," since to do so keeps the white male hegemony at the center and resists the inclusion of multiple voices and experiences. Incorporating these voices and accounting for context will reconstitute the recipe for a "good leader" and how she is evaluated. Furthermore, it will open the spaces within which women leaders can see themselves. Intersectionality will reinvigorate a field of study that relies heavily on a traditional mind-set that does not incorporate multilayered identities. American higher education, at its best, provides access to better opportunities for students regardless of gender, race, sexuality or identity. Just as our colleges and universities gradually become more accepting of diverse students from all backgrounds and from around the world, so too must we accept the diversity of experience that are beginning to characterize their leaders.

References

Anderson, E. (2010, August 12). *Feminist epistemology and philosophy of science.* Retrieved from Stanford Encyclopedia of Philosophy, http://plato.stanford.edu/entries/feminism-epistemology

Baca Zinn, M., & Thornton Dill, B. (1996). Theorizing difference from multiracial feminism. *Feminist Studies, 22,* 321–331.

Bowleg, L. (2008). When black+lesbian+woman ≠ black lesbian woman: The methodological challenges of qualitative and quantitative intersectionality research. *Sex Roles, 59,* 312–325.

Crenshaw, K. (2000). Demarginalizing the intersection of race and sex: A black feminist critique of antidiscriminatory doctrine, feminist theory and antiracist politics. In J. James & T. D. Sharpley-Whiting (Eds.), *The black feminist reader* (pp. 208–238). Malden, MA: Blackwell.

Eagly, A. H. (2007). Female leadership advantage and disadvantage: Resolving the contradictions. *Psychology of Women Quarterly, 31,* 1–12.

Fain, P. (2010, November 29). *Diversity remains fleeting on colleges' governing boards, surveys find.* Retrieved from Chronicle of Higher Education, http://chronicle.com/article/Diversity-Remains-Fleeting-on/125566/

Hassen, P. F. (2007, February 12). *College presidents aging and holding jobs longer according to a new report on the college presidency from the American Council on Education.* Retrieved from American Council on Education, http://www.acenet.edu/AM/Template.cfm?Section=Search&template=/CM/HTMLDisplay.cfm&ContentID=20430

Holmes, S. L. (2004). An overview of African American college presidents: A game of two steps forward, one step backward, and standing still. *Journal of Negro Education, 73,* 21–39.

Jackson, S. (2007). African American female college and university presidents: Experiences and perceptions of barriers to the presidency. *Journal of Women in Educational Leadership, 5,* 119–137.

Madsen, S. R. (2008). *On becoming a woman leader.* San Francisco, CA: Jossey-Bass.

McCall, L. (2005). The complexity of intersectionality. *Signs: Journal of Women in Culture and Society, 30,* 1771–1800.

Richardson, A., & Loubier, C. (2008). Intersectionality and leadership. *International Journal of Leadership Studies, 3,* 142–161.

Sanchez-Hucles, J. V., & Davis, D. D. (2010). Women and women of color in leadership. *American Psychologist, 65,* 171–181.

Shields, S. A. (2008). Gender: An intersectionality perspective. *Sex Roles, 59,* 301–311.

Spelman, E. (1988). *Inessential woman: Problems of exclusion in feminist thought.* Boston, MA: Beacon Press.

Wilkinson, J., & Blackmore, J. (2008). Re-presenting women and leadership: A methodological journey. *International Journal of Qualitative Studies in Education, 21,* 123–136.

In Their Own Voice

Catherine H. Raycroft

Leadership is the capacity to mobilize others toward a shared goal. The goal, followers, and leaders make up three equal necessary parts of leadership. These three elements inspire individuals and groups to accomplish shared goals.

Advice for young women: Relate to a female mentor who would work with you in terms of developing your skills, talents, aspirations. Mentors can be teachers, guidance counselors, family friends, or relatives who are successful in their respective fields and like what they are doing. Keep alert to opportunities for educational advancement or matriculation—community colleges, seminars sponsored by women's groups, such as the American Association of University Women and Business and Professional Women. Keep yourself *grounded* and don't take no for an answer to any of your questions (*within reason*).

Be positive!

What keeps me up at night? Just being sure that we are constantly able to evolve our ideas and our capabilities. . . . Above all, we need to bring bottom-line value for the client.

—Virginia Rometty, First Woman CEO, IBM

6

Has Judicial Thinking on Academic Freedom Impeded Gender Mainstreaming in Universities?

Breena E. Coates

Gender mainstreaming is a broad umbrella term for policies and institutional architectures that support gender equality and empowerment through raising of awareness, expansion of choices, access to resources, avenues toward wealth-creation, and decision-making processes (Coates, in press). The term *gender mainstreaming* grew out of the work of international human rights organizations (Agosin, 2001, p. 5). With this came the recognition that there is a gendered element to every human rights abuse or neglect, and to making this concept visible and obvious beyond feminist and development circles.[1] The gender mainstreaming principles, in addition, seek to reinforce statutory mandated visions of individual nation-states in their quest to mainstream women. To those neoconservatives who argue that women do not need to be mainstreamed any longer, the United Nations Development Fund for Women report in 2008–2009 notes that progress has been minimal across the globe. Arguably, "the greatest struggle has been to make human rights of women visible, whether it is with regard to the use of violence against women, or in issues of employment, education, health care, or other rights" (Gaer, 2001, p. 99). The Fourth World Conference on Women in 1995, in Beijing, produced the Beijing Platform for Action as an ongoing effort to advance gender mainstreaming.[2] Gender mainstreaming in its broad policy strategy for promoting equal opportunities on the basis of gender and diversity does not apply to a particular sex, but rather is seen as culturally and historically determined.

This chapter looks at a segment of gender mainstreaming—that is, main-streaming of female faculty in American universities. This is an important area to study in terms of women's rights, because universities are the birthplaces of constructions human and organizational behavior. It is here that leadership behavior is influenced by research inquiry that is useful for social change in workplaces. For the crusaders of gender mainstreaming, this has entailed hard work, because established, gendered, institutional structures do not overturn themselves quickly, or without a battle.

Gender mainstreaming in the United States originated from women's movements such as the Suffragette Movement and the "first Women's Movement"—roughly from the years 1840–1925. The rhetorical strategies of this movement led to the passage and ratification of the 19th Amendment to the Constitution in 1920, which was landmark legislation for women for their ability to participate in the public policy-making process via their ability to vote. Thirty-five years later, a second stream of the Women's Movement arose when women again began to voice their frustrations and demands for equality in the areas of education, employment, and housing. Under the auspices of this movement, women enunciated a vision for themselves: to define their gender, and within that context to look at roles, rights, challenges, opportunities, and threats that their female identities subjected them to. Out of this second wave, a number of other movements arose, each with distinct characteristics. The strongest of these movements continue to this day. These are: radical femi-nism, liberal feminism, structural feminism, lesbian feminism, revalorists, womanists, and power feminism (Wood, 1999). It should be noted that male endorsement of these movements spawned a movement known as the pro-feminist men's movement. One also sees a new construction of "pan global" feminism arising that feeds into the vision of the United Nations for a global focus on women in the workplace. Inquiry into the configuration of imperial-ism and the roles of females in societies (vis-à-vis their struggles against mas-culine domination as well as hegemonic institutions) has provoked stronger scrutiny.

The persuasive rhetoric, lobbying, and policy initiatives of these various movements to aid workplace mainstreaming saw victories in the form of law. Statutory laws such as the Civil Rights Act of 1964,[3] with its proscriptions against discrimination under the word "gender" brought forth a range of other unexpected positive externalities for women.[4] A final and critical piece of leg-islation for the emancipation of women, the Equal Rights Amendment (ERA),[5] has been stymied since 1982. This proposed amendment to the U.S. Constitu-tion would have had the effect of giving females equal rights under any fed-eral, state, or local law. The proposed law would have swept into its mandate female rights that are not missing from specific statutes, such as workplace justice. The bill passed both houses of Congress, but, unfortunately, it did not gain ratification before its deadline on June 30, 1982.

Gender Mainstreaming in Academia

Legislation

The concept of faculty rights for women in the academic workplace has had considerable discourse before, during, and after the passage of the Civil Rights Act of 1964. This statute was amended by Congress in 1972 to apply the law to universities and colleges. While many people are under the assumption that gender discrimination in universities has ended, this is still far from the truth, as many accounts of the struggles of female faculty in academic institutions have shown. West and Curtis (2006) observe that women earn more than half of all graduate degrees but hold only 24% of full professorships, 31% of tenured positions, and 40.9% of tenure track positions in academia. Women as assistant, associate, and full professors earn only 83% of male faculty. Other related tangible exhibitions of gender discrimination exist, such as appointment at lower rank, slower promotion rates, lower retention rates, and not being properly recognized for scholarly contributions. Women in academia have found that raising the issue of discrimination often leads to reprisals and punishments. To those who say that the vision of a level playing field has been achieved, feminists counter that discrimination exists, but it has become more subtle. How else, they ask, can one explain the gender differences still pervasive in academic institutions? As noted by Monroe, Ozyurt, Wrigley, and Alexander (2008), "overt discrimination has largely given way to less obvious but still deeply entrenched inequities." Studies show that women continue to fear direct retaliation if they advocate openly for change (Monroe et al., 2008, p. 223).

Gender discrimination is prohibited under the provisions of Title VII of the Civil Rights Act of 1964. It seems however, that courts have taken a parsimonious view of Title VII, especially in the academic arena, and have dealt with cases of female faculty in a seemingly "unsympathetic" manner (Zimmer, 2003). As understanding of the implications of this law broadens via judicial writ, two categories of employer injurious behavior are generally cited. The first is called *disparate treatment*. Under this category, an employer knowingly treats individuals differently because of gender. The second type is known as *disparate impact*. Under this classification, a policy that is intended to be neutral or appears to be so, but produces an adverse effect on a member of the protected group, is seen as being, in fact discriminatory. This was made clear in the landmark *Griggs* decision.[6]

Besides Title VII of the Civil Rights Act, several other federal laws also uphold the prohibition of gender discrimination in the workplace. Among these are Title IX of the Education Amendments of 1972, the Equal Pay Act of 1963, and John F. Kennedy's Executive Order 10925 March 6, 1961.[7] Despite these laws and the considerable discourse about female discrimination in universities, women in U.S. universities cite gender mainstreaming deficiencies as an ongoing problem. Disparities arise from a complex web of cultural assumptions and practices frequently encountered in academic institutions. They flow largely from the role that male-dominated leadership culture plays in these assumptions.[8]

Male Cultures and Hidden Biases

There is a growing literature in management and social psychology on cognitive bias on the part of males that create patterns of gender bias in organizations. Overt "hostile sexism" (Glick & Fiske, 1996, 2001) is not infrequent. Whitely and Kite (2010) explain that women in faculty positions have a harder time living up to the expectations of the male-dominant culture. In academia, as in other organizations, men in general, and men as leaders, initiate and craft the organizational culture to which women must then adjust. This culture does not favor gender mainstreaming principles. Organizational realists argue that since "men craft" what "women must accept" in the organizational culture, many manifestations of gender bias are present in today's academies. Among these are gender devaluation, punishments for women seeking change, and rejection of the status quo. The costs of women-centered participative and communal management can also be cited as areas where women get criticism. Female behaviors of nurturance, warmth, and supportiveness are in conflict with masculine expectations of directiveness, assertiveness, competitiveness, and dominance (Caplan, 1994) and are viewed as negative when looked at through a male-cultured glass.

Devaluation in particular has to do with academic leadership positions. Eagly and Karau (2002) in their seminal work on role congruity suggest that women are prejudged unfairly in two ways in organizations. First, women are generally perceived less favorably than men when in leadership positions. Second, and relatedly, in analyzing leadership behavior a preconceived (gendered) stereotype of what such leadership conduct should be is seen. Since the "norm" for the culture is male-oriented, this pattern factors into how women are perceived (Eagly & Karau, 2002). The central behavioral issues are:

(1) social conceptualizations and stereotypes about what constitutes *male and female behaviors*, and (2) what constitutes *leadership behaviors*. Since leadership is associated with "masculine" traits of decisiveness, assertiveness, and so on, women who are consensus builders, collaborators, and equality-seekers are handicapped from the very start. In this regard, women are often penalized for simply disagreeing with others, while men are seen as deliberative and analytical when confronting in the same situation. Eagly and Karau (2002) argue that it is these attitudes that account for the difficulty women face in reaching leadership positions, and furthermore, when achieving leadership status. This also contributes to perceived lack of support on the part of males when viewing their female colleagues in leadership roles.

Social psychology theory suggests that dominant group members—in this case, males—allocate scarce resources more favorably to the in-group, because this adds to their internal perception of the self (Adams, 2001). Furthermore, there is an interesting dilemma for women in academic workplaces—while they see that they are being punished for female characteristics of nurturing, communicative, participative, and communal management styles (Rosener, 1990), they are also disparaged and censured when they display the agentic styles associated with males. Dominant women learn that there is a "likeability penalty" for acting agentic (Eagly & Carli, 2007). Studies also have shown that women are punished in student ratings if they "fail to meet gender appropriate expectations" (Bennett, 1982; Kierstead, D'Agostino, & Dill, 1988, p. 344). These "gender appropriate expectations" favor male cultures. Having failed to make their cases through institutional channels, when women do make formal complaints to the courts for redress, the courts have reverted to giving "academic deference" to universities and findings in their favor, thereby diminishing the gender mainstreaming vision of the equal opportunity laws of the land.

Perceptions of Female Leadership Power

Discrimination by males is never always deliberate. Robert Reich, former secretary of labor, has argued that "subtle but pervasive patterns of discrimination" dominate institutions in all sectors of the economy, because of a "myopia" on the part of male-dominated leadership who unconsciously discriminate—without realizing that they are doing so (Manegold, 1994). Research has found that myopia to be connected to underlying unacknowledged prejudices, which also explain related social pathologies such as racism. In the case of racism, these hidden prejudices are categorized as "symbolic," or "aversive racism" (Swim, Hyers, Cohen, & Ferguson, 1995), and their attributes of marginalizing and discriminating can be applied to sexist behaviors against females as well. Myopic or unconscious bias has been shown in the work of Hart, who documents evidence for "subtle," "indirect," "hidden," and/or "second generation discrimination" (Hart, 2005, p. 749). Because antidiscrimination statutes and organizational policies are well known now, it is hardly surprising to see that employers take pains to avoid overt discriminatory tactics.

A more subtle form of bias—*unconscious* bias—is more often the norm in modern academic institutions. For courts, this subtle form of bias creates a challenge in evaluating discrimination claims courts have found. Legal scholars have recognized that outcomes of a discrimination plea depend on perceptions of the decision makers as to what actually happened in a circumstance, in addition to the law itself. Research has shown that perceptions differ markedly between males and females and blacks and whites and others. This places hurdles on the plaintiff in proving workplace discriminatory intent, and hinders gender mainstreaming.

It can be said that the power of leadership positions erodes by gender. In other words, when such jobs are held by women, they are perceived to be less powerful, easily disrespected, and often cheapened. High-status roles in organizations—such as chairs and deans—are differently perceived when held by males versus females. Women in general, while being given entry into these positions, have a harder time in maintaining their standing, dignity, and authority in these roles. As noted by one study, "gender devaluation refers to the subtle process by which administrative positions lose their aura of status, power and authority when held by women" but in contrast, they usually regain their status and power when reoccupied by men (Monroe et al., 2008, p. 219). External offers of academic leadership positions to women are often dismissed or minimized in academia as the "affirmative action effect" (Monroe et al., 2008). Eagly and Karau (2002, p. 546) have argued that, "when a stereotyped group member and an incongruent social role become joined in the mind of the perceiver, this inconsistency lowers the evaluation of the group member as an actual or potential occupant of the role" (Eagly & Karau, 2002, p. 547).

Women who occupy middle management positions such as chairs, receive additional power deficits. They are given much responsibility without resources—particularly in this educational climate of cut-backs. They are squeezed from the top by their deans and provosts, and laterally by their professorial colleagues,[9] and from below by staff and students whom they must please. Female chairs are particularly powerless as they are middle managers who get rammed from all sides with few resources to create goodwill for the policies that they must enforce (Kanter, 1989).

Academic Deference, Academic Freedom, and the Gendered Academy

The Triple Whammy on Women vis-à-vis the "Deference" Principle

The concept of academic deference took root in the case of *Farrell v. Butler University* (2005).[10] In its decision, the court ruled in favor of Butler University and rejected the adverse discrimination claim of the faculty member. In the *Farrell* case, the court gave legal standing to the term, "limited deference" in adjudicating claims against universities. The court's reasoning was that deference was necessary to preserve academic freedom when dealing with equity issues in universities. Firsthand experience shows that female faculty fail to win in civil rights cases concerning gender discrimination, which are the lion's share of such cases,[11] which begs the question: Did judicial deference play a part in these cases? Under this standard, male-centered interests of faculty who have denied tenure females are upheld first by the university's system of successive evaluations, and then by the courts via the special deference doctrine. All this provides a chilly judicial climate for equity cases in the academy. Such behavior then becomes a violation of the intent of Title VII of the Civil Rights Act.

This leads to the question, What might be judicial reasoning behind this behavior? Courts say that special deference must be given to decisions for the universities because academic disciplines are heavily specialized, requiring the special knowledge from within the academy that for obvious reasons courts do not have. To this, critics of the practice of judicial deference argue that a penalizing *triple whammy* exists for faculty women, when others outside the academy—for example, in judgments involving business corporations—are not similarly penalized. In a typical sex discrimination case in a business firm, Courts give only "limited" deference to the employer's reasons for its decision—whereas, in the case of institutions of higher education, courts have traditionally deferred to the university's right to make academic decisions.

Even though the Constitution gave the lawmaking powers to the Congress, courts have become the predominant policy-making body in the nation. The lack of judicial scrutiny on both overt and facially neutral policies, and on plaintiffs who bring charges on these grounds, have created adverse impacts for academic women, and has eroded the intent of EEO laws and regulations for legal protection of women in employment.[12] Since the discrimination cited is often subtle, it is difficult for the female plaintiff to produce sufficiently for the court's satisfaction, factual proof of the institution's "state of mind," animus, or "intent to discriminate" (West, 1994). This is all the more reason for judicial scrutiny, rather than the judicial deference doctrine.

Protection of Academic Freedom

Universities have always held the principle of academic freedom as good intellectual policy within the academy. Typically judges will not substitute their own judgments in place of the institution's defense in academic decision making. In the *Sweezy*[13] decision, it was noted that universities *should,* and *do,* provide the academic ambiance that is favorable to inquiry, experiment, and creation. To accomplish this, the court opined academic freedom is required. The courts determine that in universities "the four essential freedoms" prevail. These are determined as: *Who* may teach; *What* should be taught; *How* teaching should be done; and, *Who* may be admitted to study in the institution (*Sweezy v. New Hampshire,* 1957). These freedoms bestow property rights on the university, and it is on these freedoms and ownerships that judicial forbearance is based. Finkin finds the academic freedom/deference principle is "particularly perverse," and observes that it is "an excrescence of property rights . . . unrelated to the maintenance of conditions of academic freedom within the institution (Finkin, 1983). It is this very judicial forbearance doctrine that allows excessively subjective decision making in universities and that has led to discriminatory claims by female academics. Critics say that this falls close to illegal practice. Others claim that there is a lack of due process involved. The question has been raised freedoms of individuals and that freedoms of academic units, might well be protected under the academic freedom deference, but they often come into conflict. Then the freedom of women is stripped away from legal protection (Byrne, 1989). As noted by Melissa Hart, "the biggest obstacle plaintiffs face may not be the law, but the court" (Hart, 2005, p. 788). Whether specified or not, the deference doctrine in favor of academia has shown that legal judgments for universities in such cases demonstrate a lack of sympathy to female faculty contentions of bias, "dismissing as a matter of law claims that seemed quite strong, or at least solid enough to allow a fact finder to rule either way" (Moss, 2006). The bulk of the academic deference precedents are gender discrimination cases, which illustrates the extent to which the doctrine has been a muscular fortification against the use of statutory laws to Title VII to gender-mainstream women in the academic workplace. Citing the importance of their academic freedom, defendants and sympathetic courts have asserted that federal courts should decline to "invade" higher education with "federal court supervision."

Protection of Academic Freedom in Court Decisions

Judges began to "protect" the academic freedom concept under the judicial writ of case law since the 1950s. In *Sweezy v. New Hampshire* (1957), Earl Warren, the then Chief Justice of the Supreme Court, wrote "the essentiality of freedom in the community of American universities is almost self-evident." In *Keyishian v. Board of Regents* (1967),[14] Justice Brennan observed that the concept of academic freedom was "a special concern of the First Amendment." More recently in *Grutter v. Bollinger* (2003),[15] Justice Sandra Day O'Connor, arguing on a racial issue, stated that narrowly tailored discrimination was permitted in the Equal Protection Clause of the Constitution in university admissions, because the institution (in this instance, the University of Michigan) had in its "academic wisdom" decided that diversity should be an academic value (Balch, 2009).

The academic freedom canon has been seen by the courts as deriving from the First Amendment to the Constitution. However, the academic freedom and deference doctrine is far from being widely held and constitutes an "amorphous quasi-legal concept" that is not justified in the minds of many legal realists as well as "empty rhetoric" rather than sound judicial thinking (Balch, 2009). While used by the courts, academic freedom is not strictly a "legal" concept as it dilutes rather than strengthens workplace justice. It has grown, however, out of academic cultures in universities and the social constructions of reality of faculty and academic leadership. Institutional academic freedom means that the university is independent in actions such as selection, retention, disciplining, and dismissal of its faculty, students, administrators, and staff. However, these must be within the legal guidelines—academic freedom dilutes the statutory guidelines against workplace inequality by limiting institutional responsibility for discrimination. Furthermore, legal scholars see two different kinds of academic freedom shields: (1) protections to *individual* faculty from government intrusion and (2) protections to *institutions* from government intrusion.[16] These two principles collide with each other, as noted in *Piarowski v. Illinois Community College.*[17] It is used to denote both the freedom of the academy to pursue its ends without interference from government . . . and the freedom of the individual teacher . . . to pursue his ends without interference from the academy; and these two freedoms are in conflict" (*Piarowski v. Illinois Community College*, 1985). In general, legal scholars have argued that there has been "no adequate analysis of what academic freedom the Constitution protects, or why it protects it. Lacking definition or guiding principle, the doctrine floats in law, picking up decisions as a hull does barnacles" (Byrne, 1989). Given that the First Amendment is protection for *all* people against government intrusion of speech, it has not been seen as necessary for *special* protection only for the academy as academic deference seems to imply. This is not to say that academic freedom is undesirable, only that special treatment of universities on the part of the courts has served to validate and to maintain male-dominated cultures in these organizations, and consequently has been hostile to gender mainstreaming. This deference to the university and to academic freedom is called into question by many because the university itself is still a gendered institution, where the goal of mainstreaming academic women is tested via a flawed theory of culture. This model while generally unconscious in application, nevertheless affect interactions, and decisions throughout "the life of the relationship" (Hart, 2005, p. 746), and that it is not necessarily something that occurs only at the moment an employment decision is made (Kreiger, 1995).

University Processes and Mainstreaming of Women

It has been stated that most universities already have taken steps to promote women's participation in the arts and sciences, and to link that participation to fairness and social justice in the academic community. So why would another discussion be necessary? It is argued that the gender mainstreaming lens brings into critical focus process, production, and outcomes issues that might need scrutiny in a more deliberate way by looking into the institution's value chain, from the supply chain system and the customer relations management system to the entire enterprise resource planning systems. The dynamics of information in the value chain is from final consumption through to primary production and input suppliers and back again. Useful institutional questions would be: How inclusive, transparent, and responsive are the information flows in the chain? To what extent are stakeholders' decisions (what to produce, when to produce, how to produce) pulled by what constituents value? Customers, stakeholders, and constituents in this case are broadly defined. They consist of direct customers such as students and parents; customer/participants such as faculty and staff, and indirect constituencies such as the general citizenry. To adequately assess the value chain in terms of gender mainstreaming issues, universities must do methodical evaluation of each stage of its chain—from recruitment to retention to promotion, as well as termination strategies. Questions to ask in this regard would be: How much investment is being made in the focal area? What areas of the process add value, and what is wasteful? How is the value that is created shared along the chain? Embedding gender mainstreaming into the entire value chain, with specific mandates, is a necessary component for strategic thinking in academia. Without this vision, statements about equality are merely whitewashing. Specific attention should be given to the discriminatory pressure points in the academic value chain.

Conclusion

The phrase, "gender mainstreaming" is about a strategic vision for leveraging change, supranationally,[18] nationally, and organizationally. Some critics have asked why we even need to talk about gender mainstreaming in the 21st century. To this, proponents of the philosophy point out that the movement— which began in the late 19th and early 20th centuries to bring women into economic, political, and social power bases and mainstreams—has been only marginally successful for women around the world. Statistical evidence backs up this claim by showing that while today half the population of the world is women, only one-third of women constitute the global labor force, and women earn a meager one-tenth of global income. In the 21st century, it clear that women across the globe still do not fully and easily navigate through, and influence, political, economic, and social agendas to change the contexts of their own lives and those of other women (Moreno, 2010). Marginalization, domination, and discrimination continue to limit women, not just in political agenda setting but also in their personal spheres of decision making over their own bodies, minds, and life choices (Moreno, 2010). On a global scale, this is an issue that demands the realization of the complete spectrum of human rights touted by democracies.

In the United States, laws exist to mainstream women in the workplace in recruitment, retention, and promotion and offer proscriptions against unfair dismissal. However, these laws are hampered by the courts in their findings of constitutional protection of academic freedom, and consequent judicial deference to universities. However, such usage of academic freedom appears to be a flimsy notion at best, and has been rejected by organizational and legal pragmatists, who claim that the concept is used as a *stick* as well as a *screen*. Also key to their argument is the fact that the university organization—like any other organization—is shaped by invisible or partially visible cultural pillars that have discriminatory effects, and therefore an ongoing evaluation of university and judicial procedures is necessary to show where these procedures butt heads with public policy vision and intent.

It is suggested that academic leadership look to mainstreaming as more than a vision or a statement in the organizational mission. Public relations efforts embedded into vision statements are commonplace and have had little success in turning around the broad and deep mainstreaming efforts that public policy has sought. This chapter has suggested that organizational value chain analysis must be an ongoing concern of strategic leadership, especially when the issue of gender mainstreaming deficiencies is brought up so frequently. Such scrutiny will show weaknesses, threats, and opportunities for changing the face of universities by gender.

From a review of discrimination cases in universities, it seems that invoking judicial deference has been successful in upholding institutional judgments. Nevertheless universities need to take a second look at the following: (1) maintaining the university's integrity; (2) intellectual honesty in the academy; and (3) contractual obligations in terms of faculty resources. In terms of the latter, if universities see fit to use arbitrary judgments in tenure and promotion cases, and courts defer to this, then that is an issue that should be made transparent at the very beginning of the contract between institution and prospective faculty member. High-level employees (faculty) have a lot to lose if an employment relationship does not work out. The hardships endured may include: (1) loss of investment of 5 to 6 career years at the institution; (2) the stigma of rejection that will follow that person on seeking another academic post; and (3) the possible end of a university career that denial of tenure creates.

In sum, institutional integrity and intellectual honesty as well as justice and fairness to employees is at stake and is an important justice issue for universities to now consider instead of blindly accepting academic freedom and judicial deference mantras in their favor. In turn, courts must provide fair and unbiased scrutiny of all parties in a case and not make a special exception for universities. The court's final decision in *McConnell v. Howard University* (1987)[19] could serve as an example and a restraint to the judicial deference argument.[20]

Until universities and the courts revisit the issue of judicial deference, Title VII continues to be weakened, and judicial deference prevents society from moving forward in an important area of employment equality and equal opportunity. Moss goes so far as to argue that the application of judicial deference amounts to "a judicial repeal of Title VII" (Moss, 2006, p. 22). However, with cases like *McConnell v. Howard University*, cited above, hope exists for the "undercutting of the 'academic defense doctrine'" (Moss, 2006, p. 22).

Notes

1. The term, as it relates to global policy, had its genesis in the United Nations Third World Conference on Women in Nairobi, 1985. Subsequent to the Nairobi Conference, the United Nations developed the concept of gender mainstreaming through its various institutions.

2. The United Nations has also developed a variety of organizational structures like the UN Development Fund for Women, the UN Division for the Advancement of Women, the UN International Institute for Research and Training of Women, and other gender equality structures (Runyan, 1999, 2010) that promote, produce research, and promulgate actions on behalf of women on a global scale. The UN along with other supranational bodies, like the World Bank and the Organisation for Economic Co-operation and Development, and trade compacts between nations, such as the EU and NAFTA, have employed this phrase in advocating equality for women.
3. Civil Rights Act, Public Law 88–352, 78 Stat.214.
4. The term *gender* in the Act originally referred to the employment of women, but soon encompassed sexual harassment of women of two kinds: quid pro quo harassment and hostile work environment harassment.
5. Written by suffragist Alice Paul, the ERA in 1923 was introduced in the Congress for the first time. In 1972, it passed both houses of Congress, but expired on its June 30, 1982, deadline, due to failure to ratify.
6. *Griggs v. Duke Power Company,* 401, U.S. 424, 1971.
7. Kennedy's Executive Order 1095, 1961, envisioned social justice in the United States for all people through affirmative action by institutions. Schoen and Winocur (1988) show that by themselves affirmative action interventions cannot adjust the gender imbalance in workplaces.
8. It should be noted that the male model also ensnares male faculty and administrators into upholding conscious, and often unconscious, stereotypical roles (Monroe et al., 2008).
9. A chairman, especially a female at the associate professor level, is not in the usual sense a "manager" of the department. She is the equal or in the case of the associate professor the subordinate of full professors who must judge her for tenure purposes. Even if she is a full professor, her colleagues are equal to her, often disrespectful to her judgments, and she must humor them as she returns to their ranks when her term is over.
10. *Farrell v. Butler University*, 421 F3e 609 (7th Circuit).
11. Even if the courts do not "cite the academic freedom [argument] expressly, they certainly have proven hostile to professors' claims of discrimination, dismissing as a matter of law, claims that seemed quite strong, or solid enough" (Moss, 2006).
12. As such the prediction attributed to Thomas Jefferson that the constitution would become "a mere thing of wax in the hands of the judiciary, which they may twist and shape into any form they please," rings true in this and other instances.
13. *Sweezy v. New Hampshire,* 354 U.S. 234, 1957.
14. *Keyishian v. Board of Regents*, 345 F2d 239, 1967.
15. *Grutter v. Bollinger*, 539 U.S. 406, 2003.

16. Bryne, J. P. (1989), 99 *Yale Law Journal*, 251 255, 257.
17. *Piarowski v. Illinois Community College*, 759 F.2d. 625 (1985).
18. "Mainstreaming a gender perspective is the process of assessing the implications for women and men of any planned action, including legislation, policies or programmes, in areas and at all levels. It is a strategy for making women's as well as men's concerns and experiences on integral dimension of the design, implementation, monitoring and evaluation of policies and programmes in all economic and societal spheres so that women and men benefit equally and inequality is not perpetuated. The ultimate goal is to achieve gender equality" (United Nations, 1997).
19. *McConnell v. Howard University*, 818 F2d 58, 1987.
20. In *McConnell v. Howard University*, the court gave deference to the institution's faculty handbook in making a judgment for the university, where it was stated that the decision of the Board of Trustees of Howard University was to be final. The trial court noted it would require proof that board of trustees had acted arbitrarily or if that McConnell could present evidence of motivation that was suspect or irrational. The Court of Appeals rejected this standard presented by Howard University.

References

Adams, M. (2001). Intergroup rivalry, anti-competitive conduct and affirmative Action. *Boston University Law Review, 82,* 1089, 1118.

Agosin, M. (Ed.). (2001). *Women, gender, and human rights: A global perspective.* New Brunswick, NJ: Rutgers University Press.

Balch, S. (2009, September 7). *Constitutionalizing "academic freedom," deconstructing free speech.* Paper presented at the National Association of Scholars, Washington, DC.

Bennett, S. (1982). Students perceptions and expectations for male and female instructors: Evidence relating to the question of gender bias in teaching evaluation. *Journal of Educational Psychology, 74,* 170–179.

Byrne, J. P. (1989). Academic freedom: A special concern of the first amendment. *Yale Law Journal, 99,* 2.

Caplan, P. J. (1994). *Lifting a ton of feathers: A woman's guide to surviving in the academic world.* Toronto, ON: University of Toronto Press.

Civil Rights Act 1964, Pub.Law 88–352, 78 Stat. 241.

Coates, B. E. (in press). Gender mainstreaming. In A. Kaul & M. Singh (Eds.), *New paradigms: Study of best practices in lead organizations.* New Delhi: Prentice Hall.

Eagly, A., & Carli, L. (2007). *Through the labyrinth: The truth about how women become leaders.* Boston, MA: Harvard Business School Press.

Eagly, A., & Karau, S. (2002). Role congruity theory of prejudice toward female leaders. *Psychological Review, 109,* 3.

Equal Pay Act, U.S. Code Chapter 8, 206(d)(1963).

Farrell v. Butler University, 421 F.3d 609, 2005.

Finkin, M. (1983). On institutional freedom within the institution. *Texas Law Review,* 817, 839.

Gaer, F. D. (2001). Mainstreaming a concern for the human rights of women: Beyond theory. In F. Gaer (Ed.), *Women, gender, and human rights: A global perspective* (pp. 98–124). New Brunswick, NJ: Rutgers University Press.

Glick, P., & Fiske, S. (1996). The ambivalent sexism inventory: Differentiating hostile and benevolent sexism. *Journal of Personality and Social Psychology, 3,* 491–522.

Glick, P., & Fiske, S. (2001). Ambivalent alliance: Hostile and benevolent sexism as complementary justifications for gender inequality. *American Psychologist, 56,* 109–118.

Griggs v. Duke Power Company, 401, U.S. 424, 1971.

Grutter v. Bollinger, 539 U.S. 406, 2003.

Hart, M. (2005). Subjective decisionmaking and unconscious discrimination. *Alabama Law Review, 56,* 3.

Kanter, R. M. (1979). Power failure in management circuits. *Harvard Business Review, 57,* July–August.

Kierstead, D., D'Agostino, P., & Dill, H. (1988). Sex role stereotyping of college professors: Bias in students' rating of college instructors. *Journal of Educational Psychology, 80,* 342–344.

Kreiger, L. H. (1995). The content of our categories: A cognitive bias approach to discrimination and equal employment opportunity. *Stanford Law Review, 1161,* 47.

Manegold, C. (1994). Glass ceiling is pervasive, secretary of labor contends. *New York Times,* September 27, B9.

McConnell v. Howard University, 818 F.2d 58, 1987.

Monroe, K., Ozyurt, S., Wrigley, T., & Alexander, A. (2008). Gender equality in academia: Bad news from the trenches, and some possible solutions. *Perspectives on Politics, 6*(2), 215–233.

Moss, S. A. (2006). Against "academic deference": How recent developments in employment discrimination law undercut an already dubious doctrine. *Berkeley Journal of Employment and Labor Law, 27,* 1.

Piarowski v. Illinois Community College, 759 F.2d 625, 1985.

Rosener, S. (1990). Ways women lead. *Harvard Business Review, 68,* 119–125.

Runyan, A. S. (1999). *Women* in the neoliberal "frame." In M. Meyer & E. Prugl (Eds.), *Gender politics in global governance* (pp. 210–220). Boulder, CO: Rowman & Littlefield.

Runyan, A. S. (2010). Global feminism. In M. Paludi (Ed.), *Feminism and women's rights worldwide* (pp. 1–6). Westport, CT: Praeger.

Sweezy v. New Hampshire, 354 U.S. 234, 1957.

Swim, J., Hyers, L., Cohen, L., & Ferguson, M. (1995). Sexism and racism: Old-fashioned and modern prejudices. *Journal of Personality and Social Psychology, 68*, 2.

United Nations. (1997). "Integrating women's human rights into global health research: An action framework." *Report of the Economic Social Council, by Donna Baptiste et al.* New York: Author.

West, M. (1994). Gender bias in academic robes: The law's failure to protect women faculty. *Temple Law Review, 67 Temple Law Review* 68–178.

West, M., & Curtis, J. (2006). AAUP faculty gender equity indicators 2006. Washington, DC: American Association of University Professors.

Whitely, B., & Kite, M. (2010). *The psychology of prejudice and discrimination.* Belmont, CA: Wadsworth.

Winocur, S., Schoen, L., & Sirowatka, A. (1989). Perceptions of male and female academics with a teaching context. *Research in Higher Education, 30*, 317–329.

Wood, J. (1999). *Gendered lives: Communication, gender and culture* (3rd ed.). Belmont, CA: Wadsworth.

Zimmer, M. (2003). Systemic empathy. *Columbia Human Rights Law Review, 34*, 575, 576.

7

Inequality in the Division of Household Labor and Child Care: Causes, Consequences, and How to Change

Miriam Liss

Women's household labor has declined since 1965 while men's contribution to housework has increased over the same period (Bianchi, Milkie, Sayer, & Robinson, 2000); however, women still do more than men. Over the 40-year period explored in this longitudinal time diary study, the number of hours women have spent doing housework has been nearly cut in half (from 30 hours a week to 17.5 hours a week), while the number of hours men spent on household labor has doubled from 4.9 hours to 10 hours a week. However, this drop-off has not been consistent over time. The biggest decrease in women's relative contributions to household labor occurred between 1965 and 1975, when women went from doing 6.1 times more household labor than men to doing only 3.3 times as much. The trend continued to decrease, but the gains toward equality have been smaller with each consecutive decade. In 1985, women were doing twice as much housework as were men; however, in 1995 they were doing 1.8 times as much. Thus, one could argue that the gains toward equality in household labor that women made early in the women's movement have stagnated.

Although the ratio of household chore participation vary slightly from study to study, the pattern of women doing more than men is consistent across multiple studies and multiple countries. One study investigating division of labor across 33 countries found that wives ranged from doing 62% of the household labor in Latvia to 90% of the household labor in Japan; in the United States, women reported doing 67% of the household labor (Fuwa & Cohen, 2007). Another study, looking specifically at employed American women with high socioeconomic status and egalitarian gender attitudes, found that women reported doing 70% of the cooking, 72% of the cleaning, 64% of the child care, and 58% of the total labor in the household (Claffey & Mickelson, 2009). A recent review article spanning literature from 2000 to 2009 concluded that, overall, North American women perform about two-thirds of the routine household labor (Lachance-Grzela & Bouchard, 2010).

Although some interview studies have suggested that women do 10 to 15 hours more work than men each week when paid and unpaid labor are combined (Hochschild & Machung, 1989), more recent time diary studies do not present such a dire picture (Sayer, England, Bittman, & Bianchi, 2009). The work of Sayer et al. (2009) indicated that when paid and unpaid labor were combined, men and women generally worked equal numbers of hours and that men who worked while their wives stayed home actually worked significantly more hours than women. However, they also found that employed mothers with young children do work more total hours than do men.

Research that has investigated what full-time working couples do after work has consistently revealed that women suffer from a "leisure gap" where they engage in about 30 minutes per day less of leisure than do men (Mattingly & Sayer, 2006). Although this research is generally conducted utilizing time diaries where people report what they are doing with their time (Mattingly & Sayer, 2006), one study followed couples where both the men and women worked over 30 hours a week in order to determine how each spent their after-work hours (Saxbe, Repetti, & Graesch, 2011). They found that men spent significantly more time engaged in leisure activities than did women and women spent significantly more time in housework.

Why Is the Division of Labor Unequal?

One of the biggest reasons that women do more housework than men is that women have less power than do men (Davis, 2010). One manifestation of greater power is that the individual with more power in the relationship generally makes more of the decisions in the relationship (Fox & Murry, 2000). This means that the more powerful individual in a couple could choose to do less household labor or to do specific tasks that are found more enjoyable or occur less frequently. The influence men have over women's decision making can be subtle. One study found that wives were more likely to agree with earlier stated opinions by their spouse than were husbands (Zipp, Prohaska, & Bemiller, 2004). Regardless of whether the manifestation of power is overt or subtle, it is important to consider the source of the power.

Gender Ideology

It is typical that men hold more power in relationships, and the traditional view of gender is that men are the head of the household. Thus, individuals who hold traditional views about gender are more likely to endow the male member of the couple with more relational power. Given this, it is important to consider the role of gender ideology on the division of labor. Research has shown that couples who hold egalitarian beliefs about gender were more likely to share household chores relatively equally (Kroska, 2004; Stevens, Minnotte, Mannon, & Kiger, 2006). Men's endorsement of liberal gender attitudes may be more important than women's in determining whether housework is shared equally. Having liberal attitudes predicted husband's participation in domestic tasks considerably more than having liberal attitudes did for wives (Kroska, 2004). Another study found that men who had liberal views as adolescents participated in more household labor than did men who had held more conservative views (Cunningham, 2005). The fact that men's views about equality matter more than women's is consistent with the idea that men have more power in relationships—the men are more likely than the women to determine whether there is equality.

The relationship between gender ideology and amount of household labor completed can be seen on a cultural level as well. In a study from married women across 30 nations, a general trend was found wherein wives in nations with higher levels of gender equality tended to do fewer hours of household labor and less of the total labor in the family (Greenstein, 2009). In this international study, individual women's gender ideology was also a small, but significant, predictor of women's share of the domestic work (Greenstein, 2009).

Nevertheless, simply believing in equality in the abstract is not enough to create an equal division of labor within the family. Attitudes about division of labor tend to be considerably more egalitarian than the actual division of labor (Ferree, 1991). Some research has even found that general attitudes about the importance of equality have absolutely no relationship to the actual division of labor in the family (Wilkie, Ferree, & Ratcliff, 1998). Other sources of unequal power in the relationship also need to be examined.

Relative Resources

One source of power that has been found to relate to division of household labor is the amount of financial resources each member of the family contributes to the household. Research has consistently found that the individual who contributes more financial resources to the household does less housework (Coltrane, 2000; Kroska, 2004). This can be seen from a social exchange perspective where each member of the couple calculates the costs and benefits of being in the relationship (Nakonezny & Denton, 2008; Thibaut & Kelley, 1959).

Given that husbands tend to make more money than wives since men's earnings exceed women's (Blau & Kahn, 2006; Dey & Hill, 2007), wives may participate in household labor as a way to contribute to the marriage. Research has generally supported the idea that as women's earnings move toward being equal to the earnings of their male partners, the inequity between men and women's division of labor lessens (Brayfield, 1992; Ishii-Kuntz & Coltrane, 1992; Presser, 1994). However, the relative resources perspective is challenged by data reviewed below that when women earn more than men, their contribution to housework and child care actually increases (e.g., Brines, 1994; Greenstein, 2000)

Time Availability

A similar perspective to relative resources holds that the individual who has the greater amount of time will engage in the greater amount of household labor. Research has generally supported this perspective, showing, for example, that as women's employment hours go up, husbands' contributions to household labor go up as well (Coltrane, 2000; Ishii-Kuntz & Coltrane, 1992; Kroska, 2004). This was found in a study of employed women from 30 nations where women employed either part- or full-time had a total decrease of hours of household labor and did a smaller share of the overall household labor relative to their husbands (Greenstein, 2009). A recent time diary study found that husbands who had wives who worked more hours did more child care activities on weekdays (Connelly & Kimmel, 2009). The importance of time availability may differ depending on national context. One study found that, for women who live in more egalitarian countries, full-time employment status (and thus having less available time) was related to a more equal division of labor in the family (Fuwa, 2004). However, this was not true for women in less egalitarian countries. Women in countries characterized by more traditional gender ideologies appeared to benefit less from their individual assets (such as full-time employment) in the negotiation about who did what in the family. This pattern is also seen in Japan, where even women who work full-time and earn high incomes tend to do the great majority of household labor and child care (North, 2009). Furthermore, the research on leisure time reviewed above indicated that women are more likely to use available time to do household chores while men are more likely to pursue leisure activities (Mattingly & Sayer, 2006; Saxbe, Repetti, & Graesch, 2011).

Other Sources of Power

There are other sources of unequal power in a relationship that have been less frequently investigated as sources of the unequal division of labor in the home. For example, a frequently cited source of relational power is the principle of least interest (Waller, 1938). This is the idea that the individual in the relationship with the least investment in it has the most power in that relationship. Research has found that in couples where there was an inequality in the sense of investment in the relationship, it was usually the man who was less invested (Sprecher & Felmlee, 1997). Furthermore, in heterosexual couples, the member of the couple that was less emotionally invested in the relationship did, indeed, perceive him- or herself as having more power in that relationship (Sprecher & Felmlee, 1997; Sprecher, Schmeekle, & Felmlee, 2006). Although perceptions of who is more invested in the relationship has not been studied in terms of the division of labor among actual married couples, research among young adults suggests that there are pervasive stereotypes held by both women and men that men are less interested in marriage and children than women (Erchull, Liss, Axelson, Staebell, & Askari, 2010). Thus, both women and men assumed that the man would the least invested partner which would give the man more power in the relationship. However, these stereotypes were found to be false; both men and women were equally interested in marriage and children (Erchull et al., 2010). Furthermore, for young women, but not men, desire for marriage and children was related to willingness to participate in household and child care chores. Thus, women may feel as though they need to do more chores in order to make up for the fact that they have successfully convinced their supposedly recalcitrant husbands into getting married and having children.

Doing Gender

Although gender ideology, relative resources, and time availability do explain some of the inequity of the division of household labor, simply being a woman has been found to predict doing more household labor and simply being a man has been found to predict doing less household labor even when all the other variables are taken into account (Kroska, 2004). This has led researchers to hypothesize that men and women are socialized to enact their gender roles in certain ways and that this differential gender socialization influences the division of household labor in a variety of ways.

Women and men are socialized differently, and women may see having a clean house as an important part of their identities and part of their roles as women (e.g., Crawford, 2006; Davis, 2010; Eagly & Steffen, 1984). Research has begun to look at the role of attitudes toward housework as a predictor of how much housework is completed (Poortman & van der Lippe, 2009). Women have been found to enjoy housework more, report higher standards for that housework, and feel a greater sense of responsibility for ensuring the housework is adequately completed (Poortman & van der Lippe, 2009). Furthermore, the more positive women's attitudes and the more negative men's attitudes were toward household labor, the more household tasks the woman did relative to the man even taking into account the contribution of other predictors of division of labor such as time availability and relative resources (Poortman & van der Lippe, 2009). Some research has suggested that men's attitudes toward specific household chores may be better predictors of who completes the chores than women's attitudes (Wilkie et al., 1998). This study found that the personal preferences for household labor predicted the actual division labor for both husbands and wives, but the preferences of husbands was a better predictor than those of wives. This is consistent with the idea that men have more power in the relationship.

Despite the fact that women are socialized to associate household labor with their sense of themselves as women, research does not actually consistently show women enjoying household tasks. One study showed that women have more positive feelings toward child care and laundry, but men actually have more positive feelings toward grocery shopping, kitchen cleanup, and housecleaning (Kroska, 2003). This may be because women perform household chores out of obligation while, when men do perform these chores, they are more likely to do it out of choice.

The perspective of doing gender is evident in some research that has pointed to the limitations of the social exchange perspective and resource arguments in explaining the division of household labor. Although it is true that research suggests that as women contribute more to the household their contribution to household labor goes does, this is only true up to a certain level of contribution. In their seminal study demonstrating that women have a "second shift" of household labor after their workday, Hochschild and Machung (1989) found that in every couple interviewed where the woman earned more than the man, the woman contributed a disproportionate amount of the household labor. Equality in the division of labor was found, however, among some couples that had equal income or where the man earned more. In fact, the couples in which the husband earned the least amount of money were the ones where the wives did the most labor. Another interview study found that when women earned more than men, women participated in more of the labor to decrease the stigmatization for the man of earning less (Atkinson & Boles, 1984).

Several studies have systematically tested this hypothesis (Bittman, England, Sayer, Folbre, & Natheson, 2003; Brines, 1994; Greenstein, 2000; Lothaller, Mikula, & Schoebi, 2009). In two of these studies, a relationship was found such that when women's earnings surpassed men's earnings, men's contribution to household labor decreased (Brines, 1994; Greenstein, 2000). Unemployed men, or those who earned the least relative to their wives, contributed the least amount of household labor. A similar finding with an Australian sample indicated that among the 14% of couples in the sample in which the wives earned 51%–100% of the household income, more income was actually related to greater participation in household labor (Bittman et al., 2003). The authors of these studies proposed that couples engage in a process of gender deviance neutralization where the husbands must compensate for the threat to their masculinity of earning less money by contributing less to the household labor. It should be noted, however, that one study looking at data from Austria, Portugal, and the Netherlands did not replicate this finding (Lothaller et al., 2009).

Thus, gender roles play an important role in the division of labor. Women may do more labor than men because they claim to enjoy, feel satisfied, or feel more responsible for the care of the house—all attributes that are part of the socialization of what it means to be a female. Furthermore, when gender roles are violated in some domains, such as when women earn more than men, the need to feel like one is complying with one's gender role in other ways may increase. This explains the counterintuitive finding that greater earnings for women can translate into actually having to do more domestic labor.

An Integrative Theory

Recently, theorists from the study of communication have developed a theory which more specifically helps explain how gender socialization results in an inequitable division of labor (Alberts, Tracy, & Trethewey, 2011). They propose that women generally have a lower threshold of tolerance for when a task needs to be accomplished. So, while a man may see socks on the floor and not be bothered, a woman will be irritated by the socks enough to pick them up. The authors note that this tendency for women to have lower tolerance may have some biological/evolutionary cause (e.g., women having a keener sense of smell) but is also due to the historical social role of women being in the home and thus developing greater attunement to what needs to be done in the home (Wood & Eagly, 2002). Furthermore, women tend to have more skills and competencies in performing household tasks, due to watching their parents perform tasks in a gendered manner and being given chores to do around their childhood home that are gendered in origin. Thus, women have a lower tolerance for performing household labor, become designated as experts in these tasks, and take "ownership" in the relationship for performing them (Clair, 2011). The fact that women tend to perform tasks before men notice that they need to be done creates a self-perpetrating system. The house never gets dirty enough for men to notice that it needs to be cleaned, increasing the gendered division of labor as well as the dynamics of women feeling as though they "own" and are "experts" in the performance of household tasks.

The dynamics of gratitude also contribute to this process. Alberts et al. (2011) proposed that, for women, doing work around the house is expected and they do not expect gratitude for doing such tasks. However, when men perform chores, especially if they are performing a chore before it would naturally reach their level of response threshold, this is seen as a gift and men expect gratitude. On the other hand, many women see their ability to work as a gift given to them by their husband who may prefer that she stay at home (Tracy & Rivera, 2010). Thus, this woman may perform more household labor as a way to compensate for their guilt at being away from the home and family. Thus, the different dynamics of gratitude contributes to our understanding of why women who outearn men generally do a higher percentage of the division of labor.

Data on this integrative theory suggests that among same sex roommates, the member of the pair who has a lower threshold for tolerance of dirt and mess is the one who does more than the cleaning (Riforgiate & Alberts, 2008 cited in Alberts et al., 2011). This theory is also consistent with data that suggests that women have higher standards for household labor (Ferree, 1991). In fact, in this study, 34% of the men reported that they felt it was difficult to meet their wives' standards for housework.

Perceptions of Fairness

One of the paradoxes of the literature on the division of household labor is that few women report that the division of labor is unfair, even if they are doing most or all of the housework (Claffey & Manning, 2010). Furthermore, men and women generally have very different thresholds for what they consider to be a fair division of labor. For example, one study found that although 96.6% of the women did most or all of the housework, 70% of the women reported the division of labor to be fair (Frisco & Williams, 2003). Furthermore, 62.5% of women who saw the division of labor as fair did all or most of the housework while 62.9% of the men who saw the division of labor as fair did less than half or none of the housework (Frisco & Williams, 2003). Another study found that men believed the division of labor to be fair when they contributed 36% of time devoted to household tasks while women found it fair when they contributed 66% (Lennon & Rosenfield, 1994). A more recent study found that although women spent about three times as many hours as men on low control tasks (in other words, tasks where the individual has no control about when the task needs to be done) such as cooking, cleaning, washing, and shopping for groceries (29 hours versus 10 hours per week), there was no significant difference in the extent to which they believed that the division of labor was fair (Bartley, Blanton, & Gilliard, 2005).

There are several explanations as to why women often regard an unequal division of labor as fair. One hypothesis utilizes relative deprivation theory (Crosby, 1976). This theory holds that evaluations of fairness are subjective decisions in which one compares oneself to others (Greenstein, 1996, 2009). If a woman compares the amount of labor she does to the amount her husband does, she will perceive this as unfair. However, if she compares the amount of labor she does to other women in similar situations, she will not see the amount of work she does as unfair.

Research has suggested that women with more liberal ideologies are more likely to compare themselves to men when making judgments about fairness while more traditional women are more likely to compare themselves to other women (Greenstein, 1996). This same pattern was found in an international sample of married women from 30 nations. In nations with less gender equity, unequal division of labor was less strongly related to perceptions of unfairness than in nations with higher levels of gender equity. For example, in Mexico, if a woman increased the share of her household labor from 25% to 75%, this would only result in a small decrease in her perceptions of fairness, while in Sweden, the same increase in household labor would cause a very large decrease in a woman's perceptions of fairness (Greenstein, 2009). Thus, the national context provides a comparison point for women in making their decisions of fairness.

In addition to gender ideology, the other variables that have been associated with the actual division of labor (relative resources and time availability) have also been found to be related to perceptions of fairness (Claffey & Manning, 2010). In an international study of over 8,000 women, time availability and relative resources as well as gender ideology were significant predictors of the perceptions of fairness of the division of labor (Braun, Lewin-Epstein, Stier, & Baumgartner, 2008). The percentage of women who perceived equity in the division of labor in their family ranged from 30% in Flanders to 63% in Portugal; 41% of the participants in the United States perceived equity in their relationships. Similar to the studies discussed above, this study found that women who lived in countries in which women generally earned more were less satisfied with an unequal division of labor. Consistent with the idea of relative deprivation, the average inequality of labor in the country also influenced perceptions of fairness; if the average woman in the country had a very unequal division of labor, individual women were less likely to see their inequality as unfair. Furthermore, a woman's individual gender ideology also strongly predicted her sense of unfairness about the division of labor. The Braun et al. (2008) study also found that women who were engaged in the labor market, and thus had less time available to engage in household labor, were generally less satisfied with their division of labor. Furthermore, women who earned more money were more likely to perceive inequity in the division of labor. The importance of time available for perceptions of the fairness of the division of labor has also been found in a study of Swedish couples (Nordenmark & Nyman, 2003). This study found that couples' perception of the amount of leisure time they had in comparison with their spouse was one of the primary determinants of whether they perceived the division of labor to be fair.

Some interesting interview studies have revealed that even when women do not explicitly perceive the division of labor in their household as unfair, they do express some implicit feelings of unfairness when pressed. In the Swedish study described above, Nordenmark and Nyman (2003) described how several couples would initially describe things as fair but, when pressed, admit that it was unfair that the husband, for example, had more leisure time than the wife. The authors noted that, for many of their couples, the uneven distribution of housework may have seemed fair because while the women are more likely to do the small daily tasks of cooking and cleaning, men often participated in the "bigger" less frequent tasks such as shoveling and mowing the lawn. Since these tasks are more visible and more dramatic to perform, men would get more credit for doing them. However, it should be noted that other research has found that it is the smaller daily tasks (defined as low control tasks) that were related to feelings of inequity in both husbands and wives (Bartley et al., 2005).

Another interview study described several principles that couples used to decide whether the division of labor was fair or unfair (Gager, 2008). In those couples who used an equity principle, husbands and wives calculated all of the inputs into the marriage so that a high-paying job or occupational prestige could be levied by men in exchange for not having to do housework. Note that this is a similar dynamic to using a relative resources argument for deciding that the man should do less labor. Couples that applied an equality principle expected an equal division of labor regardless of the inputs into the relationship. In her interview of dual-earner couples, Gager found examples of both principles in action. However, many of the women in couples where an equity argument was being used were actually less satisfied upon further interview than they initially reported. For example, in one couple where the husband made double what the wife made and participated in little household labor because he felt his job was more important and valuable, the wife, although reporting being unhappy in the marriage, had begun to accept her husband's equity argument and did not see the division of labor as unfair. Factors such as the importance of promoting family harmony and the value placed on caretaking activities as well as the feeling that women had no power to change their circumstances made many women accept an unequal division of household labor and contributed to their being less likely to perceive it as unfair.

The dynamics of women finding unequal division of labor to be unfair are complex and may involve interpersonal and emotional dimensions that research does not traditionally measure. For example, one study (Kawamura & Brown, 2010) found women who believed that she "mattered" to her husband—in other words that she was respected, admired, and appreciated by him—did not find the division of labor to be unfair, even if they did the majority of the household labor and child care. The perception of "mattering" was an important factor predicting fairness above and beyond all of the other factors traditionally found to predict perceptions of fairness including actual housework performed, gender ideology, time availability, and relative resources (Kawamura & Brown, 2010). This demonstrates that emotional factors may play a role in perceptions of fairness above and beyond traditionally measured factors. It should be noted, however, that the perception that women "matter" when they perform the majority of the household labor and child care can be considered a benevolent sexist ideology (Glick & Fiske, 1996) where women are placed on a pedestal and given respect and admiration as long as they are fulfilling their traditional gender roles. Often the admiration that comes to a woman fulfilling her traditional gender roles goes hand in hand with hostility toward women who do not conform to such roles (Glick & Fiske, 1996). Showing a woman respect and admiration for doing the majority of household labor and child care is a low-cost way for men to maintain inequity within the home without wives perceiving that inequity as being unfair.

Finally, the issue of who "owns" certain tasks (Claire, 2011) combined with the dynamics of gratitude described above (Alberts et al., 2011) may contribute to perceptions of fairness. If a woman takes ownership over certain household tasks, then any contribution that a husband does, even if it is considerably less than an equitable, would result in gratitude, ameliorating any potential feelings of unfairness.

Consequences of an Unequal Division of Labor

Marital Satisfaction

Evaluations of fairness in division of labor are important because feeling that the division of labor is unfair in a relationship is an important predictor of relationship dissatisfaction and divorce. Research has suggested that feeling as though the division of labor is unfair is related to dissatisfaction in the relationship for both women and men, but it is only related to the odds of divorce among women (Frisco & Williams, 2003). Research on dual-earning Russian families also found that feelings of unfairness were related to marital contention, especially for wives (Cubbins & Vannoy, 2004). Another study utilizing an American group of high–socioeconomic status employed mothers found that an unequal division of household labor was related to feelings of marital distress and personal distress, but this was mediated by perceptions of fairness (Claffey & Mickelson, 2009). In other words, perceived unfairness was the mechanism by which someone with an unequal division of labor became distressed both personally and within the marriage. Just as the relationship between the division of labor and perceptions of inequity differ from country to country, so does the relationship between perceptions of inequity and marital satisfaction (Greenstein, 2009). In countries with high levels of gender equity, perceiving an unfair division of labor was related to lower levels of satisfaction with family life; however, women in low-equity nations were generally satisfied with their family life even if they perceived an unfair division of labor. Thus, women make appropriate comparisons within their national context when deciding both whether their unequal division of labor is fair and how perceptions of fairness should influence relationship satisfaction. It should be noted that, although accepting an unequal division of labor as fair may not lead to dissatisfaction or distress among traditional women, research has suggested that believing in equality and actually achieving it (a group called the "congruent liberals") was related to the greatest level of happiness (Crompton & Lyonette, 2005).

The role of division of labor on marital satisfaction becomes even more central when considering the transition to motherhood. Research has suggested that the transition to parenting generally involves a movement to a more traditional division of household labor (Coltrane, 2000; Cowan & Cowan, 1988) as well as the endorsement of more traditional beliefs about gender (Katz-Wise, Priess, & Hyde, 2010). However, research demonstrates that marital satisfaction decreases after the birth of a child (Twenge, Campbell, & Foster, 2003). This is especially the case for individuals in higher socioeconomic classes, is pronounced for mothers of infants, and appears to have a stronger effect on the current cohort of parents than previous cohorts (Twenge et al., 2003). One hypothesis for this trend is that women become disappointed when their expectations for an equitable division of labor after the birth of a child are not met (Cowan & Cowan, 1988; Hochschild & Machung, 1989; Twenge et al., 2003). This may be especially true for relatively well-off young women who are brought up to expect equality and have high career aspirations. For these women, the arrival of children and the transition to a more traditional domestic lifestyle may be associated with a feeling of role constriction and dissatisfaction (Twenge et al., 2003). One longitudinal study using data from the National Survey of Families and Households found that the transition to motherhood was related to an increase of housework, which was related to increased perceptions of unfairness about the division of labor, which led to decreased marital satisfaction (Dew & Wilcox, 2011).

Physical Health

In addition to causing marital strain, research suggests that an unequal division of labor may have negative physical health consequences for women. One study found that the amount of time that women spent on household chores (measured by actual observations within the home) was related to women's inability to physiologically "unwind" after work. Both men and women who spent the most time doing housework maintained higher levels of cortisol throughout the evening (Saxbe et al., 2011). Men who engaged in more leisure activities, which they did more so than women, were better able to unwind, or decrease their cortisol production, after work (Saxbe et al., 2011). In general, the ability to unwind (experience decreases in cortisol levels after work) for women was linked to doing less housework and having husbands doing more housework, while the ability to unwind for men was linked to having more leisure time and having wives who had less leisure time (Saxbe et al., 2011). Given that evening cortisol production has been linked to a number of dire health consequences, including early mortality (e.g., Sephton, Sapolsky, Kraemer, & Spiegel, 2000), it is essential to understand how women's tendency to do more housework then men, even when working full-time, may be negatively impacting their health. Furthermore, other research has suggested that wives who were able to physiologically recover from the stress of work day had higher levels of marital satisfaction (Saxbe, Repetti, & Nishina, 2008).

Psychological Health

Research has consistently shown that doing a great deal of household labor and child care is related to increased depression (Coltrane, 2000). These relationships appear to be related by perceptions of fairness such that, it is not the inequity per se that is related to depression, but the perception that the division of labor within the family is unfair (Claffey & Mickelson, 2009). Other research has also found that wives who viewed their participation in household labor as unjust were more likely to experience depression (Lennon & Rosenfield, 1994) than those who felt the division, whether equitable or not, was fair.

Recently, research has turned to the effect of inequity in the division of labor on other emotions besides depression. Research has suggested that both individuals who perceived that they under-benefited from inequity in the division of labor (usually the wife) as well as those who perceived that they over-benefited (usually the husband) experienced a variety of negative emotions (Lively, Steelman, & Powel, 2010). Specifically, perceiving that one under-benefited from the division of labor was related to distress, anger, and rage. Men who under-benefited from the division of labor experienced greater negative emotions than women who under-benefited, likely because women were resigned to this situation more than men The perception that one over-benefited from the division of labor resulted in the negative emotions of fear and self-reproach (Lively et al., 2010). Women who over-benefited generally experienced these emotions more strongly than did men. Thus, for both men and women having a division of labor that went against a traditional gendered division of labor resulted in greater negative emotions. Nevertheless, under-benefiting resulted in considerably more negative emotions than over-benefiting for both men and women.

Professional Consequences

There are profound professional consequences for the inequity in the division of labor and child care. Although women have made great strides in the workplace and now represent more than 50% of middle management positions, they continue to only represent approximately 2% of top CEO positions (Sabattini & Crosby, 2009). Research on the pay gap has found that, among college graduates, women earn 80 cents for every dollar that men earn one year after college (Dey & Hill, 2007). Ten years after college, women only earned 69 cents for every dollar that men earned (Dey & Hill, 2007). The gap in wages and difficulty in advancement is especially salient for mothers, such that some have referred to the existence of a "maternal wall" (Crosby, Biemat, & Williams, 2004). For example, working mothers have been found to earn only 60% of the wages of fathers. One investigation examining whether the motherhood wage penalty has decreased over time found that it did not. Each child significantly decreased a woman's wages, although it had no effect on men's wages (Avellar & Smock, 2003).

Many who interpret this wage gap and lack of advancement of women to the highest tiers of business success do so using the "rhetoric of choice" (Sabattini & Crosby, 2009). The assumption is that many women make an individual personal individual choice to be less invested in their job and prioritize marriage and family. The assumption is that women choose to cut back on work hours, or even leave the workforce entirely, because it is their personal choice to do so (Sabattini & Crosby, 2009). However, this choice rhetoric is misleading as women's tendency to do more housework and child care and to take "ownership" over domestic tasks is likely not fully a conscious choice but the result of a complex interweave of socialization pressures and often unspoken interactive patterns with their spouse (Alberts et al., 2011). The tendency to take on the majority of household labor and child care is a self-replicating process that continues often out of the control of the woman. For example, as discussed above, the more a woman takes on these tasks the less likely the man will, until habits of who does what becomes entrenched (Alberts et al., 2011).

Furthermore, the choice that women make to scale back their careers or even to opt out of the workforce is often not a choice made freely (Stone & Lovejoy, 2004). Often inflexibility in the workforce forces them to make the decision to opt out of the workforce despite their desire to find a solution that would allow them to continue working and spend time with family (Stone & Lovejoy, 2004). Most companies operate under the assumption that the ideal worker is fully devoted to his or her career and should be available to work as many hours as needed by the employer (Blair-Loy, 2005; Crosby et al., 2004). Given that women generally make less than men (Dey & Hill, 2007), the pressure is usually greater for women to opt out of the workforce than men. The gender difference in who takes time off after having children is dramatic. Among college graduates, 27% of mothers were out of the workforce while an additional 17% were working part-time; the corresponding numbers for fathers were 1% out of the workforce and 2% working part-time (Dey & Hill, 2007). Part-time work, even for a short period of time, can be economically devastating. One study estimated that women in the United Kingdom who moved from full-time to part-time work for one year and then moved back to full-time work would earn 10% less after 15 years than women who worked full-time for the entire time period (Sabattini & Crosby, 2009).

Although the wage gap and the choice for the mother (rather than the father) to cut back on work are mutually reinforcing, there is a social pressure for women to be the one to opt out of the workforce even if she is the primary wage earner (Blair-Loy, 2005). This pressure is both internal and external; women are socialized into believing and embracing the ideology of intensive motherhood (Hays, 1996), which holds that women should be the caretakers of their children and that mothering should be intensive, emotionally consuming, and infinitely rewarding. Although the choice to become a mother, and to dedicate oneself to one's children even at the detriment to one's career success can appear to be a free choice, some have argued that it is the result of our idealization of the motherhood role that is encouraged within a patriarchal culture

(Meyers, 2001). In one study of both career- and family-focused women, not a single seriously considered that the man quit his job and take care of the children (Blair-Loy, 2005). Women are put in an impossible situation where the notion of the ideal worker who is completely devoted to work and always available to her job is necessarily in conflict with that of the ideal mother, who is completely devoted and always available for her children (Blair-Loy, 2005; Crosby et al., 2004). Given the impossible nature of balancing these roles, many women scale back their career aspirations or opt out of the workforce entirely, with grave professional consequences. The "choice" to make professional sacrifices is hardly free but constrained by deeply entrenched cultural expectations and stereotypes (Crosby et al., 2004).

The relationship between the unequal division of labor and the pay gap represents a complex reciprocal dynamic. As reviewed above, two common explanations for the unequal division of labor is that men make more money than women having more resources and also have less time available to do household tasks. However, the fact that men tend to be the primary breadwinners and earn more money than women can be seen as a result of the socialization pressures that encourage women to take on the majority of the domestic tasks. Thus, to use relative resources and time availability as an explanation for the inequity of the division of labor and to use the unequal division and women's "choice" to take on the majority of the domestic tasks as an explanation for the pay gap ignores how these processes mutually reinforce each other. These are complex processes, entrenched in gender socialization, and while they may feel like autonomous, personal, and independent choices, the choices may not be as free as we may think.

How Do We Change?

Interpersonal Communication and Negotiation

Many individual solutions may lead to greater gender equality in the home. One possible solution is for women to assert themselves and ask for change in their households. One study found that while the majority of married women (53%) had thought about changing the division of labor in their household, only 26 of 86 reported change and only 11 reported doing so through open discussion with their husband (Mannino & Deutsch, 2007). Furthermore, the most assertive women were closer to their ideal division of labor as compared to nonassertive women.

Understanding how women and men make sense of and communicate about household labor and child care can assist men and women in their negotiations.

Understanding the dynamics of how threshold tolerance for mess contributes to an unequal division of labor can help couples more clearly and openly discuss the specific dynamics of the division of labor in the home (Alberts et al., 2011). The spouse who does less of the household labor may hold the belief that if they are not bothered by the mess that they should not be responsible for cleaning it up. Furthermore, husbands may argue that if women want to set higher standards for household chore task performance than they feel is necessary, then they should not have to perform up to those standards. However, such an argument would not work in a work environment—one would not imagine an employee telling an employer that their standards for task performance are too high and that they refuse to live up to those standards (Alberts, Riforgiate, Tracy, & Trethewey, 2011).

Women may also propagate the inequity of the division of labor by sending mixed messages to their husbands (Alberts et al., 2011). While they may say they want their husbands to do more, they may continue to want to maintain control and ownership over the household tasks. Furthermore, they may criticize their husbands for not doing the tasks up to their standards, thus causing their husbands to become discouraged and unlikely to continue to try to perform the tasks. Similar dynamics have been found with child care, in which research has suggested that women participate in "gatekeeping" in which they restrict the role of the father because of their beliefs that they are the only ones who can properly care for their children (Fagan & Barnett, 2003). Challenging these gatekeeping behaviors would lead to more equality as would challenging the idea that men are unable to participate in household chores up to the standards of their wives (Ferree, 1991).

On the other hand, it has been argued that instead of assuming that the overperforming (generally the wife) spouse's standards are correct, one should consider that perhaps the tolerance for mess should be raised and women should lower their standards in order to increase equality in household labor (Wood, 2011). Indeed, it is likely that before a home got so messy that it actually became a problem for the health of the residents, the person with the higher threshold for mess (usually the husband) would actually notice the mess and clean it up (Wood, 2011). Thus, negotiations to create a more equitable division of labor in couples should recognize the role that the tolerance for mess plays in the inequity in labor and in who takes ownership over certain tasks. Negotiations could involve both the husband raising their standards and performance levels as well as the wives lowering their standards, being willing to abdicate ownership of certain task, and accepting imperfect completion of tasks. For both members of the negotiating pair, having a clear language with which to discuss the dynamics of inequity would greatly help communication (Alberts et al., 2011).

Challenging Stereotypes

Other interventions could challenge commonly held stereotypes about men and women that lead men to hold greater power in relationships. For example, as discussed above, one source of power that men typically hold in relationships that may translate into being able to do less household labor is the belief that women want marriage and children more than men and that men are generally the least invested partner in a relationship (Sprecher & Felmlee, 1997; Sprecher et al., 2006). Nevertheless, research has suggested that, at least among undergraduates, men and women want marriage and children equally (Erchull et al., 2010). Thus, women may assume that they want marriage and children more than their spouse, and thus believe that they need to work harder in the marriage in order to justify convincing their man to settle down. This is related to dynamics of gratitude discussed above (Alberts et al., 2011). If women feel grateful for the simple fact that their husbands agreed to marry them, then they may be willing to do more in exchange. However, if they realized that the belief that their husband did not want to get married was based on an inaccurate stereotype, this may mitigate their need to perform more household labor.

Rejecting the stereotype that mothers are inherently better than fathers at parenting is another step in promoting gender equality in the home (Bjarnason & Hjalmsdottir, 2008; Crosby et al., 2004; Deutsch, 2007). Believing that women are better qualified than men to take care of children was related to expecting a more traditional division of labor among students in Iceland (Bjarnason & Hjalmsdottir, 2008). In one study among American college students, rejecting the belief that women are uniquely qualified to care for children was related to planning for an egalitarian life path in which both parents reduced their work outside of the home and shared household chores and child care (Deutsch, Kotot, & Binder, 2007). Hopefully, as more fathers become actively involved in the home, the stereotypes about parenthood will change which will further change realities (Crosby et al., 2004).

Structural Changes

To truly effect the division of labor from a societal level, social systems need to change (Lachance-Grzela & Bouchard, 2010). These systems can change both through family-friendly policies of individual companies and through national policy changes. Individual companies have attempted to create programs to allow workers to combine their work and their family life (Sabattini & Crosby, 2009). Such policies include flex-time, family or personal leave, and telecommuting. However, these work-family or work–life programs, even when available, are often underutilized. This is because the stereotype of the ideal worker as completely committed to the job fosters a corporate culture where work–life policies cannot be taken advantage of without the user appearing to be an uncommitted worker. Another barrier to taking advantage of flexible work schedules is the notion that "face time" in the office is the only way to assess how committed a worker is to his or her job (Thompson, Beauvais, & Lyness, 1999). When workplace programs appear to benefit certain groups over others (such as parents over nonparents), there tends to be a backlash against their use and a stigmatization and fear of stigmatization among those who use them (Sabattini & Crosby, 2009). Thus, workplace policy changes need to be framed to benefit all workers, not simply mothers or parents. If these policies are framed as ways to create a happier and more diverse workforce and if organizations actively encourage all workers to use policies that promote flexibility, they will be more sustainable. This would benefit the organization as well as the employee as flexible job arrangements and the ability to balance work and personal life is related to productivity and organizational commitment (Sabattini & Crosby, 2009).

National policy can also promote social equality. One way to do so is to promote equal access to the work place with policies such as affirmative action and antidiscrimination laws. Many liberal countries, such as the United States, Canada, and Australia, have implemented such policies (Chang, 2000; Fuwa & Cohen, 2007). Another dimension involves providing benefits to families, such as through extended parental leave or state-funded child care services. These benefits can be seen both in countries that are high in the first dimension of promoting egalitarianism in the workplace, such as Sweden, as well as in countries that have historically valued women's roles in the home, such as the former socialist countries of Hungry and East Germany, which provide up to 3 years of parental leave (Fuwa & Cohen, 2007). Research has found that countries that have antidiscrimination policies have more egalitarian divisions of labor (Fuwa & Cohen, 2007) than countries that solely focus on family policies. Furthermore, in countries with affirmative action policies, women who earn more money have higher levels of egalitarianism in the household. However, in countries with higher levels of parental leave, women's greater income or engagement in full-time employment did not lead to more egalitarian division of labor. Fuwa and Cohen (2007) cautioned that policies that promote women taking off years from the labor force to care for children may act to reinforce traditional gender roles and inequality in the family. Instead, they suggested that policies that would reduce the wage difference between men and women would have a greater effect in reducing inequality in the household.

Another social policy that would promote greater equality in the division of labor is offering paternal leave. This policy began in Sweden in 1974 but by 2007 had spread to 66 nations (O'Brien, 2009). Research has indicated that fathers are most likely to take this leave when it provides a high percentage replacement of their income and involves leave that can only be taken by fathers, such as "daddy days" or "father quotas" (O'Brien, 2009). Research has also shown that fathers who take leave are more involved in caretaking activities up to a year later, suggesting that these policy changes do indeed matter (Tanaka & Waldfogel, 2007). Theorists have suggested a positive feedback loop in which fathers who participate more in the home allow mothers to be more active in the workplace which then further encourages fathers to continue and increase their involvement at home (Coltrane, 2010). Thus, both corporate and social policies, in addition to individual measures, are essential in promoting equality in the household and men's involvement in household labor and child care.

This chapter has reviewed the discrepancy in household labor and child care as well as the reasons for and consequences of the inequality. As we move forward in the 21st century, families will hopefully move closer to an egalitarian division of labor. Given the manifold negative consequences both for the couple, and individual women's physical, psychological, and professional well-being, this is an important goal. However, given the pressures of social roles, often unspoken interpersonal dynamics within couples, stereotypes about women's superior capacity to perform chores and housework, as well as social forces such as the pay gap, achieving this equality might be difficult. It will take a combination of individual efforts, interpersonal negotiation, and social change to achieve equality.

References

Alberts, J. K., Tracy, S. J., & Trethewey, A. (2011). An integrative theory of the division of domestic labor: Threshold level, social organizing and sensemaking. *Journal of Family Communication, 11,* 21–38.

Alberts, J. K., Riforgiate, S. E., Tracy, S., & Trethewey, A. (2011). One more time with feeling: A rejoinder to Wood's and Clair's commentaries. *Journal of Family Communication, 11,* 60–63.

Atkinson, M. P., & Boles, J. (1984). WASP (wives as senior partners). *Journal of Marriage and the Family, 46,* 861–870.

Avellar, S., & Smock, P. J. (2003). Has the price of motherhood declined over time? A cross-cohort comparison of the motherhood wage penalty. *Journal of Marriage and Family, 65,* 597–607.

Bartley, S. J., Blanton, P. W., & Gilliard, J. L. (2005). Husbands and wives in dual-earner marriages: Decision-making, gender-role attitudes, division of household labor, and equity. *Marriage and Family Review, 37,* 69–94.

Bianchi, S. M., Milkie, M. A., Sayer, L. C., & Robinson, J. P. (2000). Is anyone doing the housework? Trends in the gender division of household labor. *Social Forces, 79,* 191–228.

Bittman, M., England, P., Sayer, L., Folbre, N., & Natheson, G. (2003). When does gender trump money? Bargaining and time in household work. *American Journal of Sociology, 109,* 186–214.

Bjarnason, T., & Hjalmsdottir, A. (2008). Egalitarian attitudes towards the division of household labor among adolescents in Iceland. *Sex Roles, 59,* 49–60.

Blair-Loy, M. (2003). *Competing devotions.* Cambridge, MA: Harvard University Press.

Blau, F. D., & Kahn, L. M. (2006). The U.S. gender pay gap in the 1990s: Slowing convergence. *Industrial and Labor Relations Review, 60,* 45–66.

Braun, M., Lewin-Epstein, N., Stier, H., & Baumgartner, M. K. (2008). Perceived equity in the gendered division of household labor. *Journal of Marriage and the Family, 70,* 1145–1156.

Brayfield, A. A. (1992). Employment and housework in Canada. *Journal of Marriage and the Family, 54,* 19–30.

Brines, J. (1994). Economic dependency, gender, and the division of labor at home. *American Journal of Sociology, 100,* 652–688.

Chang, M. L. (2000). The evolution of sex segregation regimens. *American Journal of Sociology, 105,* 1658–1701.

Claffey, S. T., & Manning, K. R. (2010). Equity but not equality: Commentary on Lachance-Grzela and Bouchard. *Sex Roles, 63,* 781–785.

Claffey, S. T., & Mickelson, K. D. (2009). Division of household labor and distress: The role of perceived fairness for employed mothers. *Sex Roles, 60,* 819–831.

Clair, R. P. (2011). The rhetoric of dust: Toward a rhetorical theory of the division of domestic labor. *Journal of Family Communication, 11,* 50–59.

Coltrane, S. (2000). Research on household labor: Modeling and measuring the social embeddedness of routine family work. *Journal of Marriage and the Family, 62,* 1208–1233.

Coltrane, S. (2010). Gender theory and household labor. *Sex Roles, 63,* 791–800.

Connelly, R., & Kimmel, J. (2009). Spousal economic factors in ATUS parents' time choices. *Social Indicators Research, 93,* 147–152.

Cowan, C. P., & Cowan, P. A. (1988). Who does what when partners become parents: Implications for men, women, and marriage. *Marriage and Family Review, 12,* 105–131.

Crawford, M. (2006). *Transformations: Women, gender, and psychology.* Boston, MA: McGraw-Hill.

Crompton, R., & Lyonette, C. (2005). The new gender essentialism—Domestic and family "choices" and their relation to attitudes. *British Journal of Sociology, 56,* 601–620.

Crosby, F. J. (1976). A model of egoistical relative deprivation. *Psychological Review, 83,* 85–113.

Crosby, F. J., Biemat, M., & Williams, J. (2004). The maternal wall: Introduction. *Journal of Social Issues, 60,* 675–682.

Cubbins, L. A., & Vannoy, D. (2004). Division of household labor as a source of contention for married and cohabiting couples in metropolitan Moscow. *Journal of Family Issues, 25,* 182–215.

Cunningham, M. (2005). Gender in cohabitation and marriage: The influence of gender ideology on housework allocation over the life course. *Journal of Family Issues, 26,* 1037–1061.

Davis, S. N. (2010). The answer doesn't seem to change, so maybe we should change the question: A commentary on Lachance-Grzela and Bouchard (2010). *Sex Roles, 63,* 786–790.

Deutsch, F. M., Kotot, A. P., & Binder, K. S. (2007). College women's plans for different types of egalitarian marriages. *Journal of Marriage and the Family, 69,* 916–929.

Dew, J., & Wilcox, W. B. (2011). If momma ain't happy: Explaining declines in marital satisfaction among new mothers. *Journal of Marriage and the Family, 73,* 1–12.

Dey, J. D., & Hill, C. (2007). *Behind the pay gap.* Washington, DC: American Association of University Women Educational Foundation.

Eagly, A. H., & Steffen, V. J. (1984). Gender stereotypes stem from the distribution of women and men into social roles. *Journal of Personality and Social Psychology, 46,* 735–754.

Erchull, M. J., Liss, M., Axelson, S. J., Staebell, S. E., & Askari, S. F. (2010). Well…She wants it more: Perceptions of social norms about desire for marriage and children and anticipated chore participation. *Psychology of Women Quarterly, 34,* 253–260.

Fagan, J., & Barnett, M. (2003). The relationship between maternal gatekeeping, paternal competence, mothers' attitudes about the father role, and father involvement. *Journal of Family Issues, 24,* 1020–1043.

Ferree, M. M. (1991). The gender division of labor in two-earner marriages: Dimensions of variability and change. *Journal of Family Issues, 12,* 158–180.

Fox, G. L., & Murry, V. M. (2000). Gender and families: Feminist perspectives and family research. *Journal of Marriage and the Family, 62,* 1160–1172.

Frisco, M. L., & Williams, K. (2003). Perceived housework equity, marital happiness, and divorce in dual-earner households. *Journal of Family Issues, 24,* 51–73.

Fuwa, M. (2004). Macro-level gender inequality and the division of household labor in 22 countries. *American Sociological Review, 69,* 751–767.

Fuwa, M., & Cohen, P. N. (2007). Housework and social policy. *Social Science Research, 36,* 512–530.

Gager, C. T. (2008). What's fair is fair? Role of justice in family labor allocation decisions. *Marriage & Family Review, 44,* 511–545.

Glick, P., & Fiske, S. T. (1996). The Ambivalent Sexism Inventory: Differentiating hostile and benevolent sexism. *Journal of Personality and Social Psychology, 70,* 491–512.

Greenstein, T. N. (1996). Gender ideology and perceptions of the fairness of the division of household labor: Effects on marital quality. *Social Forces, 74,* 1029–1042.

Greenstein, T. N. (2000). Economic dependence, gender, and the division of labor in the home: A replication and extension. *Journal of Marriage and the Family, 62,* 322–335.

Greenstein, T. N. (2009). National context, family satisfaction, and fairness in the division of household labor. *Journal of Marriage and the Family, 71,* 1039–1051.

Hays, S. (1996). *The cultural contradictions of motherhood.* New Haven, CT: Yale University Press.

Hochschild, A., & Machung, A. (1989). *The second shift: Working parents and the revolution at home.* New York: Penguin Group.

Ishii-Kuntz, M., & Coltrane, S. (1992). Predicting the sharing of household labor: Are parenting and housework distinct? *Sociological Perspectives, 35,* 629–647.

Katz-Wise, S. L., Priess, H. A., & Hyde, J. S. (2010). Gender-role attitudes and behavior across the transition to parenthood. *Developmental Psychology, 46,* 18–28.

Kawamura, S., & Brown, S. L (2010). Mattering and wives' perceived fairness of the division of household labor. *Social Science Research, 39,* 976–986.

Kroska, A. (2003). Investigating gender differences in the meaning of household chores and child care. *Journal of Marriage and the Family, 65,* 456–473.

Kroska, A. (2004). Divisions of domestic work. *Journal of Marriage and the Family, 65,* 456–473.

Lachance-Grzela, M., & Bouchard, G. (2010). Why do women do the lion's share of housework? A decade of research. *Sex Roles, 63,* 767–780.

Lennon, M. C., & Rosenfield, S. (1994). Relative fairness and the division of housework: The importance of options. *American Journal of Sociology, 100,* 506–531.

Lively, K., Steelman, L., & Powel, B. (2010). Equity, emotion, and the household division of labor. *Social Psychology Quarterly, 73,* 358–379.

Lothaller, H., Mikula, G., & Schoebi, D. (2009). What contributes to the (im)balanced division of family work between the sexes? *Swiss Journal of Psychology, 68,* 143–152.

Mahalik, J. R., Morray, E. B., Coonerty-Femiano, A., Ludlow, L. H., Slattery, S. M., & Smiler, A. (2005). Development of the Conformity to Feminine Norms Inventory. *Sex Roles, 52,* 417–435.

Mannino, C. A., & Deutsch, F. M. (2007). Changing the division of household labor: A negotiated process between partners. *Sex Roles, 56,* 309–324.

Mattingly, M., & Sayer, L. C. (2006). Under pressure: Trends and gender differences in the relationship between free time and feeling rushed. *Journal of Marriage and the Family, 68,* 205–221.

Meyers, D. T. (2001). The rush to motherhood: Pronatalist discourse and women's autonomy. *Signs, 6,* 735–773.

Nakonezny, P. A., & Denton, W. H. (2008). Marital relationships: A social exchange theory perspective. *American Journal of Family Therapy, 36,* 402–412.

Nordenmark, M., & Nyman, C. (2003). Fair or unfair? Perceived fairness of household division of labour and gender equality among women and men: The Swedish case. *European Journal of Women's Studies, 10,* 181–209.

North, S. (2009). Negotiating what's "natural": Persistent domestic fender role inequality in Japan. *Social Science Japan Journal, 12,* 23–44.

O'Brien, M. (2009). Fathers, parental leave policies, and infant quality of life: International perspective and policy impact. *Te Annals of the American Academy of Political and Social Science, 624,* 190–213.

Poortman, A.-R., & van der Lippe, T. (2009). Attitudes toward housework and child care and the gendered division of labor. *Journal of Marriage and the Family, 71,* 526–541.

Presser, H. B. (1994). Employment schedules among dual-earner spouses and the division of household labor by gender. *American Sociological Review, 59,* 348–364.

Sabattini, L., & Crosby, F. J. (2009). Ceilings and walls: Work-life and "family-friendly" policies. In M. Barreto, M. K. Ryan, & M. T. Schmitt (Eds.), *The glass ceiling in the 21st century: Understanding barriers to gender equality* (pp. 201–223). Washington, DC: American Psychological Association.

Saxbe, D. E., Repetti, R. L., & Nishina, A. (2008). Marital satisfaction, recovery from work, and diurnal cortisol among men and women. *Health Psychology, 27,* 15–25.

Saxbe, D. E., Repetti, R. L., & Graesch, A. P. (2011). Time spent in housework and leisure: Links with parents' physiological recovery from work. *Journal of Family Psychology, 25,* 271–281.

Sayer, L. C., England, P., Bittman, M., & Bianchi, S. M. (2009). How long is the second (plus first) shift? Gender differences in paid, unpaid, and total work time in Australia and the United States. *Journal of Comparative Family Studies, 40,* 523–545.

Sephton, S., Sapolsky, R., Kraemer, H., & Spiegel, D. (2000). Diurnal cortisol rhythm as a predictor of breast cancer survival. *Journal of National Cancer Institute, 92,* 994–100.

Sprecher, S., & Felmlee, D. (1997). The balance of power in romantic heterosexual couples over time from "his" and "her" perspectives. *Sex Roles, 37,* 361–379.

Sprecher, S., Schmeekle, M., & Felmlee, D. (2006). The principle of least interest: Inequality in emotional involvement in romantic relationships. *Journal of Family Issues, 27,* 1255–1280.

Stevens, D. P., Minnotte, K. L., Mannon, S. E., & Kiger, G. (2006). Family work performance and satisfaction: Gender ideology, relative resources and emotion work. *Marriage and Family Review, 40,* 47–74.

Stone, P., & Lovejoy, M. (2004). Fast-track women and the "choice" to stay home. *Annals of the American Academy of Political and Social Science, 596,* 62–83.

Tanaka, S., & Waldfogel, J. (2007). Effects of parental leave and work hours on fathers' involvement with their babies: Evidence from the millennium cohort study. *Community Work and Family, 10,* 409–426.

Thibaut, J. W., & Kelley, H. H. (1959). *The social psychology of groups.* New York: John Wiley.

Thompson, C. A., Beauvais, L. L., & Lyness, K. S. (1999). When work-family benefits are not enough: The influence of work-family culture on benefit utilization, organizational attachment, and work-family conflict. *Journal of Vocational Behavior, 54,* 392–415.

Tracy, S. J., & Rivera, K. D. (2010). Endorsing equity and applauding stay-at-home moms: How male voices on work-life reveal aversive sexism and flickers of transformation. *Management Communication Quarterly, 24,* 3–43.

Twenge, J. M., Campbell, W. K., & Foster, C. A. (2003). Parenthood and marital satisfaction: A meta-analytic review. *Journal of Marriage and the Family, 65,* 574–583.

Waller, W. (1938). *The family: A dynamic interpretation.* New York: Gordon.

Wilkie, J. R., Ferree, M. M., & Ratcliff, K. S. (1998). Gender and fairness: Marital satisfaction in two-earner couples. *Journal of Marriage and the Family, 60,* 577–594.

Wood, J. T. (2011). Which ruler do we use? Theorizing the division of domestic labor. *Journal of Family Communication, 11,* 39–49.

Wood, W., & Eagly, A. H. (2002). A cross-cultural analysis of the behavior of women and men: Implications for the origins of sex differences. *Psychological Bulletin, 128,* 699–727.

Zipp, J. F., Prohaska, A., & Bemiller, M. (2004). Wives, husbands, and hidden power in marriage. *Journal of Family Issues, 25,* 933–958.

Part Two

Steps Underway Around the World

It is impossible to practice parliamentary politics without having patience, decency, politeness and courtesy.

—Khaleda Zia
Prime Minister, Bangladesh 1991–1996; 2001–2006

8

The Silicon Ceiling: Women Managers and Leaders in ICT in Australia

Annemieke Craig, Jo Coldwell, Julie Fisher, and Catherine Lang

Women in Australia

> *When I was in high school, it was always talked up that women could do science, engineering and technical [work] too. While we are just as capable as men, when we get into these industries, we face other challenges. There have been brave women who have done their bit to overcome these challenges, but it also requires brave men to challenge the attitudes of these industries to women participating in their workplaces. (APESMA, 2010)*

> *Silicon: Elemental silicon has a large impact on the modern world economy . . . Because of wide use of silicon in integrated circuits, the basis of most computers, a great deal of modern technology depends on it. (Wikipedia, 2011)*

The chapter begins with a historical and current analysis of female participation in the workforce, in education and in leadership. The second section focuses on the information and communication technology (ICT) workforce in particular. The third section presents findings from a recent case study that gathered both quantitative and qualitative data from a diverse group of professional women in ICT. The case study provides a view into the ICT profession from the female perspective and identifies a selection of factors that would make a significant difference to female participation and longevity in the profession. The conclusion reached after this investigation is that the silicon ceiling is certainly not visible, yet remains fixed due to nonessential job characteristics that persist in the industry. The future looks bleak unless more female managers and male champions ensure that these nonessential employment characteristics are removed from ICT positions.

Female Participation in the Workforce

The Australian workforce has changed considerably over the past five decades. In 1961 women's participation rate[1] in the labor force was 34% (ABS, 2011a). At this time the standard working week was Monday to Friday from 9 a.m. to 5 p.m., with three weeks of annual leave. The labor force was characterized by a noticeable division between the sexes and their expected roles in society. The traditional role for a man was to be the breadwinner who supported his wife and children. Business documents were created by people (mostly women) in the typing pool using manual typewriters, and management had secretarial support. Women worked until they were married, and then they left paid employment to start a family. There was little part-time work available and child care was rare (ABS, 2011a), and hence mothers rarely returned to the workforce.

Fifty years later, women's participation rate in the workforce has almost doubled to 59.1%, with men's participation rate at 72.2% (ABS, 2011b). Women now account for 45% of the Australian labor force (Department of Education, Employment, and Workplace Relations [DEEWR], 2011a). Working hours are increasingly varied; there is greater availability of part-time work, flexible hours, and paid carers' leave. While four weeks of annual leave is standard, the average number of hours worked by full-time workers has increased, as has the proportion of employees working longer hours. The average number of hours worked grew from 41 hours a week to 43 hours in 1995 and declined slightly to 42 hours in 2005. However, the proportion working 60 plus hours a week continues to increase (ABS, 2010a). The typing pool has been replaced by the individual use of personal computers, and the work calendar is managed via electronic devices such as iPads and smart phones. A group of managers may share an executive assistant or may have their own personal assistant.

A recent report by the DEEWR verifies that the Australian labor market has undergone many changes: the participation of women in the workforce has increased; the workforce is aging (38% of workers are aged 45 years or older, compared with 33% 10 years ago); there is an increased focus on skilled jobs; the participation of young people choosing to be in education is increasing; and working arrangements are being transformed through

technological change, increased labor market flexibility, and economic reforms (DEEWR, 2011a).

While women now represent approximately half of the labor force,
their participation is unequal across different segments of the workforce.
Australia's workforce is more gender-segregated than that of most other
industrialized countries (Hausmann, Tyson, & Zahidi, 2011). Over half of
all female employees are employed as clerical and administrative workers, sales workers, or community and personal service workers, and these
are areas where there are substantially fewer men (ABS, 2010c). There
are fewer women who are tradespeople and fewer women who are in
science, technology, engineering, and mathematics positions. Equally there
are areas of employment where men are underrepresented: there are fewer
male teachers in the schools; there are fewer men in the health and community services sector; and there are fewer male clerks. Further, part-time
work has traditionally been dominated by women. This is still the case with
women making up almost 75% of the part-time workforce in August 2011
(ABS, 2011a).

Female Participation in Education

The 1980s and early 1990s provided a period of enormous change in the Australian education system. High school retention rates more than doubled during the 1980s, increasing from 34.5% in 1980 to 76.6% in 1993 (ABS, 2011b).
In 1987, for the first time school retention rates for girls exceeded those of
boys. Changing community expectations, a depressed teenage labor market,
and government policies encouraging students to complete their secondary
education were all contributing factors (Schofield, 2011). The result was an increased number of young people, particularly women, eligible to enter higher
education.

A university education in Australia, supported by Commonwealth-funded
grants and loans, has moved from being elitist to a universal possibility for all,
regardless of gender. Fifty years ago, only 20% of higher education students
were female (Schofield, 2011); by 1981, the proportion of female students
had increased to 45% of the student body (OSW, 2002). By 2010 more than
half of all enrolled students on campus (56%) were female (DEEWR, 2011b).
Over this time the actual number of students enrolled in universities increased
at a rapid rate, and the Minister for Tertiary Education, Senator Chris Evans,
suggested in his media release of April 2011 that an estimated 50,000 additional undergraduate students are enrolled at Australian universities compared
to 2009 (Evans, 2011).

Increased participation in education has resulted in the Australian workforce becoming more educated and more highly skilled. There has been a marked increase in the proportion of Australian workers who hold post-school qualifications. Around half of those employed in 2000 had studied after leaving school but by 2010, this had risen to around 61% (DEEWR, 2011b).

During the last decade, the likelihood of women having a post-school qualification overtook that of men. The proportion of women with a qualification increased from 58% in 2001 to 67% in 2009, compared with men from 60% in 2001 to 65% in 2009 (ABS, 2010a).

Female Participation in Leadership

> *Australian women now hold some of the most powerful positions in the country—at the time of publication . . . we had a female Prime Minister, two female state Premiers, a female Governor General and two female state Governors . . . But that doesn't mean the journey for women, particularly professional women, is now all smooth sailing. (Curtain, 2011, p. 3)*

The ABS has estimated that over 53% of professionals are women and yet women make up just 33% of managers (ABS, 2010c). It needs to be pointed out that teaching and nursing are considered professional occupations, so this may explain the higher proportion of women in the professional category. It does not, however, explain the much lower proportion of female managers.

The disparate representation of women in the professions and women in leadership roles in that profession is amply illustrated within the secondary education sector in Australia. In a report commissioned by the DEEWR, McKenzie, Kos, Walker, and Hong (2008) indicated that although female participation in teaching was greater than male participation, this was not reflected equally in leadership roles within Australian schools. At the time of the report, 79% of primary teachers and 56% of secondary teachers were female. While 57% of the leadership positions in primary schools were held by females, only 41% of leadership posts in secondary schools were held by females. The term *leadership post* includes principal and deputy-principal positions. The proportion of females in leadership positions is much lower than the proportion of female teachers. Further, of the females teachers who are in a leadership role, the majority were deputy-principals, not principals (see Table 8.1, McKenzie et al. (2008), p. 42).

The Australian Human Rights Commission has summarized a similar (if not more extreme) tale of disparate representation within the top ranks of industry. The following snapshot of women in leadership emphasizes the underrepresentation of this gender in leadership roles in a number of key sectors (Australian Human Rights Commission, n.d.):

- Public sector—In 2010, women comprised 57.8% of Commonwealth public service employees but just 33.2% of members of Australian government boards (FAHCSIA, 2010).
- Federal parliament—In 2011, women are slightly more than half the population (99.2 males to 100 females) yet make up 24.7% of elected positions in the House of Representatives and 35.5% of the Senate (APH, 2011).
- Academia—Women account for over half of all lecturing staff in Australian universities yet only 39% of senior lecturing staff and just 24.5% of staff above senior lecturer (While, 2001).
- Law—While 65% of law graduates are female (Graduate Careers Australia, 2010), women make up only 16% of the bench in the Federal Court of Australia (Federal Court of Australia).
- Sports—One in four national sport organizations have no women directors (Adriaanse, 2010).

Recent evidence suggests that the situation in academia, at least, is improving. Diezmann and Grieshaber suggest that although women continue to be underrepresented in the ranks of the Australian professoriate, the number of appointments by gender at the associate professor and professor levels is similar. They note, however, that, on average, it took women approximately 2 years longer than men to gain such an appointment (Diezmann & Grieshaber, 2010).

The Equal Opportunity for Women in the Workplace Agency (EOWA) undertook a census of women in leadership in 2010, which highlights the

TABLE 8.1
Participation of women in leadership within schools

Role	Primary School		Secondary School	
	Male (%)	Female (%)	Male (%)	Female (%)
Principal	51	49	68	32
Deputy principal	65	35	54	46
All leaders	57	43	59	41

under-representation of women in senior leadership positions for the top 200 organizations listed on the Australian Stock Exchange (ASX). Over 61% of organizations do not have any female participation in executive key management personnel. Further, women hold just over 4% of line roles within the ASX 200 organizations. This is particularly concerning since the experience provided within line management is generally considered "essential for rising to the top corporate positions, this data shows that women are largely absent from these important pathways to the most senior positions" (EOWA, 2010), suggesting that any improvement in female participation at the most senior levels is unlikely in the short term. Table 8.2 summarizes these census results.

Gender disparity between men and women in leadership roles in Australia perpetuates existing stereotypes about the role of women, both at work and in the wider society, and exacerbates gender pay inequity. Research has shown that having significant numbers of women in leadership positions encourages other women through the pipeline. By implication, unless systemic change in gender diversity in leadership is achieved, there is limited chance of the disparity improving on its own.

The business case for diversity and gender has been made by several authors. For example, Trauth (2011) states that gender diversity is an economic necessity as well as essential for social justice; "women represent half the population and in many societies half the labor force . . . the 'best brains' can be located in a variety of bodies, not just male" (Trauth, 2011, p. 2). Klawe, Whitney, and Simard (2009, p. 68) have suggested that there is a need for more women purely "out of self-interest." Diversity in design and development teams often leads to teams with "enhanced abilities to perform tasks, greater creativity, and better decisions and outcomes" for all (Klawe et al. 2009, p. 68).

The advantages of promoting women into leadership positions are summarized as follows:

TABLE 8.2
Female leadership participation in ASX 200

Role	Female (%)
ASX 200 Chairs	2.5
ASX 200 CEOs	3.0
ASX 200 EKMP	8.0
ASX 200 Board directors	8.4

- The economic and investment argument: According to Goldman Sachs, narrowing the gap between male and female employment rates would have huge implications for the global economy; for example, in Australia it would boost GDP by 11% (Goldman Sachs, 2009).
- The productivity argument: The current gender bias means that women are employed in roles where their productivity is not maximized. If the gender productivity gap was minimized, for example by increasing the number of women in leadership positions, the level of economic activity in Australia could be boosted by 20% (Goldman Sachs, 2009).
- Economic incentives would have flow-on effects for the wider society. They would assist in addressing the problem of pension sustainability, thereby reducing the dependency ratio, lifting household savings rates and increasing tax received by the government (Goldman Sachs, 2009).

Furthermore, education statistics previously presented indicate that women are more likely than their male counterparts to have relevant postgraduate qualifications. This is despite their tendency to undervalue their own skills and to be less forthcoming in pursuing leadership positions (Chesterman, Ross-Smith, & Peters, 2004). For all these reasons we need to be both vigilant and evangelistic to ensure that female participation in leadership in business and education is supported, encouraged, and advanced.

The Australian ICT Profession

The Australian Computer Society (ACS) has an obligation to the Australian community to bring about economic, social and intellectual benefits through a higher participation of women in ICT. At national, state and regional level, the ACS commits to create and support initiatives that encourage the entry, development and retention of women in ICT professions generally and within the ACS. (Motion passed unanimously by ACS National Council, November 2002; ACS, 2007)

The motion passed by the ACS in 2002 is to be commended, but in fact little has changed in gender representation in the Australian ICT workforce in the last 15 years according to an investigation into recent census data (Byrne & Staehr, 2011). Even more alarming is that in Australia "women working full time earn around 18% less than men, which means that over their working life they can be around $1 million worse off" (Byrne & Staehr, 2011). The following section provides an overview of the ICT workforce in Australia and an insight into its gender composition.

The ICT Workforce

Computing is a relatively young profession compared to medicine or law, for example. Australia moved into the modern computing era in the late 1940s with the development of the CSIR Mk1 (Pearcey, 1994). This machine, later renamed CSIRAC, was the first computer in Australia and it was arguably the fourth (Bowles, Semkiw, Spencer, & Hughes, 2002) or fifth (Pass, 2006) electronic stored-program computer ever developed in the world (Bowles et al., 2002). It provided a computing service until well into the 1960s, and by then there were a total of 34 computers in the country. From these small beginnings the industry developed rapidly and by 2006–2007, 73% of Australian households had access to a computer at home, with 64% of households having access to the Internet from home (DFAT, 2008).

Over the same period there was remarkable growth in new employment opportunities in the emerging computer industry which became known as the information and communication technology, or ICT, sector. In 2010, this sector employed more than 545,500 workers in Australia (ACS, 2010). Revenue from the ICT industry was over $85 billion (IBSA, 2010); the ICT market was the fourth largest in the Asia-Pacific region and the 11th largest in the world.

Within this time frame, however, computers and computer work had also become stereotyped as more appropriate for males (Game & Pringle, 1984; Mackinnon, 1995), and currently women account for just 23.5% of the total Australian ICT workforce (ACS, 2010). This gender imbalance in the ICT workforce is a well-documented problem in many Western cultures; however, studies such as the ones conducted by Adams, Bauer, and Baichoo (2003) in Mauritius and Ng, Das, Ching, and Chin (1998) in Malaysia suggest that the issue is not a universal phenomenon but a cultural problem. The social constructivist viewpoint suggests that the computing/ICT field has been socially constructed as a male domain. Spencer (2003, p. 63) suggests that the shifting and alternative definitions for ICT strongly support the view that the domain has been socially constructed, and this, therefore, suggests that it may be possible to reconstruct it.

Wesselius (1998) suggests it is appropriate to dichotomize gender into distinct categories for the purposes of comparison. This theorizing by women, who are the minority in the field, has made little impact into changing the male stereotype. While there is no direct evidence of overt discrimination against women in ICT—in fact any such action would be deemed illegal—Byrne and Staehr suggest that "on the income side there does appear to be a disparity" and that indirect discrimination in negotiation may disadvantage women (Byrne & Staehr, 2011).

Gender Composition of the ICT Workforce

Accurate statistics for the ICT profession are difficult to come by due to the breadth of careers classified in this domain. The term ICT "lacks clarity of definition" (Webb & Young, 2005, p. 148), and equally it is not easy to draw boundaries around what are ICT occupations (DCITA, 2006). The Australian Computer Society (2010) suggests that

> one of the significant difficulties in understanding ICT in Australia is the frequent confusion between analysis of the ICT workforce in labour market terms (e.g., what job the individual performs), and analyzing the ICT workforce in Industry terms (e.g., what kind of organisation the individual works for). There is a significant percentage of ICT professionals in the ICT industry, but ICT industry employment includes not only those professionals but also many ICT nonprofessional technical, sales, logistical and administrative staff.

Despite this ambiguity in the definition of ICT, participation of females in the ICT sector remains very low, with just under 23% in the ICT trade, technical, and professional occupations as at August 2009. However, if we focus on the Australian Bureau of Statistics categorization of the ICT sector, which includes information media and telecommunications as well as the computer system design component of professional, scientific, and technical services, women comprise just over 19% of workers. However, Innovation and Business Skills Australia (IBSA) suggests that since

> the identifiable ICT industry groups . . . leave out a significant component of software and ICT services, ICT consulting, and ICT wholesale trade, which may have higher levels of female employment, the gender balance within the ICT industry may not be significantly different to the gender balance of the ICT workforce across all industries. (IBSA, 2010, p. 10)

Of perhaps more interest is the variation of female participation in different sectors of the industry. According to IBSA, which analyzed the distribution of females in ICT occupations, approximately 44% of female participation is in the graphic and web design category (16%), software and applications programming category (12%), and management and organization analysts category (16%) (IBSA, 2010). It also suggests that the preference is for females to congregate in occupations "related to software and services, rather than hardware . . . [and] business and systems analysis" (IBSA, 2010, p. 11).

Female participation in management in the ICT sector is out of step with other sectors with a participation rate of 29%, a higher participation rate than the overall level of female participation in the industry. Another area where female participation is higher than the industrywide participation figure is in ICT education and training. It is implied that these areas demand higher levels of people skills, which generally come naturally to women more than men. It is interesting to note that "more employment growth is taking place . . . in the software and soft skills categories that already have higher female percentages than the norm" (IBSA, 2010, p. 11).

The participation of females in the various ICT sectors as categorized by IBSA (2010, p. 12) indicates that women are highly represented in the less technical areas of ICT, while men have made up the majority of the higher-level, higher-status, higher-paid ICT workforce in Australia. Further, Byrne and Staehr note that, "The proportion of all women employed in ICT occupations who are managers is 11.9% and for men the figure is 12.2% so there does not appear to be any bias preventing women entering high status occupations in the ICT workforce" (Byrne & Staehr, 2011). It appears that nonessential work practices, such as long working hours and little consideration of family responsibilities, may have an impact, and this will be discussed in more detail in the next section.

Case Study: An Investigation of the ICT workforce

The professional Australian woman is passionate, driven, focussed determined and resilient—but she has had to make a number of sacrifices in the name of success and while regret might be too strong a word, she is fully aware of these sacrifices and is striving to ameliorate them. The sacrifices she has made include time, money and personal relationships. (Curtain, 2011, p. 22)

Researchers in Australia reported findings from a survey of 289 women in ICT (Anderson, Timms, & Courtney, 2006). This survey found that 1 in 10 women reported experiencing blatant discrimination, and more than half said that "subtle discrimination" was at play in their workplace. Examples were given of important decisions being made in nonwork (male-only) social environments, as well as women being held more accountable and, apparently, to higher standards than their male peers (Timms, Lankshear, Anderson, & Courtney, 2008). In this study one respondent referred to this as a "silicon ceiling," the title we have adopted for this chapter.

The following case study reports on an investigation carried out by the authors. The aim was to explore the reality of Australian women working in ICT. We wanted to investigate the way women in the ICT workforce "engage in, interpret and mutually construct their particular realities" (Cecez-Kecmanovic, 2011). Our key research question was:

What is the experience of women working in IT particularly with respect to their workplace?

Methodology

To get a deeper insight into the current female ICT work environment in Australia, both qualitative and quantitative data were collected. The quantitative data provided a picture of what is happening in workplaces. Collecting qualitative data was important for understanding some of the key issues that impact women working in ICT and to determine if, in the 21st century, the profession is moving away from the male stereotype.

In 2008, women who were members of the Victorian ICT for Women professional network and those who had some association with the network were invited to participate in a survey. 530 women were invited, and 121 completed the survey (a 23% response rate). The survey explored a number of issues and included questions that had been used in an earlier survey of Australian women conducted by the Australian Computer Society (Bandias & Warne, 2009). The questions included:

- demographic questions such as age and qualifications;
- those with defined responses such as the gender breakdown of the workgroup, working hours, and the length of time the participant had worked in the industry;
- Likert-scale statements (on a scale of 1 to 5, where 1 was strongly disagree and 5 was strongly agree); and
- questions requiring a free text response.

Unusually for this form of survey there was a very high response to the open-ended questions. Sixty-six percent of participants entered a text response to two or more of the questions requiring a free text response.

Analysis of Quantitative and Qualitative Data

The Likert-scale questions asked the women how satisfied they were with their career choice, if working in IT gave them flexibility, if they believed they were respected in their workplace, if they believed IT gave them more opportunities than other professions, if they believed they were not discriminated against, if they were given professional development opportunities, and if they were paid at a rate similar to their male counterparts.

SPSS was used to analyze the quantitative data, and this included the calculation of frequencies and cross-tabulations. Cross-tabulations were conducted to demonstrate "the presence or absence of a relationship" between different factors (Bryman & Cramer, 1992, p. 153). A chi-squared test was applied to determine the significance of the results. The results were regarded as significant if the probability of error was equal to or less than .05 (i.e., significant at the 5% level).

Qualitative data were collected from both the survey and interviews. The data were analyzed using a meta-matrix as described by Miles and Huberman (1994). A matrix "is essentially the 'crossing' of two lists, set up as rows and columns" (Miles & Huberman, 1994, p. 93) using the key themes identified from the literature and the survey. The use of a meta-matrix allows data to be analyzed in a number of ways. Miles and Huberman (1994, pp. 246–253) argue that by using these techniques, conclusions that generate meaning can be drawn (making and interpreting findings at different levels of inference). The qualitative data were entered into an Access database according to the identified themes, in this case the themes relating to flexibility in the workplace, opportunities, and management support. The use of a database enabled reports to be generated for data analysis.

Case Study Results: Silicon Ceiling or Not?

Here we report on the results of the case study. The first section provides a demographic overview of the survey participants. This is followed by a summary of the results from the quantitative data; finally the qualitative responses are discussed.

Table 8.3 indicates that the majority of participants, more than 70%, had worked in the industry for more than 5 years, with 16% working part-time. The respondents were also well qualified, with most (54%) holding a bachelor's degree and 25% having either a master's degree or PhD. Only 12% had no formal post-school qualification.

TABLE 8.3
Length of time in the IT workforce

Time	Percentage
Less than 5 years	29
Between 5 and 10 years	25
Between 10 and 15 years	21
More than 15 years	25

What is interesting is that for most women (59%), IT was not their first career choice. This could relate to the age of our respondents and the fact that ICT is a relatively new profession.

The women worked in a range of roles, including technical roles such as programmers or IT support. Table 8.4 describes the most common roles women performed and the percentage of women in these roles. A total of 122 women answered this question, and 4 described themselves as students.

The data indicate that a few women are reaching the level of manager but not much further.

Given that the IT industry has a reputation for long hours of work and is often considered not family friendly, it was important to establish how many women were able to work in IT and manage family responsibilities. Of the 120 responses to this question, 58% of women said they did not have children, 32% had one or two children, and 8% had three or more children.

The survey explored a number of issues relating to the IT workplace. One question was "What would improve your satisfaction with IT as a career choice?" A number of options were provided for respondents to select from. Of those who answered this question: 33% said they want improved career progression, 20% want better work–life balance, and 19% want mentoring. Networking opportunities (15%) and flexibility at work (10%) were of lesser importance.

The majority of women worked in male-dominated areas. Almost 50% of the women worked in an organization where there were less than 25% women. Previous studies show that male-dominated workplaces do have an impact on the women working there. The survey asked participants to respond to a number of Likert-scale statements. Table 8.5 provides an overview of the results and is presented as percentages.

TABLE 8.4
What women do in IT (n = 122)

Role	%
Business or system analyst	16
Manager (including IT, information, general, service manager)	14
Sales and marketing	11
Project leader or project manager	11
Programmer analyst/analysis testing	9
Consulting/contractor	8
Webmaster/Internet development	4

TABLE 8.5
Results of Likert-scale responses

Statement	Strongly Agree	Agree	Neither agree nor disagree	Disagree	Strongly Disagree
I am very satisfied with IT as a career	41.6	32.6	15.7	2.2	1.1
Working in IT gives me flexibility	34.8	31.5	13.5	6.7	4.5
I am respected in my work place	39.3	36.0	16.9	2.2	1.1
I know where I am going in terms of my job	23.6	34.8	29.2	6.7	3.4
Working in IT has given me more opportunities than other professions	28.1	28.1	25.8	5.6	3.4
I never feel that I am discriminated against at work because I am a woman	22.5	22.5	25.8	18.0	6.7
I have regular professional development opportunities	11.2	38.2	24.7	14.6	3.4
I am paid at a rate similar to male counterparts	18.0	29.2	18.0	16.9	5.6

As shown in Table 8.5, the majority of women were satisfied with their choice of IT as a career and the flexibility their workplace offered, and said that they felt respected. However, for a number of women, discrimination was still an issue and many did not have professional development opportunities. It could be argued that without such opportunities, progression is more difficult in any profession.

Cross-tabulations were conducted to establish which factors impacted on women's career satisfaction. Women who said they were very satisfied with their career also said that:

- Their job offered them flexibility ($p < .001$).
- They were respected in their workplace ($p < .001$).
- There was no discrimination ($p < .043$).
- They had a plan for their career into the future ($p < .001$).

As can be seen, three of the four cross-tabulations were statistically highly significant ($p < .001$). The results indicate that flexibility at work, perceptions relating to respect, and where there was no discrimination were correlated with the level of satisfaction women felt with their career. In addition, if women were satisfied with their career, they had plans for the future, whereas women who were not satisfied did not have future career plans.

On the issue of pay where women perceived that they were not discriminated against, were respected, had opportunities, and were offered professional development opportunities, they were also more likely to say that they were paid at a rate similar to their male counterparts. All the results were either statistically significant ($p < .05$) or highly statistically significant ($p < .0001$). Of the 89 respondents to this statement, only 23% disagreed or disagreed strongly with the statement relating to pay.

Discussion: What Affects the Silicon Ceiling?

Respondents were asked:

- What are your expectations as a woman, of the industry and working or studying ICT currently?
- Would you describe your workplace as "family friendly"?
- IT workplaces have been described as "chilly" and a "boys club." To help us gain an understanding of your workplace, would you describe your workplace as "chilly" or a "boys' club."

The results indicated that three themes were most important: workplace flexibility, workplace culture, and career progression. These are certainly the most important influencers of work satisfaction for women in ICT and are now discussed in more detail.

Workplace Flexibility

It is suggested that an attractive aspect of working in IT is the flexibility of hours that it might offer. The question, then, is to what extent does this flexibility really exist and is there a price to pay?

Women clearly want more flexibility, particularly when they have a family. When asked what their expectations were, the respondents indicated that being able to work and have a family was important. For example:

> Would like to see the industry making it easier for women to work from home or part time after they have kids. This would keep more women in the industry and entice them back again.

And:

> That the industry does not support the re-integration into the work force of women after periods of leave.

Other women commented on supporting real flexibility, suggesting:

> not just lip-service but true support of flexible working and family-friendly environments. Company subsidised child-care on-site for larger companies.

On the question of how family friendly were their workplaces, the majority of women said their workplaces were family friendly; however, there was some qualification. For example, "There are 'family friendly' policies in place but these are not always implemented":

> I'm allowed a lot of flexibility (probably not sanctioned so could be cut off at any time). But I wasn't allowed to return to part time work after maternity leave; and "Yes to some degree—we have policies in place but being able to use these policies without some eyebrows being raised would be nice."

Others mentioned that flexibility comes at a cost.

Although my hours can be tweaked to allow for dropping kids at school etc (which I greatly appreciate) I still feel that I am expected to put in more hours in order to show dedication to my work and this upsets me as I don't feel the need to do this unless I have deadlines to meet or important things to complete before going home for the night. I manage my time well at work and this "unspoken" expectation puts unnecessary pressure on me and my family.

Two others commented: "In some ways yes, but overriding that is the project schedule," and "There is no appreciation of the difficulties due to early morning meetings and last minute requests to work back late. This can be very difficult for working parents."

Workplace Culture

The culture of the workplace has an impact on how well women are able to progress. It could be argued that if the culture is difficult not only will women leave, but they will find it harder to progress particularly to management positions. For many women, their workplace culture is not ideal. Of the 80 women who answered this question, more than half said that the workplace was either chilly or a boys' club or both. The two areas that best highlight the issues women face are discrimination and lack of respect and the opportunities they perceive they have to progress.

Being respected in what you can offer in terms of your skills and expertise impact on career progression. When asked what their expectations were as women in IT, an overwhelming number of women wanted respect for the skills they bring. They used words and phrases such as "the value/benefit of women's skills," "respected for the value I can offer to the organization," "expect respect." One pertinent comment highlights the fact that it isn't about reaching the very top but at least be given opportunities:

> Simply to be respected and given the freedom to contribute. To have an ICT career to the extent that you want. . . . We all don't want to be CIOs, but do want to contribute and make a difference, use our intelligence and creativity.

The language used around women or toward women is an indication of a lack of respect. For example, "he refers to us as 'darl,' 'hun,' etc." Another woman talked about prolific swearing in her workplace. Feeling that you are not being treated equally was raised by many. On the question of discrimination, one comment was that it was "Difficult—facing age and gender prejudice."

Career Progression

The opportunities women are offered at work are a key issue. Without the necessary experience, women will not move into management positions. Many women said that having the same opportunity as men was what they expected; however, this was often not the case, particularly where children were a consideration. "To be able to have the same opportunities as men for career growth and job fulfilment, even if we have to take time out to have a family."

The question of pay and progression was raised by a number of women, such as this woman who expects "Equal rights and pay based on knowledge and experience." Another expected "to be considered and hired for upper management and [general management] roles and have a seat at most boards around the world."

Von Hellens and Nielsen (2001) argue that socializing outside the workplace with colleagues is important for winning promotions. They also note that women often have fewer opportunities for such socializing Our research found that women do perceive they have fewer opportunities, particularly when it comes to networking with colleagues.

A number of women explicitly stated that they were excluded from what they perceived to be networking opportunities. For example, "They do not invite me out for Friday drinks or weekends away with them!" Another commented on feeling "excluded." Other women technically have the opportunity, but it may not be ideal or suitable. One woman said:

> Often, yes, it is a boys club, but can tend to be a more 'boys who go to the pub' club, as networking and negotiations happen as much, if not more, at after-work drinks than in the office. I am always invited to after-work drinks, so don't feel completely excluded, but there is definitely a pat-each-other-on-the-back, hands-shaking atmosphere here.

Another commented that "there is definitely a boys' club element—the team social gathering (organized by the boys) is to taste their home brew!" Another woman drew attention to what she believes is the impact of a boys' club culture: "Career progression is sometimes evident to be boys' club related."

Our case study presents a mixed picture of a profession that can be exciting, creative and powerful. We are mindful of the fact that women may have started in ICT and subsequently left the industry due to it being not family friendly or too masculinized; our sample may reflect the strongest, most persistent females in the industry. It appears that there is still a lot of work to be done before the ICT workplace is considered nongendered.

Conclusion

In this chapter we have presented a 21st-century snapshot of women managers and leaders in ICT. Our case study findings indicate that there are many nonessential blockers to women pursuing this creative and satisfying career. The ICT industry should be the most flexible of all industries due to the ability to take advantage of the technologies it created, such as social networking, synchronous and asynchronous team project communication systems, conferencing software, and hardware that connects across geographical locations. However, it appears that, despite lip-service to flexibility, it continues to be reported by many women as being inflexible, or flexible at a cost to workers who have primary carer responsibilities. Unfortunately, added to this more than half the women who work in ICT reported that their work environments were chilly or had a boys' club atmosphere. A significant number reported that they do not get the same career advancement opportunities as their male colleagues. Yet the research also shows that many women working in ICT do have a great deal of job satisfaction. These report that they have job satisfaction, career progression opportunities, and life balance, which includes a flexible work environment. The discordance in these findings, together with societal perceptions and the reporting of a persistent silicon ceiling, is alarming. None of these factors is essential to being an effective ICT professional; however, for a woman to become an ICT professional, their absence is significant.

There is much being done at many levels to support women in selecting and continuing in this career path. Some organizations apply affirmative action; attempting to ensure the number of females hired is approximately the same as the number of males hired. Networking and mentoring opportunities are greater than ever before. Despite these efforts the industry and profession continues to be male dominated and female unfriendly.

The Equal Opportunity for Women in the Workplace Agency, an Australian government agency, has a vision is to achieve equal opportunity for women in Australian workplaces. It highlights that:

Gender disparity in Australian workplaces, such as the disparity between men and women in leadership roles, perpetuates existing stereotypes about the role of women, both at work and in wider society, and exacerbates gender pay inequity. Further, research has shown that having significant numbers of women in leadership positions encourages and sustains other women. This means that unless systemic change in gender diversity in leadership is achieved, there is limited chance of the disparity improving on its own. (EOWA, 2010)

The issue is being talked about, and publications such as this will ensure it continues to be in the forefront of concern for industry and the education sector. However, if women continue to be in the minority in ICT, particularly in senior management roles, women will continue to see ICT as a poor career option and the lack of gender diversity will become self-perpetuating.

Note

1. For all groups, the labor force participation rate is expressed as a percentage of the civilian population aged 15 years and over in the same group (ABS, 2011b, p. 40).

References

ABS. (2010a). Measures of Australia's Progress Cat No 1370.0. Released September 15, 2010. *Australian Bureau of Statistics*. Retrieved from http://www.abs.gov.au/AUSSTATS/abs@.nsf/mf/1370.0

ABS. (2010b). Australia's workers; education and workplace training. Australian Social Trends. September. Cat No 4102.0 *Australian Bureau of Statistics*. Retrieved from http://www.abs.gov.au/socialtrends

ABS. (2010c). Forms of employment. November. Cat 6359.0. *Australian Bureau of Statistics*. Retrieved from http://www.ausstats.abs.gov.au/Ausstats/subscriber.nsf/0/ED7010B1774DA4D4CA2578800019CAFB/$File/63590_november%202010.pdf

ABS. (2011a). Labour force. September. Cat 6202.0. *Australian Bureau of Statistics*. Retrieved from http://www.ausstats.abs.gov.au/ausstats/meisubs.nsf/0/8C439CD898424D72C257927000DBD7A/$File/62020_sep%202011.pdf

ABS. (2011b). Fifty years of labour force: Now and then. Cat 6105.0—Australian Labour Market Statistics, Oct. *Australian Bureau of Statistics*. Retrieved from http://www.abs.gov.au/ausstats/abs@.nsf/Latestproducts/6105.0Feature%20Article1Oct%202011?opendocument&tabname=Summary&prodno=6105.0&issue=Oct%202011&num=&view=

ACS. (2007). *The Australian computer society's women's board.* Retrieved from http://www.acswomen.com/acsw

ACS. (2010). Australian ICT statistical compendium. *Australian Computer Society.* Retrieved from https://www.acs.org.au/2010compendium/ICTStatistical-Compendium2010.pdf

Adams, J. C., Bauer, V., & Baichoo, S. (2003). An expanding pipeline: Gender in Mauritius. In S. Grissom (Ed.), *Proceedings of the thirty-fourth SIGCSE technical symposium on computer science education* (pp. 59–63). Las Vegas, NV: ACM Press.

Adriaanse, J (2010, April). *Gender distribution on boards of national sport organisations in Australia,* Doctoral Study Data Stage 1, University of Technology Sydney.

Anderson, N., Timms, C., & Courtney, L. (2006). *If you want to advance in the ICT industry, you have to work harder than your male peers.* Women in ICT Industry Survey: Preliminary findings. *AusWit Conference,* Adelaide.

APESMA. (2010). *Women in the professions: The state of play 2009–10. Executive summary of the APESMA women in the professions survey report.* Retrieved from http://www.apesma.com.au/groups/professional-women/files/Womens-Survey-Report-web.pdf

APH. (2011). Politics and public administration group parliamentary library. *Composition of Australian parliaments by party and gender as at 5 January 2011.* Retrieved from www.aph.gov.au/library/intguide/pol/currentwomen.pdf

Australian Human Rights Commission. (n.d.) *Women in leadership.* Retrieved from http://www.hreoc.gov.au/sex_discrimination/programs/women_leadership.html#fnB7

Bandias, S., & Warne, L. (2009). *Women in ICT—Retain and sustain: An overview of the ACS-W Survey.* ACIS Conference, Melbourne.

Bowles, R., Semkiw, J., Spencer, J., & Hughes, J. (2002). *Provenance–Creators and custodians.* Published by the Australian Science and Technology Heritage Centre on AustehcWeb. Retrieved from www.asap.unimelb.edu.au/pubs/guides/csirac/

Bryman, A., & Cramer, D. (1992). *Quantitative data analysis for social scientists.* London: Routledge.

Byrne, G., & Staehr, L. (2011) Women and the Australian ICT industry: An analysis of ABS census and survey data. *PACIS 2011 Proceedings.* Retrieved from http://aisel.aisnet.org/pacis2011/32

Cecez-Kecmanovic, D. (2011). On methods, methodologies and how they matter. *European Conference on information systems,* Helsinki, Aalto University School of Economics.

Chesterman, C., Ross-Smith, A., & Peters, M. (2004). *Senior women executives and the cultures of management* (June).

Curtain, C. (2011). *A long way to the top.* Global Partnerships Financial Consulting. Retrieved http://www.gpfc.com.au/downloads/Women%20In%20Business%20%20White%20paper%20by%20Charmaine%20Curtain.pdf

Department of Communications Information Technology and the Arts. (2006). *Building Australian ICT Skills*, Commonwealth of Australia.

DEEWR. (2011a). Australian Jobs. *Department of Education, Employment and Workplace Relations, Australian Government*. Retrieved from http://www. deewr.gov.au/Employment/ResearchStatistics/Documents/AustralianJobs.pdf

DEEWR. (2011b). Summary of the 2010 higher education student statistics. *Department of Education, Employment and Workplace Relations, Australian Government*. Retrieved from http://www.deewr.gov.au/HigherEducation/Publications/HEStatistics/Publications/Pages/Students.aspx

DFAT. (2008). *About Australia: Information and communications technology. Australian government: Department of Foreign Affairs and Trade*. Retrieved from http://www.dfat.gov.au/facts/ict.html

Diezmann, C., & Grieshaber, S. (2010 July, 6–9). Gender equity in the professoriate; a cohort study of new women professors in Australia. In M. Devlin, J. Nagy, & A. Lichtenberg (Eds.), *Research and development in higher education* (pp. 223–234). 33rd HERDSA Annual International Conference. Melbourne, Australia.

EOWA. (2010). *Australian census of women in leadership*. Australian government. Retrieved from http://www.eowa.gov.au/Australian_Women_In_Leadership_Census/2010_Australian_Women_In_Leadership_Census/Media_kit/2010_census.pdf

Evans, C. (2011). *Record number of Australian students at university*. Media release, April 23, 2011. Retrieved from http://www.ministers.deewr.gov.au/evans/record-number-australian-students-university

FAHCSIA. (2010). *Women on Australian Government Boards Report 2009–2010*. Department of Families, Housing, Community Services and Indigenous Affairs. Retrieved from http://www.fahcsia.gov.au/sa/women/pubs/govtint/wagbr08_09/Pages/default.aspx

Federal Court of Australia. *List of appointment date of current judges*. Retrieved from www.fedcourt.gov.au/aboutct/jj_seniority.html

Game, A., & Pringle, R. (1983). Sex-typing in computerland. *Australian Society, 3,* 8.

Goldman Sachs, JBWere Investment Research. (2009, November 26). *Australia's hidden resource: the economic case for increasing female participation.*. Retrieved from www.eowa.gov.au/Pay_Equity/Files/Australias_hidden_resource.pdf

Graduate Careers Australia. (2010). *Gradsonline survey*. Retrieved from http://svc095.wic026v.server-web.com/GraDSOnline/about/about.asp

Hausmann, R., Tyson, L. D., & Zahidi, S. (2011). The global gender gap report 2011. *World Economic Forum*. Retrieved from http://reports.weforum.org/global-gender-gap-2011/

IBSA. (2010). Environment scan 2010—Information and communication technology industries. *Innovation and Business Skills Australia*. Retrieved

from http://www.ibsa.org.au/Portals/ibsa.org.au/docs/Research%20&%20Dis
cussion%20Papers/Sectoral%20report%20%20ICT%20Industry%2026%20Feb%
2010.pdf

Klawe, M., Whitney, T., & Simard, C. (2009). Women in computing—Take 2.
Communications of the ACM, 52, 68–76.

Mackinnon, A. (1995). Women and computing: An overview. In P. Bishop,
M. Dyer, & P. Griffin (Eds.), *Women, computing and culture 1994.* Research
Centre for Gender Studies and the School of Communication and Information
Studies, University of South Australia, pp. 15–22.

McKenzie, P., Kos, J., Walker, M., & Hong, J. (2008). *Staff in Australia's schools,
2007.* Department of Education, Employment and Workplace Relations.
Australian government.

Miles, M. B., & Huberman, M. A. (1994). *Qualitative data analysis.* London:
Sage.

Ng, C., Das. S., Ching. L. T., & Chin, M. A. (1998, August 4–7). Telework and
gender in the information age: New opportunities for the developing world.
Regional Conference on Gender and Technology in Asia, Bangkok, Thailand.
Retrieved from http://www.apdip.net/projects/seminars/it-policy/cn/resources/
cecilia/TWGASAT.html.

OSW (2002). *Women 2002.* Office of the Status of Women. Retrieved from http://
www.osw.dpmc.gov.au/index.htm/women_2002.pdf

Pass, S. (2006). *CSIRAC.* Melbourne School of Engineering, Department of Computer Science and Software Engineering. Retrieved from http://www.csse.un
imelb.edu.au/dept/about/csirac/#webcms-toc-1.2

Pearcey, T. (1994). Australia enters the computer age. In J. Bennett, J. Broomham,
P. Murton, T. Pearcey, & R. Rutledge (Eds.), *Computing in Australia the development of a profession* (pp. 15–32). Marrickville, NSW: Hale and Iremonger
and the ASC.

Schofield, J. (2011) Introduction to this collection. *Equality speaks: Challenges
for a fair society.* Catalyst. Retrieved from http://catalyst.org.au/documents/
equality-speaks/introduction_equalityspeaks.pdf

Spencer, S. (2003). Can you do addition? Questioning the domain of IT. In *Aus-
WIT 2003—Participation, Progress and Potential.* Hobart, Australia: University of Tasmania.

Timms, C., Lankshear, C., Anderson, N., & Courtney, L. (2008). Riding a hydra:
Women ICT professionals' perceptions of working in the Australian ICT industry. *Information Technology & People, 2,* 155–177.

Trauth, E. M. (2011). What can we learn from gender research? Seven lessons for
business research methods. *Electronic Journal of Business Research Methods,
9,* 1–9.

Von Hellens, L., & Nielsen, S. (2001). Australian women in IT. *Communications
of the ACM, 44,* 46–52.

Webb, P., & Young, J. (2005). Perhaps it's time for a fresh approach to ICT gender research? *Journal of Research and Practice in Information Technology, 37,* 147–160.

Wesselius, J. C. (1998). *Gender identity without gender prescriptions: Dealing with essentialism and constructionism in feminist politics.* Retrieved from http://www.bu.edu/wcp/Papers/Gend/GendWess.htm

While, K. (2001). Women in the professoriate in Australia. *International Journal of Organisational Behaviour, 3,* 64–76.

Wikipedia. (2011). *Silicon.* Retrieved from http://en.wikipedia.org/wiki/Silicon

A business leader has to keep their organization focused on the mission. That sounds easy, but it can be tremendously challenging in today's competitive and ever-changing business environment. A leader also has to motivate potential partners to join.

—Meg Whitman
President and CEO of eBay

9

Men's Perceptions of Women Leaders and Managers

Patti J. Berg, William E. Schweinle, and Betty A. Hulse

In 2008, Hillary Rodham Clinton nearly secured the Democratic Party nomination for president of the United States. Clinton won more than 18 million votes (including Michigan, in which her major opponent had withdrawn his name) and 46.0% of total delegate votes (Real Clear Politics, 2010). In fact, she won 48.1% of the popular primary vote (when Michigan is included), compared to the 47.4% achieved by eventual President Barack Obama, making the primary race one of the most competitive in history. As president, Barack Obama appointed Clinton U.S. Secretary of State, a position held by women (Madeleine Albright, 1997–2001, and Condoleezza Rice, 2005–2009) in two of the three 4-year terms preceding her own. Clinton had gained the confidence of the populous at large and had earned the respect of her opponent, who appointed her to the highest ranked Cabinet position within the executive branch, the fourth-ranked individual in the presidential line of succession should the president be unable to serve (U.S. Department of State, 2012). The secretary of state is responsible for developing and implementing foreign policy and oversees 30,000 employees with a budget of approximately $35 billion (White House, 2012). At the same time and until 2011, Nancy Pelosi was the first woman to serve as Speaker of the House (second in the presidential line of succession), making her the highest ranking woman in America's political history.

Clearly, women have become more visible as leaders. Furthermore, women are now as actively employed as men in the workforce. According to the 2010 U.S. Bureau of Labor Statistics, women comprise 47.2% of the labor force and hold 51.5% of management, professional, and related occupations. Arguably, such statistics are the offspring of an increasingly well-educated female work-force. Within four decades, the percentage of women in the workforce attend-ing college has grown impressively, from 22.1% in 1970 to 66.7% in 2010. Similarly remarkable, within the same time frame the percent of women gradu-ating from college with a degree grew more than three times, from 11.2% to 36.4% (Bureau of Labor Statistics Spotlight, 2011b). Despite these positive trends, chief executive positions are still predominately held by men, with the percentage of women in these positions at 25.5% (2010 U.S. Bureau of Labor Statistics). Women are even more scarcely represented among *Fortune* 500 companies' executive officers, with only 14.4% of these positions occupied by women (Catalyst Census, 2010).

The promising increase in the number of educated, employed women prompts us to ask ourselves what is responsible for the underrepresentation of women at senior levels of leadership and management. There are several possible factors that may inhibit the ascent of women into top leadership positions. Among these are societal perceptions of women leaders and the dominate leadership paradigm present in our culture. Perceptions of women by men are of particular interest since men currently hold the majority of such coveted positions and may act as powerbrokers in the promotion of women through managerial ranks. Furthermore, it is of interest to examine how the gender assignment of leadership attributes is perpetuated by mem-bers holding positions of authority. While the focus of the present chapter is on men's perceptions of women leaders and managers, we are reminded that gender and leadership identity is a dynamic process highly influenced by cultural and societal changes. In the following pages, we review and summarize findings related to men's perceptions of women in leadership positions.

Social Role Theory

According to Social Role Theory, people form beliefs about the attributes or characteristics of a person based on the roles they typically see performed by representatives of that person's gender. These exposure-formed beliefs then become widely held expectations of behaviors for people of that gender (Eagly, 1987). The homemaker-provider division of labor between women and men led women to learn domestic skills and men to learn skills that would gain them paid employment (Eagly, Wood, & Diekman, 2000). The behaviors stereotypically associated with homemaker and provider have been character-ized as communal versus agentic (Eagly et al., 2000). Communal attributes, for instance nurturance, helpfulness, kindness and interpersonal sensitivity, have traditionally been ascribed to women, whereas agentic attributes, like ambition, dominance, independence and self-confidence have traditionally been ascribed to men (Eagly & Karau, 2002). Gender roles and their associated expectations influence behavior through accepted descriptive and injunctive societal norms. Descriptive norms refer to what is usual and typical (what we *do* or who we are) and suggests a degree of uniformity within a particular group; for instance, women are compassionate and men are competitive. Injunctive norms (also referred to as prescriptive norms) refer to what is proper, expected, acceptable, and desired (what we *should do*) and holds with it a degree of approval or disapproval by its group members (Eagly et al., 2000). For instance, men should enjoy attending or watching sports while women should be interested in shopping.

While it is important to explore social roles as barriers to women with leadership aspirations, we must be careful not to oversimplify its influence in the workplace. Whitehead (2001) reminds us that gender identity is "grounded only in the incessant flux of intersubjective occurrence, identifiable only through prior social and cultural discursive configurations" (p. 94).

Role Congruity

Stereotypical gender-assigned roles may be placed upon positions in society just as they are to individuals. In doing so, a search begins, attempting to bring together an individual and a societal position that are well matched. Leadership roles have been defined as historically congruent with prescriptive stereotypes of men and incongruent with prescriptive stereotypes of women. Women are often perceived as violating their prescribed role when taking on leadership positions. For instance, historically, leadership and managerial positions have been assigned agentic qualities, such as courage, control over subordinates, assertiveness, competitiveness, and independent success with tasks. The search to find a match for such a position is likely to begin with an individual who shares such qualities—the expectation being that a man is more likely to possess them. The agentic personality has become accepted as desirable and necessary for success as a leader or manager (Eagly, 1987; Eagly & Karau, 2002). Social Role Theory suggests a defining process ensues, with workplace position defined by gender attributes and men and women further defined by their role in these gender-assigned positions in the workplace.

Not uncommonly, men choose leaders based upon observed societal norms and largely associate leadership with being male. Jackson, Engstrom, and Emmers-Sommer, (2007) asked male and female U.S. university students to identify the leader of a group based on seating arrangement and head-of-table cue.

Both male and female students chose a leader with the same gender as their own most often, but male subjects did so with significantly greater frequency than female subjects: 93.5% of the time male subjects selected a male leader, and 63.5% of the time female subjects selected a female leader (Jackson et al., 2007). When questioned about the reasons for their leadership choices, a number of male subjects indicated that men are "usually," "most likely," "generally" leaders, with none claiming or referring to males as being superior to females in leadership abilities (Jackson et al., 2007). Similar findings by Duehr and Bono (2006) indicate that male university students still view men and managers as more similar than women and managers.

Longitudinal research findings in populations of U.S. college students show attitudes toward women's roles grow more egalitarian for both genders over 4 years of college but that men's views are less egalitarian compared to women at matriculation and again 4 years later (Bryant, 2003). In other words, men's views of women's roles are more traditional upon college entry and are less likely to change as compared to women's views over this period of time.

In a more recent study, Bosak and Sczesny (2011) asked German undergraduate male and female business students to make decisions on shortlisting or hiring an applicant for a position in management. The students were also asked to rate the certainty of their decisions. Applicants were fictional and varied according to gender and role description (described as a leader or nonleader). When students were provided with evidence of an applicant's qualifications as a leader (leader role description), male and female subjects shortlisted and hired the "applicants" based on qualifications and independently of gender (Bosak & Sczesny, 2011). Female subjects shortlisted and hired nonleader male and female applicants with the same degree of certainty, and male subjects shortlisted these applicants with the same amount of certainty. However, for applicants with nonleader role descriptions, male subjects selected male applicants with greater certainty than female applicants (Bosak & Sczesny, 2011). These findings indicate that, in the absence of evidence qualifying a male or female for a leadership position, men continue to show bias for hiring men into management or leadership type positions (Bosak & Sczesny, 2011).

Prime, Carter, and Welbourne (2009) found that senior male managers perceived women leaders as possessing statistically stronger feminine leadership behaviors (supporting, rewarding, mentoring, team-building, inspiring, and networking) than men leaders. Women were in agreement, and the distinction was more pronounced for these respondents. Male respondents (senior male managers) were more likely to prescribe masculine leadership behaviors (problem-solving, delegating, and influencing upward) to men leaders than they were to women leaders. The authors also found a change in the way male managers view successful managers. Male respondents reported women leaders were more effective at supporting others and rewarding subordinates. Such biases inevitably infiltrate employment decision making.

Acceptance of leadership paradigms that are largely masculine have resulted in a perceived incongruence between feminine gender and leadership roles (Eagly and Johannesen-Schmidt, 2001). Historically, women who wished to achieve and succeed in management positions encountered the stereotype that women do not possess these agentic characteristics, and, found lacking, women were denied promotion or management positions altogether. In fact, under a paradigm that esteems leadership qualities as those that are "masculine," one of two possibilities exist for a woman interested in ascension to leadership position: (1) women demonstrate attributes imposed on the current leadership paradigm; (2) the paradigm shifts to equate leadership attributes with those that are "feminine." Acceptance of women in leadership roles would necessitate a change in how a women's sphere of competence is viewed or a shift in the perceived preferential attributes of a good leader from "masculine" to "feminine." Yet, Due Billing and Alvesson (2000) warn that modifying perceptions of the ideal leader by assigning feminine gender attributes to successful leadership may not be the best approach toward launching women into leadership positions since this reassignment does nothing to alter underlying societal norms and reinforces traditional attitudes that define idealized leadership potential by gender role divisions.

Paradigm Shifts in Role Congruity

Over the past 30 years, workplace environments have evolved; successful businesses operate in a global economy, information is available instantaneously, menial tasks are now automatized, and communication is held at a premium with new ways to communicate with others to build partnerships and launch ideas. The evolved workplace has brought with it a reformed perspective about ideal leadership skills, and a shift has emerged in male perceptions of women's suitability to hold management positions.

The GLOBE Research Project on Leadership Worldwide collected data from 17,300 managers in nearly 1000 different organizations representing 62 societal cultures to explore leadership attributes with the goal of discovering universal practices and values (Grove, 2005). A set of six Culturally Endorsed Leadership Dimensions were determined to be universal, four which were perceived to promote good leadership (Charismatic/Value Based, Team Oriented, Participative, Humane Oriented) and two which were perceived to impede good leadership (Self-Protective, Autonomous) (Grove, 2005). The character-istics, abilities, and skills associated with the leadership dimensions promoting good leadership included: ability to inspire and motivate, emphasizing team-building, involving others in decisions, supportive, considerate, compassion-ate, and generous (Grove, 2005). Characteristics describing dimensions that inhibit good leadership included: independent/individualized leadership, self-centered, status conscious, and face-saver (Grove, 2005). These results support a new appreciation for communal attributes and hold particular agentic quali-ties accountable for inhibiting good leadership.

Research using male and female nontraditional undergraduate and gradu-ate U.S. business students provides further evidence of the shift from a mas-culine leadership paradigm to a leadership paradigm with a greater balance between female and male characteristics (Atwater, Brett, Waldman, DiMare, & Hayden, 2004). Subjects utilized a modified version of Yukl's taxonomy of managerial subroles and rated each subrole as feminine or masculine. Of the 19 managerial subroles, subjects rated 7 subroles as more feminine and 6 sub-roles as more masculine (Atwater et al., 2004).

Sczesney et al., in a 2004 study of male and female management students in Germany, India, and Australia, indicated a shift in the leadership paradigm to include person-oriented traits, a traditionally communal/feminine characteris-tic, as being an important characteristic for a leader to possess. People-oriented skills were viewed as more important for leaders-in-general than task-oriented traits by Australian and Indian students; task-oriented traits were viewed as more important than person-oriented traits by German students (Sczesny, Bosak, Neff, & Schyns, 2004). In addition, male and female students from all three countries viewed women executives as having person-oriented traits to a greater degree than executives-in-general (Sczesny et al., 2004). However, male subjects of all three countries and female German subjects demonstrated bias toward men as leaders by imaging mainly male executives when consider-ing questions pertaining to leaders-in-general (Sczesny et al., 2004).

The Pew Research Center Social and Demographic Trends Survey (2008) asked adult respondents to indicate whether the characteristics presented were "more true of men or more true of women." They were then asked to rate how important these characteristics were for leadership. Traits tested were hon-esty, intelligence, hardworking, decisiveness, creative, compassionate, outgo-ing, and ambitious. The characteristics rated most important for leadership were honesty, intelligence, hardworking, and decisive, with honesty rated the highest. Respondents rated women higher than men in honesty, intelligence, being outgoing, creativity, and compassion; respondents rated women and men equally in respect to hardworking and ambitious, and respondents rated men higher than women in decisiveness.. The majority of men and women in this survey believed that both men and women make good leaders (69% of men and 68% of women); 21% of respondents favored men as leaders, and only 6% favored women as leaders (Taylor et al., 2008). Only 4% of men believed women make better leaders than men compared to 8% of women believing women make better leaders than men.

A survey distributed by Eagly and Johannesen-Schmidt (2001) prompted subjects to indicate how often a manager engaged in Transformational, Translational, and Laissez-Faire leadership style behaviors. Women were rated higher than men on several scales: the attributes version of idealized influence, inspirational motivation and individualized consideration and contingent rewards (Eagly & Johannesen-Schmidt, 2001). On perceived effectiveness measures women were also rated significantly higher than men (Eagly & Johannesen-Schmidt, 2001).

Duehr and Bono (2006) sampled male middle managers, asking them to describe "women" and "managers." They found a robust positive correlation (ICC = O.63, $p < .001$) between descriptors. Such a match between attributes of women and those of managers constitutes a dramatic shift in the views of male middle managers from previous research results (Heilman, Block, Martell, & Simon, 1989; Schein, 1973, 1975). The authors also found a change in the way male managers view successful managers. Perhaps surprisingly, the views of male middle managers resulted in a correlation between "men managers" and "managers" as .74, in contrast to Heilman et al. (1989) ICC = .86 and to their own comparison of "women managers" and "managers" with an ICC = .81. Examining mean scale ratings across study samples for trends, male managers viewed successful managers as more communal and less agentic compared to Heilman et al. (1989) means. This change suggests a shift in the leadership paradigm to include a greater balance between agentic and communal characteristics (Duehr & Bono, 2006).

Interestingly, Rudman and Glick (1999) found that the feminization of management and leadership styles may present a backlash effect for women with more agentic work styles. The authors found that agentic women were penalized for lack of communal traits (such as kindness, generosity, concern, helpfulness, and compassion, traditionally considered feminine qualities) and were viewed as possessing less social aptitude than men with similar agentic qualities. In addition, there was a broader range of acceptable cross-gender workplace behaviors for men than there were for women. The results suggest that a workplace paradigm shift toward more androgynous leadership roles may benefit aspiring women more than taking on agentic qualities to remain competitive within the workplace.

A meta-analysis performed by Koenig, Mitchell, Eagly, and Ristikari (2011) determined that though there is strong evidence suggesting leadership is still associated with masculine attributes, these qualities are becoming increasingly androgynous over time. The group concluded that today's leadership now incorporates more feminine qualities such as sensitivity, understanding, and warmth but not at the expense of masculine dominance and strength.

Impact of Experience on the Social Role Paradigm Shift

Research supports that men with exposure to working women and women managers held more positive attitudes toward women managers. Male managers with working wives and male managers with past positive experiences with female coworkers were much less likely to attribute poor performance to gender-related characteristics and were much less likely to react punitively to lower performance evaluations compared to male managers without similar experience (Eskilson & Wiley, 1996).

There is evidence that exposure to women leaders in the political realm similarly influences a change in voter attitudes (Beaman, Chattopadhyay, Duflo, Pande, & Topalova, 2009). In 1998 Indian policy established gender quotas for leadership positions in certain geographical areas and required a percentage of leadership positions be reserved for women. Indian election results in 2008 showed significant gains for women contesting unreserved positions, with 18.5% of women elected to councils where positions had been reserved in contrast to 11% women in councils in which positions had never been reserved (Beaman et al., 2009). Further, the electoral gain by women was not due to incumbent advantage, as evidenced by an observed incumbent disadvantage for both reserved and unreserved positions (Beaman et al., 2009). Beaman and colleagues asked villagers to evaluate the effectiveness of a hypothetical leader, with manipulation of gender as the only variant between participants. Men living in villages where female position reservations had never occurred perceived the leader as significantly more effective when the leader's gender was experimentally manipulated to be male. In villages where female position reservation had occurred male participants judged women and men as equally effective (Beaman et al., 2009). These results indicate that exposure to women leaders positively affects men's view of women's leadership effectiveness.

Beaman and colleagues used additional measures to investigate villagers' implicit and explicit taste for female leaders. Male and female villagers exhibited a strong same-gender preference for leadership, even in villages where reservations had occurred and male villagers explicitly admitted a preference for male leaders. This research indicates that in India exposure to women leaders does not reduce men's preference for a male leader but that exposure may make it more likely that men will associate women with leadership and leadership effectiveness (Beaman et al., 2009).

Current research reveals a paradigm shift toward a more androgynous leadership identity and points to men's evolved perceptions of women as capable, effective, and qualified for leadership positions. Also working in favor of women interested in taking on leadership positions is the improved confidence men have in their leadership abilities as men gain more experience working with women in such positions. Women are now visible in more positions of authority and power, increasing employee encounter frequencies with female leaders and redefining the leader–subordinate relationship (Koenig et al., 2011). Yet, in spite of changing perceptions and attitudes, disparities in hiring and the systematic promotion of women into management or leadership positions are statistically evident, and the marginalization of women in senior leadership positions persists.

Changing Gender Roles

The evolving organization of work has brought with it changing home dynamics and redefined family contexts. A change in the division of labor in society has accompanied the entrance of women into the workforce. Increasing numbers of men share responsibility for the care of children and domestic chores, reshaping gender roles and, in doing so, redefining masculine attributes. As men and women begin to assume roles traditionally imposed upon their counterparts, masculine and feminine roles begin to share attributes, and the extension of these newly defined social roles infiltrates the leadership paradigm.

Patriarchy

Beyond social roles, socially and culturally reinforced stratifications prop the interests of men within organizations. From this perspective, women who want to achieve must make themselves indispensable to the organizational structure, effectively breaking through the "glass ceiling" (Whitehead, 2001). Such success often requires women invest their efforts in a corporate culture that thrives on negotiation and aggressive competitiveness, occasionally at the expense of personal consideration for others. Whitehead (2001) argues that the prospects of movement within a hierarchical structures brings with it alluring seductive qualities of potency and control as well as the perceived authority to change an organization.

Women negotiating their way through the hierarchical patriarchal structure are faced with subtle barriers in their pursuits toward promotion. At each level, women are confronted with the role incongruity challenge—ascension through the hierarchy brings with it status increases, and a broader breach between social role and leadership congruity emerges for women. Men, however, enjoy a closer match as they ascend. A Koenig et al. (2011) meta-analysis found that men, who are often beneficiaries of promotion and hold ultimate decision-making authority, devalue leadership by women and that men in such positions believe women do not possess the qualities of leaders. Women battle access challenges emboldened by implicit biases about leadership attributes.

Prime, Carter, and Welbourne (2009) contend that men are in a powerful position to close workplace gender gaps. They argue that, in order to transform the current male-dominated stratification, men must understand that the status quo is not beneficial to either gender, develop an awareness of gender biases, and actively challenge such biases. According to Prime, Carter, and Welbourne (2009), men with more enlightened perspectives about gender bias viewed the exclusion of women from leadership positions as disadvantageous to corporate competitiveness. Prime et al.'s research found that men are reluctant to deviate from social gender norms primarily because of the social penalties imposed on men who do not assume the "breadwinner" role. Men who had been mentored by women were more likely to hold such enlightened viewpoints.

Joining Research with the Anecdotal

Returning to the near rise of Hillary Clinton to the most powerful office in the United States, political systems offer an insightful approach to looking at perceptions of population subgroups, in this case a Democratic subgroup, since a single vote can be viewed as an indicator of confidence. While it is not possible to determine what percentage of those votes received by Clinton were cast by men, it is unlikely that all of her support was provided by women, suggesting a subgroup of men and women agreed Clinton possessed the skills and attributes to serve in the highest-ranking executive office in the United States. Yet, during her bid, Clinton was especially vulnerable to comments by political pundits, the new media, and talk-radio hosts referring to her as "emotional," often equated negatively with women and not a quality associated with the office of president, and "shrill," an unflattering description for a woman. Clinton's press image was all at once too feminine while at the same time not feminine enough.

What the research about men's perceptions of women with aspirations to hold high-ranking leadership positions in business or politics communicates is that social norms are shifting as are leadership paradigms. It appears, however, that much of this shift is felt at foundation and middle management levels.

Executive positions within the patriarchal hierarchy continue, by and large, to promote men, perpetuating the perception that women are unsuited for such leadership positions. In spite of this exclusion, women are increasingly visible in positions of authority, and, it appears, confidence in women's leadership skills by men with experience working with women is improving as more women work side by side with their male counterparts.

References

Atwater, L. E., Brett, J. F., Waldman, D., DiMare, L., & Hayden, M. (2004). Men's and women's perceptions of the gender typing of management subroles. *Sex Roles, 50,* 191–199.

Beaman, L., Chattopadhyay, R., Duflo, E., Pande, R., & Topalova, P. (2009). Powerful women: Does exposure reduce bias? *Quarterly Journal of Economics, 124,* 1497–1540.

Bosak, J., & Sczesny, S. (2011). Gender bias in leader selection? Evidence from a hiring simulation study. *Sex Roles, 65,* 234–242.

Bryant, A. N. (2003). Changes in attitudes toward women's roles: Predicting gender-role traditionalism among college students. *Sex Roles, 48,* 131–142.

Bureau of Labor Statistics. (2011a). *BLS spotlight on statistics: Women at work.* Retrieved from http://www.bls.gov/spotlight/2011/women/pdf/women_bls_spotlight.pdf

Bureau of Labor Statistics. (2011b). *Annual averages 2010—Current population survey: Employed persons by detailed occupation, sex, race, and Hispanic or Latino ethnicity.* Retrieved from ftp://ftp.bls.gov/pub/special.requests/lf/aat11.txt

Catalyst. (2010). *Catalyst census of women corporate officers and top earners of the fortune 500.* Retrieved from http://www.catalyst.org/file/412/2010_us_census_women_executive_officers _and _top_earners_final.pdf

Due Billing, Y., & Alvesson, M. (2000). Questioning the notion of feminine leadership: A critical perspective on the gender labeling of leadership. *Gender, Work & Organization, 7,* 144–157.

Duehr, E. E., & Bono, J. E. (2006). Men, women and managers: Are stereotypes finally changing? *Personnel Psychology, 59,* 815–846.

Eagly, A. H. (1987). *Sex differences in social behavior: A social-role interpretation.* Hillsdale, NJ: Erlbaum.

Eagly, A. H., & Johannesen-Schmidt, M. C. (2001). The leadership styles of women and men. *Journal of Social Issues, 57,* 781–797.

Eagly, A. H., & Karau, S. J. (2002). Role congruity theory of prejudice toward female leaders. *Psychological Review, 109,* 573–592.

Eagly, A. H., Wood, W., & Diekman, A. B. (2000). Social role theory of sex differences and similarities: A current appraisal. In T. Eckes & H. M. Trautner (Eds.), *The developmental aocial psychology of gender* (pp. 123–174). Mahwah, NJ: Erlbaum.

Eskilson, A., & Wiley, M. (1996). The best teacher: Mediating effects of experience with employed women on men managers' responses to subordinates' mistakes. *Sex Roles, 34,* 237–252.

Grove, C. N. (2005). *Introduction to the GLOBE research project on leadership worldwide.* Retrieved from http://www.grovewell.com/pub-GLOBE-intro.html#Primary21

Heilman, M. E., Block, C. J., Martell, R. F., & Simon, M. C. (1989). Has anything changed? Current characterizations of men, women, and managers. *Journal of Applied Psychology, 74,* 935–942.

Jackson, D., Engstrom, E., & Emmers-Sommer, T. (2007). Think leader, think male and female: Sex vs. seating arrangement as leadership cues. *Sex Roles, 57,* 713–723.

Koenig, A. M., Mitchell, A. A., Eagly, A. H., & Ristikari, T. (2011). Are leader stereotypes masculine? A meta-analysis of three research paradigms. *Psychological Bulletin, 137,* 616–642.

Pew Research Center. (2008). *A paradox in public attitudes. Men or women: Who's the better leader?* Retrieved from http://pewsocialtrends.org/files/2010/10/gender-leadership.pdf

Prime, J. L., Carter, N. M., & Welbourne, T. M. (2009). Women "take care," men "take charge": Managers' stereotypic perceptions of women and men leaders. *Psychologist-Manager Journal, 12,* 25–49. doi: 10.1080/10887150802371799

Real Clear Politics. (2010). *2008 democratic delegates.* Retrieved from http://www.realclearpolitics.com/epolls/2008/president/democratic_delegate_count.html

Rudman, L. A., & Glick, P. (1999). Feminized management and backlash toward agentic women: The hidden costs to women of a kinder, gentler image of middle managers. *Journal of Personality and Social Psychology, 77,* 1004–1010. doi: 10.1037/0022–3514.77.5.1004

Schein, V. (1973). The relationship between sex role stereotypes and requisite management characteristics. *Journal of Applied Psychology, 57,* 95–100.

Schein, V. (1975). Relationships between sex role stereotypes and requisite management characteristics among female managers. *Journal of Applied Psychology, 60,* 340–344.

Sczesny, S., Bosak, J., Neff, D., & Schyns, B. (2004). Gender stereotypes and the attribution of leadership traits: A cross-cultural comparison. *Sex Roles, 51,* 631–645.

U.S. Department of State. (2012). *Diplomacy in action.* Retrieved from http://www.state.gov/ secretary

White House. 2012. *The executive branch.* Retrieved from http://www.whitehouse.gov/our-government/executive-branch#eop on January 28, 2012

Whitehead, S. (2001). Woman as manager: A seductive ontology. *Gender, Work & Organization, 8,* 84.

In Their Own Voice

Josephine C. H. Tan

The term *leadership* is often associated with the ability to command from lead positions in a political, corporate, or institutional unit. However, leadership occurs in other contexts such as in academic committees where the form of governance is more collegial-based, or in informal groups of young people (e.g., teenagers, university students) with similar interests and identification. Some leaders are formally voted, acclaimed, or appointed into designated roles that have titles and clearly defined duties. Other leaders are identified through more informal means that rely not on the number of votes received but on the degree of high influence that they have on members of the group. Regardless of the context, a leader is an individual who has the formal authority/power or the respect of others to influence their thinking and/or to mobilize them into actions (Yukl, 2009). Sitkins (2009) has a more tongue-in-cheek, albeit not totally inaccurate, definition: "Turn around and see if anyone is following you!" (p. 12).

There is an abundance of writing on leadership (e.g., Barling, Christie, & Hoption, 2011; Hollander, 2009). Different kinds of leadership styles have been identified, a variety of leadership theories have been developed and tested, and the contemporary focus in the research area now includes diversity (e.g., Ayman & Korabik, 2010). Readers who wish to learn more about the theoretical and empirical aspects of leadership are encouraged to seek out the literature. This chapter, however, takes an experiential approach in which I share my views and experiences on leadership as a minority woman. I have served in formal as well informal leadership capacity in student organizations, ad hoc and formal academic committees within and outside of my university, and on professional regulatory and psychological organizations on provincial and national levels. Looking back at my life in order to write this chapter, I am truly surprised by the degree of my participation. Leadership roles were never a part of my life ambitions.

The reader is probably asking at this point with some degree of skepticism how then did I find myself taking on leadership roles. Leadership has taught me a great of self-reflection, and using that self-reflection now, I must say that I was asked, persuaded, requested, or compelled out of a sense of duty to do something *for* the program, the society, the organization, the group, and so on. The core reason was *service to the collective.*

Leadership and Management

Leaders have the capacity to influence the group or the collective, and to set the vision and culture of the system. Duties of a manager typically consist of attending to the daily operations of a system or organization, in part through task delegation and supervision of individuals or teams assigned to the tasks. Yet for both leaders and managers, the interpersonal skills to work with people and to manage teams or the entire group are critical. In a system that has a hierarchical top-down form of governance, the leader and managers are more easily identifiable because of their formal titles and delineated roles. Moreover, the vision and goals of the system are typically defined or guided by the leader, and the implementation of most tasks to achieve those goals are normally performed by the manager and the rest of the system.

However, in contexts where the form of governance is more collegial, such as in a university setting where the members have similar credentials, it becomes tricky to differentiate the manager from the leader. How does the chair of an academic committee whose membership is voluntary in nature "command" a colleague to undertake a task? We know that that is not possible, so we do it in the form of request. If the colleague turns down the request for some reason, then what is the next step? Perhaps we might ask for a different volunteer to take on the task. How does an academic leader approach a colleague in the same department who is not doing his or her part on the team and is affecting team morale and task progress? In such cases, I have found it necessary to put on my manager hat and to utilize whatever interpersonal skills I have to address the problem.

As can be seen, the distinction between a leader and a manager can be blurred because it depends on the context, the formality of the roles, the demands of the task, and the expectations placed on the individual. Perhaps such a distinction is not possible because at critical times, a leader might have to adopt a more managerial role. Similarly, a manager might have to exhibit some leadership qualities when a leadership vacuum exists and the group cohesion breaks down.

Leadership Qualities

I have had the opportunity to work with a number of men and women leaders, observed their style, and learned from them. Some are charismatic, highly self-promoting, and rely on others to do the work. Others are quietly effective with little fanfare. Some simply do everything themselves and occasionally inform the group. Some leaders are ineffectual in that they are "laissez-faire … in which the leader avoids making decisions, abdicates responsibility, and does not use their authority" (Antonakis, Avolio, & Sivasubramaniam, 2003, p. 265). A few are destructive as defined by the ill-consequences of their leadership.

I view effective leaders to be those who can accomplish group goals with the support and efforts from a group. Almost invariably, such leaders possess emotional intelligence. These individuals are cognizant of their inner states and motives, are skilled in reading the same in others (empathy), and employ effective social skills that engage others, and able to create team cohesion and resolve problems. Research has shown that emotional intelligence predicts who becomes a leader (Goleman, 1995).

The effective leaders are also skilled in communicating with others. They listen well and make an attempt to hear what others have to say with an open mind. Their ability to read others helps them to understand the explicit and implied meanings in messages that are conveyed to them. They have strong persuasive powers and can appeal to the others on a logical, empirical, and emotional level. Their written and verbal communications are clear and well-organized, and their points are well-argued with an end goal in mind. Their excellent communication skills lend well to team building, building a following, resolving problems, and developing a vision or strategic plans.

Another characteristic that I have observed in effective leaders is their thorough knowledge of the group that they serve from a historical, current, and future perspective. Knowing the history of the group such as its origins allows one to track its developmental trajectory to the present day, and appreciate the forces—obstacles and resources—that influenced its evolution. An understanding of the group from the inside, such as its different parts and their inter-relations, is critical. Understanding of how the group maps onto the greater system at large and the types of external influences and pressures on the group that can potentially impact on its functioning and future development is equally important. Additionally, familiarity with the short-term and long-term directions of the group, along with its current focus, opportunities, and challenges, allows one to lead it in the desired direction and to make progressive milestones. In the absence of such information, the leader has the opportunity to work collaboratively with the group members to develop a vision and strategic plan.

Another attribute that I particularly admire in effective leadership is the value with which the leaders regard individual group members. The individual followers are often considered to be their most valuable resource. Enthusiastic and energetic group members contribute to team cohesion and harmony, common identity, increased productivity, sharing of creative and innovative ideas, and the renewal and sustainability of the group. These leaders engage in what Bass (1985) calls intellectual stimulation—they encourage curiosity and stimulate the individuals to develop creative and innovative ways of problem-solving and moving forward.

Several effective leaders also have the capacity to instill confidence and optimism in others which is valuable especially in times of crisis. Perhaps this might be what some researchers refer to as charisma which helps to "facilitate the followers' emotional attachment and psychological identification" (Mitchell & Boyle, 2009, p. 459). Many effective leaders are also flexible and capable of adapting to the needs of the group and rising to meet the internal and external forces on the group.

Unfortunately, I have also seen destructive leaders at work. Their characteristics include authoritarianism, defensiveness, dismissal of feedback, self-interests at the expense of the collective, dehumanization of the individual by treating them as a drain or a gain on the budget, retaliation against individuals by taking away resources that diminished their status within the system and interfered with their productivity, failure to communicate or to disclose fully or honestly, failure to consult or to consult adequately, blaming the individuals in the group instead of taking some responsibility when failure occurs, and forcing changes on the system against the will of the collective. The members under the destructive leadership become demoralized, apathetic, insecure, and depressed, and complain that they lack direction or information from their leaders. The information gap strengthens the rumor mill where gossip is unfortunately treated as the truth when it mostly reflects the pessimism and fears experienced by the collective. Whatever form of transgression the destructive leadership might make, the end result is reduced group morale, decreased productivity, and failure to meet goals.

Gender and Leadership

Are there gender differences in leadership style? This question has received considerable scrutiny and studies on gender differences in different components of leadership styles have been carried out (e.g., Eagly & Johannesen-Schmidt, 2001; Eagly, Johannesen-Schmidt, & van Engen, 2003). My experience is that generally, the men leaders tend to be more hierarchical and agentic and the women leaders to be more facilitative and communal. These characteristics can be discerned from the manner in which the leaders manage meetings, communicate with others, and resolve problems. The men are more likely to express their opinions with greater ease and in clear and direct fashion; the women do so in a tentative mitigated fashion, sometimes in the form of a question. The men also seem to have less difficulty disagreeing or even arguing with others and standing their ground. The women on the other hand, acknowledge discrepant views and in rebuttal, might reiterate their own views again in a tentative and inquiring manner. Differences in interpersonal behaviors are also evident. The men show more dominant cues (rapid speech, no hesitation) that are associated with competence and women show more warmth cues (smiling, head nodding) that reflect communality. The women are also more ready than the men to provide others with positive reinforcement and offers of assistance.

I see both the agentic and communal styles as being congruent with effective leadership as long as the leader has the flexibility to utilize both appropriately at the right time. For instance, the agentic style can be helpful in shepherding the group to arrive at a decision, while the communal style can enhance the discussion process by encouraging diverse viewpoints, facilitating consensus building, and reducing the risk of conflicts. Each style, when taken to the extreme, can potentially lead to breakdown of the group. The agentic style can turn authoritarian leading to anger and conflicts, while the communal style can lead to loss of focus and indecisiveness.

Despite general gender differences in leadership styles, it is not possible to stereotype individual men and women leaders as displaying one style or another. The ones I have worked with often incorporate both leadership styles with a proclivity toward one particular style. For the most part, they are sufficiently flexible to modify their mannerisms and actions when the situation calls for it to keep the group process on track.

There is, however, one difference between men and women leaders that I often see. After a decision has been made, the men delegate the tasks to others (usually a subordinate) for implementation and maintain a relatively hands-off approach. The subordinate is responsible for keeping the leader posted and for trouble-shooting to ensure task accomplishment. The women leaders operate differently. They supervise the tasks to greater detail, are more heavily involved in its accomplishment, and sometimes they take on the tasks themselves to ensure quality or timeliness. As a result, the women leaders have a heavier burden and a higher risk of burnout. The women attribute their deeper involvement to a sense of responsibility and commitment to the task and a grave concern for adverse consequences to the group should the tasks not be done well or on time. Of course, there are exceptions to this observation.

Challenges in Leadership Roles for Women

The role of leadership is often perceived as incongruent with the female gender role which can result in prejudicial evaluations and reactions toward women leaders (Eagly & Johannesen-Schmidt, 2001). The reactions that I have received in leadership roles are mixed. I tend to receive more support and cooperation from the younger individuals, regardless of their gender. Their interpersonal demeanor is equally respectful. As for reactions from other leaders, the women leaders generally adopt a more communal style with me. The reactions of the men leaders who are sensitive to diversity issues tend to be highly positive and supportive. Those who have less sensitivity tend to be pompous and condescending in both tone and behavior, and a couple of them have been outright dismissive toward me such as repeatedly ignoring my communications to them and choosing to respond to me only at their whim and fancy.

Several of the women leaders with whom I have worked have noted the challenges of working on a team basis. Their stories share common threads of which I can identify with some. Taking on more workload than the others on the committee and feeling underappreciated for their efforts is a frequent comment. Another has to do with the perception that others on the committee unfairly take credit for the work carried out by the women. The women also complain of some committee members not doing their fair share of the work, and expressed their own growing concern of adverse consequences to the group unless they themselves take up the slack. Yet they are aware that this might put them into an undesirable situation where their efforts are unfairly credited to someone else. The term "badge of status" has been used to refer to high positions that an individual occupies and takes credit for the work associated with that role but that were actually carried out by others.

The women also reported having the strong impression that men are automatically regarded by others as more competent and knowledgeable solely on the basis of their gender. The women mentioned that their contributions to discussions and their attempts to influence are often ignored, and that they are interrupted more frequently than men in meetings. Some of the women resented being treated like a "gofer" (someone who does menial things for others) despite occupying a lead role. Very often, they noted that their communal style of leading is misunderstood as reflecting inadequacy, ineffectiveness, failure to act decisively, and lack of confidence, all of which reduces their credibility as a leader.

The women also mentioned suffering from loss of support network when they move from a peer to a lead position within their system. The system accommodates the change by redefining the relationship that the women had with the ex-peers. The informality and spontaneity of the previous peer relationships give way to greater formality and more rigid boundaries to delineate the status difference. Unless the women can seek out other sources of support, they are likely to remain isolated and lonely in their leadership positions. A woman's transition to a leadership position is less stressful when the group to which she belongs has several women in it. The tendency for women to be communal despite status differential likely is a protective factor.

The women who change their interpersonal style to reflect more agency and more "take command and control" approach reported facing less problems in leadership positions as a result, even though they might feel some misgivings about the need to change. Anecdotal evidence shows that some women can in fact become more agentic, dominating, demanding, competitive, and authoritarian than men. In effect, the leadership role changed the women. These women are disliked unless they incorporate some facilitative and communal characteristics, such as expressing warmth and support for others (Carli, 2001).

Culture and Leadership

The need to consider culture in leadership is gaining increasing recognition (Chin, 2010; Sanchez-Hucles & Davis, 2010). The intersection of gender and culture sometimes increases the challenge for minority women in leadership positions. In my case, growing up in a traditional Asian society with parents who were schooled in the traditional Chinese educational system that is influenced by Confucianism meant that I was socialized heavily into the traditional female gender role which is antithetical to leadership aspirations. It also meant that I was not exposed to women leader role models when growing up. The Confucian values of dedicated work ethics, group harmony, and personal sacrifice for the collective good, as well as the principle that those in the highest position of authority carry the greatest responsibility to the collective were also ingrained into me. When I traveled to Canada for my university education, I was exposed to and adopted a more individualistic way of being, which made the thought of a leadership role more acceptable. I reconciled my leadership roles with the cultural forces in me by interpreting leadership positions as a duty to contribute and serve the collective, instead of promoting self-interests.

The cultural and gender influences doubly reinforced my communal and facilitative leadership style which contributed occasionally to others' devaluation of my abilities and effectiveness in my duties. My discomfort with group disharmony interfered with my ability to disagree or challenge when the need arose. The personal sacrifice work ethic was highly dominant in me as well. It led to overwork, burnout, and a realization that the inequality in workload might well in part be the product of my own work ethic. Furthermore, I grew to realize that I held unfair expectations of the same personal sacrifice work ethic from others who were not from my cultural background.

The self-reflection and insight led to a modification of my behavior and thinking in order to achieve a more realistic and balanced perspective. I attempt to combine dominant with communal cues in my interpersonal style in increase my credibility and effectiveness. My belief in self-sacrifice for the collective is reined in, the urge to jump in and take up the slack for others is decreased, and respect for others' need and desire to have a work–life balance has increased. It also helps that as I gain more experience and recognition in leadership work, any explicit or undercurrent bias against me as a minority woman leader becomes increasingly diminished.

Conclusion

Women can as effective as men in leadership roles. However, they experience problems in leadership such as reduced credibility on the basis of their gender, increased workload, reduced recognition for their efforts, and compromised social support. Their tendency to use a communal form of leadership style is sometimes mistaken for inadequacy and ineffectiveness. The intersection of culture and gender can produce increased challenges for minority women leaders.

Suggestions for Women Seeking Leadership Positions

There are several suggestions that I would offer to women who are interested in leadership positions. Be aware of why you desire the role and ask what you can offer or contribute to the group you wish to lead. Observe and learn from other women and men leaders, acquire different leadership skills and be flexible and intelligent in their employment. Be aware of the limits to which you can invest physically and emotionally into the role without incurring burnout. Avoid dual relationships, maintain professional boundaries, and do not allow social disapproval to deter you from performing effectively. One cannot please everyone at the same time. Additionally, develop strong social skills and communication skills. The presence of a strong support network can weather you through the leadership challenges that come your way. Be insightful of yourself and others, and know the forces within and without yourself that shape you and your leadership performance. Be careful about seeking a high-level leadership position immediately because it helps to begin by gaining experience at a lower level. Become familiar with the structure, function, and dynamics of the group you wish to lead before stepping into a leadership role. Leadership is a developmental process with no end point for there is no such thing as a perfect leader. However, it can be highly intrinsically rewarding for one who chooses to serve.

References

Antonakis, J., Avolio, B. J., & Sivasubramaniam, N. (2003). Context and leadership: an examination of the nine-factor full-range leadership theory using the Multifactor Leadership Questionnaire. *The Leadership Quarterly, 14,* 261–295. doi:10.1016/S1048–9843(03)00030–4

Ayman, R., & Korabik, K. (2010). Leadership. Why gender and culture matter. *American Psychologist, 65*(3), 157–170. doi: 10.1037/a0018806

Barling, J., Christie, A., & Hoption, C. (2011). Leadership. In S. Zedeck (Ed.), *APA handbook of industrial and organizational psychology:* Vol 1. *Building and developing the organization* (pp. 183–240). Washington, DC: American Psychological Association.

Bass, B. M. (1985). Leadership: good, better, best. *Organizational Dynamics, 13*(3), 26–40.

Carli, L. L. (2001). Gender and social influence. *Journal of Social Issues, 57*(4), 725–741.

Chin, J. L. (2010). Introduction to the special issue on diversity and leadership. *American Psychologist, 65*(3), 150–156. doi: 10.1037/a0018716

Eagly, A. H., & Johannesen-Schmidt, M. C. (2001). The leadership styles of women and men. *Journal of Social Issues, 57*(4), 781–797.

Eagly, A. H., Johannesen-Schmidt, M. C., & van Engen, M. L. (2003). Transformational, transactional, and laissez-faire leadership styles: A meta-analysis comparing women and men. *Psychological Bulletin, 129*(4), 569–591. doi: 10.1037/0033–2909.129.4.569

Goleman, D. (1995). *Emotional intelligence: Why it can matter more than IQ.* New York, NY: Bantam Books.

Hollander, E. P. (2009). *Inclusive leadership. The essential leader-follower relationship.* New York, NY: Routledge

Mitchell, R. J., & Boyle, B. (2009). A theoretical model of transformational leadership's role in diverse teams. *Leadership & Organization Development Journal, 30*(5), 455–474. doi: 10.1108/01437730910968714

Sanchez-Hucles, J. V., & Davis, D. D. (2010). Women and women of color in leadership. *American Psychologist, 65*(3), 171–181. doi: 10.1037/a0017459

Sitkins, R. (2009). *Rough Notes, 152*(7), 12–15.

Yukle, G. (2009). *Leadership in organizations* (6th ed.). Upper Saddle River, NJ: Prentice Hall.

10

Empowering Women Leaders and Managers to Rise above Microaggressions in the Workplace: Recommendations for Workplaces, Families, and Everyday Life[1]

Kevin L. Nadal, Vanessa Meterko, Vivian M. Vargas, and Michelle Wideman

Case

Andrea is a 20-year-old Latina American woman who grew up in a working-class neighborhood in Brooklyn, New York. Her family consists of two immigrant parents (who were born and raised in Colombia) and a brother who is five years older than her. She is currently a sophomore at a local public four-year university, where she is taking classes in fashion merchandising and design. Her parents own a small bodega in their neighborhood which has been steady and secure over the past 15 years. Her older brother, Alex, recently graduated with a master's degree in business administration, and is currently working in an entry-level position in a Fortune 500 company in the financial district of Manhattan.

Ever since Andrea was a little girl, she dreamed of being a fashion designer who lived in a high-rise apartment building in New York City. She grew up watching television shows like *Girlfriends, Sex and the City,* and *Friends,* where she saw images of successful business women living the life she had always dreamed of. At the same time, she recognized that there were many obstacles that she would have to overcome in order to achieve the career she wanted. First, she knew that as a Latina woman, there were several gender role expectations that she was supposed to abide to because of her culture. She recognized that she was often encouraged to find a good husband and raise children, while her brother was encouraged to be successful in school and in his career. This lack of support from her parents became a major conflict for Andrea because she was not interested in having a husband or in maintaining traditional gender roles. While she would consider having children in the future, her main priority was her career and not becoming a homemaker.

Second, Andrea knew that the fashion industry was dominated by white/European Americans, and that there were very few Latinas who held higher leadership positions in the field. Her older brother Alex has been a great role model for her, and has shared with her all of the obstacles that he had to overcome in graduate school and in his current position. Although she recognizes that racism and sexism may still exist in present society, she remains optimistic that she can be successful and achieve her dream.

As part of her college requirements, Andrea is required to complete a part-time internship in the field of her choice. Because she is interested in fashion, she applies for a position with a small company that is run by a flourishing fashion designer. The designer, who also serves as the CEO of the company, is a 36-year-old white American man who graduated from a fashion institute over a decade ago. Since then, he has been trying to make a name for himself by actively designing collections and market them to small high-end boutique stores in the city. The staff also consists of two full-time assistants, both white American women in their late 20s who have been working with the designer for the past six years. Chris is another intern who was hired the same time that Andrea was; he is a white American man and is likely around Andrea's age.

When Andrea first begins her job, she is given an array of assignments, which includes everything from filing paperwork to cleaning up in the design room. While Andrea knows that these are very menial tasks, she recognizes that this is just a start for her and so she accepts things in stride. The other intern, Chris, is initially given the same types of tasks, likely because they have the same levels of experience. However, as time passes, Andrea starts to recognize that Chris is given more skilled assignments, while she is not. She tries not to make a big deal out of it, because she is still optimistic that she will have more opportunities in the future. However, weeks go by, Andrea notices that there aren't any changes to her situation; in fact, she observes that Chris has been working directly with the designer more often, and that Chris is often invited to sit in on meetings that she is not.

Andrea begins to feel very upset about the whole situation. She feels like she is being treated unfairly because of her race, her gender, her age, or some combination of them all. She talks with her brother about her situation and he validates her experiences by sharing that he has often been treated as an inferior at his job, likely due to his race and his age too. Andrea is conflicted because she needs this internship to graduate, and she doesn't want to be punished for speaking her mind to her supervisor or other coworkers. So, she decides to ignore the situation and continues to complete the tasks that she is given. However, she feels sad and disappointed because she knows that she has a lot of talent that she can contribute to the company. She begins to feel hopeless that she will not be able to achieve the career she had always dreamed of.

Introduction

This informal social pressure to curb overt displays of discrimination is strengthened by increased legal efforts to minimize and prevent discrimination, particularly in the workplace. For example, sexual harassment laws and policies have been created to prevent an intimidating and hostile work environment. Because such hostile environments have been found to interfere with women's work performance (U.S. Equal Employment Opportunity Commission, 2008), many companies and institutions have made efforts to minimize overt discrimination in the workplace by creating safe environments for their employees.

Despite these great strides, discrimination still exists in the United States, but instead may take more subtle forms (Nadal, 2008; Sue & Capodilupo, 2007). For example, when a woman clutches her purse a little tighter when she sees a black man approaching her, she is indirectly communicating that she is not comfortable with his presence and fears for her safety. Similarly, when a man stares at a woman's breasts as he speaks with her, he is indirectly sending the message that she is a sexual object and that he has a right to objectify her. Neither is using racist or sexist slurs to communicate hostile or overt biases toward to the individual. However, both communicate indirect messages that biases exist. These subtle forms of discrimination can occur based on one's race, ethnicity, gender, sexual orientation, or other social identity; in recent years, such instances have been labeled as *microaggressions*.

Microaggressions are "brief and commonplace daily verbal, behavioral, or environmental indignities, whether intentional or unintentional, that communicate hostile, derogatory, or negative slights and insults toward members of oppressed groups" (Nadal, 2008, p. 23). Microaggressions occur on a daily basis and are so subtle that even the victims themselves may not know if the incident was directed at them because of their race, gender, sexual orientation, religion or if it occurred because of some other reason. As a result, unlike the blatant racism prior to, and during, the civil rights movement, microaggressions become difficult to recognize and address. For example, in the first aforementioned example, the man may notice that in his presence the woman decided to hold on to her purse a little tighter. Upon seeing this action he may wonder the following internal monologue: "Is it my appearance? Is it because I am black? Is it because I am male? Or is it because this woman has been robbed in the past and now clutches her purse whenever anyone (of any race or gender) approaches her?"

In the second example, the woman may recognize that the man is staring at her breasts. She may be able to recognize that she is being objectified, but may not know how to handle it. She may wonder if he is conscious and aware of his behavior, she may be unsure of whether or how to confront him, and she may be cognizant that there is an array of possible consequences if she does say something (e.g., if he is her boss, she could potentially lose her job; if he is her coworker, she may know there would be future tension that she would rather not deal with). Regardless of the intention of the enactor of the microaggression, these commonplace incidents of microaggressions can have a cumulative and detrimental effect on the mental health of members of nonprivileged groups.

The brief, commonplace, and subtle nature of microaggressions pose unique challenges for perpetrators and recipients alike. In contrast to overt forms of discrimination (e.g., racial slurs, sexual harassment, hate crimes), enactors of microaggressions may not recognize their behaviors and recipients may be confused and invalidated by the ambiguity of a microaggression. For example, when a white woman tells a black woman, "You're so articulate," the white person may genuinely believe that she is complimenting the person of color. However, she may not realize that her statement might actually be implying her bias that all black women are uneducated and inarticulate. On the contrary, because this statement may not be overtly racist or malicious in intention, the black woman might question whether or not she is being discriminated against. She may feel hurt while also questioning whether or not she is being "too sensitive." If she chooses to confront the individual, the white woman may rationalize or provide an explanation for the microaggression (e.g., "I was honestly just complimenting you"), which may in turn invalidate the recipient's experience of racism.

One of the biggest challenges of microaggressions is that a clash of worldviews may hinder one's ability to recognize such events. An incident that is perceived as hurtful by one individual in one context may not be perceived as harmful by another individual in another context. Moreover, an interaction that is perceived as a microaggression by an individual of the dominant identity group (e.g., whites, men, upper class, heterosexual individuals) may not be perceived as such by those of marginalized groups (e.g., people of color, women, lower class, or lesbian, gay, bisexual, or transgender). While the complexity of microaggressions make it an elusive concept, recognizing their existence is the first step in stopping continued negative messages to various marginalized groups.

This chapter will describe the ways in which microaggressions affect the lives of women. Specifically, examples will focus on ways that microaggressions may manifest itself in the workplace, as well as the ways that microaggressions may influence women's work performance and leadership potential. The chapter will address microaggressions affecting women leaders in general, and then will concentrate on the particular challenges that confront women of color, lesbian and bisexual women, and transgender women. Finally, the chapter will discuss the psychological impact of these subtle acts of discrimination, the coping mechanisms that women use, and implications and recommendations for addressing microaggressions in the workplace and in everyday life.

Gender Microaggressions and Women

Women's rights campaigns have been making progress toward equality since major milestones in history, such as the 19th Amendment and the Civil Rights Act in 1964 (Nadal, 2010; Swim & Cohen, 1997; Swim, Hyers, Cohen, & Ferguson, 2001). Despite steadfast efforts toward an egalitarian society, gender discrimination and sexism still exist today. Blatant forms of sexism are becoming increasingly less common and even looked down upon by society. However, subtle forms of sexism have become more commonplace and are harder to distinguish. Swim and Cohen (1997) define blatant and overt sexism as intentional, visible, and unambiguous, harmful, and unfair treatment of women. These forms of sexism are often easier to identify and are likely to fit the criteria for sexual harassment: unwelcome sexual advances, requests for sexual favors, and other verbal or physical conduct of a sexual nature. On the contrary, subtle or covert sexism usually goes unnoticed because it has been hidden by cultural and society norms (Swim & Cohen, 1997). Subtle sexism often does not fit the criteria for sexual harassment, even though it creates hostile work environments and has negative consequences for women (Nadal, 2010). For example, a man who makes a stereotypical comment about women or who compliments a woman on her looks may not easily be defined as an unwelcome sexual advance or verbal conduct of a sexual nature. Thus, such behavior may not be reported or addressed and the behavior may continue.

Gender microaggressions are defined as "brief and commonplace daily verbal, behavioral, and environmental indignities that communicate hostile, derogatory, or negative sexist slights and insults toward women" (Nadal, 2010, p. 155). In a qualitative study, Capodilupo et al. (2010) found that female participants endorsed two main themes of gender microaggressions: *Sexual objectification* and *Assumption of traditional gender roles*. Sexual objectification at the workplace may be exemplified by a man who comments on a woman's outfit while staring at her body. While he may be intending to pay her a compliment, he is degrading her in the process. Additionally, women are often assumed to maintain traditional gender roles. For example, when a career-driven woman is asked why she never got married or had kids, an indirect message is communicated that a woman's primary role in life is to raise children. While one may assume that asking such a question is innocuous or harmless, the woman who experiences this frequently may feel that others do not value her life choices or career.

In Capodilupo et al.'s (2010) study, participants also reported other types of gender microaggressions: *Second-class citizen, Assumptions of inferiority, Denial of reality of sexism, Denial of individual sexism, Use of sexist language, Leaving gender at the door,* and *Environmental invalidations*. An example of second-class citizenship may include a group of male employees who never invite a female coworker to join them at sporting event after work. Perhaps they assume that women would not be interested in sports, but perhaps they also exclude her because she is not viewed as important or worthy of an invitation. Additionally, women are often assumed to be inferior to men (both physically and intellectually). For example, when a woman's ideas are dismissed at a meeting, while a man's are not, it is assumed that a man's opinions are more valuable than a woman's. Similarly, when women are assumed to need a man's help with carrying boxes, opening windows, or paying for their meals, a subtle message is communicated that all women need a man's help.

Denial of reality of sexism occurs when a man invalidates a woman's experiences with sexism by labeling her as "paranoid" or "oversensitive," while denial of individual sexism occurs when a man negates a woman who confronts him for perpetuating sexist acts. Sexist language occurs in both overt and covert forms; for example, jokes which belittle women may be more intentional and explicit. However, when a man calls a female coworker "sweetie" or "honey" while he does not use the same language with male coworkers, he is unintentionally treating her in a condescending manner. Women are often asked to "leave their genders at the door." This means that they are told (directly and indirectly) to not exhibit any feminine qualities (e.g., showing emotions) or complain about sexism. Finally, environmental microaggressions are instances where microaggressions are transmitted through systems, cultural norms, or the physical environment. For example, when a woman sees that there are very few women CEOs in the Fortune 500 companies or in government positions, an indirect message is transmitted that women are inferior or do not make good leaders. Moreover, when women are portrayed as sexual objects in the media, an indirect message is sent that women are allowed to be dehumanized or sexualized.

Gender microaggressions, whether intentional or unintentional, can have a lasting negative effect on women and their psychological well-being (Nadal, 2010). This negative effect can permeate every aspect of a woman's life, including her home life, her workplace, or her roles in society. Workplace discrimination and sexual harassment toward women may lead to reports of lower job satisfaction, and significant consequences for employee health like higher levels of anxiety and depression (Fitzgerald, Drasgow, Hulin, Gelfand, & Magley, 1997; Nadal, Hamit, Lyons, Weinberg, & Corman, in press). Moreover, stereotypes and discrimination can affect a woman's ability to excel in their careers (Sipe, Johnson, & Fisher, 2009). Thus, eliminating gender microaggressions and other forms of discrimination can have beneficial effects on the workplace environment, including improved morale, organizational commitment, and retention (Sipe, Johnson, & Fisher, 2009).

Racial Microaggressions and Women of Color

Previous literature has found that people of color are often the victims of racial microaggressions. Racial microaggressions are defined as "brief and commonplace daily verbal, behavioral, or environmental indignities, whether intentional or unintentional, that communicate hostile, derogatory, or negative racial slights and insults to the target person or group" (Sue, Capodilupo et al., 2007, p. 273). As with gender microaggressions, several categories of racial microaggressions have been identified: *Alien in one's own land, Ascription of intelligence, Color blindness, Criminality/Assumption of criminal status, Denial of individual racism, Myth of meritocracy, Pathologizing cultural values/communication styles, Second class citizen,* and *Environmental microaggressions* (Sue, Capodilupo et al., 2007). Many of these categories have been validated through research with African Americans (Sue et al., 2008), Latinos (Rivera, Forquer, & Rangel, 2010), and Asian Americans (Sue, Bucceri, Lin, Nadal, & Torino, 2007).

Alien in one's own land refers to instances where individuals are treated like foreigners, even though their family may have been in the United States for many generations; this can be exemplified by an employer telling an Asian

American person that she "speaks good English" when she was born and raised in the United States and English is the only language she knows. Ascription of intelligence occurs when people assume others to have a certain intellectual capacity because of their race. For example, an employer who asks an Asian American employee to help fix a computer (who has indicated in no way that he is computer-savvy) may indicate the individual's biases or stereotypes about Asian Americans. This may be contrary to aforementioned examples of individuals assuming that African Americans are intellectually inferior or un-educated. Colorblindness may refer to instances when individuals make statements like "I don't see color" or "there is only one race—the human race." While these comments may be meant to be egalitarian sentiments, they indirectly invalidate the reality that the person of color is a racial and cultural being and that racism does exist in her or his life. Additionally, people of color are often assumed to be criminals, as exemplified by the aforementioned example of a woman holding her purse as a black man enters an elevator. But another example may include a person of color who is followed around in a store, or a police officer pulling over a person of color for not doing anything wrong. While no one in these scenarios are using racist language or overtly discriminating the people of color in these cases, all of these experiences subtly communicate negative stereotypes about people of color

The denial of individual racism occurs when an individual claims that she or he is racist, after someone confronts her or him on one's potentially racist behavior. The Myth of Meritocracy occurs when someone believes that anyone can succeed if they work hard enough. This belief suggests that if a person of color is not succeeding at work (e.g., not getting promoted), it must be due to laziness or a lack of effort on their part rather than to a systematic lack of social privilege. Pathologizing cultural values or communication styles occurs when individuals are expected to conform to White norms because their ways of doing things are unacceptable or inferior. For example, because assertiveness is an American value, it is expected that all individuals must utilize this communication style in the workplace; contrarily, while passivity may be viewed as a value in other cultures, it would be discouraged or viewed as substandard in many workplace settings. Finally, environmental microaggressions occur when cultural systems or the physical environment send negative messages to people of color. For example, seeing stereotypes of racial/ethnic minority groups on television or seeing a lack of people of color in leadership positions may send denigrating messages to individuals of those groups.

Women of color may experience microaggressions that may occur due to their gender, their race, or some combination of them all. For example, Latina and Asian American women have often reported that they feel exoticized because of both their race and gender (Rivera et al., 2010; Sue, Bucceri, et al, 2007). African American women have reported experiencing workplace microaggressions involving their hair (Sue, Nadal, et al., 2008). Specifically, many African American women have been told (explicitly and implicitly) that their hair was either "unprofessional" or "unique" and sometimes are even asked if someone could touch their hair. All of these types of microaggressions have negative implications. An African American woman who is told that her hairstyle is unprofessional is indirectly being told that she needs to conform to white norms and have a hairstyle similar to white women. Contrarily, an African American woman who is told that her hair is "unique" or asked if someone could touch her hair is implicitly being exoticized or treated like an object.

When women of color experience microaggressions, they may often question if the incident is occurring because of their race, their gender, or both. For example, when a male employer continually compliments an Asian American woman on her looks, is he treating her like a sexual object because of her race, her gender, or both? When an African American woman is overlooked for a job promotion, it is because of her race, her gender, or both? Again, it may difficult to fully answer these questions because the enactors may not recognize their behavior and sometimes may even be well intentioned. The man who continually calls attention to the Asian American woman's looks may genuinely believe that he is complimenting her, while the employer who overlooked the African American woman for a job promotion may genuinely believe there were other factors as to why she wasn't the best candidate. Nonetheless, either of these situations may leave the woman of color to feel confused, invalidated, frustrated, or saddened. As a result, these women experience discrimination that is different than their white female counterparts who only experience sexism, as well as their men of color counterparts who only experience racism. Because of this, the stress of being a "double minority" may have significant impacts on her self-esteem, her mental health, and her performance in the workplace.

Sexual Orientation Microaggressions and Lesbian and Bisexual Women

Lesbian, gay, and bisexual (LGB) individuals have been criminalized, victimized, and marginalized throughout the history of the United States. Records indicate that men were executed for the act of sodomy in colonial America as early as 1624 (Herek, 1989). In contemporary times, hate crimes toward LGB people have continued to be on the rise; while the number of hate crimes based on race has been on the decline, hate crimes based on sexual orientation have increased over the past several years (Federal Bureau of Investigation [FBI], 2008). And while these numbers are still high, it is also important to recognize that many hate crimes based on sexual orientation are underreported, which means that the number of LGB hate crimes in the United States may even be higher (Herek, 2000). However, much like sexism and racism, discrimination toward LGB persons may also take on more subtle forms. Nadal, Rivera, and Corpus (2010) outline seven recurring types of microaggressions against LGB individuals: *Use of heterosexist terminology* (e.g., people using the word "gay" to describe something negative), *Endorsement of heteronormative culture/behaviors* (e.g., LGB individuals feeling pressured to appear heterosexual in order to be considered professional), *Assumption of universal LGB experience* (e.g., others assuming that all LGB people fit into a neat stereotype or that one LGB person can speak for the entire community), *Exoticization* (e.g., others glamorizing or objectifying lesbian and bisexual women as sex symbols or gay men as comedic relief), *Discomfort/ disapproval of LGB experience* (e.g., LGB people receiving disapproving stares from strangers when out in public with their partners), *Denial of the reality of heterosexism* (e.g., a person denying that they treat LGB people any differently than they treat heterosexual people), and finally *Assumption of sexual pathology/ abnormality* (e.g., instances when LGB individuals are cast as overly sexual or sexually deviant).

There are many ways that lesbian and bisexual women experience these microaggressions twofold because the intersections of their identities. Lesbian and bisexual women have reported experiencing a variety of these types of microaggressions in the workplace, even at jobs that they describe as "gay friendly" (Giuffre, Dellinger, & Williams, 2008). These experiences have the potential to lead lesbian and bisexual women to have ambivalent or negative feelings about themselves, coworkers, their work environment, or some combination of them all. In some instances, encountering and addressing these issues directly has also been shown to facilitate learning about different groups of people in the workplace (Giuffre et al., 2008).

An example of a sexual orientation microaggression in the workplace would be a coworker asking a bisexual woman personal questions about her dating life, her sex life, or her pregnancy (if applicable). While these questions may be well-meaning or may arise out of curiosity, and while some bisexual women may not mind "teaching" their heterosexual coworkers about bisexuality, others may feel singled out because other women in the workplace do not have to field such personal questions. The woman may also feel pressure to speak on behalf of all bisexuals or act as role model to disprove negative stereotypes about lesbians and bisexuals (Giuffre et al., 2008).

Another example of a sexual orientation microaggression in the workplace involves the stereotype that LGB people embody characteristics of the opposite gender (e.g., gay men are considered feminine and lesbian women are considered masculine). This stereotype encourages a unique type of discrimination in the workplace. For instance, a lesbian woman who worked at a "gay-friendly" but male dominated company reported feeling uncomfortable when the men in the office made sexually crude comments about other women in her presence. She felt that because she was attracted to women, the men treated her as "one of the boys" and expected her to participate in the sexist objectification of other women, or at least to be less offended than a heterosexual woman might be (Giuffre et al., 2008).

A final example of a sexual orientation microaggression in the workplace is the case of a married lesbian woman working in Massachusetts who is reassigned to work in another state. The woman's heterosexual boss may not have considered the fact that her employee's legal same-sex marriage in Massachusetts would no longer be recognized as such once she relocated to another state, like California or Florida. This oversight may not be malicious, and the woman's boss may simply assume that there is little difference between one coastal city and another. However, by assuming that geography plays no part in the life of a lesbian employee, the employer indicates that she is not mindful of continued discrimination against LGB persons.

While more employees and employers are open about their sexual orientations than in years past, there is still variability in the degree of openness at work ranging from explicit openness to lying in order to be perceived as heterosexual (Croteau, 1996). This continued hesitance to disclose sexual orientation at work and fear of discrimination may stem from the overt and covert discrimination that out lesbian and bisexual women still experience. In addition to being subject to the already well-documented gender-based discrimination in the workplace (e.g., lower pay for equal work, the proverbial "glass ceiling" and the lack of accommodation of motherhood at work), lesbian and bisexual women face unique types of discrimination in the workplace. From being the only woman in the office subjected to repeated probing questions about her personal life to being inappropriately treated as one of the boys, bisexual and lesbian women continue to face sexual orientation microaggressions in the workplace.

Transgender Microaggressions and Women of Transgender Experience

The word *transgender* is considered an "umbrella term" and is used to describe people who do not conform to traditional gender roles, including transgenderists, drag queens, cross-dressers, and transsexuals (Kenagy, 2002). People of transgender experience can identify as male-to-female (MTF) or female-to-male (FTM). The former is a person who was assigned the male gender at birth but who identifies as female and the latter is a person who was assigned the female gender at birth but who identifies as male (Kenagy, 2002). Individuals in the process of transitioning from one gender to another may identify as entirely female or entirely male, both female and male, or neither (Koken, Bimbi, & Parsons, 2009). Because American society sees sex and gender roles as "inherently immutable" it is difficult for some to accept others who do not fall into a simple male or female category (Kidd & Witten, 2007/2008). As such, *transwomen* or women of transgender experience are frequently socially marginalized and persistently stigmatized because of the way they live their lives. Some have argued that the inclusion of gender identity disorder in the *Diagnostic and Statistical Manual of Mental Disorders, Fourth Edition (DSM-IV)*, has only added to the discrimination and condemnation faced by this group on a daily basis (Koken et al., 2009).

As *gender nonconformists*, transwomen are often the victims of hate crimes and especially targeted because they are generally seen as men who are acting effeminate (Koken et al., 2009; Wilchins, 2008). Transwomen often provoke disgust and hate in those who wish to see "their kind" annihilated; this prejudice and hatred often results in especially brutal hate crimes (Kidd & Witten, 2007/2008). It is often believed that there is an underlying desire in these perpetrators "to eradicate the transgender-identified individual in order to alleviate his/her disgust and to avenge the sense of betrayal that precipitated the attack" (Kidd & Witten, 2007/2008, p. 34). Due to this overwhelming violence and palpable discrimination, many in the transgender community prefer to remain silent; thus, transgender people are slowly and collectively becoming an invisible minority ignored by many in law enforcement (Kidd & Witten, 2007/2008; Wilchins, 2008).

As gender nonconformists, transwomen face an exorbitant number of challenges on a daily basis. For individuals in society who are not familiar with members of the transgender community, "oohs" and "ahs" are frequent reactions along with questions of "why" and "how" with unsatisfactory answers. For example, many individuals ask invasive and private questions to transgender individuals about their body parts or their sexual activities (Nadal, Skolnick, & Wong, under review). Because of this, many transwomen are unable to live "normal" lives, often encountering everything from stares, snickers, and insults to outright hostility, rejection and aggression. Transgender individuals also deal with everything from rejection by family to denial of employment to limited educational opportunities (Leichtentritt & Davidson Arad, 2004; Sausa, Keatley, & Operario, 2007). Because of the limited literature about the transgender community, most members of society need to be educated about this community, in order to provide safer and more welcoming environments for them.

Nadal, Skolnick, and Wong (under review) utilized focus groups with transgender women and men and found that there are several categories of microaggressions that are directed toward transgender individuals. These categories include: *Use of transphobic language* (e.g., calling individuals by incorrect pronouns or using transphobic slurs), *Endorsement of gender-normative/binary culture/behaviors* (e.g., assuming that men and women should dress a certain way), *Assumption of universal transgender experience* (e.g., assuming that all transgender persons desire hormone treatment or reassignment surgery), *Exocitization* (e.g., staring at transgender in awe or scrutiny), *Discomfort/disapproval of transgender experience* (e.g., peering at a transgender person with condemnation), *Denial of reality of transphobia* (e.g., invalidating a transgender person's experiences of discrimination), *Assumption of sexual pathology/ abnormality* (e.g., stereotyping transgender people to all HIV/AIDS or to be sex workers), *Denial of individual transphobia* (e.g., denying one's own transphobic biases), *Denial of personal body privacy* (e.g., asking a transgender person inappropriate questions about her or his body parts), and *Systemic and environmental microaggressions* (e.g., transphobic microaggressions that occur in the media, government, policies, and other institutions).

There are many ways that transgender microaggressions may occur in the workplace—on both systemic and interpersonal levels. A common example of an environmental/systemic microaggression includes how buildings usually have both a women's restroom and a men's restroom, but not a unisex option. This forced choice may cause a transgender employee to feel unwelcome or abnormal because they do not define themselves in such dichotomous terms. Moreover, when transgender individuals are transitioning from one gender to another, they may not feel comfortable using one bathroom over the other, or may be chastised in using the restroom of the gender they identify with (e.g., a transgender woman may want to use the women's restroom, but security guards may not let her). Another environmental transgender microaggression may involve a transgender employee who might also feel like a second-class citizen when she or he notices that there are no transgender CEOs or leaders within her or his company. This conspicuous absence sends the message that transgender people are invisible, less powerful, or less valued than those who endorse gender normative behaviors and identify with their biological sex.

Transgender microaggressions can also transpire through interpersonal interactions. For example, some transgender individuals report that coworkers repeatedly call them by the incorrect pronoun despite the fact that they had openly clarified their preferred gender pronoun on several occasions. When coworkers reply with "I don't even know what to call you" or continue to call the transgender person by her or his biological name and not by her or his preferred name, they are sending the message that the person's transgender experience is not valid or important. Again, although this may be explained away as confusion or carelessness, repeated microaggressions like these send the message that the transgender employee is abnormal and not worth respecting.

Women's Coping with Microaggressions

Some researchers have suggested specific actions to combat these types of subtle discrimination and create more accepting and productive work environments (see Sue, 2010 for a review). When individuals are the victims or recipients of microaggressions, there are several thought processes that may occur. Some authors have identified a "Catch 22" of whether or not they should react (Nadal et al., in press; Sue, Capodilupo et al., 2007). If they do choose to respond to the microaggression, there is a potential of endangering their physical or psychological safety. For example, if a drunken man makes sexist remarks toward a woman at a bar, she may simply choose to ignore the statements because she worries that if she starts an argument with him that he may potentially become violent. Thus, she may choose to avoid controversy and ignore him altogether in order to protect herself.

Psychological safety may be a more salient factor for addressing microaggressions in workplace settings. For instance, when a woman hears a sexist remark made by a coworker in the workplace, she has a difficult task of determining whether or not to respond. Because the remark is made by a coworker, she realizes that saying something may lead to tension between her and the individual. This tension may lead to an uncomfortable work environment, which may then negatively influence her behavior and work performance. Moreover, she may want to avoid confronting him because she does not want to be seen as "oversensitive" and does not want any hard feelings to affect her reputation or opportunities within her company. Thus, she may feel it would be easier for her to not respond at all.

However, for individuals who do not respond to microaggressions when they transpire, there are a myriad of physical and psychological consequences that may occur (Nadal et al., in press). For example, in the above illustration of the intoxicated man who makes a sexist remark at the bar, a woman may regret not saying anything to the man. While at the time, she may have been worried about her safety, upon leaving the situation, she may feel disempowered for not being able to voice her opinion. She may also feel regret and worry that he will continue to make sexist remarks to other women, making her feel guilty that she should have something to teach him a lesson. Thinking about what she "should have" or "could have" said may lead the woman to perseverate about the situation, which may then impact her self-esteem and may even negatively other aspects of her life.

Nadal et al. (in press) cite the emotional, behavioral, and cognitive reactions that women may experience in response to microaggressions. Women may experience various emotions that remain internalized (e.g., guilt, humiliation, and discomfort), as well as those that have been externalized and communicated to others (e.g., anger and fear). Women may utilize different behavioral techniques in response to microaggressions. Some women may remain passive and choose not to confront the enactor of the microaggression, while others attempt to protect themselves by actively engaging in behaviors that would make them less susceptible. For example, many women report that they walk in large groups in order to avoid being catcalled or bothered by men. Finally, women report many ways that they react cognitively to microaggressions: some become more resilient, others learn to accept microaggressions as a norm in society, and others have actively resisted microaggressions.

Finally, women of intersectional identities may cope with microaggressions in other ways. For example, Sue, Capodilupo, and Holder (2008) discuss how African Americans may deal with microaggressions. In a study with mostly female participants, many individuals report that they need a *sanity check,* in which they contact a friend or family member to confirm if their feelings and perceptions of a microaggression are valid. Moreover, this sanity check allows for these individuals to process their feelings in a safe and healing environment where they can feel validated and where they can be genuine without appearing to be an "angry minority." It is likely that women and other marginalized groups may also utilize this sanity check, in order to validate their perceptions and reactions to potential microaggressions and to verify that their reactions to microaggressions are legitimate.

Case Study Discussion

To better demonstrate how microaggressions may manifest and how it may affect women's leadership, it will be helpful to examine the case of Andrea—the young Latina woman who feels like she is not given opportunities for growth in her company. Andrea observes that she is the only woman of color in the small company she works for, and that her peer (who is white and male) is given much more leadership opportunities than she is, even though they have the same amount of work experience, talent, and leadership potential. Andrea is distressed by the entire situation and does not know how to address the situation. First of all, because she is only an intern in the company, she may feel like she does not have any power or right to say anything. She may also worry that somehow her internship will be jeopardized, which will then affect her ability to graduate in a timely manner. Also, because she is the only woman of color in the company, she runs the risk of being seen as "oversensitive" or the "angry minority" because it is possible that others will invalidate that race plays any part in the situation. Thus, she may choose to not say anything to her employer or fellow coworkers because she perceives that the cost of potentially damaging her role in the company would outweigh the benefit of feeling validated and being given more opportunities.

While Andrea appears to experience microaggressions in the workplace, it is also apparent that she may also experience microaggressions within her family. Throughout her life, her parents have encouraged her to maintain traditional gender roles, which meant that her brother, Alex, was pushed to receive his education so he could provide for his future family, while she was persuaded to engage in traditionally feminine activities so that she could become a good mother, wife, and homemaker. When Andrea tells her parents that she wants to continue her education and become a business woman, they are mildly supportive, but they would prefer for her to concentrate on her family and not on her career.

Given that Andrea comes from a Latino/Colombian family, there are many cultural factors that may influence how she deals with these microaggressions. Because of the traditional Latino gender roles of *machismo* (i.e., male dominance and males as providers) and *marianismo* (i.e., female submissiveness and women as self-sacrificing caretakers), Andrea may have difficulty in speaking back to her parents or explicitly telling them how she feels about their expectations. If she decides to argue with them each time they expect her to maintain traditional gender roles, she may be viewed as disrespectful toward authority figures, which is a big taboo in Latino culture. Moreover, if she continues to reject their gender role expectations, she may be viewed as being too "Americanized" which may also lead to further tension in her relationship with her parents. Given all of these factors, Andrea may decide that she should "pick and choose her battles" with her parents. She may want to speak her voice every once in a while, so that she doesn't feel disempowered as a woman, but she may want to withhold her feelings from them once in a while, in order to remain respectful of them and honor cultural traditions.

Regardless of how Andrea actually decides to respond to each situation (and future encounters) of microaggressions, it may be necessary that she has a support group to help her to cope with these experiences. Within her workplace, because she is the only woman of color, it may be difficult for her to confide in her coworkers about her perceptions of subtle racism in the company. As a result, it may be viewed as a healthy decision that she has chosen to share her situation with her brother, who can validate that racism and other forms of discrimination still occur in workplace settings. Perhaps she can also confide in other friends and family members who may be able to provide her with support, while also being a "sanity check" that she needs to process her perceptions and her feelings. It may be important for Andrea to have a similar type of support system to deal with the microaggressions that occur in her family. Perhaps a woman in the extended family (e.g., a female cousin, a career-oriented aunt, etc.) may be able to provide her with the space to vent or express her feelings when she feels frustrated, hurt, or exhausted by the microaggressions she experiences at home. And although her brother is not a woman, he may serve as an ally who can address microaggressions in the family and serve as a middle person who can help their parents understand how their actions affect her.

Finally, through examining the case of Andrea, one can notice the negative impacts that microaggressions may have on women's leadership and work performance. Because her parents encourage her to maintain traditional gender roles, her capacity to continue school and enter the career field of her choice may be hindered. Thus, she may not have been encouraged to reach her full potential as a leader in her school settings and now in the workplace. Moreover, because of her parents' minimal support, she may feel isolated and may not feel able to talk with them about her problems at work. As a result, when she does experience microaggressions at her job, she may not have a support system to deal with them at home, which may then affect her mental health and her work performance.

In the workplace itself, experiences with microaggressions may have a direct impact on Andrea's leadership potential and career opportunities. Because women are often viewed as intellectual inferiors or second-class citizens in the workplace, employers and institutions may not even be aware that women are not encouraged to succeed in the same ways that men are. For example, it is a well-known fact that women earn 70–75 cents for every dollar that a man makes. It can be argued that this is not a conscious decision on the part of every employer or human resources office. Rather, it can be argued that it is the unconscious bias held by institutions and employers that allows individuals to pay women less, even though they work just as hard (or harder) in the same type of positions as these men.

Recommendations for Women's Leadership

In order to prevent microaggressions toward women (and other marginalized groups) and to promote women leaders in society, there are many changes that can be recommended for workplace settings, families, and in everyday life.

Although sexual harassment laws and policies are established and enforced in most states, microaggressions must also be discussed in workplace settings because sexual harassment laws and policies do not protect against subtle forms of discrimination. For example, because many microaggressions are so subtle and seemingly innocuous, it would be difficult for individuals to contend these instances in court. As a result, many workplace microaggressions are underreported because women and other marginalized persons do not feel that reporting such instances will lead to positive outcomes. Specifically, workplaces can implement many programs and policies to prevent or minimize microaggressions altogether. Some examples include:

1. Integrating microaggressions into human resources diversity training programs. By discussing that subtle forms of discrimination is harmful in the same way that sexual harassment and overt discrimination is, the company is communicating that it is intolerant of discrimination and that they promote culturally competent work environments.

2. Incorporating microaggressions into sexual harassment policies and procedures. In the same ways that employees are informed about sexual harassment policies upon hiring, they should also be educated about microaggressions and subtle forms of discrimination. Again, this will serve as a way of promoting multiculturalism and social justice within the company.

3. Creating safe environments where individuals can feel comfortable in discussing issues of race, gender, sexual orientation, and culture in the workplace. By being able to discuss cultural influences on communication styles, power dynamics, and other factors, institutions allow opportunities for individuals to address microaggressions as they occur. In doing so, individuals may feel more "safe," which would then lead to more productive working environments.

For families, there are many ways that individuals can address microaggressions in order to promote women's leadership and growth. However, one difficulty with addressing microaggressions in family systems is the complexity of family dynamics, gender roles, and culture. Each family is different because of their individual structures (e.g., whether it is a single-parent home, a two-parent home, or a home with guardians), gender roles (e.g., how much a family abides by traditional gender roles in behaviors, household chores, career choices, etc.), and culture (e.g., how one's ethnic and cultural values impact how individuals communicate, behave, and perceive each other). Despite these unique factors, there are several ways that families of all kinds can promote women's leadership and minimize or prevent microaggressions:

1. Teaching one's children about culture from an early age and encourage all children to succeed regardless of their gender, race, age, or social class. Doing so will allow children to develop a healthy self-esteem, which will hopefully lead to self-confidence, a good work ethic, and capacity for leadership.

2. Helping children to understand the obstacles that may hinder their success, due to their gender, race, age, social class, or other identities. Some individuals may believe that social justice issues should not be taught to children because they fear that it will confuse them or taint their innocence. However, teaching them in small ways about social justice at early ages can help them to be prepared to deal with discrimination when they face it as adults. Sometimes, adults have difficulty discussing issues of race, gender, and culture because they never learned to language to discuss it in their formative years. Teaching children how to do so in their early years will hopefully allow them the comfort in discussing such issues as adults.

3. Being aware of one's biases about gender and gender role expectations. In maintaining such awareness, individuals can be cognizant of how these biases affect the ways they encourage (or discourage) their children from engaging in behaviors or activities, as well as making career choices and striving for success.

In terms of everyday life, there are many ways that microaggressions can be minimized or diminished altogether. School systems can teach students about social justice issues from an early age and even well into adolescence. Religious institutions must be aware of ways that they perpetuate rigid roles, particularly in hindering women's leadership; perhaps changes can be made to empower women in a way that may not completely disregard tradition. The media must be more responsible regarding the sexist images that they portray about women, as well as the negative and stereotypical images they also portray of various racial/ethnic groups, LGBT people, and other socio-cultural groups. Positive images and role models of women, including women of color, LGB women, and transgender women will help to dispel stereotypes and negative assumptions about these groups. Government policies should reflect women's rights and encourage women to become leaders in all sectors; thus, perhaps this will foster more women's leadership and result in more women as elected officials. Finally, individuals must be cognizant of their interpersonal interactions, and how gender and other cultural identities may influence relationships. When microaggression inevitably occur, it would be important for individuals to discuss such instances, in order to foster continued awareness and serve as "teachable moments" for continued personal growth.

Note

1. Portions of this chapter were published in M. Paludi and B. Coates (Eds.), *Women as Transformational Leaders* (Westport, CT: Praeger, 2011). This chapter is reprinted here with permission from Praeger, Westport, CT.

References

Capodilupo, C. M., Nadal, K. L., Corman, L., Hamit, S., Lyons, O., & Weinberg, A. (2010). The manifestation of gender microaggressions. In D. W. Sue (Ed.), *Microaggressions and marginality: Manifestation, dynamics, and impact.* New York: Wiley.

Croteau, J. M. (1996). Research on the work experiences of lesbian, gay, and bisexual people: An integrative review of methodology and findings. *Journal of Vocational Behavior, 48,* 195–209.

Federal Bureau of Investigation (FBI). (2008). *Hate crime statistics, 2007.* Washington, DC: Author. Retrieved from http://www.fbi.gov/ucr/hc2007/index.html

Fitzgerald, L. F., Drasgow, F., Hulin, C. L., Gelfand, M. J., & Magley, V. J. (1997). Antecedents and consequences of sexual harassment in organizations: A test of an integrated model. *Journal of Applied Psychology, 82,* 578–589.

Giuffre, P., Dellinger, K., & Williams, C. L. (2008). No retribution for being gay? Inequality in gay-friendly workplaces. *Sociological Spectrum, 28,* 254–277.

Herek, G. M. (1989). Hate crimes against lesbians and gay men: Issues for research and policy. *American Psychologist, 44,* 948–955.

Herek, G. M. (2000). The psychology of sexual prejudice. *Current Directions in Psychological Science, 9,* 19–22.

Kenagy, G. (2002). HIV among transgendered people. *AIDS Care, 14,* 127–134.

Kidd, J. D., & Witten, T. M. (2007/2008). Transgender and trans sexual identities: The next strange fruit-hate crimes. Violence and genocide against the global trans-communities. *Journal of Hate Studies, 6,* 31–63.

Koken, J. A., Bimbi, D. S., & Parsons, J. T. (2009). Experiences of familial acceptance-rejection among transwomen of color. *Journal of Family Psychology, 23,* 853–860.

Leichtentritt, R. D., & Davidson Arad, B. (2004). Adolescent and young adult male-to-female transsexuals: Pathways to prostitution. *British Journal of Social Work, 34,* 349–374.

Nadal, K. L. (2008). Preventing racial, ethnic, gender, sexual minority, disability, and religious microaggressions: Recommendations for promoting positive mental health. *Prevention in Counseling Psychology: Theory, Research, Practice and Training, 2,* 22–27.

Nadal, K. L. (2010). Gender microaggressions and women: Implications for mental health. In M. A. Paludi (Ed.), *Feminism and women's rights worldwide,* Vol. 2: *Mental and physical health* (pp. 155–175). Westport, CT: Praeger.

Nadal, K. L., Hamit, S., Lyons, O., Weinberg, A., & Corman, L. (in press). Gender microaggressions: Perceptions, processes, and coping mechanisms of women. In M. A. Paludi (Ed), *Managing diversity in today's workplace.* Westport, CT: Praeger.

Nadal, K. L., Rivera, D. P., & Corpus, M. J. H. (2010). Sexual orientation and transgender microaggressions in everyday life: Experiences of lesbians, gays, bisexuals, and transgender individuals. In D. W. Sue (Ed.), *Microaggressions and marginality: Manifestation, dynamics, and impact* (pp. 217–240). New York: Wiley.

Rivera, D. P., Forquer, E. E., & Rangel, R. (2010). Microaggressions and the life experience of Latina/o Americans. In D. W. Sue (Ed.), *Microaggressions and marginalized groups in society: Race, gender, sexual orientation, class and religious manifestations* (pp. 59–83). New York: Wiley.

Sausa, L. A., Keatley, J., & Operario, D. (2007). Perceived risks and benefits of sex work among transgender women of color in San Francisco. *Archives of Sexual Behavior, 36,* 768–777.

Sipe, S., Johnson, D. C., & Fisher, D. K. (2009). University students' perceptions of gender discrimination in the workplace: Reality versus fiction. *Journal of Education for Business, 84,* 339–349.

Sue, D. W. (2010). *Microaggressions in everyday life: Race, gender, and sexual orientation.* New York: Wiley.

Sue, D. W., Bucceri, J. M., Lin, A. I., Nadal, K. L., & Torino, G. C. (2007). Racial microaggressions and the Asian American experience. *Cultural Diversity and Ethnic Minority Psychology, 13,* 72–81.

Sue, D. W., & Capodilupo, C. M. (2008). Racial, gender, and sexual orientation microaggressions: Implications for counseling and psychotherapy. In D. W. Sue & D. Sue (Eds.), *Counseling the culturally diverse* (5th ed.). New York: Wiley.

Sue, D. W., Capodilupo, C. M., & Holder, A. M. B. (2008). Racial microaggressions in the life experience of black Americans. *Professional Psychology: Research and Practice, 39*(3), 329–336.

Sue, D. W., Capodilupo, C. M., Torino, G. C., Bucceri, J. M., Holder, A.M., Nadal, K. L., & Esquilin, M. E. (2007). Racial microaggressions in everyday life: Implications for counseling. *The American Psychologist, 62,* 271–286.

Sue, D. W., Nadal, K. L., Capodilupo, C. M., Lin, A. I., Rivera, D. P., & Torino, G. C. (2008). Racial microaggressions against black Americans: Implications for counseling. *Journal of Counseling and Development, 86,* 330–338.

Swim, J. K., & Cohen, L. L. (1997). Overt, covert, and subtle sexism: A comparison between the attitudes toward women and modern sexism scales. *Psychology of Women Quarterly, 21,* 103–118.

Swim, J. K., Hyers, L. L., Cohen, L. L., & Ferguson, M. J. (2001). Everyday sexism: Evidence for its incidence, nature, and psychological impact from three daily diary studies. *Journal of Social Issues, 57,* 31–53.

U.S. Equal Employment Opportunity Commission. (2008). *Sexual harassment.* Retrieved from http://www.eeoc.gov/types/sexual_harassment.html

Wilchins, R. (2008). An invisible war. *Advocate, 1005,* 33.

We must not, in trying to think about how we can make a big difference, ignore the small daily difference we can make which, over time, add up to big differences that we often cannot foresee.

—Marion Wright Edelman
Children's Defense Fund

I never did anything alone. Whatever was accomplished in this country was accomplished collectively.

—Golda Meir

Somewhere out in this audience may even be someone who will one day follow in my footsteps, and preside over the White House as the President's spouse. I wish him well.

—Barbara Pierce Bush; Remarks at
Wellesley College commencement

International Insights on Women and Transformational Leadership[1]

Florence L. Denmark, Jessica B. Brodsky, and Shanna T. German

Dimensions/Elements of Transformational Leadership

Transformational leaders have a specific vision about an organization. They further their followers' goals by creating mutual interests between individuals. In so doing, they provide employees with a sense of purpose and feeling of family. As leaders incorporate transformational features into their management style, followers develop intrinsic motivation and increased long-term commitment to the company. Furthermore, research suggests that leadership style is a relatively stable trait in individuals (Eagly, Johannesen-Schmidt, & van Engen, 2003). Bass and his colleagues (Bass, 1998; Bass & Avolio, 1994a) have condensed transformational leadership qualities into the four Is:

- *Idealized Influence*—Leaders are role models to their followers by displaying consistency in portraying high moral and ethical standards.

  Key features: proud, respectful, trusting, risk taking, dependable

- *Inspirational Motivation*—Leaders enhance motivation from their followers by providing them with meaningful and challenging work. In turn, a shared vision is generated.

  Key features: enthusiastic, optimistic, visionary, empowering

- *Intellectual Stimulation*—Leaders encourage creativity and innovation from their followers in order to undertake old problems in new ways.

  Key features: nurturing, challenging, approachable, innovative

- *Individualized Consideration*—Leaders carefully account for individual followers' needs for achievement and growth through open communication.

  Key features: empathic, supportive, respectful, communicative, attentive good listener

Transformational vs. Transactional Leadership

In conjunction with transformational leadership, Burns (1978) recognized transactional leadership as a second style of interaction in an organization. Transactional leadership involves the exchanging of work for reward, without the aspiration of a greater, shared goal. It emphasizes the transaction between the leader and the follower. Research has indicated that through this type of leadership style, commitments are short-term with individual self-interests in mind, motivation to work being contingent upon a reward (Contingent-reward), job assignments explicit, rules followed, and relationships contractual (Bass & Avolio, 1993, 1994b).

Geijsel, Sleegers, and van den Berg (1999) contest that although "transactional leadership fosters the *basic* needs of followers," transactional leadership is dependent upon transformational leadership. Moreover, these authors consider while transactional leadership is "generally sufficient to maintain the status quo . . . in order to achieve change and innovation; however, transformational leadership is necessary to 'motivate others to do more than they originally intended and often even more than they thought possible'" (p. 310).

Measuring Leadership

The most widely utilized tool to measure transformational and transactional leadership is the Multifactor Leadership Questionnaire (MLQ Form 5X; Bass & Avolio, 1991). The MLQ-5X is a multiple rater survey consisting of questions in which items are evaluated on a 5-point Likert scale ranging from 0 (not at all) to 4 (frequently, if not always). The MLQ-5X is completed by individuals and their superiors, contemporaries, and/or subordinates to assess leadership behaviors. The MLQ-5X consists of six dimensions based on a factor model analysis (Avolio, Bass, & Jung, 1999). The six factors include: Charisma/Inspiration, Intellectual Stimulation, Individualized Consideration, Contingent Reward, Active Management-by-Exception, and Passive-Avoidant Leadership. The MLQ-5X is used all over the world and has been translated into nearly thirty languages (Mind Garden, 2009).

Other leadership measures utilized to assess leadership in the field are the Leadership Practices Inventory (LPI; Kouzes & Posner, 1990) and the Global Transformational Leadership Scale (GTL; Carless, Wearing, & Mann, 2000). The LPI assesses five leadership behaviors consisting of six items each. The leadership practice identified are: Challenging the Process, Inspiring a Shared Vision, Enabling Others to Act, Modeling the Way and Encouraging the Heart. The GTL is a short measure to evaluate transformational leadership through seven items. It focuses on the extent to which leaders are visionary, innovative, supportive, participative, and worthy of respect. Both the LPI and the GTL are less frequently administered to assess leadership qualities in comparison to the MLQ-5X.

Transformational Leadership and Women

In his 20-year review of worldwide research on transformational leadership, Bass (1999) concluded that women "tend to be somewhat more transformational than their male counterparts" (p. 17). According to Rosener's transcontinental study (1990), female managers perceived leadership behaviors to be in line with qualities representative of the transformational style. The author found that women were more likely to motivate others based on the individuals' own self-interests, encourage participation, and empower their followers. Moreover, they credit their success as leaders to their interpersonal and unifying skills. Men, on the other hand, embraced transactional leadership behavior, ascribing their power to position and authority. Denmark (1993) suggests that effective feminist leaders must empower others, specifically those who are less empowered themselves, including women and members of ethnic minorities. The numerous studies in which women exhibit, report, and reflect transformational qualities have been undertaken around the globe and in a variety of fields.

After 582 male and 219 female subordinates evaluated 150 male or 79 female managers from six Fortune 500 companies, Bass and Avolio (1994a) provided significant corresponding evidence to corroborate Bass's (1999) declaration above. They proffered that "women managers, on average, were judged more effectively and satisfying to work for as well as more likely to generate *extra effort* from their people" (p. 555). In their aptly titled article, "Shattering the Glass Ceiling: Women May Make Better Managers," women were also rated higher than men on three of the "4 Is" of transformational leadership.

The largest meta-analysis, consisting of 45 studies, compared gender difference and leadership styles, from diverse organizations throughout the United

States, Canada, English and non-English-speaking European countries (Eagly et al., 2003). The authors determined that female leaders exhibited more characteristics related to transformational leadership than males. Such qualities included: Charisma, Idealized Influence, Inspirational Motivation, Intellectual Stimulation, and Individualized Consideration. They also found female leaders to be more likely to demonstrate Contingent Rewards, which is more reminiscent of transactional leadership behaviors. Transformational qualities plus Contingent Rewards have been viewed as creating the most effective leadership for an increased commitment from followers. Certainly, individuals require some form of reward for their work. It is in conjunction with the transformational traits, however, that followers will share in a desire of the betterment of organizations. Moreover, males were more inclined to exhibit the inferior leadership behaviors related to transaction traits—Management by Exception (active and passive) and laissez-faire.

Furthermore, in the United States, sales groups from IBM and Southern Bell participated in a study in which 15 female managers were evaluated by one female and one male subordinate using the MLQ-5X. Results indicated a positive correlation between transformational and contingent-reward leadership behaviors and female leaders' effectiveness. Female managers were regarded as demonstrating interpersonal characteristics, thus creating affective bonds with their followers. Moreover, transformational and contingent reward leadership styles positively related to subordinate commitment and performance. Authors suggested that "allowing female leaders to engage in more one-on-one working relationships with subordinates may enhance both leader and subordinate effectiveness . . . regardless of the gender of the subordinate" (Yammarino, Dubinsky, Comer, & Jolson, 1997, p. 219).

A common question to such robust findings is, why are women liable to exhibit more transformational leadership behaviors than men? Burke and Collins (2001) proposed that women are more inclined to be "accessible to subordinates while making efficient use of their time" (p. 254) because they are comfortable and familiar with frequently balancing competing tasks, such as a family and a profession. Eagly, Johannesen-Schmidt, and van Engen (2003) surmised that women utilize a transformational style in an attempt to circumvent role incongruity. By incorporating interpersonal characteristics, therefore, women will not have to conform, to either their gender or leader role.

What's Wrong with This Picture Then?

Although women have been accepted into management positions, a "glass ceiling" still exists in most industries, precluding them from reaching the highest levels (Bass, 1999). Others such as Eagly and Carli (2007) believe that a more fitting image to describe women's challenges is a labyrinth. A labyrinth conveys the complexity and range of challenges that can emerge and passage through a labyrinth requires persistence, awareness of one's progress, and a foresight into the challenges that lie ahead. Eagly and Karau (2002) also suggest that there is also a perceived incongruity between the female gender-role and leadership, perhaps despite the use of transformational leadership behaviors. This leads to two forms of prejudice: Perceiving women less favorably than men as potential occupants of leadership roles, and evaluating behavior that fulfills the prescriptions of a leader role less favorably when it is performed by a woman. If transformational leadership in general has been found to be the most effective method of leading others, and women demonstrate more transformational leadership qualities, why, then, is the ratio of women to men in these positions not inverse?

Van Engen, van der Leeden, and Willemsen (2001) contested that the difference between the manner in which men and women lead is negligible. In their study, consisting of 30 female and 40 male managers and 253 female and 74 male shop assistants from four large department stores in the Netherlands, the manager's gender did not significantly predict the type of leadership behaviors. They viewed female managers to be vigorous and goal-oriented, as well as socially and charismatically as skilled as males. Moreover, shop assistants, using the Dutch translated version of the MLQ, rated their managers similarly, despite gender. These authors do qualify their findings by indicating that the organizational context of a department store is different than other industries. Nevertheless, they state that "sex discrimination in hiring, and promotion based on either a lack of a 'masculine mode of management' or a surplus of a 'feminine mode of management' is . . . proved unfounded" (p. 595).

Research involving an international bank in Australia examined the leadership styles of female and male managers from multiple perspectives (Carless, 1998). One hundred and twenty female and 184 male bank managers were evaluated through superior ($n = 32$), self, and subordinate ($n = 588$) assessments using several leadership surveys (MLQ-5X, LPI, and GTL). Self-evaluations revealed that female managers reported to utilize more transformational leadership qualities, such as being interpersonally interested and encouraging participation from their subordinates than their male counterparts.

Nevertheless, male and female managers were deemed similar by subordinates in transformational leadership qualities such as effectively communicating a vision, inspiring respect and trust, innovative problem-solving, and maintaining consistency. Similarly, female managers were observed to demonstrate more transformational leadership qualities than males, according to the superiors' ratings. Subordinate staff, however, did not experience a difference in leadership style and equally evaluated their male or female managers. The author explained that, "subordinates evaluate equally the leadership capabilities of female and male managers" implying that "women are accepted as managers in the banking industry . . . [and they do not] rely on stereotype expectations when rating their manager" (p. 899).

Similarly, Manning (2002) evaluated 64 individuals from a health and human services agency in the United States and found that managers, despite gender, correspondingly viewed themselves as transformational leaders. Specifically, those in higher managerial positions were more inclined to rate themselves as a transformational leader when compared to mid-level managers. However, observer raters, which included other managers, behavioral observations by the author, and peers, did not experience the social services managers to demonstrate such qualities. Interestingly, male manager self-ratings were more closely analogous with that of the observers, while females rated themselves as being significantly lower in transformational leadership than their evaluators viewed them.

In a nationwide survey, Burke and Collins (2001) also studied gender differences in leadership styles. Participants consisted of 711 female and 320 male accountants from public, industry, and not-for profit organizations in supervisory positions. Through managers' self-reports from the MLQ-5X, a small, but significant difference was discovered in favor of female managers. They were found to utilize the more effective leadership styles than males, emphasizing transformational behavior first and contingent reward next. The female accountants were less likely to practice the least effective management style, management-by-exception, than males in that position. Such behaviors include active monitoring and intervening to correct followers' mistakes. However, both male and female managers emphasized transformational leadership and contingent rewards as priority. Based on their findings, the authors stressed the importance of gender neutral hiring and promoting of accountants throughout the United States.

Maher (1997) presents a critical aspect to consider before accepting the research findings on leadership and gender differences. The article suggested, "gender differences in transformational and transaction leadership are far from universal" (p. 220). In her study, participants consisted of 133 female and 129 male undergraduate students at a Midwestern urban university, in which 73% worked full-time and 23% worked part-time. They rated their current managers' (163 male, 99 female) leadership styles with the MLQ-5X. Results revealed that in actuality, no significant gender difference existed by raters of their specific managers with regard to leadership style. In general, females, however, expected more stereotypic leadership characteristics from female (transformational and transactional) compared to male managers (laissez-faire).

Cultural Values and Transformational Leadership

Transformational leadership has generally been viewed as a strong leadership style in United States, Canadian, and Western European management literature. The benefits have been studied and tend to include broadening and elevating the interests of followers, generating awareness and acceptance among followers for the purpose and mission of the group, and motivating followers beyond their own self-interests in support of the group goals (Bass, 1997). While many researchers have found that the existence of transformational leadership extends beyond the United States to other countries, far fewer have examined its effectiveness (Spreitzer, Pertulla, & Xin, 2005). Why is it important to expand our knowledge to that of other countries, one might ask? The answer lies in our understanding of cultural values and their impact on how various people view their environment.

Leadership is often seen as a fit between a person's characteristics and leadership behaviors and the perceiver's beliefs of what a leader should be like (Den Hartog et al., 1999). In many cases, this is influenced by both individuals' cultural values, those beliefs central to a culture that influence the way members of that cultural group should lead their lives. Values act as guides for the behaviors, preferences, and judgments one makes while affecting how one evaluates his or her own life experiences (Wan et al., 2007).

Cultural groups may often vary in their beliefs as to what characteristics make one an effective leader. For example, in some cultures, one might need to make strong decisions without consulting those around him or her to be seen as an effective leader; however, in others, an appreciation for the opinions of others marks effective leadership. Furthermore, the actions of leaders may be interpreted differently in different cultures as a result of their values. For example, cultural sensitivity may be interpreted as weakness in an authoritarian society, while the same act applauded for effectiveness in a democratic one (Den Hartog et al., 1999). Similarly, in some non-Western societies who subscribe to an age-based hierarchy, the desire to transform others into leaders may be perceived as disrespectful to tradition

The marketplace of today has become more global than ever. In it, employees of multinational organizations are often obliged to worldwide travel as a necessity of doing business. The workforce is becoming more culturally diverse, as a result of more mergers and acquisitions, joint ventures, buyer-supplier cross-national relationships, and employee movement to seek greater opportunities for advancement (Bartlett & Ghoshal, 1998). Thus, the need to understand how cultural values influence styles of leadership becomes extremely important.

The literature available on the effect of cultural values on leadership suggests that there are two perspectives: the universal and the culturally specific. The universal perspective states that some concepts are generalizable across cultures and organizations (Bass, 1997; Spreitzer et al., 2005). The culturally specific perspective suggests that there are differences across cultures that will inevitably cause people to view leadership differently. Many leadership styles were developed in North America and other Western societies. Therefore, these theories may not be generalizable when implemented by leaders from different cultures (Spreitzer et al., 2005).

Support for the Universal Perspective

Bass (1997) supports a universal perspective based on the beliefs that leadership is a universal phenomenon. Some research suggests that leaders may be born predisposed to lead and the fact that pop culture and fads spread worldwide generates commonalities amongst people of different cultures. Bass also points to research from the United States, Canada, Taiwan, New Zealand, India, Japan, and Singapore supporting the universal effectiveness of transformational leadership.

Walumbwa, Orwa, Wang, and Lawler (2005) found that both Kenyan and American transformational leaders had strong and positive effects on organizational commitment and job satisfaction in both cultures. Muenjohn and Armstrong (2007) studied the relationship between subordinates' work values in Thailand and leadership behaviors exhibited by their expatriate managers from Australia. The authors suggest support for the universal perspective, in that the culture of Thai subordinates, which is different than that of their expatriate managers, played a limited role in influencing the leadership behaviors and effectiveness of expatriate managers. There was very little influence of cultural values on leadership style when expatriate managers used either transformational, transactional, or nonleader leadership behaviors.

Proponents of a universal perspective on transformational leadership believe that those who are, in fact, transformational leaders, have the ability to lead and inspire any group of people despite cultural differences. One such person is Mother Teresa. Mother Teresa was an exceptional leader who displayed charisma and had the ability to inspire others to transcend their own self-interests in order to achieve beyond their expectations. She dedicated her life to helping the poor, the sick, and the dying first in India and then around the world. She was able to transcend cultural, geographic, and political boundaries. As an ultimate universal transformational leader, Mother Teresa is a model for helping others aspire to and attain higher levels of performance for themselves or an organization.

Rosener (1990) conducted a study with prominent female leaders from four different continents. They were asked about their leadership styles and based on self-reports, it was found that despite the continent the women were from, female leadership could be characterized by attempts to encourage participation, share power, energize, and enhance the self-worth of others. As a contrast, male counterparts were also surveyed and their leadership style, across continents, consisted of a series of transactions using rewards and punishments with subordinates.

Similarly, Gibson (1994) looked at the leadership behaviors emphasized by males and females across four countries that were matched by cultural similarities into dyads (Norway and Sweden; Australia and U.S.). The questionnaires explored multiple leadership behaviors including goal setting, interaction facilitation, work facilitation, supportive behavior, and personal development. In addition, it explored six leadership styles that ranged from autocratic to laissez-faire. Male and female leaders demonstrated divergent leadership behaviors in all instances. While males mostly emphasized goal-setting behaviors, females tended to facilitate interaction. Australians differed from the other three nations studied in placing significantly more emphasis on the benevolent autocratic style and less on laissez-faire. Americans did not differ greatly in terms of style from the Norwegians and Swedes in the study. With this information, we can see that although there is a lot of support for a universal perspective, there may be unique differences amongst individual countries or cultures, a topic that will be discussed in the next section.

Support for the Culturally Specific Perspective

In the most widely cited study on cross-cultural comparisons of leadership prototypes, Gerster and Day (1994) compared ratings of 59 leadership attributes from a sample of students from multiple countries, including the United States. Characteristics of business leaders were rated on a most, moderate, or least basis. They determined that these attributes varied based on the respondents' culture/country of origin. Kaifi and Mujtaba (2010) further contend that these differences may relate to the degree of cultural deference afforded to elders. They surveyed Americans and Afghans to better understand their orientation toward transformational leadership. The Afghan participants indicated a greater tendency toward transformational leadership, though both groups scored highly. In addition, female American and male Afghan respondents had elevated transformational leadership orientation compared to their female Afghan and male American counterparts. The authors believe that Afghans are inclined to be transformational leaders because their culture places a strong emphasis on respect for those with knowledge, wisdom, and experience. Other differences besides respect for elders have been shown to greatly influence the way in which cultures view leadership. In general, two dimensions where cultures, beliefs, and actions often vary, and, therefore, lead to differences in leadership style, are power distance and collectivism.

Power Distance and Collectivism

Much of the research linking culture and leadership points to Hofstede's (1993) dimensions of power distance and group level collectivism. They are the two most significant cultural variables impacting effective leadership. Power distance is the extent to which power should be unequally distributed in a culture. Cultures high on power distance accept a hierarchy that separates superiors and subordinates, affording special privileges and ultimate power to the upper strata (Waldman et al., 2006). Subordinates with a high power distance orientation expect more, and are more receptive to one-way, top-down leadership from their superiors (Javidan et al., 2006). However, transformational leaders focus on stimulating subordinates in challenging ways and work most effectively with two-way leader-follower relationships (Bass, 1997). Accordingly, one would expect that cultures that place a higher value on power distance would be less likely to engage in transformational leadership.

In a study of 561 financial firms in 15 different countries, Waldman et al. (2006) found that managers in cultures stressing greater power distance tended to devalue three aspects of transformational leadership: providing a sense of mission or purpose in the larger environment, articulating an inspirational vision, and showing determination when accomplishing goals. They argue that managers with power may lack concern for broader stakeholder groups, and the community or society as a whole when making decisions. Therefore, in these societies, there may be more of a tendency for managers to abuse that power. Furthermore, Kirkman, Chen, Fargh, Chen, and Lowe (2009), studying Chinese and American respondents, found that at the individual level, power distance orientation moderated the reactions to transformational leaders. When power distance orientation was low for individuals, reaction to transformational leadership behaviors was more positive. When power distance orientation was high for individuals, reaction to transformational leadership behaviors weakened. Interestingly, this finding only held for individual power distance orientations and was not supported for country level power distance orientation.

However, Schaubroeck, Lam, and Cha (2007) found quite the opposite. When looking at the relationship between transformational leadership behavior and group performance in 218 financial service teams in Hong Kong and the United States, higher power distance teams exhibited stronger positive effects of transformational leadership on team potency. This was supported by teams in both Hong Kong and the United States. They argue that teams with higher power distance have greater respect for authority and, therefore, may be more open to leaders' influence attempts. In addition, they may be more willing to emulate their leaders and follow through on suggestions to work collaboratively. In contrast, teams with lower power distance may embrace transformational leadership behaviors to a lesser extent and may respond to them more weakly.

Collectivism is a construct that supports the importance and loyalty to a group over the individual as opposed to the converse, individualism. Because transformational leaders inspire others by emphasizing the importance of group values and interests, collectivist cultures should be more susceptible to and supportive of this leadership style. Thus were the findings of Jung, Bass, and Sosik (1995). Their research concluded that transformational leadership emerges more readily in the collectivistic societies of East Asia. Jung and Avolio (1999) further examined the moderating influence of collectivism and individualism on transformational and transactional leadership. Their results showed that collectivists who worked with a transformational leader generated more ideas than with a transactional leader.

Walumbwa and Lawler (2003) researched the inherently collectivist cultures of China, India, and Kenya to examine the moderating effect of allocentrism (collectivism at the group level) on leadership. Transformational leadership explained a greater proportion of variance in organizational commitment, satisfaction, and withdrawal behavior for those who scored higher on allocentrism.

Conclusion: Future Directions on Leadership

As part of the Global Leadership and Organizational Behavior Effectiveness Research Program (GLOBE), Den Hartog et al. (1999) collected response samples of middle managers from countries in Africa, Asia, Europe, Latin America, North America, the Middle East, and the Pacific Rim. Results support the perspective that specific aspects of transformational leadership are strongly and universally endorsed across cultures. These aspects include items reflecting integrity, honesty, charisma, inspiration, and visionary leadership. In addition, features included team-oriented leadership, decisiveness, and intelligence. Some items, however, were deemed "culturally contingent," contributing to or impeding leadership. Items included in transformational leadership were enthusiasm, risk taking, sincerity, intra-group conflict avoidance, compassion, and participation.

The research that has been done on this topic leads to an argument over whether leadership behaviors and styles are universal or culturally specific. The GLOBE study shows us that there is mixed support for both perspectives and, therefore, it may be necessary to develop a new way of defining the relationship between culture and leadership. Many have been redefining the term "universal." A *simple universal* is the phenomenon that is constant throughout the world. A *variform universal* is one in which subtle modifications of a simple universal can be seen when on studying that principle in different cultures. For example, transformational leadership may exist in individualistic cultures, such as the United States, as well as collectivist cultures such as China. The specific behaviors put forth by those leaders, however, may vary slightly. This is indicated in the GLOBE study where specific aspects of transformational leadership were endorsed universally across cultures (Den Hartog et. al., 1999). A third type of universal is *functional universal* in which patterns and relationships are consistent across cultures without regard to situational factors (Bass, 1997). Different forms of the "universal" are emerging in an attempt to explain the variances that exist in the research that has been done on this matter.

Researchers have also argued for the existence of multiple styles of leadership within cultures and individuals. Hollander (2009) suggests that transformational leadership may even be just an extension of transactional leadership, by means of including greater leader intensity and follower arousal. In a study of female ratings of leadership styles at all levels of business in Thailand, Chirametakorn (2001) found that both transformational and transactional leadership styles were being used and were also both associated with positive outcomes such as extra effort, effectiveness, and satisfaction. There was a negative relationship found between laissez-faire leadership and two outcomes: extra effort and effectiveness. The author described a positive relationship between transactional leadership and outcome variables as consistent with the cultural values of high power distance and high collectivism. This finding that both transactional and transformational leadership behaviors can be present simultaneously is in line with Bass (1997) who argued that transformational and transactional leadership are separate dimensions, and, therefore, a leader can use both styles. While there is no one consensus on what leadership style is most effective, there seems to be a movement toward an eclectic approach in which various styles are used in conjunction with one another to best suit the population.

Note

1. Portions of this chapter were published in M. Paludi and B. Coates (Eds.), *Women as Transformational Leaders* (Westport, CT: Praeger, 2011).

References

Avolio, B. J., Bass, B. M., & Jung, D. I. (1999). Re-examining the components of transformational and transactional leadership using the multifactor leadership questionnaire. *Journal of Occupational and Organizational Psychology, 72,* 441–462.

Bartlett, C., & Ghoshal, S. (1998). *Managing across borders.* Boston, MA: Harvard Business School Press.

Bass, B. M. (1985). *Leadership and performance beyond expectations.* New York: Free Press.

Bass, B. M. (1997). Does the transactional-transformational leadership paradigm transcend organizational and national boundaries. *American Psychologist, 52,* 130–139.

Bass, B. M. (1998). *Transformational leadership: Industrial, military, and educational impact.* Mahwah, NJ: Erlbaum.

Bass, B. M. (1999). Two decades of research and development in transformational leadership. *European Journal of Work and Organizational Psychology, 8,* 9–32.

Bass, B. M., & Avolio, B. J. (1991). *Multifactor leadership questionnaire* (Form 5X). Binghamton, NY: Center for Leadership Studies.

Bass, B. M., & Avolio, B. J. (1993). Transformational leadership: A response to critiques. In M. M. Chemmers & R. Ayman (Eds.), *Leadership theory and research: Perspectives and directions* (pp.49–88). San Diego, CA: Academic Press.

Bass, B. M., & Avolio, B. J. (1994). *Improving organizational effectiveness through transformational leadership.* Thousand Oaks, CA: Sage.

Bass, B. M., & Avolio, B. J. (1994). Shattering the glass ceiling: Women may make better managers. *Human Resource Management, 33,* 549–560.

Burke, S., & Collins, K. M. (2001). Gender differences in leadership styles and management skills. *Women in Management Review, 16,* 244–256.

Burns, J. M. (1978). *Leadership.* New York: Harper & Row.

Carless, S. A. (1998). Gender differences in transformational leadership: An examination of superior, leader, and subordinate perspectives. *Sex Roles, 39,* 887–902.

Carless, S. A., Wearing, A. J., & Mann, L. (2000). A short measure of transformational leadership. *Journal of Business and Psychology, 14,* 389–405.

Chirametakorn, R. (1991). *Transformational leadership and women leaders in Thailand* (Doctoral dissertation). Nova Southeastern University.

Den Hartog, D. N., House, R., Hanges, P. J., Ruiz-Quintanilla, S. A., & Dorfman, P. W. (1999). Culture specific and cross-culturally generalizsble implicit leadership theories: Are attributes of charismatic/transformational leadership universally endorsed? *The Leadership Quarterly, 10,* 219–256.

Denmark, F. L. (1993). Women, leadership, and empowerment. *Psychology of Women Quarterly, 17,* 343–356.

Eagly, A. H., & Carli, L. L. (2007). *Through the labyrinth: The truth about how women become leaders.* Boston, MA: Harvard Business Publishing.

Eagly, A. H., Johannesen-Schmidt, M. C., & van Engen, M. L. (2003). Transformational, transactional, and laissez-faire leadership styles: A meta-analysis comparing women and men. *Psychological Bulletin, 129,* 569–591.

Eagly, A. H., & Karau, S. J. (2002). Role congruity theory of prejudice toward female leaders. *Psychological Review, 109,* 573–598.

Geijsel, F., Sleegers, P., & van den Berg, R. (1999). Transformational leadership and the implementation of large-scale innovation programs. *Journal of Educational Administration, 37,* 309–328.

Gerster, C. R., & Day, D. V. (1994). Cross-cultural comparison of leadership prototypes. *Leadership Quarterly, 5,* 121–134.

Gibson, C. B. (1994). An investigation of gender differences in leadership across four countries. *Journal of International Business Studies, 2,* 255–279.

Hofstede, G. (1993). Cultural constraints in management theories. *Academy of Management Executive, 7,* 81–94.

Hollander, E. (2009). *Inclusive leadership: The essential leader-follower relationship.* New York: Taylor & Francis.

Jung, D. I., & Avolio, B. J. (1999). Effects of leadership style and followers' cultural orientation on performance in group versus individual task conditions. *Academy of Management Journal, 42,* 208–218.

Jung, D. I., Bass, B. M., & Sosik, J. (1995). Collectivism and transformational leadership. *Journal of Management Inquiry, 2,* 3–18.

Kaifi, B. A., & Mujtaba, B. G. (2010). Transformational leadership of Afghans and Americans: A study of culture, age, and gender. *Journal of Service, Science, and Management, 3,* 150–158.

Kirkman, B. L., Chen, G., Fargh, J., Chen, Z., & Lowe, K. B. (2009). Individual power distance orientation and follower reactions to transformational leaders: A cross-level, cross-cultural examination. *Academy of Management Journal, 52,* 744–764.

Kouzes, J., & Posner, B. (1990). *Leadership practices inventory (LPI): A self-assessment and analysis.* San Diego, CA: Pfeiffer.

Maher, K. J. (1997). Gender-related stereotypes of transformational and transactional leadership. *Sex Roles, 37,* 209–225.

Manning, T. T. (2002). Gender, managerial level, transformational leadership and work satisfaction. *Women in Management Review, 17,* 207–216.

Mind Garden. (2009). Retrieved from http://www.mindgarden.com/translations.htm#mlq

Muenjohn, N., & Armstrong, A. (2007). Transformational leadership: The influence of culture on the leadership behaviours of expatriate managers. *International Journal of Business and Information, 2,* 265–283.

Rosener, J. B. (1990). Ways women lead. *Harvard Business Review*, November–December, 119–125.

Schaubroeck, J., Lam, S. S. K., & Cha, S. E. (2007). Embracing transformational leadership: Team value and the impact of leader behavior. *Journal of Applied Psychology, 92,* 1020–1030.

Spreitzer, G, Perttula, K. H., & Xin, K. (2005). Traditionality matters: An examination of the effectiveness of transformational leadership in the U.S. and Taiwan. *Journal of Organizational Behavior, 26,* 205–227.

van Engen, M. L., van der Leeden, R., & Willemsen, T. M. (2001). Gender, context and leadership styles: A field study. *Journal of Occupation and Organization Psychology, 74,* 581–598.

Waldman, D. A., deLuque, M., Washburn, N., House, R., et al. (2006). Cultural and leadership predictors of corporate social responsibility values of top management: A GLOBE study of 15 countries. *Journal of International Business Studies, 37,* 823–837.

Walumbwa, F. O., & Lawler, J. J. (2003). Building effective organizations: Transformational leadership, collectivist orientation, work-related attitudes, and withdrawal behaviors in three emerging economies. *International Journal of Human Resource Management, 14,* 1083–1101.

Walumbwa, F. O., Orwa, B., Wang, P., & Lawler, J. J. (2005). Transformational leadership, organizational commitment, and job satisfaction: A comparative study of Kenyan and U.S. financial firms. *Human Resource Development Quarterly, 16,* 235–256.

Wan, C., Chiu, C., Tam, K., Lee, S., Lau, I. Y., & Peng, S. (2007). Perceived cultural importance and actual self-importance of values in cultural identification. *Journal of Personality and Social Psychology, 92,* 337–354.

Yammarino, F. J., Dubinsky, A. J., Comer, L. B., & Jolson, M. A. (1997). Women and transformational and contingent reward leadership: A multiple-levels-of-analysis perspective. *Academy of Management Journal, 40,* 205–222.

Whether there are innately female leadership styles . . . is not really the right question. It is more important to ask why there has been so little attention paid to women leaders over the years as well as why the styles of leading more often exhibited by women are particularly useful at this critical moment in history.

—Charlotte Bunch
American Activist and Organizer

12

Successful Strategies for Women in International Business

Karen Dill Bowerman

Strategies for effectiveness in global business activity are essential even though not every business organization is multinational with facilities and other assets in at least one country other than its own. All businesses, however, are increasingly dependent on global activity "whether it is importing parts, exporting merchandise, outsourcing offshore, hiring employees from other nations, dealing with consequences of the value of the dollar, or simply facing multinational competition relative to their product or service" (Bowerman & VanWart, 2011, p. 306). To deal with the wide range of international business issues, we need strong global leaders, whether they are men or women.

You are likely reading this book set and this chapter because you care about helping women in international business become successful since there is benefit both to the individual and the organization. Therefore in this chapter we will not just *talk at* the issues in theory. You are asked to engage with the material. Following a few introductory paragraphs, I will ask you to think about an issue based on the discussion points provided. These are the kinds of questions you may think through individually or talk through with others. I will then provide the beginnings of an action plan and I ask you to add to the plan—in writing—based on your answers to the discussion points. Spend some time with this material and by the conclusion of this chapter, you will have developed successful strategies for women in international business from several different perspectives. Think of the process as a skill-building process for yourself so that you end up with a strategic action plan you own that is built on the sound ideas in this chapter.

Men and women find that most activities are in common for most basic preparation and career development associated with international business. Examples of basic activities that apply to both genders include developing an understanding of global cultures, maintaining trust across national boundaries despite cultural differences, participating in global organizational networks and mastering language ability (Bowerman & VanWart, 2011). When giving advice on effective preparation for international trips (Alsup, 2011), there is not a gender distinction. Both men and women are advised to utilize technology effectively by utilizing telephone apps or downloads for a world clock with all destinations shown, a weather monitor for all destinations and travel guides and email subscriptions for U.S. Department of State information on all destinations. They need to make at least two copies of certain information before departing on an international trip including the Passport, emergency contact information, itinerary and medical prescriptions, etc. These kinds of basic guides are important for all; they should be included as leadership preparation for men and women alike.

The above activities are examples of basic undertakings that are gender-neutral, as already stated. However, as we dig more deeply into issues associated with women in international business, we find situations emerge with the need for some unique strategic attention. The first of these that we shall discuss is the need for strategies that continue our focus on improving gender diversity in international organizations. Then we shall turn our attention to career development strategies to help prepare women for international service.

Issue: Strategies for Increasing Gender Diversity in International Organizations

In a recent McKinsey survey, almost three-fourths of executives responding said that companies are more financially successful when they are more diversified by gender (Werner, Devillard, & Sancier-Sultan, 2010). They found that in these challenging economic times the strategic importance of gender diversity was even more important in Asia-Pacific (Australia, Hong Kong, Taiwan, Japan, South Korea, etc.) and in developing markets than in other areas such as China, India, Europe, and North or Latin America.

Chief Executive Officer Peter Voser of Royal Dutch Shell is conscious of his organization's leadership team remaining concerned about the percentage of women in senior positions: "I've ... indicated that [having] a higher percentage [of women] aligns our corporate thinking with that of our customers and key stakeholders, and stimulates better decision-making. But there's another reason for employee attraction and retention" (Voser, 2011). Various studies provide quantitative substantiation of the executives' opinion in the McKinsey survey cited above. For example, Ross and Dezsö (Dezsö & Ross, in press) found that among the largest 1,500 U.S. companies, all with international activity and most with global management reflected in their structure, those with the highest percentage of women in top management (excluding CEO per se) showed a positive relationship to high performance on organizational factors such as the market-to-book ratio, return on assets, return on equity, and annual sales growth from 1992 to 2006.

While making a pitch to include more experienced women in top military positions for fresh thinking on waging war, creating peace and influencing international security, the author of *Porcelain on Steel: Women of West Point's Long Gray Line* (Fortis Publishing, 2010) concluded by way of analogy, "Several private and academic studies conducted by Catalyst and Harvard Business Review empirically demonstrated that Fortune 500 companies 'with the highest female representation at top management levels consistently and significantly outperformed companies with the lowest level of women executives.' The Harvard study found that companies with the most female leadership performed up to 69% better than their competitors as measured by ROI and shareholder value. Yet women make up less than 3% of CEOs and hold less than 17% of corporate board seats" (McAleer, 2011).

Another study confirmed further quantitative substantiation of the executives' opinion, but from the different perspective of problem solving. Study participants from age 18 to 60 were assigned randomly to teams. Each team was asked to complete several tasks including brainstorming, decision making, visual puzzles and solving one complex problem. Teams with members that had higher individual IQs did not do substantially better on problem solving; however, teams with more women members scored higher on problem solving (Woolley & Malone, 2011). Furthermore, teams that had smart people dominating the conversation did not function as highly intelligent groups. It is curious to note that while individual women on average have higher social sensitivity than do men, and women's presence was needed for higher scores on problem solving, factors such as group satisfaction, group cohesion and group motivation were not correlated with collective intelligence of the team in problem solving.

Are such positive results in problem solving by the team achieved because of individual perspectives and inputs of very bright women? Perhaps in part, but research points to the diverse perspective of a team achieved by *mere presence* of women that gives the team heightened focus on listening to diverse contributions. The concept is that groups valuing diversity give heightened value to different perspectives of members and the benefit in discussions comes from differences actually being contributed and exchanged among team members.

Are such positive results achieved because of individual perspectives and inputs of very bright women? Perhaps in part, but research points to the diverse perspective of a team achieved by mere presence of women that gives the team heightened focus on listening to diverse contributions. The concept is that groups valuing diversity give increased value to different perspectives of members and the benefit in discussions comes from differences actually being contributed and exchanged among team members (Ramarajan & Thomas, 2011).

Perhaps it is not surprising that when gender diversity is a strategic priority, company leadership is more diverse, including leadership at the senior management level, despite the fact that women are not yet well represented in top management in companies overall. Transparency of data is essential so that managers can align actual organizational results to their desired results and stated targets. Desired results should be stated and tracked with transparency at all levels of a organization, including top senior management positions. Actual results for women in senior management positions in global organizations lag considerably behind well-meaning but poorly tracked intentions. Fewer than 500 of the largest 1,500 U.S. companies have *one woman or more* in senior management (Dezsö & Ross, in press).

We may deduce that it is important for companies to become more diversified by gender at all levels of the organization including where it is apparently most difficult—yet very important—at the executive level. Remember, improved financial success is thought to result in a benefit to the organization itself, and increased numbers of women in leadership positions benefit the career path of other women themselves. Thus, increasing gender diversity in global organizations will be the first component of an action plan designed to overview successful strategies for women in international business.

Discussion Points

- Why do you think gender diversity was found to be important in developing markets where discrimination against women is frequently harsh, particularly in basic areas of health care and education?
- How could you convince your top management to actively support a goal of increasing gender diversity in international activity of the organization?
- In your own setting, what programs could be undertaken to make international roles for women more attractive?
- What should be done in order to help make women successful in international roles they take on in your organization?

- If you set out to increase gender diversity in international activity of your organization, how would you measure results and specifically how would you use the data?

Action Plan

Strategies for increasing gender diversity in international activity of the organization

a. Invite and lobby top management to support gender diversity as a strategic priority, telling them that without their involvement quality results would likely not be achieved. Encourage them to ensure that a high proportion of candidates being considered for advancement are women so that the odds improve for qualified women to be selected. Ask them to become involved in serving as a role model for women and to visibly supporting the action plans below. Request that they evaluate middle and upper level managers based in part on their accomplishments relative to this action plan, perhaps in the manner that Shell adopted. Achieving worldwide data of more than 25% of their supervisors and professional staff being women, and 15% of their senior executives being women (up 5% in 5 years), Shell got to that result by setting long-term targets (not quotas) and evaluating managers based in part on their results relative to the targets (Barsh & Yee, 2011).

b. Encourage management to consider programs that can benefit all employees, including women, such as: accommodating flexible hours and sites, thinking *family life* so that facilities increasingly accommodate reconciliation of family–work balance (addressed in greater detail in the final section of this chapter), supporting networking and in-person or online meetings of women employees, mentoring for managers when they are relatively new on the job, offering support for women reentering after parental leave and coach supervisors that such leave is neutral in any evaluation to take place (Werner et al., 2010). These kinds of programs may make it more attractive for a woman to participate in international activity that would otherwise rob them of time with family.

c. When women are assigned to serve international roles, give training that will help them thrive on a personal level—particularly when stationed abroad for an extended period—so they can be successful for the organization. Openly discuss what works and does not work relative to spouse and children. When women serve as expatriates, sent to live and work in a different country from which they are born, they have the same family and spouse needs as do men. That is, the spouse must be comfortable with assimilation, safety and happiness in the country where they are sent. We know that a primary reason for expatriate dissatisfaction is because the spouse or family is not happy and has not adjusted. An international company often has staff to assist expatriates and their family members from tasks as large as buying property to as small as learning the monetary system so they can easily go grocery shopping or eat out (Bowerman & VanWart, 2011).

d. Track the management actions taken by date in attempts to bring improvement to gender diversity and the corresponding numbers of women by level within the organization; appropriately and transparently publish the data on results. Assess which programs yielded the greatest results and institutionalize them as best practices wherever appropriate.

e. Add here to the plan based on your own answers to the discussion points above:

_____
_____
_____
_____

In addition to developing strategies for an intraorganizational environment that fosters improved gender diversity in top leadership positions, as well as a positive interorganizational environment for women in international business, we must look beyond environment to the preparation that women themselves receive for leadership in international business.

Most of the leadership that women should exhibit when involved with international business does not differ from that exhibited by men. However, there are a few gender-specific leadership issues that should be given thought. From personal experience in Japan, I recall learning the formal way of drinking tea and then trying my best to be proper. It was months later when I found out that I had not been using traditional conduct for a woman since I had been modeling the men with whom I spent time on the job. Indeed that was a gender-specific situation that was both humorous and embarrassing, but proper tea-drinking methods are not at the top of the list of essential earth-shaking qualities for leadership in the international setting; nevertheless this type of episode is analogous to other gender-specific situations that arise in business.

There are situations that a woman might face that require strong communication skills in order to be prepared to lead. For example, a female sales manager was sent to close a large deal in an Asian country where many managers lacked both experience and willingness to deal with women in business. At dinner one evening when she realized there was a wandering hand under the table, it was important to emerge from the informal situation by cutting the unwanted behavior while simultaneously building the professional relationship and mutual respect that would be necessary the next morning for leadership and mutual respect during business discussions. This can be complex when working in an international setting with others who have lived for years believing that women are not desired as business partners. If this woman is to be successful in closing the deal for which she was sent overseas, she must find an artful manner to be clear and resolute in communication without offending the potential international associate.

A similar situation could present itself in many ways, some of which are covert and difficult to recognize. Instead of overt flirting, a situation might be more challenging to identify clearly (and correctly) as a gender issue such as covert dismissal from the "real" business discussion. Again, the woman must be sensitive to recognize the dynamic and then artful to weave her way into the discussion without being abrasive in her communication and therefore ineffective.

There are endless career development strategies that could be considered for women preparing for leadership in international business, many of which will be discussed later in this chapter. Women and men both need to be preparing to be multilingual, educating themselves in the cultures of other peoples and nations, traveling independently without encumbrance and assistance of tours and developing beliefs in global shared humanity. The strategies selected for discussion here are relevant in some way to her gender, whether real or perceived and whether active concerns or issues of historical importance that carry different weight in different cultures and with women of different backgrounds. They include (1) honest feedback for advancement, (2) being true to one's values, (3) and understanding the intersection of career life and personal life.

Issue: Strategies for Receiving Honest Feedback for Advancement That Is Essential for Women in International Business to Become Better Prepared to Lead

First, in corporate environments where there are few female senior leaders dealing with international activity, women may find that the percentages of women decline as we look up the hierarchy because it is felt *women are just not right for those roles.*

Alternatively in organizations where there are few female senior leaders, some even well-intended individuals may say that they know that *really women don't want advancement.* In actuality, we have found that the percentages of men and women who wish to advance to the next level are almost identical; specifically in the 24 to 34 age group, 98% of men and 92% of women agreed or strongly agreed that they wanted to move up (Barsh & Yee, 2011).

Whether for one of the paternalistic reasons cited above, or because of remnants of outright bias, or for other reasons, women may be given feedback on job performance that is not helpful to their achieving more lofty goals. After all, soft and lenient feedback is the easiest feedback to give to anyone, including women. Feedback that is not challenging typically does not lead to a push for professional development and a drive toward mutual goal setting for professional advancement. Lenient feedback may, in fact, be passive because performance is viewed by the supervisor or manager as "good enough to get by." However, for the recipient of the feedback, it may lead to maintenance behavior rather than assertive behavior for experiences that will bring new skills with new levels of cultural understanding and the opportunity for advancement.

We know that on occasion managers who are not properly schooled in giving appraisals fail to give women in-depth critical feedback because they fear an emotional response. Giving feedback to persons working with international matters is particularly challenging because it must go beyond feedback on mere numeric goals to touch also upon sensitive cultural issues that may be more difficult for some people to discuss critically.

Thus, the first strategy is for a woman to seek feedback that has a level of honesty to match the woman's goals for professional growth within the international arena. Beware: when you seek direct feedback, you may get it. When you get it, you must react with appreciation and stated desire to work with the company to construct a plan for professional growth that addresses areas of deficiency or perceived deficiency. The corollary to this strategy is for leaders to initiate giving honest and direct feedback to the woman in international business whether she requests it or not, remembering to utilize appraisal systems that cover all important aspects of performance including matters pertaining to the international dimension of the work. These same leaders who give feedback that is truly helpful are probably the same individuals who are clear about overcoming invisible barriers for women in the business.

Discussion

Assuming there are actually leadership issues that are different for women than for men in international business, does this imply that women should consider distinctive communication strategies?

Discuss why lenient feedback given to women in international roles may ultimately lead to lowered ambition or lowered performance.

Have you ever personally experienced or seen emotion in a feedback or evaluation situation? Did you see it as appropriate? Why or why not? Was the subject was female?

Feedback is a normal part of performance appraisal in corporate life. What are some factors that can explain why the feedback loop may be imperfect for women in international business?

Action Plan

Strategies for receiving honest feedback for advancement that is essential for women in international business to become better prepared to lead:

a. In the course of supervisory and managerial training that is given, include segments on career development emphasizing that supervisors should serve as coaches by giving employees regular feedback informally, outside of the formal structure of annual performance appraisals. Do not assume that supervisors and managers feel comfortable giving frequent feedback, and do not assume that they realize coaching should include feedback on career opportunities beyond only current performance. International firms should include coaching on career development for international positions that may be open for employees when the time is right for their advancement, and feedback to employees on how they need to improve or position themselves in order to take advantage of such opportunities. During the training sessions with supervisors and managers, explore for any hidden attitudes (such as "really women don't want advancement") they may have that result in spending disproportionate quality time coaching men.

b. Ensure that persons whom you supervise receive regular training on performance appraisal. Trainees should be taught sensitivity in having no gender bias when giving feedback—not just in the sense of becoming unduly critical but also in regard to withholding needed feedback. Some of the best training programs on this subject are taught via role play in order to help each trainee become more skilled in being honest and direct in giving objective feedback.

c. Coach women to seek honest and direct feedback. Assist by helping them to act on the feedback by developing a plan for improvement, and discussing the plan with the supervisor or manager who gave the suggestions. It is not just women who may need this coaching, but ensure that women are included as recipients.

d. Encourage women to utilize self-assessment on their performance in international business. A 360-feedback mechanism can be used so the individual can compare feedback from her supervisors, her peers, her clients and other stakeholders to her own assessment of her strengths and areas for improvement. Peter Drucker (2005) wrote an often-quoted article on managing oneself, concluding that leaders must discover their strengths, and the only path for this is utilizing feedback analysis. Encourage her to utilize the results of the self-assessment as a planning tool for building an action plan of personal career development. After conducting the surveys and developing a personal plan built on the findings, the final steps of the process will be to carry out the plan and then to reassess for improvement and for areas that need additional development.

e. Add here to the plan based on your own answers to the discussion points above: _____

_____

_____

_____

Issue: Strategies for Being True to One's Values for Confidence in Leading in International Business

Next we shall turn to issues of personal integrity and self-awareness that women in the international setting report as qualities they find essential. Integrity is associated with independence of decision making and involves incorruptibility and soundness of thought. Integrity is sometimes defined as consistent adherence to a code of moral values, regardless of whether the code is externally or internally derived. Clearly, personal integrity and independence in decision making are important for both male and female leaders and for any working environment, domestic or international. These characteristics are singled out for this discussion because thoughtful women in international business designate them as especially important. The woman with clarity on who she is and what her values are can operate independently and confidently within a known value structure.

Women have not always recognized these characteristics as critical for themselves, and society has historically associated factors like independence more with men than with women. Independent decision making, for example, was historically credited to men as a stereotypical trait, whereas dependence was a stereotypical trait associated with women in general. Dependence in decision making can interfere with one acting clearly and confidently within a known value structure. Over the last 50 years or more, there has been a thread in literature pointing to women defining themselves in terms of the roles they play relative to others (mother, daughter, worker, wife, Scout leader, etc.) rather than defining themselves in terms of who they are inside of their own souls. Also a fascinating but disturbing phenomenon called the Cinderella Complex (Dowling, 1981) was named in 1981 by a therapist who identified a deeply seated and subconscious fear that women had of becoming unloved and alone if they were to blossom as independent thinkers. To the extent that this complex, studied only 30 years ago, remains as a vestige anywhere in the world where a woman conducts business, the fear renders the woman to act dependent and to subordinate herself to others and even to seek protection in what she identifies as a hostile world. Remnants of the Cinderella Complex that may remain in today's world interfere with independent development of strength from knowing who you are and then being true and honest to yourself through self-sufficiency and independent free thinking.

The need for clarity of the woman's values was expressed in an interview with Jean Stephens who is CEO of the U.S. firm RSM International, based in London, and is the first woman to lead a Top Ten accounting network. She is responsible for the firm's international strategy and for overseeing more than 700 offices in 86 countries, with more than 32,500 employees. Because she deals with such a diverse set of cultures, I asked her for insight into what she sees as the keys to leadership success in dealing with people worldwide who have such different reactions to dealing with an American businesswoman. She said that "Yes, there are different styles in different cultures, and leaders have to be sensitive to this. But people are people around the world. Informal relationships and good camaraderie help to maintain trusting partnerships. But there are also tough issues, and as long as I'm true to myself and honest, we can get through even the toughest of them" (Bowerman & VanWart, 2011).

While Stephens emphasized that building international trust must be an upfront and transparent process with no hidden agendas, the ability to communicate consistently in an upfront manner begins within by knowing who you are and what you stand for. Values must be so crystal clear to the woman in international business that she is absolutely confident in not veering from them. She must have thought this through in advance with great clarity. In this way can she exhibit personal integrity and remain true to herself, keeping in mind that the woman in an international setting is likely to have her integrity tested on several fronts.

As was written in the movie *V for Vendetta*, "Our integrity sells for so little, but it is all we really have."

Discussion Points

We have established that the woman with clarity on who she is and what her values are can operate independently and confidently within a known value structure. Discuss personal development of these characteristics.

Describe the Cinderella Complex and your assessment of its impact on a woman's self-confidence and independence in decision-making in today's global business environment (emphasis on both "today" and "global").

From your point of view, describe the relationship between a woman's independence of thought and her potential for integrity. Have U.S. women become more independent of thought in the last couple of decades?

If your answer to the last question was "yes," then have there been increasingly high levels of integrity shown? Explain.

Action Plan

Strategies for being true to one's values for confidence in leading in international business:

a. A website on values development states "Attention to our values helps us become more self-aware, make ethical decisions … and develop credibility as a leader. First, understanding one's own core values is integral to becoming self-aware" (Gountanis, 2011). Gather together some of the many materials that are available on personal values development and identify the portions of those materials that address the stages of moral development. These stages correspond somewhat to the stages we pass through in our lives. (Even though there is typically some relationship to age as outlined here, there are certainly examples of young people at the highest level of moral development and examples of seniors who have not progressed through the stages.)

Children make choices based on immediate consequences. Teens may choose ethically when it is in their immediate self-interest to do so. Young adults at a conventional level tend to make decisions based on norms or rules for ethical conduct even if their self-interest dictates otherwise. A few people reach a level for acting within their own code for high level principles of human rights, fairness and justice; when they see society's conventions are in opposition to their own code of ethics, they may work to improve society's rules. People who reach this level do not bend with the winds of peer pressure or kickbacks or sweet inducements because they act in the context of their ethical code and moral values.

Women who read more about the stages of moral development, should be asked to analyze frankly where they are as individuals in their development and what would move them higher on the scale.

b. As a coach or supervisor of a woman, give opportunities for them to have a realistic preview of scenarios that could logically occur when involved in international activity based on the particular countries with which they will be involved. The previews should give the woman feedback from trusted co-workers on her natural instincts in the scenarios so that she can think through in advance how to frame her communication for the best leadership results, which implies that she will remain true to her values.

c. Women should find successful and trusted mentors who can be counted on for honest, objective and thorough feedback, and if they do not give it, seek it. Sometimes those trusted individuals will be in the woman's hierarchy, but sometimes not. As long as they have a clear perspective on both performance and how the woman is received within the organization and by the cultural groups with whom they are working, their feedback will be helpful. The feedback requested should not be just about performance per se, but also objective observations about the confidence with which they project that they remain true to their values within the organization and within their international environment—for example, with clients or customers. Women should not forget to thank those mentors for taking seriously the desire for direct communication relative to their career in international business because there is no doubt that their level of caring is special in that not every manager would spend the time to give detailed, serious and insightful support.

d. Add here to the plan based on your own answers to the discussion points above:

_____

_____

_____

_____

Issue: Strategies for Understanding and Supporting a Healthy Intersection of Career Life and Personal Life

International business can be intrusive into one's personal life because it creeps into our daily schedule more than a domestic job. Take the simple common instance of wanting to call clients in, say, Shanghai from an office in Seattle before they leave work in the evening; the worker will take needed materials home in order to set the alarm and be organized to call around 1:00 a.m. A career in international business has impact on a woman's personal life, and vice versa. If the woman has a spouse who expects her to serve dinner or care for the children every night, she will not be able to handle international activity without family impact. If she carries on international responsibilities freely, there are not enough hours in the week for the job not to impact her personal life. However, today in some companies and with "the right" spouse, a woman does not have to choose one or the other—career or marriage, career or children. For example, Facebook COO Sheryl Sandberg (formerly Vice President of Global Online Sales and Operations) who is married to SurveyMonkey

CEO David Goldberg, have prioritized both of their careers and do the obvious things that are necessary toward that end such as splitting their responsibilities at home. Ms. Sandberg makes the point that the old adage is no longer true that if you are being promoted at work, you can have no personal life (i.e., you can "have it all"). Search Facebook for her excellent interview on December 5, 2011, "Facebook COO Sheryl Sandberg and Her Husband Have Done the Impossible," in which she explains that what we need to reach in order to allow women to "have it all" is to work toward an even division of labor in the home. She makes the point that men assume that they can have it all (i.e., a flourishing career and a happy family life) but women do not. This phenomenon is so great that individuals alone cannot control for the desired result—organizations must give men choices too if we are to get to a balanced point. It should be pointed out that couples at the executive level may enjoy personal assistance (and assistants) that help make possible "having it all," but still the point remains that when there is an even division of labor in the home each party in the couple has greater opportunity to prioritize his or her career. For almost 20 years, we have heard about the *glass ceiling* in which seemingly invisible barriers prevent qualified women from advancing into top leadership and executive positions at the same rate as qualified men. When the Federal Glass Ceiling Commission was established in 1991 under President George Bush, its 1995 report highlighted survey data such as the fact that then in the top Fortune 1000 companies, 95% of the senior level management positions were held by men. At that time Senator Robert Dole who introduced the Act that established the Commission, wrote in the report's introduction, "For this Senator, the issue boils down to ensuring equal access and equal opportunity" (Glass Ceiling Commission, 1995).

Less than 15 years from the time of that writing, considerable research turned to a study of *self-imposed* limitations on advancement. It is not uncommon to find studies substantiating that women are disproportionately represented in top management because women *have chosen* a personal life that is inconsistent with high level and executive leadership (Bowerman & VanWart, 2011). This does not mean the end of emphasis on equal access and opportunity, but rather the addition of a well-rounded assessment of the discrepancy in data on percentages of women in senior level management positions. Such research offers meaningful inquiry and should not be dismissed as bias that exudes only from a traditional belief system about the role of women in the workplace.

Whereas marriage and parenting are linked with higher salaries for men, it is opposite for women. Furthermore, we know that personal choices including the number of hours one works per week and the continuity of one's career are related both to salary and advancement. With that base understanding, we can then turn to long-term studies showing that women MBAs with children work fewer hours per week and interrupt the continuity of their career more frequently than do men. Male and female MBAs had comparable salary after graduation, but a gap between their salaries developed soon after the women had children (Bertrand, Goldin, & Katz, 2008).

Ibarra and Obodaru (2009) conducted an interesting study with implications on perceptions of gender relative to perceived performance. Thousands of 360-degree evaluations were conducted in 149 countries, and it was learned that women outscored men in nine of ten leadership dimensions, ranking lower only in *envisioning* or the selling of their vision to various stakeholders (Bowerman & VanWart, 2011). Clearly, the selling of a vision requires a different set of skills than what is required for management toward achieving measurable objectives. The finding that women outscored men in nine of ten leadership dimensions is a resounding affirmation of both perceived and actual performance and does not help to explain why there are fewer numbers of women rising to the top of the hierarchy. The authors concluded that if women focus on communicating organizational vision, they are more likely to be perceived as leaders, so adding this skill set may help them even more in perception of performance, but its absence does not explain the fewer numbers of women rising to the top of the hierarchy.

It is time to think about your own situation, and why there may be additional personal choices that you need to work through in order to achieve a healthy intersection of career life and personal life. It is evident that a career choice for maximum upward mobility impacts family plans. For the individual woman, choosing maximum upward mobility may be a positive or negative. We all know that parental involvement by the father and mother with their children during their formative years is extremely important; but exactly how this is accomplished varies greatly. We also know that choosing maximum upward mobility may mean that the woman chooses not to marry or not to have children; it may mean, however, that she earns more. The Bureau of Labor Statistics found that women who have never married earn over 94% of their male counterparts' earnings, while married women, in the aggregate, earn only 75.5% as much as married men (Wolgemuth, 2009). If the individual woman had to make a choice to identify which is more important to her, would it be marriage or earnings? But why should she have to choose if both the husband's and wife's careers are given top priority? A young woman should think through these kinds of issues when she is still young enough to make choices that reflect personal values. She will achieve a healthy intersection of career life and personal life on her own terms and her partner's terms only if they come to grips with a variety of personal issues such as when to have children as her biological clock moves forward, knowing that her choices become limited—or gone at some point—by virtue of waiting.

A young man should think through these kinds of issues as well, because the choices he will make influence both his future career and his family. In fact, the choices he makes on this important issue may even define the energy of the life partner he will seek.

If a woman is married with children, one of her personal choices is to stop out while the children are young. Again, she should think through these issues so she is clear on her personal values and her partner's personal values and they make the decision that is right for each partner. If she stops out from a career fast track, chances are her upward mobility will be slowed, as we see in the data. On the other hand, if she seeks the fast track because she is on an alluring career track, the clock remains in motion so that she quickly will have made personal decisions by default, placing career above personal time with children.

Brief stop outs are common throughout the world, usually in the form of maternity and paternity leave along with family leave. Northern and Central European nations are known for relatively generous parental leave. It is interesting that it has been reported even in countries such as Sweden that strive for gender-equality, where both parents are given 16 months of paid parental leave, fathers take only 20% on average of the sixteen months of paid parental leave, and transfer remaining days to their spouse (Wikipedia, 2011). The fact that transfer of days between parents is allowed is important in itself for the organization helping to insure a significant amount of parental leave is taken.

A personal case may help to illustrate what was a healthy choice for Karen, given her personal values. A different person might consciously make different choices that would bring them to a different healthy intersection of professional and personal life. Karen realized at about age 20 before she was married that she would not be a happy person over the long term if she made a black and white choice between career fast-tracking and time with children. So after she married, she sought gray; she talked with her husband about how they could both have a more leisurely paced personal life and still remain engaged with their careers in order to continue bringing home the same salaries to which they had become accustomed while keeping themselves prepared to move up in the organization later when the time was personally right for them. Seeking this middle ground would not immediately include the feverish pace of international work which she had come to love. Because she was a manager responsible for vendor relations in a manufacturing firm when she bore her first child, she knew that if she pushed now for the international career that interested her, she would have some extraordinarily long workweeks in addition to international travel. In contrast, if she remained in her current position and did not seek higher level work for now, she would have hours that were somewhat flexible. She was aware that if she did not seek a higher level international position within vendor relations for another 10 years or so, she have jumped off the fast track. To her, the latter was perfectly fine because her values were such that she valued leisure time with family when her girls were young. Therefore, although she did not opt for a complete stop out, she did not choose a path of immediate economic maximization.

By remaining a manager for vendor relations, and of course continuing to do quality work, she acted upon an understanding of what constituted for her a healthy intersection of a successful career and unrushed time with family. She and her husband chose a similar path for him, prioritizing their careers in similar manner, and they shared their responsibilities at home; had they not chosen comparable paths, by default, one of their lives would have moved closer to the career stopping out. When the girls were in college, Karen ultimately returned to a faster pace of international travel and less flexible hours invested weekly in work; although her career had been slowed and perhaps she would not rise in management as high as she would have if she had made different choices relative to career, she achieved happiness and was extremely successful in her career.

If you do not identify with this illustration for yourself, it is probably because you do not subscribe to the "middle ground" that was appropriate for Karen and her spouse; if "stopping out" or "having it all" is right for you, the point is for you to know and follow the values that carry you in the direction that is right for you.

Discussion Points

Knowing that a salary gap between men and women typically develops, in the aggregate, soon after women have children, is this something you classify as understandable and perhaps reflecting the choice that most women make to work fewer hours than men work? Explain.

Make a list of reasons why international business is often considered more intrusive on one's personal life than domestic business.

Do you believe that women and men can make a choice to "have it all?" Would such a choice demand too much of an individual? Would it demand too much of you or your partner?

Research shows that if women "stop out" yet wish to return to the same point from which they depart their career track, they should remain involved in their profession in an appropriate manner. How could that be done for someone who is stopping out?

It has been found that self-employed women choose to work fewer hours per week than males who are self-employed. They also spend six more hours per week caring for their homes than do their male counterparts and they spend more time providing child care, including multitasking when they keep the child with them during business hours (Gurley-Calvez, Harper, & Biehl, 2009). Thus, it is not only in women in the corporate world who work fewer hours per week, but also women entrepreneurs. Discuss the extent to which this choice may have bearing on the growth of their businesses. How about impacts on revenue or on financing for their businesses?

Action Plan

Strategies for understanding and supporting a healthy intersection of career life and personal life:

a. Structural improvements that support work–life balance can be carried out by principled companies and those finding it in their interest to keep women advancing professionally; those companies can help to make it possible for their workers to put family number one in their life by not requiring that they work such excessively long hours that personal life is cheated. The company must remember that structural improvements for work–life balance should be fair-minded and put in place to benefit both men and women because if they do not benefit men, the men in turn will not be able to make the choices that bring the family to balance.

b. The woman herself should give early consideration to her values on the mix of career and family life that is right for her. This is like the planning that Alice ran into with the Cheshire Cat when Alice asked if the Cat could help her find her way, and the Cat responded that it depends on where you want to get and if you don't really know then it really does not matter which way you go. In this case, it does really matter, and it matters that the woman—and her partner if already in the picture—consciously blend career and personal life for consistency with values and desire.

c. MBA and other graduate programs with many students who will be on the fast track in their careers should create forums in which to discuss the issue of life balance. Even though the topic does not constitute an academic course, it should not be overlooked. Some students graduate and tend to roll on to job interviews and then roll on in their job without ever thinking about the importance of discussing this topic and thoughtfully finding what is right for themselves.

d. Add here to the plan based on your own answers to the discussion points above:

_____

_____

_____

_____

Summary of Successful Strategies for Women Leaders in International Business

Just four potential issues for women in international business have been discussed in this chapter. You should now have developed an action plan with steps in at least each of these strategic areas:

1. Strategies for increasing gender diversity in international organizations.
2. Strategies for receiving honest feedback for advancement that is essential for women in international business to become better prepared to lead.
3. Strategies of being true to one's values for confidence in leading in international business.
4. Strategies for understanding and supporting a healthy intersection of career life and personal life.

Of course, the success from your plan for both yourself and your family and your company shall come only with the plan's implementation. Whether this plan is for you personally, or as a supervisor to support women, implement with the gentle strength that brings continuous improvements for our daughters and granddaughters, their families, and the organizations in which they serve.

References

Alsup, R. (2011). *International study trip preparation—12 Tips for MBA Students*. Retrieved from http://blog.myeemba.com/2011/11/30/international-study-trip-preparation%E2%80%9312-tips-for-mba-students/?utm_source=feedburner&utm_medium=feed&utm_campaign=Feed%3A+Myeemba+%28MyeEMBA%29

Barsh, J., & Yee, L. (2011). *Changing companies' minds about women*. Retrieved from http://www.mckinseyquarterly.com/Changing_companies_minds_about_women_2858

Bertrand, M., Goldin, C., & Katz, L. (2008). *Dynamics of the gender gap for young professionals in the financial and corporate Sectors*. Retrieved from http://emlab.berkeley.edu/~webfac/moretti/e251_f08/katz.pdf

Bowerman, K., & VanWart, M. (2011). *The business of leadership.* Armonk, NY: M. E. Sharpe.

Dezsö, C., & Ross, D. (in press). *Does female representation in top management improve firm performance? A panel data investigation.* Retrieved from http://www1.gsb.columbia.edu/mygsb/faculty/research/pubfiles/3063/Perf-FemonTMT_SMJ_Final_Prepub.pdf

Dowling, C. (1981). *The Cinderella complex: Women's hidden fear of independence.* New York: Summit Books.

Drucker, P. (2005). Leadership fundamentals—Managing oneself: Best of HBR 1999. *Harvard Business Review*, 3–16.

Glass Ceiling Commission. (1995). *Good for business: Making full use of the nation's human capital.* A Fact-Finding Report of the Federal Glass Ceiling Commission, U.S. Department of Labor.

Gountanis, C. (2011). *Personal values development.* Retrieved from http://www.chrisgountanis.com/written-works/88-personal-values-development.html

Gurley-Calvez, T., Harper, K., & Biehl, A. (2009). *Self-employed women and time-use.* U.S. Small Business Administration Office of Advocacy No. 341, February.

Ibarra, H., & Obodaru, O. (2009). Women and the vision thing. *Harvard Business Review,* 62–70.

McAleer, D. (2011). *Reshaping pentagon leadership.* Retrieved from http://www.atlantic-community.org/index/articles/view/Reshaping_Pentagon_Leadership

Ramarajan, L., & Thomas, D. (in press). *A positive approach to studying diversity in organization.* Harvard Business School Working Paper.

Voser, P. (2011, June). *Engaging and retaining women.* Paper presented at Catalyst Europe Regional Symposium, The Hague.

Werner, C., Devillard, S., & Sancier-Sultan, S. (2010). *Moving women to the top: McKinsey global survey results* (pp. 1–2). Retrieved from https://www.mckinseyquarterly.com/article_print.aspx?L2=18&L3=31&ar=2686

Wikipedia. (2011). *Male–female income disparity in the United States.* Retrieved from http://en.wikipedia.org/wiki/Male%E2%80%93female_income_disparity_in_the_United_States

Wolgemuth, L. (2009). *Young women closing in on gender wage parity.* Retrieved from http://money.usnews.com/money/blogs/the-inside-job/2009/07/31/young-women-closing-in-on-gender-wage-gap

Woolley, A., & Malone, T. (2011). *Defend your research: What makes a team smarter? More women.* Retrieved from http://hbr.org/2011/06/defend-your-research-what-makes-a-team-smarter-more-women/ar/2

Freedom is never granted. It is earned by each generation . . . in the face of tyranny, cruelty, oppression, extremism, sometimes there is only one choice. When the world looks to America, America looks to you, and you never let her down.

—Hillary Rodham Clinton
Secretary of State
United States

13

Women and Management in Japan: Weight of Tradition, Prospects for Change

Ödül Bozkurt and Motoko Honda-Howard

While the underrepresentation of women in paid employment and management continues to be a universal trend in the 21st century, Japan has long stood
out in this regard with its particularly poor performance among comparably
developed economies. As recently as 2006, the country's impressive ranking
as 7th in the world in the United Nations Human Development Index was
problematically matched by a ranking of 69th in the Gender Related Development Index and a ranking of 42nd in the Gender Empowerment Index (United
Nations Development Report, 2006, as reported in Courmadias, Fujimata, &
Härtel, 2010, p. 104). In the World Economic Forum's Gender Gap Index released in 2009, Japan ranked 101st out of 134 countries. The rather anoma-
lous discrepancy between Japan's overall level of economic development and
the position it accords women in the world of paid employment is further ac-
centuated still in the case of women in management. Admittedly, even countries with far greater gender equality in terms of total labor force participation
register wider gaps between male and female employees in the higher ranks
of managerial ranks, but once again, the level of inequality seen in Japanese
workplaces outstrips that seen in any of the other comparably developed economies and indeed that in some far less developed country contexts as well. In
2005, Japan ranked at the bottom of the list of female board representation at
Fortune Global 200 companies in a survey by the nonprofit Corporate Women
Directors International (Kageyama, 2005). Observers have commented that
Japan has been "arguably exceptional among advanced industrial countries in

the attitudinal and institutional constraints it imposes on its own women managers" (Volkmar & Westbrook, 2005, p. 465).

Against this rather bleak backdrop of the traditionally widespread and persistent underrepresentation of women in the working life of Japan, however, there are also reasons to anticipate some fundamental changes in the near future. In academic, policy and popular forums alike, the question being posed increasingly more often and more vocally is if, in light of drastic demographic shifts, possible social and cultural transformations around gender roles, and the greater exposure to the diversity agenda espoused by contemporary global business thinking, gender discrimination at work will finally show signs of erosion.

"The Japanese Miracle" and the Systemic Subordination of Women in the Japanese Employment System

In the post–World War II period, Japan's rapid rise as an economic superpower was widely regarded as something of a "miracle," and especially the rather envious and curious Western audiences saw the Japanese employment system as key to the country's phenomenal success (Dore, 1973, 1989). As the efforts to identify ways forward through the limitations of largely Fordist production systems and their mostly Tayloristic employment practices turned to the Japanese model as possibly one to emulate at the enterprise level, "Japanization," that is, the transplantation of key elements of the operations of Japanese corporations, and especially the manufacturers, became a defining trend in the rest of the advanced capitalist world. Key among the foci of attention was the employment model, and lifelong employment, seniority-based pay, teamwork and continuous improvement all became Japan's conceptual exports to competitors in thinking about work organization in a novel and, apparently, highly successful way. While it was certainly more at the level of abstract debate than actual implementation of practices, the wisdom of Japanese ways of organizing work became one of the most hotly debated "solutions" to the economic impasse of the 1970s and 1980s.

Yet this much-studied and heralded employment system has crucially been characterized, as well as the lauded tenets mentioned above, by traditionally low rates of labor force participation by women, their relegation to the peripheral, temporary and marginal positions in the workforce and their near-absence from managerial posts. Taylor has argued that, far from being an unintended consequence, the peripherality of women need in fact be seen as central to the core logic of the Japanese model (Taylor, 2006). Similarly, Lam has noted that the Japanese employment system in its core involved active discrimination against women (Lam, 1992). These observations linking the heavily gender-unequal nature of the Japanese approach to employment to the logic of the system, rather than merely cultural understandings of gender in Japan, are especially important for underlining that institutional and structural, and not merely cultural, obstacles have long stood in the way of greater gender equality in the Japanese workplace.

The subordination of women in that workplace is well documented, visible to such an extent that it takes on an almost exotic and incomprehensible quality to most outside analysts. In large corporations, central to the resilience and robustness of the Japanese model of employment, most women employees were traditionally "office ladies" whose job was to serve tea to the male managers (Toshiko, 1983). The hidden or, often explicit, expectation for working women was, and largely continues to be, that they will "retire" upon marriage (Hiroshi, 1982). While women's labor force participation in Japan was noticeably low and short-lived across the life-course during the reputational heyday of the Japanese model, figures for women in management have been even more dire. Renshaw found during her fieldwork, as late as 1999, that "the belief that there are no women in management in Japan is widely held," herself being asked in the course of her research "whether there were any" (Renshaw, 1999, p. 4). In this account from the mid-1990s, a decade after the legislative changes that were to promote greater gender equality in the Japanese workplace first came into effect, Renshaw tellingly observed that while women constituted around 40% of the workforce in Japan fewer than 10% of managers were women, noting,

> Japanese women are among the best educated in the world, but their talents remain largely unused and underutilized. They have been exploited as a buffer for economic cycles, serving as temporary, and therefore less expensive labor, and then cast out at marriageable age for a new, younger crop of women college graduates. . . . The fabled foundations of Japanese management—lifetime employment, the seniority system, and the bureaucratic, tightly knit nature of industrial policy—have served as barriers to women's entry into management. (Renshaw, 1999, p. 3)

Renshaw adds that institutional discrimination by employers compounds the issue.

The institutional discrimination against women in the workplace in general, and women in management in particular, appears to have been directly and systematically linked to one of the core tenets of the Japanese employment model, that of lifetime employment. Employers' commitment to male workers' lifetime employment has been rendered possible by the employment of women on a needs-based manner, "exploited as a buffer for economic cycles" (Renshaw, 1999, p. 3). In 1990 Saso called the position of Japanese women in large companies "abysmal" (Saso, 1990, p. 226), observing that "egalitarianism does not extend to Japanese women" (Saso, 1990, p. 224). Brinton (1993) has argued that Japan's status as a leading world economic power has, in fact, systematically depended on the unpaid and under-rewarded labor of women, both at home, as domestic workers and psychological support, and at the workplace, as workers in low-paying jobs with little or no serious career prospects. In short, rather than being an idiosyncratic footnote in the largely successful Japanese model, women's subordination across the ranks, and particularly in management, has been in fact been its "hidden pillar."

Prospects for and Limits and Obstacles to Change

The celebratory accounts of the Japanese model of employment that were so prevalent in the 1980s now feel superbly anachronistic, since the reversal of fortune experienced by the Japan in the early 1990s with the bursting of the "Japanese bubble." Van Maanen notes how, correspondingly, the "intense attraction, sense of awe and rather stunned appreciation" turned critical (Van Maanen, 2006, p. 281) over the subsequent decade. The views of the approach to organizing work which had once been widely seen as one to be emulated in Western firms "became a negative model almost overnight" (Van Maanen, 2006, p. 281). Rather than being upheld now as a blueprint to be exported to the rest of the world, the Japanese approach to managing human resources have more recently been the subject to inquiries around whether they are converging with other practices globally (Jacoby, 2005).

While the difficulties encountered by the Japanese economy and therefore the increased criticisms of some tenets of its employment system have naturally caused considerable degrees of concern about the continued competitiveness of Japan as an economic superpower, the state of flux in the Japanese model and its employment system also raises the possibilities of more positive change, including in the position of women in the workforce and in management. The debate on the continuity of traditional practices versus the ground gained or to be gained by fundamentally new ones is an ongoing one, and any definitive calls to say *sayanora* to salarymen, and therefore the peripheral female worker in the Japanese workplace, are at best premature. Indeed, Morris et al. note how, while some elements of the Japanese employment model may indeed be undergoing radical transformation, some of the traditional approaches in these areas may have been abandoned only to ensure the continuity of others, particularly the lifetime employment of male white-collar workers (Morris, Hassard, & McCann, 2006).

If the overall decline in the economic prowess of Japan (recently undertaken by China as the second largest economy in the world) is the core driver of discussions about change and the need for change, this is critically accompanied by the demographic factors in the country which involve a sharply declining fertility rate and a consequent shrinkage of the working age population in the coming several decades. The looming need for the same or even growing number of workers from ever smaller demographic cohorts also happens to dovetail, not coincidentally, by the increasingly popular discourse around the "business case" for greater diversity in the Japanese workplace. Indeed, the well-educated female population of the country, which has been in steady and sharp rise in the recent decades, constitutes obvious candidates for future workers and managers, compensating for the anticipated staffing shortages (Prideaux, 2007). Taken together, these recent changes hint at growing prospects for gender equality in the Japanese workplace, supported by demographic, economic, legislative, social and cultural transformation in Japanese society at large.

The recent data on various key indicators of gender equality reveal largely a continuing case of overwhelming disadvantage and underrepresentation by women in the Japanese labor market, but nevertheless also depict a certain momentum of change. Indicators such as the rise of the percentage of women in the overall labor force from 33.06% in 1970 to 40% in 2000 (Web Japan, 2008) certainly suggest a clear trajectory of change, for example. At the same time, however, as the Japanese economy is restructured firms adopt various new employment practices and most notably the increased use of nonregular, and especially part-time workers at the expense of regular, full-time workers. This makes the nature and quality of women's jobs more problematic than the figures about their overall labor force participation rates may initially suggest. We, therefore, review data on three key indicators of gender equality and the direction of their change in recent years next and discuss possible interpretations.

The casualization of employment practices through the increased use of contingent employment arrangements (which in particular include part time work) is a significant process impacting careers for the entire labor market. Nevertheless, the trend is much more marked for women workers. Though proportionately much increased, for example, for the under-45 age group of male workers, contingent workers account for less than 10%. By contrast, over 50% women over the age of 35 have been employed as part of the contingent workforce for several years, and the proportion of younger women in contingent employment has also grown very rapidly.

Beyond revealing that women workers as a group continue to be integrated into the labor market in Japan in a far more peripheral way than their male counterparts, the increased numbers of women in contingent, and especially part time, employment also has implications for the eventual number of women in management. As Japanese firms by and large continue to rely on internal labor markets for promotions leading to more senior managerial careers, and part-timers are typically *categorically* ineligible to pursue such career tracks, the increased participation of women in the labor force does not appear to be as promising for increased numbers of women in management as it may first appear. If the trends continue, in fact, there may be proportionally fewer women on managerial tracks than employed part time than before, as the rate of casualization outstrips the rates of increase in women's labor force participation.

A Ministry of Health, Labour and Welfare survey has found that although the proportion of women managers increased from 4.1% to 6.7% between 1992 and 2005, the respective proportions for women in junior, middle and senior management were 11.5%, 5.3%, and 2.8% (as cited in Benson, Yuasa, & Debroux, 2007, p. 899). To date we do not have research to support definitely that there is a "glass ceiling" effect where relatively higher numbers of women managers in the lower managerial ranks simply are not translated into correspondingly high numbers in the higher ranks, due to the various factors that lead to women's withdrawal from the labor market mid-career, especially marriage and motherhood (Roberts, 1994), or whether we are looking at a "cohort effect" where we have yet to witness how the increasing numbers of lower and middle-managerial women employees in time will also register higher numbers in senior management.

There are numerous factors that restrain the greater participation of women in paid employment and particularly in management, despite the demographic and economic factors that would otherwise be expected to lead to far more substantial change than what Japan has experienced thus far. These include, most notably, the difficulties around child and elderly care responsibilities that are expected, more so than in comparably developed economies, to be borne by women; consolidated and perpetuated by the cultural and social norms that have traditionally expected women to be "good wives and mothers" first. Despite increasing numbers of women returning to employment after childbirth, for managerial careers, such "disruptions" complicate women managers to pursue the rather strictly structured internal labor market training and promotion stages, and in the day-to-day dictates of working life, their ability to adhere to the long-working-hours culture in Japan. Balancing the act of demonstrating commitment to the employer in the traditional Japanese way, especially in the large corporations, by staying at work for very long hours, especially when coupled with the longest daily commutes in the world in Tokyo, and delivering on the domestic expectations, where men's uptake of household chores significantly lags behind that observed in advanced Western economies, proves extremely tricky and in effect discriminatory against women in management. Due to the transformation of the extended family structures, elder members of families who may be one potential source of support for care responsibilities are not likely to reside within easy travel distances to working couples, and the provision of government supported and private childcare services remains out of synch with the needs of women managers, both in terms of numbers and availability and in terms of the hours they are able to offer services. In short, factors ranging from the practical arrangements of paid and domestic work to social and cultural understandings of women's roles in the workplace continue to hinder more rapid and fundamental transformation of the traditional gender inequality in the Japanese workplace.

The Institutional Work of Gender Equality at Work and in Management

While we argue that numerous obstacles remain real and significant, as our discussion of trends above shows, change is nevertheless underway. We contend that the opening up of further opportunities for women to take up managerial careers in Japan is going to be informed especially by the institutional work to be carried out by key actors. We identify, in particular, the government and the legislative apparatus, large corporate employers, workers' unions, and foreign employers as some of these key actors, and briefly discuss some of the ways in which they are implicated in the prospects for greater female participation in work and management next.

The Government and the Legislative Apparatus

Seeing gender inequality in the workplace as an increasingly important problem in light of the demographic shifts that have been well documented, a series of Japanese governments have attempted to remedy the situation through legislation. The 1985 Equal Employment Opportunity Law (EEOL) was enacted by the Japanese legislature with claims that it would provide an "effective long term solution to gender inequity" (Araki, 2000, p. 466; Parkinson, 1989 as reported in Courmadias et al., 2010, p. 104). Still held up as the main reference point for the way Japanese government has attempted to eradicate gender discrimination in employment, the EEOL was to rectify the legal room left for overtly discriminatory acts allowed by Japanese Civil Law and to bring Japan in line with the United Nations conventions of the last 1970s aiming to eliminate gender discrimination (Nakakubo, 2007, p. 9). As Nakakubo (2007) notes, however, the legislative was met with intense opposition on the grounds that the originally intended changes "conflicted with the traditional employment practices and social values of Japan" (p.10), and consequently the final version of the EEOL became very much a compromise, requiring employers to merely "endeavor to treat men and women equally during the recruiting and hiring process (Nakakubo, 2007, p. 11). While some commentators have argued that the low demands included in the EEOL have set a standard for legislation that fails to lead societal change (Courmadias et al., 2010), it is worth noting that a series of subsequent reforms could be seen to have substantially improved the legal protection of gender equality in Japanese employment. Concerned with the falling fertility rate in the country and in anticipation of the workforce shortages in the coming decades, further legislation particularly concerned with making it possible for women to have careers was passed addressing issues around their care responsibilities. The Law for Child Care Leave in 1992 allowed maternity leave for up to a year, while legislation in 1995 targeted increasing nursery facilities. The 1997 revisions to the EEOL established rules about the implementation of positive affirmative action on behalf of women workers, in 2000 the Basic Law for Gender Equal Society confirmed the significance of gender equality as a key policy issue and in 2001 a report by the Government Tax Commission underscored that a "double income family" ought to become the new "standard" (Nakakubo, 2007, p. 11).

Courmadias et al. (2010) observe, however, that, despite the initial expectations and the high hopes placed on the legislative changes that were implemented from the mid-1980s onward, governments' efforts to ensure gender equality in the workplace have been largely unsuccessful (p. 105). This they attribute to the "soft law approach," whereby legislation has not been adequately radical and not equipped with sufficient sanctioning mechanisms and power to ensure more immediate and comprehensive translation into practice. Courmadias et al. also argue that more fundamental changes against gender discrimination in the Japanese workplace could have been executed "with the support of the ruling elites (Courmadias et al. 2010, p. 106), which they claim has been far from forthcoming.

The government's institutional work in ensuring greater gender equality in employment in Japan can also be said to remain wanting in the example it sets as an employer as well. Women's participation in the higher echelons of public sector organizations and in politics has indeed often been lower than observed in the private sector. Further problems in the implementation of the equal rights legislation also crucially include the general context of the economic downturn that has been at play in Japan since the mid-1990s. Indeed, the legislative efforts to encourage more women in paid employment and in management clash with other defining legislative changes that the government has undertaken in order to allow for flexible restructuring of corporations (Yuasa, 2008, p. 70). The deregulation made possible by these changes is largely implicated in the casualization of employment and the rise of part-time workers, and particularly among women, as demonstrated above.

Notwithstanding such limitations of the institutional work carried out by the government and particularly the legislative, it is possible, as Nakakubo (2007) is, to remain cautiously optimistic, and that "slowly but steadily" (p. 26) legislation protecting and promoting greater gender equality in employment has been involving in the right direction. For the position of women in management, the impact of legislative work can only be observed with a further time lag, as for women taking up managerial positions, especially at the higher levels, the passage of time will offer the more accurate picture.

Large Corporate Employers

The Japanese employment model, and the accompanying constraints on women's greater participation in paid work in general and management in particular, have largely been shaped in the domain of large Japanese corporations. Although these large corporate employees do not generate the largest proportion of jobs in the Japanese economy, the most prestigious and desirable management careers are to be found in these well-established companies, even more so than is generally the case in advanced economies where entrepreneurial businesses may also be held in high esteem. Within this context, the growing espousal of the "diversity agenda" by an increasing number of corporate employers in their public discourse, in line with the aforementioned changes in governmental and legislative discourse, is a development with significant implications for the prospects of changing fortunes for female workers in Japan. "Diversity management" is increasingly debated as widely accepted "best practice" in business circles, forums for the discussion of related topics typically hosting spokespeople from several of Japan's largest corporations. As a country with no substantial history of migration, including labor migration, the diversity agenda in Japan typically entails a tripartite discussion about the need for changing attitudes toward gender, but also toward nationality and age in Japanese working life. By and large, the promoted approach, in line with the stated grounds for legislative changes and governmental policy, is predicated on the "business case" approach to diversity, where the increased integration of women into paid labor and into management is argued with reference to this making "good business sense."

There are clearly problematic aspects of corporate endorsement of diversity policies on the business case alone (as opposed to equal opportunity being a social goal in and of itself), but even on their own merits the calls for greater gender equality for improved financial performance appear not to have been taken up extensively. Practice does not correspond to the increasingly prevalent discourse around large employers' having to tap into the potential of a well-educated female workforce. Not only has the growth in the number of women managers over the past decade been less than intended by the policy initiatives, but the number of companies with a positive action program for the promotion of women has in fact decreased from 40.6% in 2000 to 21.4% in 2003 (Ministry of Health, Labour, and Welfare [MHLW], 2004).The very terms of a survey on affirmative action reveals the bare minimum terms of the gender equality debate as it relates to large corporate workplaces vividly: In 2002, 72.1% of companies were "trying, or going to try, to prohibit male workers from calling women workers 'our girls' "; 61% had "recently stopped or were going to stop requiring uniforms only for female workers"; 80.3% were "trying, or were going to try, to share tasks such as making tea and cleaning"; and 61.6% were "trying, or were going to try, to teach managers to regard women as useful human assets" (Japan Institute of Workers' Evolution, 2002, as reported in Benson et al., 2007, p. 899). Graham's (2003) account of her own experience working for a large Japanese financial corporation shows that women's jobs within large, global Japanese companies continue to be overwhelmingly in the less secure, lower prestige and lower pay job categories. In this case, of those women who started out in the same category as men, from which one could advance to management, almost all had quit within two years of being hired (Graham, 2003, pp. 37–43). In our own research interviews, we found that top-level women managers in some of the largest Japanese corporations were typically one or one of only several women in comparable positions, including in cases where the workforce employed by the corporations exceeded 40,000.

The limited experiences available to women in large corporations not only hinder their opportunities to develop the skills then demanded by employers for managerial progression, but these also have repercussions for women's ability to undertake entrepreneurial efforts outside the large corporations. For example, in a report from a recent international conference on women and business held in Tokyo, representatives of a nongovernmental organization promoting women's entrepreneurial activity noted that "women in big companies tend to have fewer opportunities to take management roles such as by making business plans, and that the lack of such experience later becomes a disadvantage for women who leave the corporate world to start their own businesses" (Sakamoto, 2010).

In our view, while the diversity discourse has become increasingly more popular partially because of the felt need for a certain corporate presentation-of-self by large Japanese corporations, it is not merely insincerity on these employers' part that get in the way of greater progress in actual practice. We see, instead, the institutional work the large corporations can (and ought to) play as key in the large scale improvement of women's participation in management, but also that their ability to carry out such work is constrained by the institutional context in which they are embedded, on the one hand, and prevailing social and cultural stereotypes, held by both male and female workers, on the other. For example, given the significance of recruitment of cohorts into permanent, management-track posts by the large corporations during the final year of studies at university, the availability of a pool of female applicants is informed by the kind of degrees female students acquire at university, as well as their willingness to apply for the most competitive jobs. Despite growing incidences of mid-career employment, by and large the long-term view of large corporations toward developing managers through their internal labor markets still remains the dominant approach, and therefore the entry moment into graduate employment sets the baseline from which the possibilities for more women in future executive ranks can possibly be drawn. These initial dynamics then interact not only with the unequal treatment of graduate women workers in the large corporations, mostly entailing gender-segregated task allocation that hinders women's progress up the career ladder, but also with the aforementioned difficulties with care arrangements in the domestic sphere. Furthermore, the lack of women managers in the highest positions of large Japanese corporations also obstructs any well-intended attempts to move forward with career development programs inspired by the diversity management agenda, as the mentors and role models are often too few and far between. Nevertheless, we would wish to think as optimistically as possible about the prospects of large Japanese corporations carrying out further institutional work opening up managerial career opportunities to women in the coming years, given that at the very least there is far greater and far more public embracement of ideas about encouraging and promoting women as part of the diversity agenda.

Much of the commentary on the underrepresentation of women in paid work and in management in Japan have largely focused on these two institutional actors that we have just discussed, in relation to the larger social and cultural contexts that inform women's roles in the workplace. Although we also believe that the roles of the government and of the large corporations are particularly salient in the transformation of gender inequality in Japanese employment, in the remainder of this chapter we more briefly discuss two additional institutional actors who are implicated in any possible progress or, indeed, the lack thereof; namely workers' unions and foreign employers.

Workers' Unions

Although the unionization rate in Japan had exceeded 50% in the postwar growth period, mimicking the trajectory in most other advanced economies, this plummeted rapidly after the 1980s and by 2001 stood at a mere 20.7% (Mouer & Kawanishi, 2005, p. 200). This obviously puts the unions on a rather defensive state, and their top priorities, both at the enterprise level and at the national level, are understandably concerned more with the retainment of hitherto gained and taken-for-granted rights. One of the biggest challenges for unions is their declining participation, at least partially attributable to the rise of part-time workers who are typically less prone to become members. Union championship of women's equality in the workplace is therefore further trivialized by the fact that a far greater proportion of part-timers are women and therefore they constitute a much smaller proportion of unions' immediate constituencies than male workers.

Nevertheless, the Japan Trade Union Confederation's (JTUC's) action plan for 2006–2012 does pay particular attention to gender equality issues. Most notably, the first item on the agenda under "Promoting equal participation toward the realization of gender equality and equal treatment for women and men" is a commitment by the confederation to increase the number of female executives among its own ranks, where a numerical target for at least one female executive is set for all affiliates, enterprise-based unions and all Confederation locals (RENGO, 2006). Other action plan items include the confederation's involvement in addressing the gender wage gap, supporting gender equality through labor laws, developing women among its own ranks and networking with international partners. Clearly, the target of one woman representative is not highly encouraging for the level of ambition on the unions' part for promoting women in management, and the rather general and generic tone of the action plan suggests that the policies around promoting gender equality are not particularly clear or rigorous.

In our interviews carried out with the representatives of JTUC, we observed that women's equality in the workplace did figure rather prominently on their action agenda. Of particular interest to the union executives was the handling of the cases of dismissals and also addressing the gender pay gap. At one level, given the highly gender-segmented nature of the labor force in Japan, the emphasis on ensuring the rights for the greatest group of women workers, who are in part-time and other forms of peripheral forms of employment, seems well justified. On the other hand, our inquiry about unions' involvement in promoting greater representation of women in management revealed that, given their limited resources, coupled with the small proportion of women who partake in employment in managerial roles, rendered this a minor concern for the most organized representation of workers' voice. Despite the declining power of unions in Japan overall, we do believe that their committed participation in the transformation process is necessary for progress. However we remain measured in expectations that unions can play a role particularly for women in management in Japan. Here, their main potential input appears to us to be in the possible changes they can implement in their own ranks, thereby opening up managerial positions to women in a key organizational sphere in Japan's economic life, and also by the longer-term consequences of their support for women at work. Given the priorities the unions currently, and we think quite justifiably, place on protecting the rights of nonmanagerial women workers, their institutional work for ensuring greater gender equality in management will likely be a more indirect than direct one.

Foreign Employers

Despite Japanese firms' increasingly public claims to have embraced diversity practices to entice more women workers into their ranks (Kageyama, 2007; *Kyodo News*, 2008), the popularity lists of preferred employers by professional Japanese women are nearly monopolized by foreign employers (Takahara, 2008). Although foreign employers have traditionally been less desirable than large Japanese employers for graduates, there have been exceptions, "a notable example of this" being highly skilled women working for foreign employers (Ono, 2007, p. 275). The notion of this serendipitous fit is not new. In 1988, Lansing and Ready pointed at it as a prescription for foreign employers' recruitment problems in Japan. Foreign employers could remedy the difficulty they experienced in hiring male Japanese workers by actively pursuing women, because the local employers were "reluctant to hire them even if they may be better qualified than male graduates," and left a "large untapped pool of well-qualified people who may be willing to forego traditional prejudices about foreign firms" (Lansing & Ready, 1988, p. 112).

The subsequent decades have, if anything, made qualified Japanese women an even more widely and immediately recognized source of staff for foreign employers. The available statistical evidence on foreign employers' employment of women managers supports this general impression and suggests that they are ahead of their Japanese counterparts in this area. The Japan Institute of Labour found that the proportion of women among managers in foreign affiliated companies in Japan was as high as 17%, with almost a quarter of the companies having 20% or more female management (Japan Institute of Labour, 2001).

In a very concrete way, it can be said that foreign employers in Japan offer certain "relief routes" for women who may found managerial career paths otherwise blocked (Bozkurt, 2010). Nevertheless, our interviews with representatives of foreign employers and with women working for foreign employers (some of whom having previously worked for domestic employers while others having built their entire careers with foreign firms) also highlighted several constraints on the significance of such relief routes. First, the alternative paths offered to women by foreign employers in Japan remain severely restricted in terms of size, with two implications. On the one hand, because in sheer numbers foreign firms' employment in Japan remains very small in comparison with that of domestic firms, they cannot possibly provide sufficient volumes of relief routes for the radically increased number of women with university degrees. On the other hand, foreign employers also tend to be small organizations in their Japan operations, typically unable to offer the depth and range of occupational development opportunities found in large Japanese companies. Second, as long as large domestic companies remain the most respected and sought-after employers in Japan, the pairing up of highly educated women with foreign employers could amount to simply the elective affinity of outsiders. If women take up these jobs primarily because they have "less to lose" (Iwao, 1993, p. 169), they do so at their own risk. Foreign firms in Japan offer far less security and permanence then large Japanese employers (Ono, 2007) and, as the latter still only engage in limited mid-career hiring, the frequent decisions by foreign firms to quit the Japanese market (as evidenced in the mobile telecommunications and retail sectors in recent years), women who build managerial careers with foreign employers enjoy a rather precarious position within the context of corporate hubs for the region moving from Japan to other country locations. Finally, it is not clear if foreign employers are interested in carrying out any institutional work for the transformation of gender roles in Japanese workplaces, or are merely able to offer some opportunities for managerial careers because high-skilled women workers in Japan offer a local advantage to "exploit."

Foreign firms' practices nevertheless constitute an important element in the institutional transformation of the employment opportunities for women, because these practices offer concrete examples of human resource management strategies that make "business sense." In addition, we have found that women who have experience in management in foreign firms are also active and key figures in the increasing number of nongovernmental and nonprofit organizations that aim to promote greater gender equality in the Japanese workplace. What may be quantitatively small opportunities afforded to women by foreign employers may therefore very well have larger implications for the institutional work these firms can play in a context where change in the established traditions of domestic employers may be slower in the absence of real-life examples and external reference points.

Conclusion

In this chapter, we have assessed the current situation in Japan for women's employment in management roles. We have argued that the notoriety of Japan as persistently the advanced economy with the most restricted opportunities for women to pursue managerial careers can best be grasped within the context of the traditional Japanese employment model that had been seen as the secret to its rapid rise to economic power in the postwar era. We have further argued that the increased criticisms about the traditional Japanese model and the concurrent changes it is undergoing in terms of some of its key pillars, coupled with the demographic shifts in the country, could possibly be opening up the space for more rapid and fundamental transformation of the gendered nature of employment in the country. We have demonstrated some of the central indicators of continuing gender inequality in paid employment, linking these with the rising but still very low female participation rates in management roles. Although much of our analysis of the state of affairs has thereby revealed that the reversal of dire gender inequality in Japanese working life has not proceeded at the pace it might have been expected to, given the seriousness of the surrounding factors, we have also claimed that the trajectory is nevertheless one that holds promise. Gender equality at work and in management in Japan will demand change in multiple elements of a complex institutional web, including cultural and social gender stereotypes and expectations, arrangements for the undertaking of care responsibilities in a context of rapidly declining fertility rates and dissolution of extended families living in proximity, career ambitions among female students in higher education and indeed earlier, the long working hours culture, and the popular representations of womanhood and paid employment. In this chapter, we have therefore also discussed a number of institutional actors whose actions we see as key for the prospects for change—the government and the legislative, the large corporate employers, workers' unions, and foreign employers—and provided an overview of the institutional work they may or may not be undertaking. A still better rounded discussion ought to also consider additional actors such as educational institutions and the popular media, the latter of which, for example, still includes, since 1969, weekly television broadcast of the adventures of Sazae-san, which portrays the women of the Japanese household as full-time care providers for children in the home, and the men as breadwinners. We do believe that Japan is undergoing societal change that seriously challenges the permanence of notions of women as having to be confined to domestic, unpaid work. How that change will be reflected in working life is in good part dependent on how the interplay between the institutional work carried out by key actors will manifest itself.

References

Araki, T. (2000). Papers of the joint US-Japan-EU project on labor law in the 21st century: Equal employment and the harmonization of work and family life: Japan's soft law approach. *Comparative Labour Law and Policy Journal, 21,* 451–466.

Benson, J., Yuasa, M., & Debroux, P. (2007). The prospect of gender diversity in Japanese employment. *International Journal of Human Resource Management, 18,* 890–907.

Bozkurt, Ö. (2010). Foreign employers as relief routes: Women, multinational corporations and managerial careers in Japan. *Gender, Work and Organization, 18,* 225–253. doi: 10.1111/j.1468–0432.2009.00503.x

Brinton, M. C. (1993). *Women and the economic miracle: Gender and work in postwar Japan*. Los Angeles, CA: University of California Press.

Courmadias, N., Fujimata, Y., & Härtel, C. E. J. (2010). Japanese equal employment opportunity law: Implications for diversity management in Japan. In M. Ozbilgin and J. Syed, *Managing gender diversity in Asia: A research companion* (pp. 104–118). Cheltenham, UK: Edward Elgar.

Dore, R. (1973). *British factory, Japanese factory*. Berkeley, CA: University of California Press.

Dore, R. (1989). *How the Japanese learn to work*. London: Routledge.

Graham, F. (2003). *Inside the Japanese company*. London: Routledge Curzon.

Hanai, K. (2004). Lifting women's job status. *The Japan Times Online,* July 26. Retrieved from http://search.japantimes.co.jp/cgi-bin/eo20040726kh.html

Hiroshi, T. (1982) Working women in business corporations: The management viewpoint. *Japan Quarterly, 29,* 319–323.

Iwao, S. (1993). *The Japanese women*. Cambridge, MA: Harvard University Press.

Jacoby, S. (2005). *The embedded corporation: Corporate governance and employment relations in Japan and the United States*. Princeton, NJ: Princeton University Press.

Japan Institute of Labour. (2001). *Ministry of Health, Labour and Welfare Survey results of labour-management relations in foreign affiliated companies in*

Japan (7th ed.). Retrieved from http://www.jil.go.jp/english/laborinfo/library/documents/sr_survey1.pdf

Kageyama, Y. (2005). Japan Inc. still makes little room on the board for women. *The Japan Times Online,* January 13. Retrieved from http://search.japantimes.co.jp/cgi-bin/nb20050113a5.html

Kyodo News. (2008) Resona to increase women execs. *The Japan Times Online,* March 5. Retrieved from http://search.japantimes.co.jp/mail/nb20080305a5.html.

Lam, A. (1992) *Women and equal employment opportunities in Japan.* Oxford: Nissan Institute of Japanese Studies.

Lansing, P., & Ready, K. (1988) Hiring women managers in Japan: An alternative for foreign employers. *California Management Review, 30,* 112–127.

Ministry of Health, Labour, and Welfare (MHLW). (2004). *Result of 2003 Basic Statistical Survey on employment and management of women workers.* Retrieved from http://www.mhlw.go.jp/houdou/2004/07/h0723–2.html

Morris, J., Hassard, J., & McCann, L. (2006). New organizational forms, human resource management and structural convergence? A study of Japanese organizations. *Organization Studies, 27,* 1485–1511.

Mouer, R., & Kawanishi, H. (2005). *A sociology of work in Japan.* Cambridge: Cambridge University Press.

Nakabuko, H. (2007). *"Phase Three" of the Equal Employment Opportunity Act.* Retrieved from http://www.jil.go.jp/english/JLR/documents/2007/JLR15_nakakubo.pdf

Ono, H. (2007). Careers in foreign-owned firms in Japan. *American Sociological Review, 72,* 267–290.

Parkinson, L. (1989). Japan's Equal Employment Opportunity Law: An alternative approach to social change. *Columbia Law Review, 89,* 604–661.

Prideaux, E. (2007). Major workforce disruptions looming over Japan. *The Japan Times Online,* January 1. Retrieved from http://search.japantimes.co.jp/cgi-bin/nn20070101a3.html

RENGO (Japanese Trade Union Confederation). (2006). *TUC action policies 2010–2011—Action Policy 5 promoting equal participation toward the realization of gender equality and equal treatment for women and men.* Retrieved from http://www.jtucrengo.org/about/actionpolicy/print/pr_a_policy05.html

Renshaw, J. R. (1999). *Kimono in the boardroom: The invisible evolution of Japanese women managers.* Oxford: Oxford University Press.

Roberts, G. S. (1994). *Staying on the line: Blue-collar women in contemporary Japan.* Honolulu, HI: University of Hawaii Press.

Saso, M. (1990). *Women in the Japanese workplace.* London: Hilary Shipman.

Takahara, K. (2008). P&G, IBM most "woman-friendly." *The Japan Times Online,* April 5. Retrieved from http://search.japantimes.co.jp/cgi-bin/nb20080405a5.html

Taylor, B. W. K. (2006). A feminist critique of Japanization: Employment and work in consumer electronics. *Gender Work & Organization, 13,* 317–337.

Toshiko, F. (1983). Women in the labour force. *Kodansha Encyclopedia of Japan, 8,* 261–269.

United Nations Development Report. (2006). *Human development report.* London: Palgrave Macmillan.

Van Maanen, J. (2006). Rediscovering Japan: Some thoughts on change and continuity in traditional Japanese careers. *Career Development International, 11,* 280–292.

Volkmar, J. A., & Westbrook, K. L. (2005). Does a decade make a difference? A second look at Western women working in Japan. *Women in Management Review, 20,* 464–477.

Web Japan. (2008). *Japan fact sheet—women's issues: changing roles in a changing society.* Retrieved from http://web-japan.org/factsheet/pdf/38WomensIssues.pdf

Yuasa, M. (2008). The changing face of women managers in Japan. In C. Rowley & V. Yukongdi (Eds.), *The changing face of women managers in Asia* (pp. 68–95). London: Routledge.

I didn't want anybody to give me anything. I didn't want any special treatment. I just wanted the opportunity to have the job, to do the job and to get compensated.

—Lilly Ledbetter
Pursed equal pay rights for 10 years in the United States
President Barack Obama signed into law the
Lilly Ledbetter Fair Pay Act in 2009.

14

Women Managers and Leaders in the Dominican Republic

Jenny K. Rodriguez

Scholars (i.e. Murray, 2010) challenge the messianic view of globalization as an encompassing phenomenon. Feminist scholars in particular highlight its uneven impact, and the ways it interacts with the fragmented nature of women's lives, opportunities, and experiences. Debates on global feminism, gender democracy, and more specifically the feminization of work and the new worker, hint at a cautious approach when assuming that many, most or all women have new, created and discovered opportunities in the labor market as a result of globalization (Bolton & Muzio, 2008; Ferre, 2006; Johanson, 2008; Vargas, 2003).

El-Bushra (2000) has noted that there is confusion in the use of gender in the development literature, where it is assumed that gender equals women's economic development. A central point here is that the macro rhetoric has not translated into changes to realities at the micro level, especially for women in developing countries. Women have been the big losers in the globalizing game because even with a steady participation in the labor market in the last two decades (United Nations, 2010), access has not meant equality in opportunities of upward mobility, salary and status in the workplace. Women remain underrepresented in managerial and leadership roles and overrepresented in vulnerable employment such as part-time, low-skilled, and low-status jobs (Alvesson & Due Billing, 2009; Dolado, Felgueroso & Jimeno, 2004; Schein, 2007; Vinnicombe & Singh, 2002).

The previous paragraph provides a conceptual and practical justification for ideas discussed in this chapter. Globalization rhetoric could easily mislead us into thinking that things have dramatically improved for women everywhere. The reality is that mapping features of work in general and managerial work in particular, as enacted and performed by women in developing countries remains largely ignored in the literature. The literature (i.e. Kinnear, 2011) focuses on the struggles a large majority of women in developing countries face with basic individual and economic rights. However, in essentializing women in developing countries as poor, uneducated and oppressed the diverse nature of their lives and experiences is invisibilized. This limits the exploration of local gender hierarchies as well as a much-needed wider interpretation that incorporates intersections beyond culture and socioeconomic factors.

This chapter takes an important step in advancing understanding of how women navigate and challenge dynamics that place them in a disadvantaged position in the workplace. It does so by writing the lives of women managers in a developing country. More importantly, organizations are spaces where societal values and structures are reproduced, and distinct dynamics of gendering are performed (Acker, 2003, 2006; Alvesson & Due Billing, 2009). Consequently, taking a closer look at the way in which the managerial and leadership roles are enacted as part of intersecting structures of power and dimensions of difference in the workplace provides much needed insight into the micropolitics of gender democracy, which is a fundamental issue that affects women's credibility and legitimacy in the managerial role.

In this chapter I report on empirical research into discourses and tensions of women managers that emerge from gender constructions and dynamics within public organizational settings in the Dominican Republic. I analyze these at structural, cultural (ideological), and identity levels using Joan Acker's (1990, 1992a, 2003) framework of gendered hierarchies in organizations. In the chapter, I argue that the major challenge faced by the women managers in the public sector in the Dominican Republic is the institutionalized patriarchal system which is reproduced by both men and women and imposes strict gender role dynamics based on sexist ideologies. I also argue that women managers discursively resist and bypass these dynamics by playing identity games which allow them to navigate the system. The chapter is organized in five sections. After this introduction, which frames the problem and identifies a gap in the literature pertaining to the writing of professional women's lives in developing countries, the second section conceptually addresses women in management and gender dynamics. A third section focuses on the context, discussing Latin American's women's lives and work, providing specific insight into Dominican women. The fourth section reports on discursive constructions and tensions associated with being a woman manager and leader in Dominican public sector, and the last section concludes.

Throughout the chapter, I shall draw on arguments pertaining to the complex, multidimensional realities women managers experience as a result of how perceived expectations of their social and family roles interplay vis-à-vis with work identities. Given that in developing countries women face social realities filled with inequalities and lack of opportunity, experiences in the workplace are relevant not only to identify suitable ways in which women can be supported but also to understand how women themselves construct their work identities and challenge existing assumptions within the social system. In the following section, I review key propositions about women in management, positioning the discussion as part of the interplay between women in management and gender dynamics.

Women in Management and Gender Dynamics

There are conflictive positions about women's accomplishment in the workplace. On the one hand, there are views contending that "women have made it" while on the other, questions remain about the extent to which achievements identified are misleading and this view make assumptions, especially of woman as a universal, homogeneous category (Hughes, 2002, pp. 32–34). One thing that remains certain is that women do not stand on a level playing field with male counterparts. The managerial role continues to be problematic for women mainly because organizations remain a male site so men are the norm against which women are compared (Due Billing, 2011). The achievement of gender democracy at work remains in question given the pervasive nature of stereotypes, barriers, and cultural models that put women in a disadvantaged position in the workplace (Barreto, Ryan & Schmitt, 2009; Blair-Loy, 2001; Heilman, 2002). Despite an increase in overall numbers in general and numbers of women qualified for management positions in particular, as well as the feminization of leadership (Höpfl & Matilal, 2007), women now experience complex, more subtle barriers to upward mobility and advancement in their careers (Blum, Fields, & Goodman, 1994; Davidson & Burke, 2004; Duehr & Bono, 2006; Helgesen, 2003; Kirchmeyer, 2002).

Much literature on management and leadership has traditionally emphasized similarities and differences between men and women's styles (i.e. Alimo-Metcalfe, 1995; Carli & Eagly, 2007; Eagly, Johannesen-Schmidt & van Engen, 2003) and what needs to be done to foster the development of female leadership in organizations (i.e. Valerio, 2009). However, an important aspect that merits further scrutiny is the gendered nature of these constructs and how they permeate the constitutive features of organizational life.

Gender shapes and creates organizational processes (Acker, 1999) and organizational settings play a fundamental role in this; they have been traditionally structured on masculine terms, reproducing paternalistic assumptions about women and men's roles in society (Kanter, 1994). Organizational dynamics are particularly strong mechanisms for reproduction of these assumptions and they reflect the hegemonic masculinity (Connell & Messerschmidt, 2005) and heteronormativity (Jackson, 2003, 2006) present in both division of labor and gender dynamics at work. As a result, special roles and positions, as well as several limitations have historically affected women at work and continue to make them a disadvantaged group in the labor market.

Inequality in access to certain positions and organizational levels is linked to reinforced notions of female inadequacy to deal with the pressures and demands of managerial work and a perceived lack of strategic acumen and mindset (Ibarra & Obodaru, 2009). There is indeed a strong case for the latter as women struggle to find suitable mentors to help them develop their skills and support them to advance in their careers (Ehrich, 2008; Linehan & Scullion, 2008; Sealy & Singh, 2006) so their access to and visibility in the managerial domain is limited. Dominant constructions of the managerial identity follow the "think manager, think male" (Schein, 2007) pattern that assumes that the characteristics of successful managers are more similar to and have more in common with men than with women, thus making women unnatural for the role.

However, the issue should not be framed in dichotomous terms. Some discussions (i.e. Bourdieu, 2004; Bourdieu & Wacquant, 2004; Mavin, 2006a, 2006b, 2008) recognize that in order to understand and transform unequal gender relations, it is important to scrutinize the dynamics enacted within the wider system of gender relations. Two things are important here; first, the shift in the literature from women in management to gender in management as it recognizes that both femininities and masculinities struggle for power and resources (Lupton, 2000), and second, the relevance of the agentic role of women in articulating and perpetuating gender dynamics. The latter is particularly linked to unraveling the intricacies of solidarity behavior amongst women in organizations.

The strength of men and masculinities in organizational discourse can no longer be understood as an unquestioned force (Collinson & Hearn, 1994) and instead, gender discourses seem more appropriate to account for the multifaceted experiences of both women and men. Organizations are gendered because they are not only the source of gender dynamics but they also reproduce them through the creation of cultural meanings that draw upon gendered ideas, values and assumptions shared by its members (Alvesson & Due Billing, 2009; Ely & Meyerson, 2001).

I noted at the start of this chapter that I use Joan Acker's (1990, 2003) framework of gendered hierarchies in organizations to explore discursive constructions at structural, cultural (ideological) and identity levels. In the following section, I briefly discuss the notion of gendered organizations as a backdrop to address Acker's work.

Gendering Organizations

The analysis of organization from a gender perspective is central to highlight the way gender identity construction and relations result in specific social arrangements in organizations that sustain unequal power relations that affect certain groups, primarily women. Rao and Kelleher (2005) have noted that "power hides the fact that organizations are gendered at very deep levels" (p. 64). The suggestion of an inherent structural gendering is in line with research that has found that prevalent masculinized notions respond to the way organizations perpetuate the status quo of dominant groups which in most cases are men (Kanter, 1977).

Rao and Kelleher (2005) have argued that there are four factors that prevent women from challenging masculinized dynamics in organizations; political access, accountability systems, cultural systems, and cognitive structures. The issue of political access is one of the most fundamental ones as women lack support systems or individuals to facilitate that their interests and perspectives become visible because organizations engage in processes of silencing (Simpson & Lewis, 2007) that maintain dynamics of power, exclusion, and invisibility.

Organizational cultures are one of the strongest mechanisms through which gendering takes place in organizations; it not only helps to shape beliefs about work identities, but it also entails mechanisms of justification and creation of values to reinforce those beliefs. Specific ideas and understandings about women and men, in particular expectations about femininity and masculinity (Acker, 2003, 2006; Alvesson & Due Billing, 2009), then become the "right way" to perceive, think, and feel in relation to the organization and embedded in the subjective way in which people in the organization (i.e. Gherardi, 1995; Schein, 1985; Smircich, 1983).

However, the gender subtext is often unacknowledged or suppressed (Martin, 1990), which helps to perpetuate the idea of organizations as gender-neutral spaces where structures and processes are simply operational creations rather than sites of gendered sense-making. In addition, the pervasive influence of societal assumptions sees gendered patterns of thought and actions (re) produced in organizations and the perpetuation of systems of inequality and oppression for women.

Acker's work is of seminal importance in broadening the scope of the study of gender in organizations and has been used to highlight the gendered nature of organizations (i.e. Metcalfe & Linstead, 2003; Singh, Anderson, & Vinnicombe, 2006). In this chapter, its use has both a conceptual as well as a practical justification. Conceptually, Acker's argument results from identifying gendered occurring processes in organizational settings, which she organizes in three different levels: structural, cultural (ideological), and identity. This helps to inform analysis of concrete or symbolic subordination of women (Acker, 1998, p. 251).

As a patterned, socially produced phenomenon (Acker, 1992b, p. 250), gender is central to understanding how people make sense of their identities, roles, and overall presence in organizations. Acker has drawn on the assertion that gender is omnipresent in social life and consequently in its institutions and organizations, hence the term "gendered institutions" (1990, p. 567). She argued that an organization is gendered when "advantage and disadvantage, exploitation and control, action and emotion, meaning and identity, are patterned through and in terms of a distinction between male and female, masculine and feminine." Based on this idea, she argues that there are five interacting processes where gendering takes place (pp. 146–147):

- *Construction of divisions along the lines of gender* → divisions of labor, of allowed behaviors, of locations in physical space, of power.
- *Construction of symbols and images that support the existence of these divisions* → language, ideology, popular and high culture, dress, the press, television.
- *Interactions between men and women, women and women, and men and men* → patterns that enact dominance and submission and produce gendered social structures.
- *Production of gendered components of individual identity* → choice of appropriate work, language use, clothing, gendered presentation of self.
- *Creation and conceptualization of social structures* → work rules, labor contracts, managerial directives, and HR systems.

Acker's constructions present us with the idea that there are ways in which organizations understand and act upon gender so in all cases, either when gender is assumed, when it's not assumed, when it's neglected or when it's addressed; messages regarding understandings about men, women, masculinity, and femininity are being sent. In that sense, organizational culture can obscure gender through gendering dynamics that embed images of the male manager as the desirable identity.

An important point in Acker's work has referred to "significant boundaries we have crossed in putting these fields together" (1998, p. 195). Acker agrees that organizations are not rigid structures but that they rather operate as processes and as such; they not only develop within themselves but also in relation to their environment. Drawing on this idea, she identifies boundaries linked to the processes that affect the integration of gender and organizations through "transcending the gender subtext of central theoretical categories and concerns [and instead putting it to use to illuminate] broader or deeper meaning of a phenomenon" (Alvesson & Due Billing, 2009, p. 192).

Her analysis has identified three accomplishments and three challenges; the accomplishments relate to crossing the boundaries of discursive constructions that generate conceptual distance, theoretical developments that compartmentalize phenomena, and separation between the public and private spheres. The challenges pertain to the understanding of the gendered substructure of organizations, the implications of globalization and its effects in gendering terms, and the role of pleasure and violence in organizations. In using her framework for the analysis of women managers, this chapter addresses the first challenge: to understand the gendered substructure of organizations.

Having set the conceptual foundations of the topics relevant to the themes discussed in the chapter, I will now provide a brief overview of the context. In the next section I provide an overview of the situation of women at work in the Dominican Republic and place this discussion within the wider regional context of Latin America and the Caribbean.

Latin American Women's Lives and Work: A View of Dominican Women

The realities of women in Latin America and the Caribbean are uneven and fragmented. The great Mexican writer Octavio Paz (2000) has noted that in the region, women are imprisoned in the image that masculine society imposes on them. The mix of conservative views on matters related to gender roles which are reinforced by a Roman Catholic religious heritage, and the prevalence of machismo (Gonzalbo Aizpuru, 1997; Inglehart & Carballo, 1997; Inglehart & Norris, 2003) has resulted in a considerable lag in gender equality. Consequently, individuality is a struggle where women must dismantle the representation of stereotypes constructed, framed and projected by dominant masculine ideologies (Ortega & Saporta-Sternbach, 1989, p. 14) before they can move to articulate other identities as workers, managers, or leaders.

The participation of Latin American women in the labor market has increased in the last decades with many women becoming head of households. It is estimated that at least one in every five of urban households (20%–30%) has a female head (Oficina Nacional de Estadísticas, 2007). The previous trend has been explained (Therborn, 2004) as a result of changes in the composition of families with a prevalence for informal couplings and unstable relationships. However, women are mostly employed in the services and informal sectors in low-paid, sex-segregated occupations (Abramo, 2006; Abramo & Valenzuela, 2005; Candia, 2003; de Oliveira & Ariza, 1997; Freeman, 2000; Oficina Nacional de Estadísticas, 2007). Their presence decreases at higher hierarchical levels (Zabludovsky & de Avelar, 2001) and while there has been an increase in women in management and other executive positions, there is scarce qualitative or quantitative data available on this (Ulshoefer, n.d.).

Women in the region experience exclusion and segregation from the labor market as a result from pressures to remain primarily or exclusively within the domestic domain (de Oliveira & Ariza, 2000). These pressures are associated with the idolization of biological politics (de Oliveira & Ariza, 2000) that sees womanhood usually constructed through motherhood; it is expected that women prioritize reproduction over production and therefore their "place" is usually assumed/thought to be in the private sphere taking care of the children and maintaining the household (Parrado & Zenteno, 2001). There is clear spillover that limits their ability to negotiate work identities; as a result, women face a double jeopardy with simultaneous demands from the private and the public spheres that make it difficult for them to develop distinct role identities. The existence of barriers at corporate level has been reported by Zabludovsky and de Avelar (2001) in their study of Mexican and Brazilian executives. Prejudices and stereotypes as well as lack of planning and counterproductive behavior by male colleagues were identified by their sample as the main obstacles. In that sense, while there is a multidimensionality of situations of power, subordination, and exploitation that affect women in all aspects of their lives (Vargas, 1989), it all primarily starts with challenges associated with the separation and reconciliation of family and professional roles.

Dominican women are no exception to these stereotypes and realities, and the increasing number of women in the workplace has not meant an increase in gender equality. There has been resistance to the stereotypes, but this has not translated into formal articulation of voices of dissent in the workplace at managerial level. Dominican women have been generally absent as creators of legitimate identity discourses, and their presence in the literature (i.e. Julia, 1990) has normally been limited to descriptions of their supportive roles as mothers, sisters, and wives of men who played decisive roles in the historical, social, political, and cultural aspects of the country, praising their merits as caring members of society, examples of virtue and supportive to men's patriotic ventures. Anim-Addo (2004) has noted that the world of African Caribbean women has not been given scope for theoretical academic development, which could explain why the lives of women remain undocumented and marginally addressed. This sets the tone for an anecdotal approach that systematically repeats generalized ideas about women's lives and experiences.

Nevertheless, according to Candelario (2005, pp. 43–46), Dominican women have been "doing feminism" since the end of the 19th century; first by participating in the Liga Internacional de Mujeres Ibéricas e Hispanoamericanas [International League of Iberian and Hispanic-American Women] and later organizing the first feminist assembly in the Dominican Republic in 1932. This was the start of what culminated in 1940 with the first bill of civil rights for Dominican women. This bill was a defining point for feminism in the Dominican Republic as for the first time in Dominican history, women had the same rights and civil duties as men. However, the civil rights law continued to perpetuate patterns of female subordination and dependency.

In that sense, the idea of late modernity of Latin American states (i.e. Pou, 1987) becomes relevant as well for the case of women's issues as their struggles pertains to dimensions that have been long institutionalized in industrialized contexts. For example, in 1981 the Movimiento Feminista de América Latina y el Caribe [Feminist Movement of Latin America and the Caribbean] established the International Day for Nonviolence against Women to be commemorated each year on November 25. According to Báez and Tapia (2002, p. 72), this is an important date for the feminist movement in the Dominican Republic because violence against women and girls is a widespread phenomenon that has been naturalized and is considered as a private matter within poor uneducated families or among "dysfunctional" women. According to newspaper reports, in the Dominican Republic at least nine women are murdered each month by husbands or former partners and it has been noted (Pola Zapico, 2003) that the issue only gains public relevance as a result of the voyeuristic interest of the media in the dramatic and sadistic nature of cases.

In terms of work trends, the inclusion of Dominican women in paid employment has increased over the years; however, they remain, alongside young people, the most vulnerable to unemployment (Martí, 2006). Women represent 51% of professional and technical workers, but only account for 32% of legislators, senior officials, and managers. In terms of political empowerment, there are only 20% of women in parliament with only 14% holding ministerial

TABLE 14.1
Labor force indicators, 2006–2011

Year	Participation rate (%)			Employment rate (%)			Unemployment rate (%)		
	Total	Male	Female	Total	Male	Female	Total	Male	Female
2006	56.0	68.6	43.6	46.9	62.3	31.9	16.2	9.2	27.0
2007	56.1	69.3	43.2	47.4	62.8	32.2	15.6	9.3	25.4
2008	55.6	67.9	43.5	47.7	62.2	33.5	14.1	8.5	22.8
2009	53.8	67.4	40.3	45.8	60.8	31.0	14.9	9.8	23.2
2010	55.0	67.8	42.4	47.1	61.1	33.3	14.3	9.8	21.4
2011[a]	56.2	68.8	43.7	48.0	62.1	34.0	14.6	9.7	22.3

Note. From Central Bank of Dominican Republic (2012).
[a] Preliminary figures for April 2011.

positions (Hausmann, Tyson, & Sahidi, 2008, p. 72). Table 14.1 provides an overview of labor force indicators for 2006–2011.

Dominican Workplaces: The Public Sector

Very little is known about dynamics in Dominican workplaces, particularly in the public sector. Some exceptions include the works by Montesino (2002) and Rodriguez (2010, 2011). An important finding in Montesino's (2002) work is the identification of authoritarian traits in the manager/worker relationship in his study of organizational behavior traits in the Dominican Republic which included a state bank branch as part of the sample.

However, it is relevant to briefly discuss the development of the public sector in the Dominican Republic to understand how it becomes a site for reproduction of societal gendered norms. The history of Dominican public sector has been fragmented and has mainly responded to demagogic political rhetoric. Some authors have associated this with the authoritarian and centralized political administrative heritage of Spanish colonialism that saw the development of a societal structure based on personal interest and gain. The outcome is a sector with a historical lack of credibility, integrity, and efficiency (Finkel, Sabatini, & Bevis, 2000) where decisions and actions respond to the personal interests of powerful individuals and groups.

There is an authoritarian and excessively centralized political tradition which has resulted in limited institutionalization and managerial capability of State institutions to comply with social demands and aspirations). In structural terms, the organization of the public sector has been fragmented and

TABLE 14.2
Public administration and defense employment, 2008–2010

Year	Employed			Unemployed (dismissed)		
	Total	Male	Female	Total	Male	Female
2008	4	67	33	4	58	42
2009	5	64	36	4	36	64
2010	5	68	32	2	40	60

Note. Data from the National Labour Force Survey, Central Bank of Dominican Republic (2012).

inconsistent. Efforts to standardize the public sector through the instauration of a system of civil service and administrative career can be traced back to the mid-19th century and beginning of the 20th century, being the first one oriented to develop the principle of stability in public sector posts. Other numerous efforts are also recognized yet the pivotal moment came in 1991, when Congress approved the bill for Civil Service and Administrative Career which was presented by the Oficina Nacional de Administración y Personal [National Office for Administration and Personnel] (ONAP).

The Civil Service Act was seminal in recognizing that the Dominican State should overcome politicized approaches to the management of public office and develop a sense of social responsibility, credibility and transparency. However, Kearney (1986) has argued that the major constraint in the implementation of civil service is the tradition of patronage associated with the presidential figure. Indeed all decisions related to recruitment, selection, promotion and termination are signed off by the president's office. The Act confers discretionary power upon the Office of the President to directly appoint and terminate a wide range of civil servants. According to the World Bank (2004), "the weight of such executive privilege weakens the institutional mandate of ONAP and undermines the authority of agency heads over their staff" (p. 106).

Although there are no trustworthy sources to establish the number of workers who actually get their salaries from the state arks (World Bank, 2004, p. 127), data from the National Labour Force Survey suggests that 4%–5% of the employed population works in the public sector. Table 14.2 provides an overview of employment data in the sector for 2008–2010.

Research Framework

Data used for the analysis presented in this chapter derive from research on gender construction in organizational culture in the public sector in the Dominican Republic. The research had the aims of examining how the process of gender construction takes place within public organizational settings at structural, cultural (ideological), and identity levels; exploring the ways in which gender dynamics operate within organizational culture, and recovering the experiences of gender identity construction of women working in organizations in the public sector. The research was conducted between 2004 and 2007 and included 40 in-depth interviews with 27 women and 13 men, of whom 5 and 6 respectively held managerial posts that included line management responsibilities. All participants worked in Santo Domingo, capital city of the Dominican Republic, in governmental institutions in the areas of education, women's issues, and banking/finance.

Questions at interviews covered an array of topic primarily related to their working lives, experiences, and interactions in the workplace. Analysis was conducted using discourse analysis. Fairclough (1992) has argued that discourse is both a political and an ideological practice as it not only establishes, sustains, and changes power relations and the collective entities between which power relations are obtained, but also constitutes, sustains, and changes significations of the world from different positions within power relations (p. 67). The use of discourse analysis facilitated approaching the research problem accounting for the relevance of power in the enactment of gender relations.

As previously indicated, I used Acker's gendered processes as a framework for the discussion of discourses and specific themes within them. By means of highlighting recurrent themes within broader discourses, I identify gender discursive constructions and by using Acker's processes, it was possible to establish a clear map of the specific aspects of structural, cultural (ideological), and identity levels and the intertextuality between the discursive practices. These reflected generated by these discourses show a sexualized, paternalistic core around which organizational processes, structures, and identities revolve. In the next section I move to discuss discursive constructions and tensions in more detail.

Being a Woman Manager and Leader in the Dominican Public Sector: Discourses and Tensions

Themes that emerged from the data were organized as part of an interconnected web of institutional, relational, and self-discursive constructions. *Institutional discourses* articulated organizational culture as masculinized and established clear distinctions between women and men based on sexualized assumptions about labor appropriateness and affinity. *Relational discourses* emerged from the exploration of the interplay of femininities and masculinities and highlighted games of domination/passivity in relationships as well as conflictive enactment of solidarity and competitiveness. Finally, *discourses of the self* explored articulations of womanhood and manhood, reflecting fixed understandings of woman and man as distinct categories positioned as binary opposites.

Institutional Discourses

Gender plays a significant role in the social structure of public sector organizations. A salient feature is the masculinized organizational culture. Structures, processes, and dynamics validate and prioritize masculinity as traits inherent to the public sector. There is a general sense that the primary public servant is male, and laws, regulations, and procedures are articulated around the use of masculine terminology to refer to workers in the sector. Underlying messages of men as primary workers are therefore identified and this is the first conflict women managers faced as dominant masculine ideologies are constant reminders that they need to adjust to a masculinized role in order to meet expectations of performance. In the organizations studied, this masculinized culture was reinforced through management artifacts and creations, which dominated organizational life and structured it in a way that reinforced existing gendered distinctions. For instance, one woman manager noted that upon mentioning the impersonal feel of her office given the choice of color, she was told that "it was not supposed to be a home; that it was an office with a professional look, a look to send a message of efficiency."

This message of separation of home/work hints at the masculinization of the workplace in contrast to the presumed feminization of the home. There is a dichotomization where home and work are placed at opposing ends of the spectrum and the distinction created through the artifact of decor in dark colors, which is assumed to be "professional" and "efficient" and distances the workplace from a home environment, which might then be colorful and thus "unprofessional and inefficient." The use of a uniform was another example of gendered artifacts and creations; while men did not have to wear uniforms, it was compulsory for all women, creating a gender force field (i.e. Williams, 2000) in the regulation of physicality in the organization. The uniform consisted of a feminized version of the male power suit. Forcing all women to wear the same clothes in colors that resembled what men usually wear in office environments highlights the attempted elimination of femininity and the homogenization of women's organizational identities.

As part of this gender force field, women managers also struggled with other forms of symbolic allocation of status (i.e. Weick, 1979, 1995). One explained that while she had been given a separate space when promoted, her office did not have a door even when her role included regular meetings of a confidential nature. She raised this issue with the institutional director and was told that she should just make the best of it. Conversely, a similarly recently promoted male manager in an open space had demanded to be built an office. Recounting this event, a male employee commented that the whole office space had been rearranged to fit an office where there was not enough space to do so and this had resulted in desks and filing cabinets being cramped to make room for the office. He further added the following:

> [the manager] is the luckiest one [. . .] he has his own office and his door is always closed so nobody bothers him. The rest of us are common employees and nobody cares if we are like sardines. (JN, aged 41, single, 17 years working in the sector)

These accounts suggest the preferential use and allocation of institutional space as the symbolic discursive framing used to objectify roles and positions, which also legitimize gendered organizational social practices that focus on perceived entitlements of femininity and masculinity (Ertürk, 2004; Pels, Hetherington, & Vandenberghe, 2002).

Another indicator of the masculinization of the culture was the segregated nature of occupational distribution; the majority of organizational directors were men, all secretaries were women, all security personnel were men, all gardeners were men, and all cleaners were women. This distribution was justified on assumptions about labor appropriateness/affinity, where men are seen as more effective in decision making and women at providing support. Similarly the gendered subtext hinted at essentialist notions of women as emotional and generally inadequate for the demands of the sector. The following comments from male managers demonstrate this:

> It's better to have a male boss because with a man you know where you stand. Women are OK today then cry tomorrow. . . . how can you handle that? (AM, aged 38, married, 7 years working in the sector)

> The public sector is too aggressive; you need to have a tough character and women are too susceptible. (CP, aged 60, married, 20 years working in the sector)

Individuals engaged in this sexualization of occupational roles, embrace and reproduce the gendered assumptions that underlie them. Interestingly, women managers who were in positions that conflicted with these roles did not clearly associate themselves with powerlessness. Instead, they justified their positioning adjusting to the institutional construction of femininity as a primary trait of their organizational persona. However, there was also fluidity in the way they performed the role; for instance, while complying with the expected role (caring woman with concerns for others), women managers also played other roles (tough boss who behaves in a demanding manner). In doing so, women managers navigated perceived feminine and masculine dimensions of the role; this suggests that they engaged in identity games, transforming the role into a fluid site of gender (re)construction.

Relational Discourses

Most accounts of relational dynamics problematized women managers' struggles to be respected and "get on with the job." Construction of role adequacy is based on gendered assumptions and relational dynamics articulated as a result. Relational discourses seemed articulated following a patriarchal structure where men dominated the direction and pace of interaction. Women generally assumed passive roles and vertical domination was identified in the ways in which men dominate conversations, topic selection, and space/time allocation of interactions. Women were generally expected to comply with sexualized roles despite their hierarchical status. For example, women managers made the following comments:

> In my experience, women are expected to be there serving coffee or taking notes. In meetings, sometimes they expect that because I am the only woman and sometimes suggest indirectly that I should, but I don't accept that. (AA, aged 61, married, 41 years working in the sector)

> I take the notes in the meetings with other Directors . . . I guess since I am HR they think I'm the best person to do it. Sometimes I wish others would take notes to make it more even so that I can participate more in discussions. (YM, aged 52, divorced, 30 years working in the sector)

These comments highlight the heterogeneity in approaches by women managers. The fragmented nature of their experiences in the managerial role suggested that there was no single approach to dealing with this. Some of the women felt that male managers undermined their voice and authority; one reported that on several occasions her views had been criticized by male colleagues who considered her "too soft," and during a meeting she had been cut short by a male colleague who jokingly said that she needed to "stop being the Mother Teresa of employees." Despite the evidence of indirect aggression showcased in their accounts, some women adopted a noncritical approach when reporting interactions where they felt undermined, indicating that they did not interpret them as deserving special attention because they detracted from the job. A reading of this could instead suggest that women managers avoided confrontation related to aspects of the meaning of, and their entitlement to the role.

Relationships between women managers and others were fragmented and dynamics revealed power struggles for legitimacy. Women managers acknowledged using discretionary strategies in order to validate their role where they felt others did not do so. For example, one commented the following:

> I know if I say something straight, they think I'm being bossy. Sometimes it's necessary that you act as if you're asking them to do things, but what you're really doing is telling them to do it. (AA, aged 61, married, 41 years working in the sector)

This was confirmed by a male employee who indicated that he recognized that part of his female line manager sometimes changed her tone, depending on what she wanted. An important aspect of relational discourses was the way in which the leadership dimension was articulated. Women managers' strategies were construed as conflictive insofar as they presented as incongruent in relation to the role (Eagly & Karau, 2002). In all cases, women managers showcased agentic consciousness and interpreted their behavior as adaptive; for instance, while a woman manager assessed her behavior as assertive and task-oriented, a male manager commented that:

> She is a bit aggressive and that doesn't go down well with women, let alone men. (RA, aged 37, 5 years working in the sector)

The previous comment illustrates the point made by Eagly and Karau (2002) that women struggle to exercise control and authority because what is acceptable for male leaders is considered "bossy" or "domineering" when performed by women. However, comments by female employees suggest that they assume the managerial role to be inherently masculine. The following comment demonstrates this:

> She [the line manager] behaves as if she were scared of them [the other directors]. Right now, most of them are men and there are two other women. But those are like men, they are not afraid of anybody. My boss is the contrary and that's why nobody respects her. (OP, aged 29, single, 4 years working in the sector)

Both relationships between women managers as well as between women managers and other women were conflictive, which challenges ideas of female solidarity. Mavin (2006a) has argued that when women enter the managerial arena they destabilize the gendered order, which puts them in a no-win situation because in adapting to their new environment, they adopt masculinized behaviors which conflict with both men and women. Women managers acknowledged that they felt misunderstood by other women; in particular perceptions of entitlement to the role varied and generated resentment and distrust. Some highlighted that their credibility was always questioned as the sector had a bad reputation. With the latter, the change in dynamics following a promotion to a management role was problematized with their personal integrity at times put into question. A comment by a female employee suggests this:

> It's tough to know that some people talk to you and inside are asking themselves who you slept with to be here. You spend most of the time trying to prove them wrong. (DB, aged 31, single, 3 years working in the sector)

Similarly, women managers felt conflicted by perceived demands from other women who seemed to take for granted their accomplishments and assume that the category of "woman" in itself created a duty of solidarity. The following remark demonstrates this:

> Women expect something from you, as if they expected that you treated them better because you're a woman and they are too. I got where I am because I respected and asked to be respected both by men and women. (AA, aged 61, married, 41 years working in the sector)

These accounts reveal the discursive practices that both women managers and their staff engage in. More importantly, they highlight the complexity in the construction of managerial leadership. Women managers struggled to legitimize their position while others struggled to make sense of their presence. As a result, dynamics were fragmented and the relationship was neither dialogical nor relational (Cunliffe & Eriksen, 2011).

Discourses of the Self

The fluidity of women managers' work identities was central to the way women engaged with the role. Women reflected on their role using terms such as "changing modes" and "chameleon" yet somehow distanced from this as a fixed way to articulate their identities. Instead, they suggested that this was the result of the pressures in the work environment and noted that at work they were someone different from the person they were at home. This was problematized by one woman manager who commented the following:

> I don't like feeling inferior so I have a strong personality here. But I am not the same person at home because there I don't have to be on guard all the time. (AA, aged 61, married, 41 years working in the sector)

The poignant reference to feelings of inferiority and insecurity is fundamental to understand the level of self-awareness of women managers in relation to their identities in the role. Nonetheless, despite this and contrary to a different interpretation (i.e. Whitehead, 2001), women managers did not see themselves as the embodiment of a counter-hegemonic statement. Instead they revealed a double conscience; on the one hand, they showcased awareness of the operating restrictions to their roles and identities, at times in the form of ambiguous messages and responses. On the other hand, by engaging in masculinized behavior they became complicit in the violence exercised against them (Bourdieu & Wacquant, 2004). The next comment suggests this:

> When I speak to my subordinates I can tell them when I want things and how I want them but when I speak to other heads of department I have to adapt my style [. . .] you have to find the right time for things. (AC, aged 45, married, 2 years working in the public sector)

Women managers acknowledged that they negotiated their identities and while this could be interpreted as undermining, a reading of resistance could also be made. In playing identity games women managers negotiated challenging dimensions of both their role and work identity. This is indeed problematic because in terms of identity, women managers are women first so given cultural constructions of woman in the Dominican context, sexualized embodiment becomes intertwined with the meaning attributed to the role. Women acknowledged that being a manager combined physical appearance, behaviors, and negotiation of constructions as understood to inherently define what a woman look like and be like.

The previous was highlighted by a woman manager who recounted that upon her promotion, a fellow woman manager at another institution had advised her to change her hair and pay more attention to her grooming (makeup, clothes, jewelry, etc.) because as a manager she would be on everyone's radar and she needed to play the part. This was also hinted by a female employee who commented that her line manager lacked finesse because she wore very

TABLE 14.3
Discourse constructions

Acker's gendered processes	Discourse	Themes
Division along gender lines	Institutional Labor appropriateness/ affinity	Masculine hegemony Women's inadequacy for the managerial role Segregation
Construction/ reproduction of gendered symbols and images	Institutional Masculinized organizational culture	Office as a power/ status symbol The power suit
Interactions between women managers with men and other women	Relational Domination/passivity Solidarity	Symbolic violence against women managers Lack of solidarity behavior between women
Gendered construction of individual identity	Self Womanhood	Identity games Negotiation of femininity and masculinity
Role of gender in social structure/ construction	Institutional Masculinized organizational culture	Masculinized norms Gendered structures

little makeup and looked like any woman walking out on the street. In that sense, part of the successful enactment of the role seemed to be associated with a "polished" version of the physical self.

Having discussed the discursive constructions, Table 14.3 summarizes the main discourses and themes. In the next section I move to address the main tensions identified in the analysis of discursive practices.

Discourse Tensions

The main tension identified was related to the ambiguity and fluidity in the way women managers played with their identities and reconstructed them based both on their needs as well as the needs of others. Generally, this refers to how fragmented and contradictory the lives of women and men are in and around organizations (Collinson, 2003). In particular, it hints at how women managers negotiate their organizational presence. However, within the apparent homogeneity of fragmented experiences, women's strategies were diverse and showcased various ways in which their behavior challenged cultural assumptions and expectations. In the Dominican context, female roles and women's identities are primarily associated with motherhood and wifehood. Other tensions pertain to the masculinization of women, the challenges in the relationship between women managers and other women, and the tensions surrounding role subversion.

The problematization of the *masculinization of women managers* is central to how the gender order is subverted in this context where a good woman is understood to be submissive and compliant. Both men and women identified the "noise" created by these women due to their behavior which was considered to be at odds with what was expected of them. However, even when women managers were considered too weak or too sensitive, their masculinized behavior was not considered positive or desirable. On the contrary, it was assumed as an appropriation that generated confusion as to the real identity of the women because they did not comply with the gender role attached to their sex identity. This reveals the gendered nature of organizational culture because women are penalized for being too emotional, for being too insensitive, for being too weak, or for being too strong (see Maddock, 1999).

Indeed, the underlying assumption seemed to be that distinctions between masculine and feminine are strict in the Dominican context and women are outsiders to the ways in which these public sector organizations define desirable worker identities. Many women who implicitly acknowledged the masculinized traits of the work environment felt that women managers were not being true to their femininity by behaving in a masculine manner, stereotyping them as renegades of femininity or men wannabes (Rodriguez, 2011). In that sense, though there is an apparent contradiction between the way both women and men feel about the environment and the way identities are enacted within it; there are some definitive features of gender roles, sexual roles, and stereotypes. However, participants did not seem to be able to attribute these differences to the gendered nature of organization but rather to individual aspects of behavior. The idea of collective agreements seemed to operate as a justification to the way men and women behaved as groups.

A second tension is related to the *construction of otherness*. Women outside of management circles did not seem to acknowledge the pressures and struggles faced by women in positions of authority to be accepted as "one of the guys." Aspects such as the strict enforcement of rules seemed more notice-able in the case of women managers than in the case of their male counterparts, which resulted in other women vilifying women managers. The responses of other women came by the hand of feelings of betrayal and lack of solidarity, as they interpreted that once these women reach the top, they forgot all the practical struggles they once faced. However, women managers were not im-mune to struggles, yet these were less evident because they did not operate on the material level of organizational culture but rather on the level of underly-ing assumptions (they are asked to play assistant/secretarial roles in meetings with peers, they are ridiculed and treated as intellectually inferior, and they are regarded as organizationally ineffective).

In addition, the problematization of the lack of support for women in posi-tions of authority was perpetuated due to women managers' inability to sup-port others. As women managers lacked power, they remained organizationally inferior in relation to their male peers even when they were seen as organiza-tionally successful by some of the other women. In many ways, the gendered nature of organizational practices created segregation among the women be-cause in order for a woman to be successful, she had to resign to herself and move to the other side, leaving her femininity and all the other women behind.

The final tension is related to *role subversion*. This role subversion oc-curred not only in terms of identity, but also in economic terms; it includes among other things mothers who become heads of household and women managers who embrace a masculine style of management. The main tension generated by role subversion relates to the economic implications as it under-mines the myth of the male breadwinner and gives women greater economic autonomy. In this sense, cultural assumptions about women's dependency on men and men's perception that they articulate women's identities through the roles they create for women as wives and mothers of their children, are shat-tered and contribute to a change in gender relations. The resulting dynamics are ones permeated by a combination of performance and resistance where women play identity games according to gender and role expectations yet also show ways of contesting these identities by disrupting the gender order with ways that transgress notions of femininity and masculinity.

Conclusion

The experiences of women managers in Dominican public sector suggest that the major challenge they face is the institutionalized patriarchal system which is reproduced by both men and women and imposes strict gender role dynamics based on sexist ideologies. These ideologies reproduce paternalistic assumptions and beliefs about the roles of women which are embedded in Dominican society.

Gendered organizational thinking is identified through reinforced ideas of men as more capable and consequently more powerful than women. Masculinity and masculine features in actions and behaviors are embodied to construct managerial appropriateness and both women managers construct their work identities based on these prescriptive notions as enforced by different aspects of organizational culture. However, women managers in particular, experience dissonance in relation to the expectations others have of them and the way they separate "woman" and "manager" as conflicting categories. As a result, they articulate the managerial role as a site of fluidity, discursively resisting and bypassing dynamics through playing identity games that allow them to navigate the system.

To conclude, this research highlights that workers are not disembodied. Embodiment is central to the articulation of the managerial role because it is not only related to naming the part but also to playing the part. When performed by women, managerial roles are sites of contestation where dynamics of exclusion and resistance coexist alongside dynamics that enable the perpetuation of the patriarchal construction of the gender order. A point forward in this discussion is to expand understanding of women managers' experiences through the use of an intersectional framework that helps to approach how different dimensions have an impact on dynamics of oppression and disadvantage that affect women managers.

References

Abramo, L. (Ed.). (2006). *Trabajo decente y equidad de género en América Latina*. Santiago: Oficina Internacional del Trabajo.

Abramo, L., & Valenzuela, M. E. (2005). Women's labour force participation rates in Latin America. *International Labour Review, 144*, 369–399.

Acker, J. (1990). Hierarchies, jobs, bodies: A theory of gendered organisations. *Gender & Society, 4*, 139–158.

Acker, J. (1992a). From sex roles to gendered institutions. *Contemporary Sociology, 21*, 565–569.

Acker, J. (1992b). Gendering organisation theory. In A. Mills & P. Tancred (Eds.), *Gendering organisation analysis* (pp. 248–260). London: Sage.

Acker, J. (1998). The future of "gender and organisations": Connections and boundaries. *Gender, Work and Organisation, 5*, 195–206.

Acker, J. (1999). Gender and organisation. In J. S. Chafetz (Ed.), *Handbook of the sociology of gender* (pp. 177–194). New York: Springer.

Acker, J. (2003). Hierarchies, jobs, bodies: A theory of gendered organisations. In R. J. Ely, E. G. Folly, M. A. Scully, & The Centre for Gender in Organisations, Simmons School of Management (Eds.), *Reader in gender, work and organization* (pp. 49–61). Oxford: Blackwell.

Acker, J. (2006). Inequality regimes: Gender, class and race in organisations. *Gender & Society, 20,* 441–464.

Alimo-Metcalfe, B. (1995). An investigation of female and male constructs of leadership. *Women in Management Review, 10,* 3–8.

Alvesson, M., & Due Billing, Y. (2009). *Understanding gender and organisation.* London: Sage.

Anim-Addo, J. (2004). Sister Goose's sisters: African-Caribbean women's nineteenth century testimony. *Woman: A Cultural Review, 15,* 35–56.

Báez, C., & Tapia, M. (2002). Estudio de caso 1: La construcción de una política pública contra la violencia de género. In D. Paiewonsky (Ed.), *El género en la agenda pública dominicana: Estudios de casos y análisis comparativo* (pp. 67–131). Santo Domingo: INTEC.

Barreto, M., Ryan, M. K., & Schmitt, M. T. (2009) Introduction: Is the glass ceiling still relevant in the 21st century? In M. Barreto, M. K. Ryan, & M. T. Schmitt (Eds.), *The glass ceiling in the 21st century: Understanding barriers to gender equality* (pp. 3–18). Washington, DC: American Psychological Association.

Blair-Loy, M. (2001). Cultural constructions of family schemes: The case of women finance executives. *Gender & Society, 15,* 687–709.

Blum, C. T., Fields, D. L., & Goodman, J. S. (1994). Organisation-level determinants of women in management. *Academy of Management, 37,* 241–268.

Bolton, S., & Muzio, D. (2008). The paradoxical processes of feminisation in the professions: The case of established, aspiring and semi-profession. *Work, Employment & Society, 22,* 281–299.

Bourdieu, P. (2004). Gender and symbolic violence. In N. Scheper-Hughes & P. Bourgois (Eds.), *Violence in war and peace: An anthology* (pp. 339–342). Oxford: Blackwell.

Bourdieu, P., & Wacquant, L. (2004). Symbolic violence. In N. Scheper-Hughes & P. Bourgois (Eds.), *Violence in war and peace: An anthology* (pp. 272–274). Oxford: Blackwell.

Candelario, G. E. B. (2005). Al eco de su voz allende a los mares: La primera etapa en el pensamiento feminista dominicano. In G. E. B. Candelario (Comp.), *Miradas desencadenantes: Los estudios de género en la República Dominicana al inicio del tercer milenio* (pp. 43–50). Santo Domingo: Centro de Estudios de Género, INTEC.

Candia, J. M. (2003). Sector informal ¿treinta años de un debate bizantino? *Nueva Sociedad, 186,* 36–45.

Carli, L. L., & Eagly, A. H. (2007). Overcoming resistance to women leaders: The importance of leadership style In B. Kellerman & D. L. Rhode (Eds.), *Women and leadership* (pp. 127–148). San Francisco, CA: John Wiley.

Central Bank of Dominican Republic. (2012). *Labour market.* Retrieved from http://www.bancentral.gov.do/english/statistics.asp?a=Labor_Market

Collinson, D. L. (2003). Identities and insecurities: Selves at work. *Organisation, 10,* 527–547.

Collinson, D., & Hearn, J. (1994). Naming men as men: Implications for work, organisation and management. *Gender, Work and Organisation, 1,* 2–22.

Connell, R. W., & Messerschmidt, J. W. (2005). Hegemonic masculinity: Rethinking the concept. *Gender & Society, 19,* 829–859.

Cunliffe, A. L., & Eriksen, M. (2011). Relational leadership. *Human Relations, 64,* 1425–1449.

Davidson, M., & Burke, R. J. (2004). *Women in management worldwide: Facts, figures and analysis.* Aldershot: Ashgate.

de Oliveira, O., & Ariza, M. (1997). División sexual del trabajo y exclusión social. *Revista Latinoamericana de Estudios del Trabajo, 3,* 183–222.

de Oliveira, O., & Ariza, M. (2000). Género, trabajo y exclusión social en México. *Estudios Demográficos y Urbanos, 15,* 11–33.

Dolado, J. J., Felgueroso, F., & Jimeno, J. F. (2004). Where do women work? Analysing patterns in occupational segregation by gender. *Annals of Economics and Statistics/Annales d'Économie et de Statistique,* No. 71–72, 293–315.

Due Billing, Y. (2011). Are women in management victims of the phantom of the male norm? *Gender, Work & Organisation, 18,* 298–317.

Duehr, E. E., & Bono, J. E. (2006). Men, women, and managers: Are stereotypes finally changing? *Personnel Psychology, 59,* 815–846.

Eagly, A. H., Johannesen-Schmidt, M. C., & van Engen, M. L. (2003). Transformational, transactional, and laissez-faire leadership styles: A meta-analysis comparing women and men. *Psychological Bulletin, 129,* 569–591.

Eagly, A. H., & Karau, S. (2002). Role congruity theory of prejudice toward female leaders. *Psychological Review, 109,* 573–598.

Ehrich, L. C. (2008). Mentoring and women managers: Another look at the field. *Gender in Management: An International Journal, 23,* 469–483.

El-Bushra, J. (2000) Rethinking gender and development practice for the twenty-first century. *Gender & Development, 8,* 55–62.

Ely, R. J., & Meyerson, D. E. (2001). Advancing gender equity in organisations: The challenge and importance of maintaining a gender narrative. *Organisation: Interdisciplinary Journal of Organisation, Theory and Society, 7,* 589–608.

Ertürk, Y. (2004). Considering the role of men in gender agenda setting: Conceptual and policy issues. *Feminist Review, 78,* 3–21.

Ferre, M. M. (2006). Globalisation and feminism: Opportunities and obstacles for activism in the global arena. In A. M. Tripp (Eds.), *Global feminism: Transnational women's activism, organising, and human rights* (pp. 3–23). New York: New York University Press.

Finkel, S., Sabatini, C., & Bevis, G. (2000). Civil education, civil society and political mistrust in a developing democracy: The case of the Dominican Republic. *World Development, 28,* 1851–1874.

Freeman, C. (2000). *High tech and high heels in the global economy: Women, work and pink-collar identities in the Caribbean.* Durham, NC: Duke University Press.

Gherardi, S. (1995). *Gender, symbolism and organisational cultures.* London: Sage.

Gonzalbo Aizpuru, P. (1997). *Género, familia y mentalidades en América Latina.* San Juan: Editorial de la Universidad de Puerto Rico.

Hausmann, R., Tyson, L. D., & Sahidi, S. (2008). *The global gender gap report 2008.* Geneva: World Economic Forum. Retrieved from https://members.weforum.org/pdf/gendergap/report2008.pdf

Heilman, M. E. (2002). Description and prescription: How gender stereotypes prevent women's ascent up the organisational ladder. *Journal of Social Issues, 57,* 657–674.

Helgesen, S. (2003). The female advantage. In R. J. Ely, E. G. Folly, M. A. Scully, & The Centre for Gender in Organisations, Simmons School of Management (Eds.), *Reader in gender, work and organization* (pp. 26–33). Oxford: Blackwell.

Höpfl, H., & Matilal, S. (2007). "The lady vanishes": Some thoughts on women and leadership. *Journal of Organisational Change Management, 20,* 198–208.

Hughes, C. (2002). *Women's contemporary lives: Within and beyond the mirror.* London: Routledge.

Ibarra, H., & Obodaru, O. (2009). Women and the vision thing. *Harvard Business Review,* January, 2–9.

Inglehart, R., & Carballo, M. (1997). Does Latin America exist? (And is there a Confucian culture?): A global analysis of cross-cultural differences. *PS: Political Science and Politics, 30,* 34–47.

Inglehart, R., & Norris, P. (2003). *Rising tide: Gender equality and cultural change around the world.* Cambridge: Cambridge University Press.

Jackson, S. (2003). Heterosexuality, heteronormativity and gender hierarchy: Some reflections on recent debates. In J. Weeks, J. Holland, & M. Waites (Eds.), *Sexualities and society: A reader* (pp. 69–83). Cambridge: Polity Press.

Jackson, S. (2006). Gender, sexuality and heterosexuality: The complexity (and limits) of heteronormativity. *Feminist Theory, 7,* 105–121.

Johanson, J. C. (2008). Perceptions of femininity in leadership: Modern trend or classic component? *Sex Roles, 58,* 784–789.

Julia, J. J. (1990). *Haz de luces.* Santo Domingo: Centro de Investigación para la Acción Femenina (CIPAF).

Kanter, R. M. (1977). *Men and women of the corporation.* New York: Basic Books.

Kanter, R. M. (1994). Men and women of the corporation. In H. Clark, J. Chandler & J. Barry (Eds.), *Organisation and identities: Text and readings in organisational behaviour* (pp. 152–164). London: Chapman & Hall.

Kinnear, K. (2011). *Women in developing countries: A reference handbook.* Westport, CT: Praeger.

Kirchmeyer, C. (2002). Gender differences in managerial careers: Yesterday, today, and tomorrow. *Journal of Business Ethics, 37,* 5–25.

Linehan, M., & Scullion, H. (2008). The development of female global managers: The role of mentoring and networking. *Journal of Business Ethics, 83,* 29–40.

Lupton, B. (2000). Maintaining masculinity: Men who do "women's work". *British Journal of Management, 11* (Special Issue), S33–S48.

Maddock, S. (1999). *Challenging women: Gender, culture & organisation.* London: Sage.

Martí, A. (2006). Anexo E: Características del mercado de trabajo en la República Dominicana. In C. Dore Cabral, L. Artiles, F. Cáceres, & P. Ortega (Eds.), *Actitudes hacia el trabajo en la República Dominicana: Reflexion sobre las percepciones y orientaciones en el mundo laboral* (pp. 151–176). Santo Domingo: Fundación Global Democracia y Desarrollo (FUNGLODE) and Instituto Nacional de Opinión Pública (INOP).

Martin, J. (1990). Deconstructing organisational taboos: The suppression of gender conflict in organisations. *Organisation Science, 1,* 339–359.

Mavin, S. (2006a). Venus envy: Problematising solidarity behaviour and queen bees. *Women in Management Review, 21,* 264–276.

Mavin, S. (2006b). Venus envy 2: Sisterhood, queen bees and female misogyny in management. *Women in Management Review, 21,* 349–364.

Mavin, S. (2008). Queen bees, wannabees and afraid to bees: No more "best enemies" for women in management? *British Journal of Management, 19,* S75–S84.

Metcalfe, B., & Linstead, A. (2003). Gendering teamwork: Re-writing the feminine. *Gender, Work & Organisation, 10,* 94–119.

Montesino, M. U. (2002). A descriptive study of some organisational behaviour at work in the Dominican Republic: Implications for management development and training. *Human Resource Development International, 5,* 393–409.

Murray, G. (2010). Framing globalisation and work: A research agenda. *Journal of Industrial Relations, 52,* 11–25.

Oficina Nacional de Estadísticas. (2007). *Monografía sobre jefatura femenina de hogar en República Dominicana. Un estudio a partir de datos censales.* Santo Domingo: Departamento de Investigaciones.

Ortega, E., & Saporta-Sternbach, N. (1989). At the threshold of the unnamed: Literary discourse in the eighties. In A. Horno-Delgado, E. Ortega, N. M. Scott, & N. Saporta-Sternback (Eds.), *Breaking boundaries: Latina writings and critical readings* (pp. 2–23). Amherst: University of Massachusetts Press.

Parrado, E. A., & Zenteno, R. M. (2001). Economic restructuring, financial crises, and women's work in Mexico. *Social Problems, 48,* 456–477.

Paz, O. (2000). *El Laberinto de la Soledad.* México: Fondo de Cultura Económica.

Pels, D., Hetherington, K., & Vandenberghe, F. (2002). The status of the object. Performances, mediations and techniques. *Theory, Culture and Society, 19,* 1–21.

Pola Zapico, M. J. (2003). *La mujer dominicana en la relación de pareja: Respuesta de justicia a la violencia de género.* Santo Domingo: INTEC.

Pou, F. (1987). Aspectos teóricos y metodológicos. In F. Pou, B. Mones, P. Hernández, L. Grant, M. Dottin, A. Arango, B. Fernández, & T. Rosado (Eds.), *La mujer rural dominicana* (pp. 13–39). Santo Domingo: CIPAF.

Rao, A., & Kelleher, D. (2005). Is there life after gender mainstreaming? *Gender and Development, 13,* 57–69.

Rodriguez, J. K. (2010). The construction of gender identities in public sector organisations in Latin America: A view of the Dominican Republic. *Equality, Diversity and Inclusion: An International Journal, 29,* 53–77.

Rodriguez, J. K. (2011). Joining the dark side: Women in management in the Dominican Republic. *Gender, Work & Organisation, 18.* doi: 10.1111/j.1468–0432.2010.00541.x

Schein, E. H. (1985). *Organisational culture and leadership.* San Francisco, CA: Jossey-Bass.

Schein, V. E. (2007). Women in management: Reflections and projections. *Women in Management Review, 22,* 6–18.

Sealy, R., & Singh, V. (2006). Role models, work identity and senior women's career progression—Why are role models important? In K. M. Weaver (Ed.), *Academy of Management Annual Meeting Proceedings, 11–16 August, 2006.* Atlanta, GA: Academy of Management.

Simpson, R., & Lewis, P. (2007). *Voice, visibility and the gendering of organisations.* New York: Palgrave Macmillan.

Singh, V., Anderson, D., & Vinnicombe, S. (2006, September 12–14). *Stepping out from gendered cultures: Fond farewells from successful women.* Paper presented at the Annual Conference of the British Academy of Management. Belfast: British Academy of Management.

Smircich, L. (1983). Concepts of culture and organisational analysis. *Administrative Science Quarterly, 28,* 339–358.

Therborn, G. (2004, October 28–29). *Families in the world. History and future on the threshold of the 21st century.* Presented at the CEPAL's Reunión de expertos "Cambio de las familias en el marco de las transformaciones globales: Necesidad de políticas públicas eficaces." Santiago de Chile.

Ulshoefer, P. (n.d.). *Perfil de la mujer empresaria ejecutiva a nivel latinoamericano.* Paper presented at the Seminar: "Aportes y desafíos de la mujer empresaria en el mundo moderno." Santiago: Servicio Nacional de la Mujer (SERNAM) and Universidad Diego Portales.

United Nations. (2010). *The world's women 2010: Trends and statistics.* New York: Department of Economic and Social Affairs.

Valerio, A. M. (2009). *Developing women leaders: A guide for men and women in organisations.* Chichester: John Wiley.

Vargas, V. (1989). *El aporte de la rebeldía de las mujeres.* Lima: Ediciones Flora Tristán.

Vargas, V. (2003). Feminism, globalisation and the global justice and solidarity movement. *Cultural Studies, 17,* 905–920.

Vinnicombe, S., & Singh, V. (2002). Developing tomorrow's women business leaders. In R. J. Burke & D. L. Nelson (Eds.), *Advancing women's careers* (pp. 206–219). Oxford: Blackwell.

Weick, K. (1979). *The social psychology of organising.* New York: McGraw-Hill.

Weick, K. (1995). *Sensemaking in organisations.* Thousand Oaks, CA: Sage.

Whitehead, S. (2001). Woman as manager: A seductive ontology. *Gender, Work and Organisation, 8,* 84–107.

Williams, J. (2000). *Unbending gender: Why family and work conflict and what to do about it.* Oxford: Oxford University Press.

World Bank. (2004). *República Dominicana: Informe sobre el gasto público: Reformando instituciones para una mejor administración del gasto público, Informe No. 23852-DO.* Retrieved from http://www-wds.worldbank.org/external/default/WDSContentServer/WDSP/IB/2005/10/11/000160016_200510 11130854/Rendered/PDF/238520SPANISH0REVISED0DR0grey1cover.pdf

Zabludovsky, G., & de Avelar, S. (2001). *Empresarias y ejecutivas en México y Brasil.* México, D. F.: Miguel Ángel Porrúa Grupo Editorial and Facultad de Ciencias Políticas y Sociales, UNAM.

15

Women in Management in Britain

Natasha S. Mauthner and Sophie Alkhaled-Studholme

The picture that emerges from our chapter is one of both growing equalities and inequalities between women and men. On the one hand, women are now outstripping men at all levels of their education. Women are successful at school, at university, and in their early careers. Male and female graduate entry into the workforce is relatively equal, as is their representation in junior management positions. On the other hand, significant gender differences and disadvantages remain. These include the gender pay gap, occupational segregation, poorer conditions of employment for part-time workers, most of whom are women, and gender-related barriers for women entrepreneurs. Furthermore, as women progress through an organization, their attrition rates increase, giving rise to what Lord Davies, in his recent report on *Women on Boards,* characterizes as a "leaking pipeline" (Davies, 2011).

In their overview of women's representation in positions of authority, power, and influence in the United Kingdom, *Sex and Power 2011*, the Equality and Human Rights Commission (EHRC, 2011) paints a similar picture of women "flooding the junior ranks of law firms, accountancies and medical practices," stepping "onto the career ladder" and working hard, "with a position at the top firmly in sight" only to later disappear "from the paid workforce or remain trapped in the 'marzipan layer' below senior management, leaving the higher ranks to be dominated by men" (p. 1). The report measured the number of women in positions of power or influence in Britain in 2010/2011 by reviewing 27 occupation categories. The results show there are more women in top posts in 17 of the 27 categories compared to 2007/2008. However, increases have been small in most areas and in many cases are attributable to just one or two women joining senior posts. On the other hand, there have been drops in women's participation in 10 sectors, including members of cabinet, local authority council leaders, and editors of national newspapers. Citing the EU European Economic and Social Committee (2009), the EHRC (2011) notes that "Women are underrepresented in all forms of leadership positions: political leadership, the senior civil service and corporate boardrooms. At the same time, the companies where women are most strongly represented are also the companies that perform best financially."

It is important to celebrate the gender equality achievements that have come about over the past 40 years through legislative, policy and organizational efforts, and other initiatives and campaigns. Nevertheless, our chapter serves as a reminder that enduring inequalities of opportunity remain for women and men in the labor market. Moreover, it draws attention to the retrograde gender equality steps taken by the current government in their efforts to recover from the economic slowdown, with the burden of deficit reduction strategies and policies falling disproportionately on women.

Women in Education

The proportion of young people (aged 18 or 19) entering higher education in the United Kingdom has increased from 30% in 1994/1995 to 36% in 2009/2010. Over this time period, young women have been more likely to enter higher education than young men. Currently 40% of young women enter higher education compared to 32% of young men. The participation rate of young men now trails that of young women by a decade, and over the past 15 years around 270,000 fewer young men than young women have entered higher education (HEFCE, 2010). There are also important gender differences in educational outcomes, with girls outperforming boys routinely at age 5, at age 16 and at degree level throughout Britain (EHRC, 2010). Alongside these gender advantages for women, significant gender differences and disadvantages remain. In terms of their career aspirations, for example, boys are more likely than girls to expect to work in engineering, ICT, skilled trades, construction, architecture, or as mechanics. Girls are more likely to expect to work in teaching, hairdressing, beauty therapy, child care, nursing, and midwifery. These career choices have major implications for employment trajectories and income levels (EHRC, 2010, p. 423). These gender differences are echoed in tertiary education, where women remain less likely than men to study science, technology, engineering, and maths (STEM) subjects, making up 48% of first degree students in STEM despite comprising 55% of first degree students overall. Thus, while gender differences in first degree subject choice are declining over time, extremely high gender segregation in vocational training remains (EHRC, 2010). Furthermore, a higher proportion of men than women attend the leading U.K. universities known as the Russell Group (EHRC, 2010). Overall, the educational environment has become increasingly enabling for girls and women, but differences in the nature and quality of tertiary education and training for females and males continue to pose obstacles for many women during recruitment and later in their careers when vying with men for promotion to professional and managerial positions (EHRC, 2010). Moreover, persistent gender segregation in subject choices and occupational training set the scene for the gender pay gap.

Women in Employment

One of the most significant social changes over the last three decades has been the increase in women's employment, and particularly mothers' employment. According to the U.K. Office for National Statistics (ONS), the employment rates of women with and without dependent children are now virtually the same. In 2010, 66.5% of mothers and 67.3% of women without a dependent child were in paid work (ONS, 2011a). With men's employment rate standing at 75.2 percent (ONS, 2011b), this means that women now make up nearly half of the labor force. While men are performing 12.8 million jobs, women occupy 12.7 million positions, although almost half of these are part time (ONS, 2011a). Underlying these figures are important ethnic and life-stage variations. While black Caribbean women are more likely to be in full-time work than any other group of women, only 1 in 4 Bangladeshi and Pakistani women works, and almost half of Bangladeshi (49%) and Pakistani (44%) women are looking after the family or home, compared to 20% or fewer of other groups. Muslim women have the lowest rate of employment of any religious group, with just 24% in employment (EHRC, 2010). Women's employment patterns also vary across the life cycle: they are much less likely than men to be employed full-time or self-employed in their early 30s (due to caring responsibilities), and if they return to work they are more likely to take and remain in part-time employment (EHRC, 2010). Furthermore, despite significant progress in terms of labor market participation, women continue to face numerous forms of inequality, disadvantage, and discrimination in the labor market, including: the gender pay gap, occupational segregation, part-time work, and restricted access to senior management positions.

Gender Pay Gap

While the gender pay gap has gradually been narrowing since the introduction in the United Kingdom of the Equal Pay Act (1970), women continue to be paid less than men for doing similar types of work (Blau & Kahn, 2007).

Women in the United Kingdom face the highest gender pay gap compared to others in European Union countries (Wilson, 2011). In 2011, men's median hourly earnings were £12.42 compared to £10.00 for women (ONS, 2011c). The gender pay difference between full- and part-time men's and women's hourly rate was 19.5%, a decrease from 19.8% in 2010 (ONS, 2011c). The reduction in earnings gap since the 1970s is mainly due to increased employment of women in traditionally male intensive occupations, such as management, engineering, and law. These overall figures mask important differences depending on age, life stage, educational qualifications, and employment sector. The gender pay gap is lowest for the under-30s, rising more than fivefold by the time workers reach 40 (EHRC, 2010). Even highly educated women graduates do not enjoy the same rates of pay on entering the labor market (Wilson, 2011). Women with children also experience a higher earnings penalty, the size of which varies according to their educational qualifications. Women with degrees are estimated to face only a 4% loss in lifetime earnings as a result of motherhood, while mothers with mid-level qualifications face a 25% loss and those with no qualifications a 58% loss. This is due to better educated mothers' greater ability to retain a strong position in the labor market (EHRC, 2010). There are also differences between the public and the private sector. In 2011, the median gender pay difference in the public sector for full-time employees was 9.2%, down from 9.9% in 2010. In the private sector, the pay gap was 18.4%, down from 19.7% in 2010 (ONS, 2011c). This has raised concerns about the potential impact of the current economic recession on the future employment and pay prospects for women, given that they are more likely than men to be employed in the public sector and may be increasingly forced to seek employment within the private sector (TUC, 2010; see also Davidson & Burke 2011). Over 40% of female jobs compared to 15% of male jobs are in the public sector, making women particularly vulnerable to public sector cuts (EHRC, 2010).

Occupational Segregation

A continuing factor influencing the gender pay gap is occupational segregation, especially in the private and voluntary sectors, where at age 40 men are earning on average 27% more than women (EHRC, 2010). Women remain concentrated in lower paid industries, sectors, and jobs: typically, clerical and secretarial work, personal and protective services, sales and retail, hospitality, and health and social work (Wilson, 2011). For example, women make up 83% of people employed in personal services, and 77% of those in administration and secretarial posts. Women comprise just 6% of engineers and 14% of architects, planners, and surveyors (EHRC, 2010). In sum, women are working in occupations that reflect their perceived role in society, and they are generally found servicing and caring for others. Thus while the growth of the service sector has increased employment opportunities for women, many of these have been relatively low paid positions.

Women in Part-Time Work

A further growth area has been part-time work. The United Kingdom has one of the highest levels of part-time working in Europe, and many women with young children work part-time to combine work and caring responsibilities (Lyonette & Baldauf, 2010). Thus, the number of people in part-time employment in the United Kingdom in 2011 was 7.82 million, of which 5.84 million were women and 1.98 million were men (ONS, 2011b). These figures reflect wider trends within the European Union where just under a third (32%) of women employed worked part-time in 2009 compared to 8% of men (EHRC, 2010). Part-time workers, however, continue to experience disadvantages compared to full-time employees, including lower pay, lower status, poorer conditions of employment, erosion of skills, and reduced chances of promotion (Lyonette & Baldauf, 2010; Sandor, 2011). This is despite the adoption of the Part Time Workers Directives in 2000 which sought to grant equal rights and conditions to part- and full-time workers in accordance with the European Union Directive on Part Time Work agreed in 1997. Specifically, this new legislation introduced new rights for part-time workers to ensure they are treated the same way as their full-time counterparts in terms of hourly pay rates, access to pension schemes, annual leave, maternity/parental leave, sick pay, and training and promotion.

For women occupying highly skilled positions the move into part-time work as a result of family responsibilities can lead to "occupational downgrading," with women moving back into positions for which they are overqualified. Based on a review of research in the United Kingdom, Lyonette, Baldauf, and Behle (2010) suggest that around 25% of women who move from full-time to part-time work change to an occupation where the average qualification level is below that of their previous full-time job. In addition, they find that those most likely to downgrade are women working in smaller-scale managerial positions, and that half of these women give up their managerial responsibilities and revert to standard personal service or sales assistant jobs, well below their skill levels. Apart from giving up their management responsibilities, these employees are likely to reduce their earnings by, on average, 32%, and when (and if) they move back to full-time, the increase in earnings is just around 19%.

Women in Management

Over recent decades, a growing proportion of managerial and professional positions have been taken up by women. The proportion of female managers, professionals, and associate professionals increased by 3% between 2002 and 2009 (EHRC, 2010). This overall increase over recent years is due a number of factors: greater numbers of women in higher education leading on to managerial and professional careers; economic growth which has lead to increased demand for managers; the move from a manufacturing to information- and service-based economy, which has benefited women's employment in management positions; legislation and social policies promoting equal employment opportunities; and the presence of women at higher managerial levels influencing the entry and retention of women at lower managerial levels.

Overall, however, in 2009 only a third of managerial jobs were gains with increases of 11% and 13%, respectively. Indian and Chinese women have made the greatest women and other Asian women saw declines of 9% and 7% in managerial and professional occupations (EHRC, 2010). Across all ages, women are underrepresented in managerial and professional jobs and over-represented in sales and unskilled occupations. In 2007–2009, the proportion of women in associate professional jobs peaked between 26 and 44 years (at 19%), tailing off subsequently to reach 12% of those aged 56–59 years. In 2009, women held just over a third (34%) of managerial positions, just over two-fifths of professional jobs, (43%), and half of associate professional jobs (50%) (EHRC, 2010). Furthermore, the gender pay gap in management positions remains strong. Female managers earned an average of £43,521 in the year to January 2006, which was £5,147 less than the male equivalent and it represents an 11.8% difference. It is estimated that women across the United Kingdom will have to wait 187 years before their take-home pay outpaces men's (Wilson, 2011).

Women in Senior Management

Despite increased access to middle management positions, women continue to be underrepresented in better paying, higher-status managerial and professional occupations. In 2010/2011, women comprised just 12.5% of directors of FTSE 100 companies, and 7.8% of directors of FTSE 250 companies, and results that indicate that women's participation on corporate boards in the United Kingdom is lagging behind Europe (EHRC, 2011). Furthermore, Sealy and Vinnicombe (2010) noted a disappointing decline in the number of companies with *multiple* women on their boards. This figure peaked in 2008 at 39 of the 100 FTSE companies, but in 2009 had declined to 37. This is significant, they suggest, as research indicates that with just one female on the board, the effects of tokenism are often in play, whereas once multiple women are present both their presence and their contribution become normalized. Other areas where they remain in the minority include: as members of Parliament (22.2%), local authority council leaders (13.2%), senior police officers (16.8%), senior judiciary (12.9%), university vice chancellors (14.3%), and editors of national newspapers (9.5%) (Lane, 1999). Even in traditionally female occupations, women are underrepresented at senior levels. For example, they account for the majority of full-time teachers across the United Kingdom, but just over a third of secondary school head teachers (ERHC, 2011). Similarly, despite the numerical predominance of women in nursing there is a marked concentration of women, especially those working part-time, in the lower echelons of the profession (Lane, 1999). Ethnic minority women are further disadvantaged compared to their white counterparts (Davidson, 1997). Where women do occupy positions of power and influence, this tends to be in the public and voluntary sectors: one example is that 48% of chief executives of voluntary organizations are women. These results, and other research, point to a growing gap between the public and the private sectors in terms of opportunities for women (EHRC, 2011). The United Kingdom's Equality and Human Rights Commission's report on *Sex and Power* (2011) concludes that "the progress of women to positions of authority in Britain has been tortuously slow . . . women are making progress in some sectors, that progress regularly stalls or even reverses in other sectors" (EHRC, 2011, p. 1). While many barriers within employment are breaking down, evidence suggests that the "glass ceiling" (the invisible barriers that prevent women from being promoted to top corporate and management positions) remains in place and that women continue to face significant difficulties accessing senior career opportunities and positions, a trend that is seen worldwide (Wirth, 2002). The Equality and Human Rights Commission suggests that "it will take another 70 years to achieve an equal number of women directors in the FTSE 100 and another 45 years to achieve an equal number of women in the senior judiciary. It will take another 14 general elections—that is, up to 70 years—to achieve an equal number of women MPs" (EHRC, 2011, p. 3). This is despite the fact that companies with a strong female representation at board and top management level perform better than those without and that gender-diverse boards have a positive impact on performance (Davies, 2011).

The Glass Ceiling and Barriers to Women's Progression

Gendered organizational cultures, defined by Lewis (2001) as a deep level of shared beliefs and assumptions that often operate unconsciously and are developed over time in an organization's historical experiences, have been a persistent theme in understanding barriers to women's career progression (Broadbridge & Simpson, 2011). Kanter's (1977) was one of the earliest studies to show how women's employment experiences were deeply shaped by the organizational culture. This culture is expressed through preferential treatment of men over women, gendered practices, and the use of masculine models, stereotypes, and symbols in management. Senior managers play a key role in framing this culture, thereby influencing women's organizational success (Broadbridge & Simpson, 2011). This gendered organizational culture can take many forms. Because men numerically dominate most organizations, at least in the most powerful positions, the culture can often reflect male ways of thinking and behaving which in turn make it difficult for women either to be perceived as competent or to feel as if they fit in. Informal communication processes in organizations may favor men because the sort of language used reflects male interests. In some occupations, the culture emphasizes those aspects of the job that men prefer. For example, male engineers tend to emphasize the importance of playing about with machinery and getting dirty; and the police overemphasizes the physical aspects of the role such as dealing with violence. Women, who are less likely to enjoy such aspects of their roles, may therefore not be perceived as being as competent as their male colleagues. Many women may find it difficult to know how to behave in a male-dominated environment and striking the right balance between maintaining femininity and appearing competent can be difficult. By being perceived as too feminine they run the risk of not being taken seriously while if they are not feminine enough they run the risk of being perceived as uncomfortably masculine and aggressive (Ragins, Townsend, & Mattis, 1998). In a survey of women who broke through the glass ceiling, 96% said adapting to a predominantly white male culture was an important factor in their success (Ragins, Townsend, & Mattis, 1998).

Old boys' networks have been identified as a continuing factor in preserving male privileges at work (Oakley, 2000; Wajcman, 1998). These networks are informal and frequently invisible. They date from school and university and are reinforced by semisocial activities. Such networking often occurs on the basis of shared social interests, informal social gatherings, conversations about sport, male only social outings, and participation in sports such as golf or football. It is argued that these sorts of activities can exclude women: either because women are less interested in these sorts of activities or because they are restricted from taking part in them due to domestic and caring responsibilities (Linehan, 2001). Exclusion from these networks can make it more difficult for women to get noticed or feel accepted within an organization; can exclude women from the work and business that gets done through these networks; and can impact on women's career progression because recruitment into senior posts often takes place through these networks. Senior posts tend to be unadvertised, and the higher the position within the managerial ranks, the less importance is attached to "objective" credentials such as education and the more likely it is that promotion is influenced by networking with the "right" people (e.g., senior managers) (Davies, 2011). Furthermore, recruitment into top managerial positions tends to be relatively unstructured and unscrutinized, potentially allowing decision-makers to make biased decisions without fear of retribution. This leaves recruitment processes open to the influence of what Kanter (1977) has called "homosocial reproduction": the tendency for people to employ other people like themselves. This compounds women's difficulties entering the male-dominated ranks of top management.

The characteristics and expectations of senior positions present further challenges for women. Managers and senior officials work the longest paid and unpaid hours of all occupational groups (ONS, 2011d). This long-hours culture places a disadvantage on those who have family responsibilities, and who are mainly women given that they continue to shoulder the bulk of domestic and care work (Rutherford, 2001). Indeed, women in management positions are less likely than men and women in other jobs to have dependent children (Wajcman, 1998). In a study of women working in a U.K. bank, the women described their employment situation as "think female manager, think childless superwoman" (Liff & Ward, 2001). At the same time, formal family-friendly policies and provisions (such as career breaks) may not be taken up by women if they feel that it might be construed as evidence that they are not able to compete on the same terms as men (Liff & Ward, 2001). More generally, opportunities to work flexible hours are more restricted in senior positions. A survey of European companies suggests that three quarters do not have any part-time workers in positions that need high qualifications or management experience (Sandor, 2011). Figures for the United Kingdom indicate that 14% of companies surveyed said it was common for them to have staff in highly qualified positions or in positions with a supervisory role working part-time, while 22% said they did so only in exceptional cases (Sandor, 2011). Indeed, the pursuit of a work–life balance is one of the reasons women leave organizations to set up and run their own businesses (Patterson & Mavin, 2009). These debates have drawn attention to the ongoing masculinization of management (Mauthner & Edwards, 2007, 2010), despite suggestions that organizational needs for interpersonal qualities more commonly associated with women, such as cooperation and collaboration, may give women a leadership advantage (Broadbridge & Simpson, 2011).

A range of other factors have been attributed to women's difficulties progressing their careers: women in managerial positions being provided with fewer opportunities than men in relation to training programs, professional conferences, and developmental experiences (Vinnicombe & Colwill, 1995). The latter include "stretch" or international assignments, and relocation, all of which are seen as important for career progression (Linehan & Scullion, 2008; Lyness & Thompson, 2000). Women's limited access to these often reflects unfounded gendered assumptions that women are less willing to accept these opportunities due to family commitments and responsibilities. Some also note a tendency for lower-level female managers not to be groomed for top management jobs in the same as lower-level male managers. Finally, there are also suggestions that women face greater barriers than men to developing formal and informal mentoring relationships mentoring that are helpful in overcoming obstacles to attaining top management positions. This means that female managers are less likely to be mentored than male managers (Linehan & Scullion, 2008).

Underlying many of the barriers to women's career progression are gender stereotypes. These preconceived ideas and assumptions about men and women, what they can do and how they behave mean they may want or be encouraged to study different subjects and receive different career advice. They may also have different employment and career expectations, with men more likely to put themselves forward for promotion while women are more inclined to wait to be asked to be promoted. Furthermore, ambition in women is likely to be seen as aggressive and unfeminine behavior. Stereotypes of being unfit for management roles disadvantages women at all levels of management. Moreover, knock-on effects of gender role stereotypes have a major impact not only on selection but promotion and evaluation of managerial performance, and therefore, cause a hindrance to women's promotion prospects (Vinkenburg, Jansen, & Koopman, 2000). The stereotypes appear to be most invoked when women are being considered for top level management positions because their presence at those levels violates the norm of male superiority (Powell & Graves, 2003). Women are not seen to have the necessary characteristics for leadership in senior or middle management positions compared to men. Sealy and Vinnicombe (2010) argue that there are enduring myths about women and senior positions, unfounded assumptions that women do not aspire to board directorships, that they lack the necessary skills to sit on boards, that they do not have the right leadership style, that they do not have the right experience, and that they are risk averse.

A recent government-commissioned review of women's progress onto corporate boards in the United Kingdom, *Women on Boards*, confirms that many of these barriers remain in place and account for women's slow progress in reaching the boardroom (Davies, 2011). The report suggests that the low number of women on boards is in part a symptom of insufficient numbers emerging at the top of the management structure and the underrepresentation of women in senior management generally. A number of reasons are outlined for this female attrition at senior levels, including lack of access to flexible working arrangements, difficulties in achieving work–life balance, or disillusionment at a lack of career progression. Extensive consultation with various stakeholders revealed that women with corporate experience were frequently overlooked for development opportunities and that there were differences in the way that men and women were mentored and sponsored, which gave men the edge over their female peers. Some respondents suggested that gender behavioral traits were a key issue, with women tending to undervalue their own skills, achievements, and experiences. Also, the relatively low number of successful female role models often compounds stereotypes and reinforces perceived difficulties in rising up the corporate ladder. Meanwhile, there is a perception that the many women in leadership positions in academia, the arts, the media, the civil service, or professional services are often overlooked because they do not have specific corporate experience and chairmen fear that they will not understand corporate issues or corporate board governance. The consultation also found that the informal networks influential in board appointments, the lack of transparency around selection criteria, and the way in which executive search firms operate posed significant barriers to women reaching boards (Davies, 2011, p. 17).

Women Entrepreneurs

One of the ways in which women are responding to the challenges they face in progressing their careers is to move into entrepreneurship and self employment. Research into the motivation behind female entrepreneurship suggests that, in United Kingdom, many women are "pushed" into entrepreneurship (Hughes, 2003) with self-employment a means of escaping the persistent gender discrimination and inequalities in the occupational confines of the labor market, including the glass ceiling (Moore & Buttner, 1997). Another reason for women pursuing self-employment is flexibility of working hours in order to accommodate family-related obligations (Boden, 1999; Caputo & Dolinsky, 1998). Indeed, one study noted that the most commonly cited reasons for women's exit from corporate life are the desire for greater freedom, autonomy, work–life balance, and professional development (Patterson & Mavin, 2009).

Women-owned businesses are one of the fastest growing entrepreneurial populations in the world, offering significant contributions to innovation, employment, and wealth creation in all economies (Brush, Bruin, & Welter, 2009; Kelley, Brush, Greene, & Litovsky, 2011). The numbers of women entering self-employment has risen significantly in the United Kingdom since the 1980s. In the 1990s, women's self-employment increased by 70% while men's increased by 30% (Allen & Truman, 1993; Moore and Buttner, 1997). Black and minority women have also turned to self-employment and managing their own, usually very small units (Bruegel, 1994). Overall, however, women do not participate in entrepreneurship to the same extent as men. Figures from the Labour Force Survey for the period 2006–2008 suggest that, in the United Kingdom, 14% of working age men are in self-employment compared to 5% of women (EHRC, 2010, p. 389). Figures from the OECD suggest that in 2009, self-employment rates among men in the United Kingdom were 18% compared to 8.5% for women (OECD, 2011, p. 43).

Despite suggestions that women may be turning to self-employment as a way of seeking refuge from gender-related disadvantages and discrimination in the labor market, the latter persist for women in self-employment. Female entrepreneurs tend to earn less than their male counterparts and encounter problems securing funding for start-up capital (Fielden & Davidson, 2006). Ongoing finance is less available for female entrepreneurs than male entrepreneurs in part because of sexual stereotyping and discrimination (Fielden & Davidson, 2006). Women enter self-employment with fewer financial assets, less experience in management, and with less network and family support. Moreover, women entrepreneurs tend to have smaller and less diverse networks than their male counterparts. They seek guidance from family and spouses, where men tend to draw on the advice of friends, business colleagues, and professional advisors (Kelley et al. 2011). A further issue concerns the sustainability of women's enterprises. Harding's (2007) report on the *State of Women's Enterprise in the UK* suggests that while female start-up activity is at 44% of the rate of male activity, female established business ownership (of business entities greater than 42 months) is just 33% of the rate of male established business ownership, prompting calls for an increased public policy focus on *sustainability* rather than start-up of businesses. This view is echoed in a report on global female entrepreneurship suggesting that fewer women than men run established businesses (Kelley et al. 2011).

It is worth highlighting here that a number of researchers criticize scholarship on entrepreneurship for its lack of attention to female business ownership and women's experiences as entrepreneurs. Some also argue that this research area investigates male-dominated sectors; lacks theoretical grounding;

neglects the importance of structural, historical, and cultural factors; uses male-gendered measuring instruments, a masculine concept of entrepreneurship, and paradigms and theories that focus on men's experiences more than women's; and overlooks the influence of power (Ahl, 2006; Bruin, Brush, & Welter, 2007; Marlow, 2002; Stevenson, 1990).

Legislation and Social Policies Promoting Equal Opportunities in the Workforce

It is over 40 years since equal opportunities legislation was first introduced in the United Kingdom. This was the Equal Pay Act (1970), which came into force in 1975 providing for equal pay on an equal treatment basis—that is, the same pay for doing the same. The Sex Discrimination Act of 1975 soon followed, making discrimination against women or men (including discrimination on the grounds of marital status) illegal in the areas of employment, education, and the provision of goods, facilities, and services and in the disposal or management of premises. Since then, the United Kingdom has seen the implementation of successive pieces of legislation seeking to address labor market inequalities resulting not only from gender differences, but also other forms of diversity including race and ethnicity (1976 Race Relations Act), able-bodiedness (1995 Disability Discrimination Act), sexual orientation (2003 Employment Equality [Sexual Orientation] Regulations), religion (2003 Employment Equality [Religion or Belief] Regulations), and age (2006 Age Diversity Legislation). Furthermore, legislative amendments have also been introduced. For example, occupational segregation means that the original legislation on equal pay had little impact on pay differentials because women are rarely in the same jobs as men. The Equal Pay Act 1970 (Amendment) Regulations 2004 rules that people in different jobs involving comparable skills, responsibility, working conditions, and effort should receive equal benefits in terms of pay (examples of other amendments include 2000 Race Relations [Amendment] Act; 2004 Amendments to the Disability Discrimination Act 1995).

One of the problems with these legislative approaches to handling unfair discrimination in the workplace is that they rely heavily on individuals taking action to challenge discrimination. However, many people find the idea of taking legal action on their own very daunting. Also individual cases have a limited impact on systematic causes of discrimination. For example, one employee could win an equal pay case but this would not necessarily mean that the person at the next desk or the next department would not suffer unequal pay as a result. In 2006, the Gender Equality Duty was introduced as part of the Equality Act 2006 as an additional tool for tackling discrimination and promoting equality. It requires all public-sector bodies and private-sector, voluntary, or charity organizations providing public services to take gender into consideration when providing employment services and service provision. It imposes a legal duty on these agencies to give "due regard" to the impact on women of all their policies and services, to promote gender equality, and to mitigate policies and practices that will have an adverse effect on women. The novelty of the act is that it shifts responsibility from individuals to the state. It puts the onus on public authorities to be proactive in promoting equality. The act has recently been used by the feminist Fawcett Society who are seeking a judicial review of the government's 2010 emergency budget, proposing an initial deficit reduction strategy of tax and benefit changes which would disproportionately affect women. The Society is arguing that, under equality laws, the government should have assessed whether its budget proposals would increase or reduce inequality between women and men. The government has admitted that it did "not hold an Equality Impact Assessment for the June 2010 budget" (Campbell, 2010).

Due to the escalation and complexity of existing legislation, in 2010 the British Government introduced a new Equality Act 2010 designed to consolidate and clarify the existing discrimination legislation concerning sex, race, disability, sexual orientation, religion or belief, and age. The Act seeks to adopt a *single* approach, harmonize existing discrimination legislation, and strengthen the law to support progress on equality. The Act requires organizations of all sizes and types to promote equality and avoid discrimination in the workplace. The Act applies equally to employers, workers, and those who are self-employed. The Equality Act 2010 covers the same groups protected by existing equality legislation. These are now called "protected characteristics" and include: age, disability, gender reassignment, race, religion or belief, sex, sexual orientation, marriage and civil partnership, and pregnancy and maternity. The Act also includes some changes to the existing legislation. One example is that the new law makes pay secrecy clauses unenforceable (but does not ban them altogether). The aim is to reduce the pay gap through increased transparency. The Act also requires private-sector employers with at least 250 employees to publish details on gender pay differences. (For more details see: http://homeoffice.gov.uk/equalities/equality-act/.)

Given that domestic and caring responsibilities continue to be a key factor in understanding gender differences in the labor market, it is worth highlighting the U.K. Employment Act 2002 which introduced new employment legislation designed to help working parents. This gave parents of children aged under 6 and of disabled children aged under 18 the right to *apply* to work flexibly, and conferred a statutory duty on their employers to consider requests seriously.

Maternity leave was increased to 26 weeks' ordinary maternity leave (paid) and 26 weeks' additional maternity leave (unpaid). Standard statutory maternity pay was increased (to £100 a week in 2003). A new right to 2 weeks' paid paternity leave was introduced to be taken within 8 weeks of the birth of a child or the placement of a child newly placed for adoption. Payment will be at the same standard rate as statutory maternity pay. The Employment Rights Act 1999 made regulations entitling a female or male employee who satisfies certain conditions to take unpaid parental leave of up to 13 weeks for the purpose of caring for the child.

Initiatives to Support the Advancement of Women

There are many initiatives within the public, private, and voluntary sector seeking to promote gender equality and the advancement of women. We can only highlight some of these here. The *Equality and Human Rights Commission* (EHRC, http://www.equalityhumanrights.com/) is an independent body that has a statutory remit to promote and monitor human rights; and to protect, enforce, and promote equality across the nine "protected" grounds—age, disability, gender, race, religion and belief, pregnancy and maternity, marriage and civil partnership, sexual orientation, and gender reassignment. It was established in 2007 by merging what were then three distinct equality commissions: the Equal Opportunities Commission (set up in 1975), the Commission for Racial Equality, and the Disability Rights Commission. The EHRC seeks to secure an effective legal and regulatory framework for equality and human rights by influencing legislative and policy developments and by using their statutory powers; provide advice and guidance on rights, responsibilities, and good practice based on equality law and human rights commission research; and provide publications to support their priorities.

Opportunity Now (http://www.bitcdiversity.org.uk/) is a gender campaign from Business in the Community, a business-led charity focused on promoting responsible business practice. Opportunity Now works with their membership of employers, from private, public, and education sectors to offer tailored, practical and pragmatic advice on workplace issues, and seeks to empower employers to accelerate change for women in the workplace. Founded in 1991, the original aim of Opportunity Now was to maximize the potential of female employees and improve their recruitment and retention prior to the start of the new millennium. Over 20 years on, the need for the work of Opportunity Now remains just as strong. For the period 2011–2012, Opportunity Now is focusing on three themes: balanced boards, flexible working, and equal pay.

The U.K. *Women's Budget Group* (www.wbg.org.uk) is an independent, voluntary organization which brings together individuals from academia, non-governmental organizations, and trade unions. The group has been engaged in scrutinizing the gender implications of the budgets and spending plans of U.K. governments since the early 1990s. Its Gender Impact Assessment of the coalition government's Spending Review (WBG, 2010) suggests that the record cuts to the public sector services and welfare budget announced will impact disproportionately on women's incomes, jobs, and the public services they use. They point out that the cuts represent an immense reduction in the standard of living and financial independence of millions of women, and a reversal in progress made toward gender equality. Their analysis suggests that the cuts will lead to hundreds of thousands of women losing their job. Among all, 53% of the jobs in the public sector services that have not been protected from the cuts are held by women and the pay and conditions of employment of all public sectors workers, 65% of whom are women, are likely to deteriorate.

Following his independent review into *Women on Boards* in February 2011, Lord Davies recommended that FTSE 100 listed companies should aim for a target of at least 25% of women on their boards by 2015. He also recommended that all chairmen of FTSE 350 companies should set out the percentage of women they aim to have on their boards in 2013 and 2015. The report also called for increased transparency with regards to: the proportion of women on the board; women in senior executive positions and female employees in the whole organization; how company and board appointments are made; how diversity issues are being addressed; what company diversity policies are in place and how they are being implemented and monitored. The steering board (experts drawn from the business world and academia) meet every 6 months to consider progress against the outlined measures and will report annually with an assessment of whether sufficient progress is being made. In October 2011, Sealy, Doldor, Singh, and Vinnicombe (2011) reported on progress over the previous 6 months. They noted that the percentage of FTSE 100 board seats held by women rose to 14.2% (up from 12.5%). Since publication of the Davies Report, 21 new female appointments had been made. These new appointments represented 22.5% of all appointments since March 1, 2011, to FTSE 100 boards. On FTSE 250 boards 28 new female appointments were made since March 1, 2011, representing 18% of all new appointments. 8.9% of all board seats on FTSE 250 boards were then held by women; up from 7.8% in late 2010. For the first time it was the minority of FTSE 250 companies that have all-male boards.

In September 2011, the government's Equalities Office launched a new *Think, Act, Report* framework aimed at improving transparency on gender equality issues, such as pay and position, in both the private and voluntary sectors. The initiative followed the quota targets set by Lord Davies to increase the number of women on boards. The framework provides a step-by-step approach for businesses through which they can recognize the barriers facing female employees, take action to address the issues raised, and then report on the progress they make. The scheme is voluntary, but a number of large British companies (including TESCO, BT, Unilever, Eversheds, and the National Grid) have already signed up. The initiative is the result of consultations with industry about the best way to boost the number of women in business, in particular those in the top jobs. Though focused especially on large and medium-sized businesses, it is open to all firms.

Concluding Comments

The picture that emerges from our chapter is one of both continuity and change. There is little doubt that women have made significant progress in the labor market. They are equally represented within the workforce, have made inroads into traditionally male sectors and occupations, are increasingly taking up managerial and professional positions, and are more able now than ever before to combine paid work with domestic and caring responsibilities. Nevertheless, they continue to face significant disadvantages and discrimination. They are still paid less than men; overrepresented in stereotypically female jobs and sectors; and underrepresented in senior management posts and the boardroom. They continue to be hampered at all levels by enduring gender stereotypes that create a seeming lack of fit between femininity and paid work, management, and leadership. Providing women with equal labor market opportunities as those enjoyed by men is likely to depend on further government legislative and policy efforts; changes in organizational cultures, policies, and practices; and significant shifts in domestic divisions of care and household labor.

References

Ahl, H. (2006). Why research on women entrepreneurs needs new directions. *Entrepreneurship Theory and Practice, 30,* 595–623.

Allen, S., & Turman, C. (Eds.). (1993). *Women in business: Perspectives on women.* London: Routledge.

Blau, F. D., & Kahn, L. M. (2007). The gender pay gap: Have women gone as far as they can? *Academy of Management Perspectives, 21,* 2–23.

Boden, R. J. (1999). Flexible working hours, family responsibilities and female self-employment. *American Journal of Economics and Sociology, 58,* 71–83.

Broadbridge, A., & Simpson, R. (2011). Twenty five years on: Reflecting on the past and looking to the future in gender and management research. *British Journal of Management, 22,* 470–483.

Bruegel, I. (1994). *Labour market prospects for women from ethnic minorities in institute for employment research.* Warwick University: Labour market Structures and Prospects for Women, Institute for Employment Research/Equal Opportunities Commission.

Brush, C. G., Bruin, A., & Welter, F. (2009). A gender-aware framework for women's entrepreneurship. *International Journal of Gender and Entrepreneurship, 1,* 8–24.

Campbell, B. (2010). The Fawcett Society takes the cuts to court. *The Guardian,* October 22. Retrieved from http://www.guardian.co.uk/lifeandstyle/2010/oct/22/yvette-cooper-fawcett-society-cuts

Caputo, R. K., & Dolinsky, A. (1998). Women's choice to pursue self-employment: The role of financial and human capital of household members. *Journal of Small Business Management, 36,* 8–17.

Davidson, M. (1997). *The black and the ethnic minority women manager: Cracking the concrete ceiling.* London: Paul Chapman.

Davidson, M. J., & Burke, R. J. (Eds.). (2011). *Women in management worldwide: Progress and prospects* (2nd ed.). Farnham: Gower.

Davies, L. (2011). *Women on boards February 2011.* Retrieved from http://www.bis.gov.uk/assets/biscore/business-law/docs/w/11-745-women-on-boards.pdf

EHRC. (2010). *How fair is Britain?* Retrieved from http://www.equalityhumanrights.com/uploaded_files/triennial_review/tr_execsumm.pdf

EHRC. (2011). *Sex and power 2011.* Retrieved from http://www.equalityhumanrights.com/uploaded_files/sex+power/sex_and_power_2011_gb__2_.pdf

Fielden, S., & Davidson, M. (Eds.). (2006). *Internal handbook of women and small business entrepreneurship.* New York: Edward Elgar.

Harding, R. (2007). *State of women's enterprise in the UK.* Norwich: Prowess. Retrieved from http://www.womenable.com/userfiles/downloads/PROWESS_State_of_Wmns_Enterprise_UK_2007.pdf

HEFCE. (2010). *Trends in young participation in higher education: Core results for England.* Retrieved from http://www.hefce.ac.uk/pubs/hefce/2010/10_03/10_03.pdf

Hughes, K. (2003). Pushed or pulled? Women's entry into self-employment and small business ownership. *Gender, Work and Organization, 10,* 433–454.

Kanter, R. M. (1977). *Men and women of the corporation.* New York: Basic Books.

Kelley, D. J., Brush, C. G., Greene, P. G., & Litovsky, Y. (2011). *Global entrepreneurship monitor. 2010 Women's Report.* London: Global Entrepreneurship Research Association.

Lane, N. (1999). Sources of career disadvantage in nursing. A study of NHS Wales. *Journal of Management in Medicine, 13,* 373–389.

Lewis, S. (2001). Restructuring workplace cultures: The ultimate work-family challenge? *Women in Management Review, 16,* 21–29.

Liff, S., & Ward, K. (2001). Distorted views through the glass ceiling: The management positions. *Gender, Work and Organisation, 8,* 19–36.

Linehan, M. (2001). Networking for female managers' career development: Empirical evidence. *Journal of Management Development, 20,* 823–829.

Linehan, M., & Scullion, H. (2008). The development of female global managers: The role of mentoring and networking. *Journal of Business, 53,* 29–40.

Lyness, K. S., & Thompson, D. E. (2000). Climbing the corporate ladder: Do female and male executives follow the same route? *Journal of Applied Psychology, 85,* 86–101.

Lyonette, C., & Baldauf, B. (2010). *Quality part-time work: An evaluation of the Quality Part-time Work Fund.* London: Government Equalities Office.

Lyonette, C., Baldauf, B., & Behle, H. (2010). *Quality' part-time work: The evidence review.* London: Government Equalities Office.

Mauthner, N., & Edwards, R. (2007). Feminism, the relational micro-politics of power and research management in higher education in Britain. In V. Gillies & H. Lucey (Eds.), *Power, knowledge and the academy* (pp. 168–190). London: Palgrave Macmillan.

Mauthner, N. S., & Edwards, R. (2010). Possibilities and practices of feminist research management in higher education in Britain. *Gender, Work and Organisation, 17,* 481–502.

Moore, D. P., & Buttner, H. B. (1997). *Women entrepreneurs: Moving beyond the glass ceiling.* Thousand Oaks, CA: Sage.

Oakley, J. (2000). Gender-based barriers to senior management positions: Understanding the scarcity of female CEOs. *Journal of Business Ethics, 27,* 321–334.

OECD. (2011). Self-employment rates. In OECD, *Labour Force Statistics 2010,* OECD Publishing. doi: 10.1787/lfs-2010–17-en-fr

ONS. (2011a). *More mothers working now than ever before.* Retrieved from http://www.nomisweb.co.uk/articles/ref/stories/3/Mother%20story.pdf

ONS. (2011b). *Statistical bulletin: Labour market statistics: December 2011.* Retrieved from http://www.ons.gov.uk/ons/dcp171778_245812.pdf

ONS. (2011c). *Annual survey for hours and earnings, November 2011.* Retrieved from http://www.ons.gov.uk/ons/dcp171778_241497.pdf

ONS. (2011d). *Hours worked in the labour market—2011.* Retrieved from http://www.ons.gov.uk/ons/dcp171776_247259.pdf

Patterson, N., & Mavin, S. (2009). Women entrepreneurs: Why women enter into entrepreneurship: An explanatory model. *International Small Business Review, 2,* 173–192.

Powell, G. N., & Graves, L. M. (2003). *Women and men in management.* London: Sage.

Ragins, B., Townsend, B., & Mattis, M. (1998). Gender gap in the executive suite: CEOs and female executives report on breaking the glass ceiling. *Academy of Management Executive, 12,* 28–42.

Rutherford, S. (2001). Are you going home already? The long hours culture, women managers and patriarchal closure. *Time and Society, 10,* 259–276.

Sandor, E. (2011). *European Company Survey 2009. Part-time work in Europe.* European Foundation for the Improvement of Living and Working Conditions. Retrieved from http://www.eurofound.europa.eu/pubdocs/2010/86/en/2/EF1086EN.pdf

Sealy, R., Doldor, E., Singh, V., & Vinnicombe, S. (2011). *Women on boards: Six month monitoring report October 2011.* London: Government Equalities Office.

Sealy, R., & Vinnicombe, S. (2010). Women on top corporate boards: The slow progress and initiatives that provide change. In L. Husu, J. Hearn, A. Lämsä, & S. Vanhala (Eds.), *Leadership through the gender lens: Women and men in organisations.* Hanken School of Economics Research Reports 71, Helsinki. Retrieved from https://helda.helsinki.fi/bitstream/handle/10227/753/71-978-952-232-101-\5.pdf

Stevenson, L. (1990). Some methodological problems associated with researching women entrepreneurs. *Journal of Business Ethics, 9,* 439–446.

TUC (Trade Union Congress). (2010). *Women and recession: One year on.* Retrieved from http://www.tuc.org.uk/extras/womenandrecessiononeyearon.pdf

Vinkenburg, C. J., Jansen, P. G., & Koopman, P. L. (2000). Feminine leadership— A review of gender differences and in managerial behaviour and effectiveness. In M. J. Davidson, and R. J. Burke (Eds.), *Women in management: Current research issues* (Vol. 2, pp. 120–137). London: Sage.

Vinnicombe, S., & Colwill, N. (1995). *The essence of women in management.* London: Prentice Hall.

Wajcman, J. (1998). *Managing like a man: Women and men in corporate Management.* Cambridge: Polity Press.

WBG. (2010). *The Impact on Women of the Coalition Spending Review 2010.* Retrieved from http://www.wbg.org.uk/RRB_Reports_4_1653541019.pdf

Wirth, L. (2002). Breaking through the glass ceiling: Women in management. *International Labour Office, 137,* 93–103.

16

Gender Discrimination and Sexual Harassment: Insights through a Comparison of the United States and Germany

Lukas Droege

Germany and the United States both had to overcome public discrimination against minorities in the past and are therefore of special interest. Looking at some of the key elected politicians in Germany and the United States, one may think that unfair discrimination is a thing of the past in Europe's and North America's largest economies: Heading the German government, the incumbent chancellor is a woman, the vice-chancellor and foreign minister is openly gay, the minister of economics is of Vietnamese origin, and the minister of finance is bound to a wheelchair. Three of the last four American secretaries of state are female and the first African American president was inaugurated in 2009. In the business world, however, women and minorities often face prejudices, which can make it difficult for them to excel in their jobs.

Although women were granted their right to vote in the United States in 1920 and hold the same constitutional rights as men, women were often restricted to certain jobs and roles in real life. The same holds true for African Americans and other minorities. The Civil Rights Act of 1964 is a landmark in the legislative history of the United States and was signed to fight these injustices. Title VII explicitly prohibits discrimination at the workplace based on race, color, religion, national origin, and sex. Additional legislations like the Age Discrimination in Employment Act of 1967 (ADEA), Title I and V of the Americans with Disabilities Act of 1990 (ADA), and Title II of the Genetic Information Nondiscrimination Act of 2008 (GINA) have further strengthened employee's rights by adding protected categories. Based on these legislations, an employee may contact the Equal Employment Opportunity Committee (EEOC) whenever he or she feels discriminated against, which in turn can file a lawsuit against the company.

The American judicial system struggles with granting the same protection to additional groups. Federal law, for example, does not explicitly protect people with alternate sexual orientation. The Employment Nondiscrimination Act (ENDA) is an initiative to protect gay, lesbians, and transgender employees from discrimination at the workplace on a national level. It was first introduced in Congress in 1994 but was never passed. Although the legislation was reintroduced in every single year until 2010, a majority of senators and representatives always voted against it. Today, only 21 mostly liberal states enacted laws protecting people from sexual orientation discrimination. The majority of 29 states do not offer a specific protection. In 8 states, gender identity is protected, as well.

Interestingly, the German parliament did not pass any specific antidiscrimination law in the decades following the Second World War. In 1949, the Federal Republic of Germany was founded based on the articles of the Basic Law. Article 3, which consists of just five sentences, guarantees equal treatment for all persons, regardless of his or her sex, descent, race, mother tongue, country and origin, faith, religious or political beliefs, and disability. Although the article is held very general and does not specify just and unjust behavior, it does provide a very general protection against discriminatory treatment. Other articles in the Basic Law support and expand this protection in civil life and at the workplace. Certain laws like the Gleichbehandlungsgesetz (Equal Treatment Act) of 1958 specify this protection to a limited extent. Until the 1990s however, most German policies focused on the traditional family role model with the husband being the breadwinner and his wife caring for household and children.

Today, the Allgemeines Gleichbehandlungsgesetz (AGG), the General Equal Treatment Act, protects employees and applicants from unfair treatment based on race, ethnicity, sex, religion or ideology, handicap, age, and sexual identity. The articles are much more specific than the Basic Law and additionally cover age and sexual identity. The AGG was not introduced until 2006, decades after the enactment of the Civil Rights Act in the USA. European directives from 2000 to 2004 forced Germany and other European countries to enact these antidiscrimination laws. Therefore, antidiscrimination laws across the European Union are fairly similar (European Commission, 2008). Although the public opinion generally supports the law, Germany would probably not have introduced this legislation without the directives from Brussels. Further European directives, which would guarantee a better protection of all groups in public life, are planned for the future. The European Union clearly serves as a catalyst for new policies in its member states. However, Germany is among the nations that prefer to enact antidiscrimination initiatives on a national level and fear too much regulation through the growing influence of the European Union (Pöll, 2008).

Opponents of the AGG argue that enacting the law was unnecessary, that the law will have little impact and will greatly increase bureaucracy and judicial efforts for companies. According to the new legislation, employers need to prove in a lawsuit that they have acted objectively at all times and did not discriminate against certain groups or individuals. Like in the United States, this proof is often difficult if not impossible to provide and a cause for many discussions (Rühl, Viethen, & Schmid, 2007). However, the Federal Anti-Discrimination Agency in Germany found no proof for a great increase in the number of lawsuits based on antidiscrimination laws since 2006 (Antidiskriminierungsstelle des Bundes, 2008). Germans usually consider high remedies, as they are common in the United States, to be excessive and not justified. Therefore, most affected employees seek amicable agreements instead of costly lawsuits with unpredictable outcomes (Dernbach, 2008). The coming years will show if the number of lawsuits based on the AGG will increase.

Table 16.1 provides an overview overprotected categories in the discussed legislations. Please keep in mind that categories might be defined and interpreted differently in Europe and the United States. For example, the category "color" is specifically mentioned in the Civil Rights Act of 1964 while it is silently included in the category "race" in Germany.

It is important to note that neither country covers all listed categories. Differences can partially be explained with historic events and cultural backgrounds. While American lawmakers paid special attention to "color" due to widespread discrimination against African Americans and their darker skin color in the past, the German word Weltanschauung is based on popular fundamental philosophical concepts from the 18th and 19th centuries. The English calque is "world view" and describes "a comprehensive conception or apprehension of the world especially from a specific standpoint" (Merriam-Webster Online Dictionary, 2011).

The EEOC publishes annual statistics about the number of individual charge filings in eight different types of discrimination. Based on this data, an employee's sex is the second most common trigger for discriminatory behavior at the workplace. What's more, the monetary benefits gained by sex-based charges exceed the benefits in race-related discrimination charges by $129.3 million to $84.4 million (Equal Employment Opportunity Commission, 2011a). Thus, charges based on sex discrimination tend to result in paybacks, which are almost twice as high as race-related charges. In total 100,000 charges were filed in 2010. This is a record high in the statistics, which have been recorded since 1997.

TABLE 16.1

Comparison of covered categories in selected American and German legislatures

	Race	Color	Religion	Weltanschauung	National origin /ethnicity	Mother tongue	Sex	Age	Disability	Sexual orientation or sexual identity	Genetic information
U.S. Civil Rights Act of 1964	x	x	x		x		x				
Additional acts in the United States								x	x	x	x
Basic Law 1949 in Germany	x		x	x	x	x	x		x		
European Directives 2000–2004	x		x	x	x		x	x	x	x	
AGG of 2006 in Germany	x		x	x	x		x	x	x	x	

Similar statistics are not available in Germany. Since many discrimination charges are filed under the category of "mobbing," these statistics would be vague and misleading.

A survey conducted by the European Union in 2008 indirectly proves that discrimination is still widespread in Germany and Europe and quantifies the extent of each category during the hiring process. The results correspond with subjective opinions and show clear trends. The average numbers for other European countries were fairly similar. Even though respondents identify multiple sources of unfair discrimination, most Europeans would not know their rights in the case they would be harassed or discriminated against. Only 33% would be prepared for such a case. Germany had one of the lowest scores of about 26% (European Commission, 2008). Although no significant improvement could be derived in comparison with data from 2006, the long-term impacts of the AGG and the continuous implementation in different companies might cause an increase in these numbers.

Twenty-three percent of respondents fear that the candidate's gender will have a negative effect on the selection process. As no gender was specified, this number includes both possible discrimination against women and men. Although this is a fairly high number, discrimination based on the candidate's age, ethnicity, or a disability is far more likely according to the survey. Only a minority of 3% does not expect any discrimination against any candidate. Clearly, Europeans and Germans in particular are generally aware of discriminatory behavior of companies. What's more, managers who are ultimately responsible for the hiring process tend to respond very sensitively to the question, that is, the listed percentages for managers were 1 to 13 points higher than the European average. These findings suggest that either the public does not recognize gender discrimination in particular or gender discrimination is a problem blown up in public discussions. As we will see, the latter suggestion is not supported by other statistics and many experts.

The hiring process is arguably the key element in the relationship between employer and employee and therefore deserves special scrutiny. Employers and their HR officers need to make sure that no applicant is treated better or worse due to discriminatory attitudes. Recent surveys like the one mentioned in Chapter 3 show that actions like the introduced laws against discriminatory behavior are necessary to ameliorate this issue.

Surprisingly, there are striking differences between German and American hiring practices. For example, a typical German résumé features both a picture of the candidate and his or her birthdate. Most companies specifically require this information on online application interfaces. On the other hand, American HR professionals explicitly forbear from asking for these elements as they might trigger discriminatory reactions like the preference of younger candidates. For Germans, this practice seems to be redundant as HR professionals can easily calculate the age of most applicants by looking at the issue date of high school or college diplomas. The estimates will only differ from the real birth year by negligible margins. The same might hold true for the exclusion of a picture on the résumé as the candidate has to "reveal" her face during the job interview anyway. During the interview, a candidate has no possibility to hide his or her gender, if he or she might fear disadvantages based on this information.

On the other hand, a recent field study, which received much attention in Germany, found that applicants with a German-sounding name had a 14% higher chance to be invited to a job interview than applicants with Turkish-sounding names. The researchers used identical résumés only varying the names and send them to various HR departments without mentioning the scientific study (Kaas & Manger, 2010). The experiment followed the example of researchers from Harvard who conducted a similar study in the United States in 2004. The researchers found that "white" names receive stunning 50% more callbacks than African American–sounding names (Bertrand & Mullainathan, 2003). Similar results can be expected with varying pictures of the applicant, different genders or other aspects, which might trigger stereotype-motivated reactions.

The Antidiskriminierungsstelle (ADS), the Federal Anti-Discrimination Agency and the German equivalent to the EEOC, is currently field-testing anonymous applications with growing success. In cooperation with five renowned companies and other government offices, 4,000 actual applications were edited. Despite their anonymous applications, 111 people found a new job through the pilot program (Schöbel, 2011). Although the participants of the study agreed that the anonymous application helped to focus on the candidate's qualifications, they were fairly reserved about a permanent installation of the practice, which is used by many corporations in the United States. Company representatives stated that they would like to wait for more results from this and similar studies before implementing the practice (Schöbel, 2011). This resistance to change clearly indicates a lack of interest in the issue. Most German companies are expected to change their application process according to the American model in the near future.

On the other side of the Atlantic, standardized applications have been in use for many years. In addition to the interdiction to gather certain data, companies are not allowed to ask specific questions (e.g., regarding possible disabilities) during the application process itself. Questions about ethnicity and gender are not forbidden, but many companies restrain from asking such questions voluntarily. In Germany applicants of certain groups are somewhat protected against unjust questions during interviews as well. A pregnant woman, who fears not to be accepted due to her upcoming leave of absence, may legally lie about her pregnancy if asked about her future family plans.

Not using certain questions has shown to help women and other groups during an application process. In one exemplary American study, the authors found that female musicians, who played their instruments behind a screen so that the auditors were not able to identify their sex, were 50% more likely to survive the preliminaries (Goldin & Rouse, 2000). The study proves that the orchestra's managers would have discriminated against women if they were able to do so. Standardized forms and questionnaires can thus greatly help to focus on the applicant's résumé.

A recent study finds that the "think manager, think male" attitude among (male) management students has not significantly changed over the last 30 years. Typical managers are described with characteristics, which are more commonly ascribed to men than women. This attitude can be observed in Germany, the USA, the United Kingdom, China, and Japan (Schein, 2007).

In this environment, women continuously have to break stereotypical views and prove themselves to reach high management positions.

As a consequence of these attitudes, women are a rare sight in top management positions in Germany, the United States, and in most other industrialized countries. Only 8 out of 184 (4.3%) of all board members in the 30 companies in Germany's leading stock index DAX are female (Sorge, 2011). No significant trend can be observed over the last decade and percentages remain on a very low level. By law, German supervisory boards consist of both stockholder and employee representatives. Since employee representatives are more likely to be female, the percentages for supervisory boards are significantly higher. While 19.3% of employee representatives on supervisory boards were female in 2010, the total percentage among stockholder representatives was less than one fourth (4.4%) (Lindstädt, 2011).

The female share increases with decreasing management levels: In 2010, women held 28.2% of medium management positions but only 11.5% of German top management positions (Hoppenstedt, 2010). Although the rates increased significantly over the last decades—the overall percentage of women in management more than doubled compared to 1995—women are still underrepresented in management positions as 45% of Germany's workforce consists of women (Bundesagentur für Arbeit, 2010).

Similar trends can be observed in the United States. In 2011, only 16% of S&P 500 board members were women. For 2007, the U.S. Government Accountability Office estimates that women comprised a steady 40% of managers and 49% of nonmanagers. Although specific findings cannot directly be compared with other nations due to different definitions and premises, the meta-analysis of different statistics seems to suggest a greater gap in Germany than in the United States. This is supported by The Global Gender Gap Report, which indicates a higher female-to-male ratio in jobs like "legislators, senior officials and managers" in the United States (0.74) than in Germany (0.61) (Hausmann, Tyson, & Zahidi, 2010). However, Germany is placed better in overall gender equality taking other political, economic, educational, and health criteria and dimensions into account. Similar results can be found in the Human Development Report of the United Nations Development Program where Germany is ranked 7th and the United States a poor 47th in the gender inequality index (United Nations Development Program, 2011).

In order to counter the lack of diversity in leadership positions, the Glass Ceiling Act was added to the Civil Rights Act in 1991. A "glass ceiling" refers to an imaginary boundary, which prevents most women and minorities from climbing to top positions on the job ladder. In 1995, the newly founded Glass Ceiling Commission found that discrimination against female managers

364 Women and Management

significantly hurt the American economy and suggested companies in the private sector to "make full use of the nation's human capital" with a stronger focus on diversity management (Federal Glass Ceiling Commission, 1995). The impact of the Glass Ceiling Commission on American corporations will hardly be measurable. Nevertheless, the initiative helps and focuses political efforts to diminish invisible boundaries. A similar commission, which can help to educate about benefits of a diverse management team, cannot be found in Germany. Without strong governmental help, Germany's private sector will have to teach itself the benefits of higher percentages of women in leadership positions. With many other pressing issues and no great incentives, most male top managers will not try to stamp on the glass ceiling wholeheartedly.

Politicians across all parties, women's right activists, and union officials have noticed the reluctance of most companies to welcome more female managers in top positions. Possible solutions are often discussed vigorously in public and discussion panels. The most popular proposal in Germany is the introduction of a quota for women in management positions. Although politics have repeatedly threatened to introduce such rules, no binding legislation has been put into practice yet. According to a federal study, 70% of German citizens would support the introduction of a quota while a vast majority of 92% thinks that many women are generally qualified for such leadership positions (Welt am Sonntag, 2011). With an introduction of a quota Germany would follow the lead of other European countries like Norway, France, the Netherlands, Belgium, and Austria, which already have or are about to introduce a binding gender quota ranging between 20% and 40%. In July 2011, members of the European Parliament agreed on the ambitious goal to increase the proportion of women in European management positions from currently 10% to 40% until 2020. They urge the European Commission to "propose legislation including quotas by 2012" if voluntary measures will not have the desired effect (European Parliament, 2011). The issue will be reviewed in March 2012 by the European Committee, and might follow a similar course as the general discrimination directives, which finally forced the introduction of the AGG in 2006.

In 2001, the German government and leading economic organizations signed a first agreement with the intention to ameliorate promotion chances for women on a voluntary basis. The effects of the agreement, however, have been very scarce and can be seen as a failure (Holst & Wiemer, 2010). Today, the Deutsche Telekom AG, known in the United States for its T-Mobile branch, is the first DAX company in Germany, which committed itself to increase the percentage of female managers in leadership positions to at least 30% until 2015 (Sachverständigenkommission, 2011). While this attempt is a sign for a growing support for quotas even among corporations, most German companies do not intend to introduce a rigid quota although they officially strive for a higher representation of women in management positions. Dieter Zetsche, CEO of Daimler AG, which produces cars under its Mercedes-Benz brand, recently taunted the gender quota and publicly wondered how he could possibly lay off so many skilled male managers to conform to a gender quota. A strict gender quota would simply not be realizable in the male-driven automotive industry (Die Zeit, 2011).

In a meeting with German ministers that received much media attention in October 2011, major corporations repeatedly promised to increase their percentages of women in leadership positions. Instead of a nationwide quota, corporations will be benchmarked against industry-specific targets. Again, the government threatened to penalize companies not conforming to the targets. Critics argued that low monetary punishments and hardly binding targets will fail to significantly increase the percentages over the coming years. Since members of the current government do not share a uniform view of the necessity of quotas, the pressure on companies is fairly low and the critics' predictions will most likely come true.

Although the private sector is not willing to introduce quotas, many companies actively assist both male and female talents on their way to leadership positions through a range of programs designed to promote equal opportunities for both sexes. These often include mentoring programs with top managers as mentors and alternate working time models that allow more flexible family planning (Riedel, 2010). These career-planning programs ameliorate the negative effects caused by common breaks in female careers due to the need of raising children. As it will be discussed later, German laws guarantee a better protection for new parents and allow far longer leaves for giving birth to a child than their American counterparts.

In recent years, especially large companies have set up diversity offices like in the United States to monitor and guide the development of equal employment and promotion opportunities within the company. The initiatives have proved that companies that are willing to actively promote equal opportunities can indeed increase the share of women in management positions. Very slowly but steadily, the share of female top executives will increase in the future.

Rigid quotas can hardly be observed in the United States since the Supreme Court declared this type of measure helping women or ethnic minorities to be unconstitutional in 1978. The judges found that the quota system, which was used by a medical school to guarantee the acceptance of traditionally discriminated-against minorities, violated the Equal Protection Clause of the Fourteenth Amendment (*Regents of the University of California v. Bakke*, 1978).

Compared to the situation in Germany, the discussion about a forced introduction of quotas for women or minorities in companies is diminishing small.
The strong opposition against quota and affirmative action policies probably
originates in the popular American belief that every man and woman is the
only architect of his or her fortune—for the good and for the bad. Every citizen has the possibilities to fulfill his or her dreams but neither the government
nor corporations have the duty to guarantee success. In this meritocracy rigid
quotas have a tough standing as they contradict this principle and will restrain
the independence of the private sector.

Instead of introducing quotas, corporations and public institutions have put
affirmative action programs into place, which may benefit certain groups with
the purpose to promote equal opportunity. Contrary to public belief, these
programs do not simply imply a quota for certain groups (Pincus, 2003). Nevertheless, minorities can often benefit from affirmative action programs. Affirmative actions have often been criticized as positive discrimination and have
been subject of numerous court cases. While the public largely supports affirmative actions for women, the opinions are split about the introduction of
affirmative action policies designed to promote ethnic minorities (USA Today,
2005).

Although quotas have helped to increase the number female executives in
the mentioned European countries and the number of female board members
in Germany and Europe (Green, 2011), many commentators seem to forget
that while quotas and affirmative action policies can perfectly fix symptoms,
they might fail to cure the basic prejudices against female managers. Women
will be accused of being promoted not for their skills but for their gender and
talented men may sense reverse discrimination. Recent studies in the United
States propose that white men derive a psychological benefit from the common
belief that affirmative actions imply quotas for women and minorities. White
men's self-esteem is strengthened through this belief as it boosts self-perceived
competence (Unzueta, Lowery, & Knowles, 2008). Nevertheless, quotas can
be a great stepping-stone for women to gain access to high management positions and prove stereotypes to be false.

Educating employees about the benefits of a diverse leadership team can
counter this common belief. The best possible way to promote more women in
management in Germany will not be a rigid quota but a better understanding
of the benefits of diverse leadership teams as American Glass Ceiling Commission is trying to promote. The current corporate initiatives paired with governmental pressure have shown first successes. Typical American approaches,
which can partially be observed in Germany with different emphases as well,
can be categorized into three groups (Kalev, Dobbin, & Kelly, 2006):

- Programs designed to establish organizational responsibility for diversity.
- Programs to moderate managerial bias through training and feedback.
- Initiatives to reduce social isolation of women and minority workers.

In general, one initiative alone does not guarantee equal employment opportunities. Experts recommend executives to follow multidimensional approaches to achieve sustainable results.

Compared to other industrialized nations, the United States is known for its high level of income inequality as measured with the Gini coefficient. As women and certain minorities are less promoted to high management positions, it is not surprising that their average salary is lacking behind, as well. What's more, however, women with similar qualifications as men and on similar management positions often receive less money for their work. In the United States, female managers only earn 71 cents for every dollar earned by their male counterparts in 2007 (Sherril, 2010). Only 10 cents of this gap can be explained by nondiscriminatory factors like age/experience, hours worked beyond full-time, and education. Many female managers are clearly discriminated against through their paychecks—especially when they additionally have to care for children in their household or are a member of a certain minority. Taking all full-time employees and not just managers into account, the U.S. Census found an (unadjusted) average earning gap between males and females of 23% (DeNavas-Walt, Proctor, & Smith, 2010). Again, the gap is even greater for African American and Hispanic women as various scientific studies have shown (Semyonov & Lewin-Epstein, 2009). Although the gender gaps decreased over time, especially in the 1960s and 1970s, this positive development has slowed down over the last decades. The Civil Rights Movement during the 1960s and the Equal Pay Act of 1963 in particular seem to have had a strong impact, which is fading away. President Obama signed the Lilly Ledbetter Fair Pay Act of 2009, which will facilitate lawsuits against discriminatory salaries in the future. This might help to abate the gender pay gap although it will still be difficult for attorneys to prove that certain salaries are unjustified and discriminatory.

The unadjusted average gender pay gap in Germany was 23.2% in 2009, which is higher than in the European Union (18%) but comparable to the United States (Körner, Puch, & Wingerter, 2010). Interestingly, the wage gap is only 6% in the states of former communist East Germany. The former pursuit of equality for all citizens and employees might have had a positive effect on the gender gap. Before the AGG was signed in 2006, (West) Germany had no specific legislation for fighting wage gaps. Nevertheless, disadvantaged employees were able to sue employers on the basis of the Basic Law.

In a landmark lawsuit in 1981, 29 female employees of a film laboratory successfully sued their employer for paying higher wages for male coworkers. Although male employees essentially had the very same tasks, they received a 27% higher paycheck on average. The employer's argument that he would not be able to find qualified men who were willing to work for the lower wage was held to be invalid by the judges (Schumm-Garling, 2005).

The German government is trying to lower this gap further with different initiatives. One popular example is the so-called Girls' Day during which female high school students can experience traditional "male" jobs with scientific and technical backgrounds. The climbing numbers of female science students seem to prove the success of this initiative (Sachverständigenkommission, 2011). Breaking the image of traditional "male" and "female" jobs will greatly contribute to more equal salaries as jobs with a high percentage of females are generally underpaid. Critics argued that the Girls' Day would assist only one gender and would therefore disadvantage boys who generally score lower in school anyway. As a response, grassroots initiatives organized the Boys' Day as a counterpart.

A very similar development can be observed in the United States: After the Ms. Foundation for Women founded the Take Our Daughters to Work program in 1993, many companies also allowed sons to participate in the programs. The program was consequently renamed Take Our Daughters and Sons to Work. This example demonstrates the very similar fears in Germany and the United States that helping one gender might involuntarily result in disadvantages for the other gender.

Women willing to give birth to a child often have to quit their job or reduce their hours thus receiving reduced salaries. In contrast to the United States, German laws make it easy to take a leave of absence to care for the family without great monetary losses. New mothers may take up to 17.5 months of paid vacation when giving birth. Employers are not allowed to lay off the new parent and have to offer the same or a similar job after the leave of absence. In contrast, new mothers in the United States can only take 12 weeks of unpaid maternity leave based on the Family and Medical Leave Act of 1993. Out of 173 countries studied, the United States is one of only four nations which do not guarantee a paid leave during childbirth. The other three countries are Liberia, Papua New Guinea, and Swaziland (Heymann, Earle, & Hayes, 2007). This monetary loss is especially crucial for low-income workers and their families.

German and American approaches toward preventing sexual harassment are very distinct from each other although surveys show that about the same percentage of women in Europe and the United States have experienced some sort of sexual harassment at work (Zippel, 2006). The EEOC defines sexual harassment as "unwelcome sexual advances, requests for sexual favors, and other verbal or physical harassment of a sexual nature" (Equal Employment Opportunity Commission, 2011b). In the United States, employees can file lawsuits on sexual harassment with the help of the EEOC resulting in monetary benefits of about $50 million every year. These benefits partially consist of punitive damages, which are illegal in Germany and other European countries. While mostly women suffer from sexual harassment by men, every sixth charge in the United States is filed by a male. The total number of receipts has decreased over the last 10 years from under 16,000 in 2000 to less than 12,000 in 2010. According to legal scholars, this drop is a result of the Supreme Court decisions in 1998 in *Faragher v. City of Boca Raton* and *Burlington Industries Inc. v. Ellerth*, which while supporting the rights of the victims made it more difficult for victims to win sexual harassment cases (Zippel, 2006). Most sexual harassment claims, however, are not brought to court but are settled without public notice (Equal Employment Opportunity Commission, 2011a). With these and other cases in the American legal system based on common law, the United States has been a forerunner in trying to solve sexual harassment issues.

Like in Europe, judges often struggle with the precise definition of sexual harassment. Many defendants argue that they simply did not realize that their behavior was unwelcome. An unknown number of victims of sexual harassment do not accuse their coworkers at all and often have to cope with the problem themselves. A main reason for this passive behavior is fear of retaliation. Whistle blowers may lose respect, be demoted by their supervisor, or even laid off. The same fears exist on the other side of the Atlantic, as well. Both Americans and Germans agree that a (male) supervisor is not authorized in any way to abuse his position for retaliation against (female) employees who are not willing to offer sexual services.

Since 2006, the German AGG explicitly prohibits any forms of sexual harassment at the workplace. The official definition is fairly similar to the American version but highlights the victim's dignity, a central element in German legislatures. It specifically mentions that employers are encouraged to penalize unjust behavior with appropriate measures ranging from warnings to an immediate layoff.

However, these laws are not strictly enforced. Few cases are brought to court and there is no public discussion about the problematic situation as few politicians actively address the issue. It is a popular public belief that sexual harassment is a bigger problem in the United States or in other countries than it is in Germany. Politics will need to propose more binding rules if it wants to fight sexual harassment. Furthermore, the AGG might not comply with all points of a European directive and does not explicitly force companies to take "reasonable care" to prohibit sexual harassment although it explicitly defines a hostile environment to be unjust.

Despite the similar official definitions of sexual harassment, there are key differences in the perception of sexual harassment in daily life in the United States and Europe. While flirting, soft approaches, and compliments are silently accepted in most European countries, these actions might already be treated like sexual harassment in the United States. The argument that these activities belong to the culture especially in southern European is often used to justify these practices and is widely accepted.

The difference in cultural depictions of sexual harassment is a reason why the European Union did not agree on developing detailed guidelines against sexual harassment and therefore does not serve as a catalyst for sexual harassment policies. Without increased pressure from the EU and without the feeling that quick actions are necessary, Germany will not enact further antiharassment policies in the near future. Due to the lack of a public belief that sexual harassment is a major problem in the society, little will be done over the course of the next years.

While European practices are considered to be too liberal by many Americans, the American approach gains negative reactions in Germany and Europe, as well. Why should an employer have the right to interfere in someone's private feelings for a coworker? Is an employer really obliged to stop flirting and soft approaches when the feelings are consensual? How can the fear of high punitive damages overshadow the joy for two employees who found each other? American policies go way too far for many Germans and can lead to an invasion of privacy. Fearing high monetary punishments, many American employers are doing just this and follow a zero-tolerance policy.

Although anti–sexual harassment policies do not have the same scale as in the United States, German and European employees are probably more protected against retaliation than they are across the Atlantic: Employment protection laws are much more employee-friendly than they are in the United States. In contrast to the employment-at-will doctrine in the United States, German employers have to justify any layoffs with specific criteria, for example. Many layoffs have been ruled to be unjust by employment tribunals and layoffs as a mean of retaliation will generally be identified as such. In contrast to the United States, most employment contracts in Germany and in most European countries are not formed on an at-will basis.

Companies themselves should not only comply with antiharassment laws for the sake of formality but should have an interest in controlling the issue since sexual harassment, just like discrimination, disturbs the work environment, hurts individuals, and harms their economic output. German companies are free to develop their own policies and strategies against sexual harassment, which they usually do in cooperation with unions. In general, however, little has been done to restrain sexual harassment at work. In the private sector, employers usually tolerate workers putting pictures of half-naked photo models on lockers or semi-open areas on shopfloors creating a questionable atmosphere. As a result, sexual comments, which can be considered as sexual harassment according to the American definition, are common. Until today, few women have used the law to hold their employers responsible in court (Zippel, 2006).

In order to defend themselves in lawsuits, American companies need to prove that they took reasonable care to protect their employees against discrimination and injustice. Reasonable care includes, at a minimum (Paludi et al., 2011):

- Establishing and enforcing an effective antidiscrimination and antiharassment policy.
- Establishing and enforcing effective investigative procedures.
- Facilitating trainings in workplace discrimination in general and in the organization's policy and procedures specifically.

These guidelines are based on rulings in the earlier mentioned cases *Burlington Industries, Inc. v. Ellerth* and *Faragher v. City of Boca Raton* from 1998 and are still not fully implemented in most companies. They are, however, more specific and binding than legal requirements in Germany.

The EEOC and leading experts strongly recommend regular trainings to educate employees about discrimination and harassment as a strong pillar of taking reasonable care. Various recent studies have shown that diversity trainings are generally effective although they are not without flaws (Antecol & Cobb-clark, 2003; Kalev et al., 2006; Pendry, Driscoll, & Field, 2007; Perry, Kulik, & Schmidtke, 1998). California, Connecticut, and Maine officially require companies to regularly conduct trainings. Trainings are not legally required in Germany although most employees would not know their rights in such cases (European Commission, 2008). The obvious need is not met due to the high costs of conducting such trainings.

The analysis demonstrated that neither Germany nor the United States is alone with its discrimination problems. There is no absolute measure for the scale of the problems so this essay tried to break gender discrimination into smaller parts for a better comparison. Although the different dimensions are fairly similar in both countries, the perception and the initiative differ significantly from each other, which can be explained by different cultural heritages and history.

While discrimination has been a publicly discussed topic in the United States since the Civil Rights Movement, Germany was occupied with the fostering of its economy after World War II and did little to address the issues. Politicians relied on the power of the Basic Law and failed to enact more specific legislations. Although some judicial efforts were made, the German AGG was almost reluctantly introduced 42 years after the Civil Rights Act. The coming years will show how effective this legislation is going to be.

The United States has been a forerunner for antidiscrimination efforts but may have carried it to excess in the view of many Europeans. Following strict policies that include various trainings can be costly for companies and some of the measures discussed earlier seem to be ineffective or even heartless. However, strong actions are required to ameliorate the situation of minorities and women.

While the American approach is certainly more effective in limiting sexual harassment in corporations, it is not necessarily the better one. The idea of generally restraining employees in from following their natural instincts sounds very strange to the German mind. On the other hand, American human resources officers and women rights activists would strongly disagree with the German inactivity. Zippel contrasts both approaches calling the American approach "politics of fear" and the German "politics as usual" finding flaws in both (Zippel, 2006). According to Zippel, the German approach combining sexual and gender harassment with mobbing and moral harassment can prompt U.S. advocates to reexamine their current policies.

Antidiscrimination initiatives in companies should not be enacted simply in order to comply with national laws but with the goal to foster a great place to work which takes into account the needs of all employees. The American concept of reasonable care is a good guideline to examine and monitor daily routines in the office and check if they promote equal employment opportunities for men and women. Supplemented by initiatives like the Girls' Day or better parental leave planning, companies can greatly contribute to better opportunities for women while strengthening their own business.

There are positive signs that gender discrimination is slowly but steadily decreasing in both Germany and the United States. Among all, 74% of Germans state that discrimination based on one's gender was "slightly less widespread" or "far less widespread" in 2008 compared to 2003 (European Commission, 2008). The number of women in top management positions continues to rise, the wage gap decreases slowly in both analyzed countries, and new laws were designed to promote equal opportunities. This development, however, is very sluggish and needs continuous efforts by politicians, corporations, women's rights activists, and unions to become a successful movement.

References

Antecol, H., & Cobb-clark, D. (2003). Does sexual harassment training change attitudes? A view from the federal level. *Social Science Quarterly, 84*, 826–842.

Antidiskriminierungsstelle des Bundes. (2008). *Nutzen und Kosten des Allgemeinen Gleichbehandlungsgesetzes (AGG).* Berlin: Nomos Verlag.

Bertrand, M., & Mullainathan, S. (2003). Are Emily and Greg more employable than Lakisha and Jamal? A field experiment on labor market discrimination. *NBER Working Paper, 9873,* 1–27.

Bundesagentur für Arbeit. (2010). *Der Arbeitsmarkt in Deutschland—Frauen und Männer am Arbeitsmarkt im Jahr 2010.* Nuremberg: Author.

DeNavas-Walt, C., Proctor, B. D., & Smith, J. C. (2010). *Income, poverty, and health insurance coverage in the United States: 2009.* Washington, DC: U.S. Government Printing Office.

Dernbach, A. (2008, August 15). Gleichheit kommt doch nicht teuer. *Der Tagesspiegel.*

Die Zeit. (2011, September 24). Daimler-Chef Zetsche kritisiert Frauenquote. *Die Zeit.*

Equal Employment Opportunity Commission. (2011a). *Charge statistics.* Retrieved from http://eeoc.gov/eeoc/statistics/enforcement/charges.cfm

Equal Employment Opportunity Commission. (2011b). *Sexual harassment.* Retrieved from http://www.eeoc.gov/laws/types/sexual_harassment.cfm

European Commission. (2008). *Discrimination in the European Union: Perceptions, experiences and attitudes.* Directorate General Employment, Social Affairs and Equal Opportunities European Commission.

European Parliament. (2011, July 6). *Women in business: Parliament calls for quotas.* Retrieved from http://www.europarl.europa.eu/news/en/pressroom/content/20110706IPR23412/html/Women-in-business-Parliament-calls-for-quotas

Federal Glass Ceiling Commission. (1995). *A solid investment: Making full use of the nation's human capital.* Washington, DC: U.S. Government Printing Office.

Goldin, C., & Rouse, C. (2000). Orchestrating impartiality: The impact of "blind" auditions on female musicians. *American Economic Review, 90,* 715–741.

Green, J. (2011, June 16). *Women lose out on U.S. boards as Europeans get quota help—Bloomberg.* Retrieved from http://www.bloomberg.com/news/2011–06–16/women-losing-out-on-u-s-boards-as-europe-gets-help-from-quotas.html

Hausmann, R., Tyson, L. D., & Zahidi, S. (2010). *The global gender gap report.* Geneva: World Economic Forum.

Heymann, J., Earle, A., & Hayes, J. (2007). *How does the United States measure up?* Montreal: Institute for Health and Social Policy.

Holst, E., & Wiemer, A. (2010). Frauen in Spitzengremien großer Unternehmen weiterhin massiv unterrepräsentiert. *Wochenbericht des DIW Berlin, 4,* 2–10.

Hoppenstedt. (2010). *Hoppenstedt-Studie "Frauen in Führungspositionen": Frauenanteil im Management steigt weiter—an der Spitze sind Frauen aber weiterhin rar.* Darmstadt: Hoppenstedt Firmeninformationen.

Kaas, L., & Manger, C. (2010). Ethnic discrimination in Germany's labour market: A field experiment. *IZA Discussion Paper Series, 4741,* 1–20.

Kalev, A., Dobbin, F., & Kelly, E. (2006). Best practices or best guesses? Assessing the efficacy of corporate affirmative action and diversity policies. *American Sociological Review, 71,* 589–617.

Körner, T., Puch, K., & Wingerter, C. (2010). *Qualität der Arbeit: Geld verdienen und was sonst noch zählt.* Wiesbaden: Statistisches Bundesamt.

Lindstädt, H. (2011). Frauen in Führungspositionen—Status quo in Deutschland und Europa. *Forum "Frauen in Führung" des BMAS.* Cologne.

Merriam-Webster Online Dictionary. (2011). Retrieved from http://www.merriam-webster.com/dictionary/weltanschauung

Paludi, C., Paludi, M. A., Strauss, S., Coen, P., Fuda, M., & Gerber, T. (2011). Exercising "reasonable care": Policies, procedures, and training programs. In M. A. Paludi, J. Carmen, A. Paludi, & E. R. DeSouza (Eds.), *Understanding and preventing workplace discrimination: Legal, management, and social science perspectives* (pp. 276–283). Westport, CT: Praeger.

Pendry, L. F., Driscoll, D. M., & Field, S. C. (2007). Diversity training: Putting theory into practice. *Journal of Occupational and Organizational Psychology, 80,* 27–50.

Perry, E. L., Kulik, C. T., & Schmidtke, J. M. (1998). Individual differences in the effectiveness of sexual harassment awareness training. *Journal of Applied Social Psychology, 28,* 698–723.

Pincus, F. L. (2003). *Reverse discrimination: Dismantling the myth.* Boulder, CO: Lynne Rienner.

Pöll, R. (2008, October 1). EU: Widerstand gegen gleiche Rechte. *Die Presse.*

Regents of the University of California v. Bakke, 438 U.S. 265 (1978).

Riedel, D. (2010, March 16). Frauenquote? Deutsche Unternehmen winken ab. *Handelsblatt.*

Rühl, W., Viethen, H. P., & Schmid, M. (2007). *Allgemeines Gleichbehandlungsgesetz.* Munich: Beck.

Sachverständigenkommission. (2011). *Neue Wege—Gleiche Chancen—Gleichstellung von Männern und Frauen im Lebensverlauf—Erster Gleichstellungsbericht.* Berlin: Bundesministerium für Familie, Senioren, Frauen und Jugend.

Schein, V. E. (2007). Women in management: Reflections and projections. *Women in Management Review, 22,* 6–18.

Schöbel, S. (2011, June 16). *Studie zu anonymisierten Bewerbungen—Karrierebremse Personalbüro.* Retrieved from http://www.n-tv.de/ratgeber/Karrierebremse-Personalbuero-article3595266.html

Schumm-Garling, U. (2005). Frauenbild im Wandel der Zeit. *Bezirkskonferenz der DGB-Frauen in Magdeburg.* Magdeburg: Deutscher Gewerkschaftsbund.

Semyonov, M., & Lewin-Epstein, N. (2009). The declining racial earnings' gap in United States: Multi-level analysis of males' earnings, 1960–2000. *Social Science Research, 38,* 296–311.

Sherril, A. (2010). *Women in management: Female managers' representation, characteristics, and pay.* Washington, DC: U.S. Government Accountability Office.

Sorge, N. -V. (2011, July 5). Wo Frauen (fast) nichts zu sagen haben. *Manager Magazin.*

United Nations Development Program. (2011). *Human development report 2011.* New York: Palgrave Macmillan.

Unzueta, M. M., Lowery, B. S., & Knowles, E. D. (2008). How believing in affirmative action quotas protects white men's self-esteem. *Organizational Behavior and Human Decision Processes, 205,* 1–13.

USA Today. (2005, May 20). *Gallup poll results.* Retrieved from http://www.usa today.com/news/polls/tables/live/0623.htm

Welt am Sonntag. (2011, July 30). Deutsche sind für Frauenförderung per Gesetz. *Welt am Sonntag.*

Zippel, K. S. (2006). *The politics of sexual harassment: A comparative study of the United States, the European Union, and Germany.* Cambridge: Cambridge University Press.

Appendix 1

Human Resource Audit Checklist: Women Managers and Leaders

Michele A. Paludi

A human resource audit outlines (1) vulnerability in the organization for women managers and leaders and (2) changes that need to be made in the organization, so any discriminatory practices may be corrected. Sample audit questions are provided below for several human resource management functions in an organization.

General

Does the organization examine practices to ensure that women and men have equal opportunity for advancement?

Does the organization examine practices to ensure that white women and women of color have equal opportunity for advancement?

Is there an orientation program for all new women managers and leaders?

Is there an orientation program for women employees who are promoted?

Do you seek feedback from women employees regarding communication in the workplace?

Are the company's actions consistent with its communications to women managers and leaders?

Are the following discussed during orientation programs for women leaders and managers?

Harassment and discrimination

Unemployment insurance

Disability insurance

Safety saws

Copies of Equal Employment Opportunity policies

Does the organization ensure that its recruitment practices reach the widest array of women and women of color for managerial and leadership positions?

Do you give an employee handbook to women leaders and managers?

Do you have a:

Company intranet?

Employee newsletter?

Employee bulletin board?

Employee suggestion box?

Electronic mail system?

Do you have a mentoring program for women leaders and managers?

Have you obtained metrics on the success of the mentoring program for women leaders and managers?

Do you have a mentoring program for leaders and managers who are women of color?

Have you obtained metrics on the success of the mentoring program for leaders and managers who are women of color?

Do you have a networking system for women leaders and managers throughout your organization?

Does your organization understand and respect different career paths taken by women, including women managers and leaders, including time off to care for children and/or aging parents?

Do you provide succession plans that include time off for career interruptions with rewards attached for reentry?

Do you monitor the number of women and men in management and leadership positions in your organization?

Wages and Benefits

Do you conduct salary studies to determine if there is a wage disparity for managers and leaders due to sex? Race?

Do you include the Ledbetter Fair Pay Act as well as the Equal Pay Act in your policies and procedures?

Do you create reward systems based on outcomes and actual performance rather than "face time" at the office?

Do you provide benefits such as tuition reimbursement programs for children of employees and managers?

Does the organization ensure that salaries are based on skill, responsibility, effort, and working conditions?

Expatriate Assignments

Do you have women leaders and managers on expatriate assignments?

Did you offer an extensive pre-departure training program for women that included a unit on gender stereotyping, sexism, sex discrimination, and sexual harassment?

Does your expatriation training include the following?

Child care provisions

Elder care provisions

Job assistance for accompanying mate/spouse

Do you contact women expatriates on a regular basis to determine if they are experiencing sexist treatment in the host country?

Do you have a mentoring/coaching program for women expatriates while they are on assignment?

Do you have a repatriation program for women expatriates?

Do you recruit candidates from a pool of employees who have indicated their interest in an expat assignment?

Do you recruit potential expats from good performers?

Do you include repats in your recruitment process?

Do you use multiple interviewers of potential expats?

Have you rejected certain employees because of their sex, race, or religion? Is this justified?

Personal

Do you meet with all women managers and leaders at least quarterly?

Do you encourage women managers and leaders to walk through the office or facility to visit with employees?

Does upper management know women leaders and managers by their first names?

Policies and Procedures

Do you review periodically with women managers and leaders such key policies as:

Sexual harassment

Nondiscrimination

Workplace bullying

Workplace violence

Equal compensation

Family and medical leave

Parental leave

Do you have the following policies in place and on which women managers and leaders have been trained?

Nondiscrimination

Sexual harassment

Americans with Disabilities

Workplace violence

Intimate partner violence as a workplace concern

Equal compensation

Health and safety

Smoking

Alcohol/drug

Bullying

Hazing

HIV/AIDS

Family and medical leave

Parental leave

Do you have signed acknowledgment forms from women managers and leaders who have received policies?

Do you have procedures for assisting women with intimate partner violence that spills over into the workplace?

Work/Life Integration Policies and Procedures

Do you have flexible work policies? For example:

Telecommuting

Desk sharing

Job sharing

Time off/career break

Compressed work week

Family and medical leave

Parental leave

On-site child care

Do you have the human resource department trained on these work/life integration policies?

Are women managers and leaders who use work/life integration policies valued? Are they treated respectfully? Are they provided with periodic updates about the organization?

Do you ensure women managers and leaders (as well as women employees) may breast-feed or pump breast milk when they return from parental leave?

Do you have a support group for women managers and leaders, that is, an organization-backed group dedicated to the advancement of women?

Do you ensure women managers and leaders are not penalized and/or retaliated against for using work/life integration policies?

Do you use metrics to determine the success of the work/life integration programs?

Training

Do you facilitate training programs on:

Nondiscrimination

Sexual harassment

Americans with Disabilities

Workplace violence

Intimate partner violence as a workplace concern

Health and safety

Smoking

Alcohol/drug

Bullying

Hazing

HIV/AIDS

Do you have signed acknowledgment forms from women leaders and managers who have been trained on:

Nondiscrimination

Sexual harassment

Americans with Disabilities

Workplace violence

Intimate partner violence as a workplace concern

Health and safety

Smoking

Alcohol/drug

Bullying

Hazing

HIV/AIDS

Complaints

Do you provide an avenue of complaint for women managers and leaders who believe they have experienced:

Discrimination

Harassment

Sexual harassment

Do you have records kept based on investigations of complaints that meet the necessary compliance?

Is confidentiality maintained during investigations?

Is retaliation prohibited for being a party to a complaint?

Generational Differences

Do you conduct regular training programs on intergenerational differences and potential conflicts?

Do you conduct anonymous surveys and focus groups to determine the needs of women managers and leaders from different generations (veterans, baby boomers, Gen X, millennials)?

Additional Considerations

Word-of-mouth recruitment through the organization's current employees replicates the composition of the existing workforce. Do you use a variety of recruitment resources that are targeted at diverse applicant pools?

Has your organization established effective, objective criteria for evaluating job candidates?

Have you established criteria for evaluating employees' performance that are reliable, valid, and free from bias?

Do you learn what employees from different national origins expect from managers, performance appraisals, decision making, implementing change, and building working relationships?

About the Editor and Contributors

Editor

Michele A. Paludi was the Elihu Root Peace Fund Visiting Professor of Women's Studies at Hamilton College for 2011–2012. Dr. Paludi is the author/editor of 46 college textbooks and more than 180 scholarly articles and conference presentations on sexual harassment, campus violence, psychology of women, gender, and workplace violence. Her book, *Ivory Power: Sexual Harassment on Campus* (1990, SUNY Press), received the 1992 Myers Center Award for Outstanding Book on Human Rights in the United States. Dr. Paludi served as chair of the U.S. Department of Education's Subpanel on the Prevention of Violence, Sexual Harassment, and Alcohol and Other Drug Problems in Higher Education. She was one of six scholars in the United States to be selected for this subpanel. She was also a consultant to and a member of former New York State Governor Mario Cuomo's Task Force on Sexual Harassment. In addition, Dr. Paludi has held faculty positions at Franklin & Marshall College, Kent State University, Hunter College, Union College and Union Graduate College, where she has directed graduate certificate programs in human resource management and leadership and management. She has taught in the School of Management, Union Graduate College.

Contributors

Sophie Alkhaled-Studholme is a Syrian British researcher. She is currently completing her PhD in management studies at the University of Aberdeen. Her interdisciplinary research interests are feminism, patriarchy, and women in the Middle East. Her doctoral research explores female entrepreneurship and gender identity negotiation in Saudi Arabia. Alkhaled-Studholme has presented her work at the British Sociological Association Annual Conference and the British Federation for Women Graduates' PhD research presentations day.

Patti J. Berg is a PhD student within the University of South Dakota educational psychology program. She serves as assistant professor in the University of South Dakota School of Health Sciences. Ms. Berg has been recognized by the American Physical Therapy Association as a neurologic clinical specialist, and her interest areas include neurology, infant and child development, memory, and motivational attributes.

Meredith Harper Bonham, EdM, is the Senior Associate Dean of Students for Strategic Initiatives at Hamilton College. She is a part-time PhD student in the Syracuse University Graduate School of Education, with a research focus on the intersection of gender and academic leadership. For 12 years, she served in the president's office at Hamilton, most recently as chief of staff and secretary to the board of trustees under President Joan Hinde Stewart. Prior to her time in the president's office, she held positions as assistant dean of admission and then as associate director of annual giving in the development office. She obtained her BA cum laude with high honors in history from Kenyon College, and her EdM in administration, planning, and social policy from Harvard University's Graduate School of Education. As part of her extensive committee service at Hamilton, she managed all senior-level searches while in the president's office and is co-chair of the college's bicentennial celebration. She has participated in several external Middle States Reaccreditation teams and chaired the 2010 Board Professionals workshop for the Association of Governing Boards. Actively involved in her local community, she currently serves as vice president of the board for the YWCA of the Mohawk Valley.

Karen Dill Bowerman is dean emeritus of the College of Business and Public Administration at California State University (CSU), San Bernardino, having served in the CSU system for 32 years. Under her leadership, the college was named one of the top 18 in the world for innovation by *European CEO Magazine,* in part because of creativity of international study both in the classroom and abroad and applied learning by working in conjunction with businesses, especially in the MBA program. She has taught leadership to professionals in the United States and Asia, with scholarly work in fields of strategic management, human resources, organizational theory, and leadership. Before earning the doctorate in administration at Texas A&M University, she led organizations in business and in state government. She blogs on "Leadership and Politics" and provides consulting services through her site at www.karenbowerman.com.

Ödül Bozkurt is senior lecturer at the University of Sussex, Department of Business and Management. She received her PhD in sociology, from the University of California, Los Angeles. Her main research interests are the organization and experience of work inside multinational corporations, and the role multinational corporations play in perpetuating and/or transforming national employment practices. She has carried out fieldwork on related topics in Japan, Turkey, Sweden, Finland, and the United States. Her research has been published in edited volumes and in journals including *Gender Work and Organization, International Journal of Human Resource Management, International Journal of Management Reviews, Human Resource Management Journal,* and *Society.*

Jessica B. Brodsky is a doctoral student in the School-Clinical Child Psychology graduate program at Pace University. Jessica graduated with a bachelor of arts in psychology and a markets and management certificate from Duke University in 2005. After receiving her BA, Jessica worked in marketing and promotions for 3 years before deciding to continue on her studies in psychology. She volunteered on Project RAP (Real Adolescent Perspectives) at the New York University Center for Research on Culture, Development, and Education, assisting in various phases of the research process. Brodsky later worked as an instructional aide in a first-grade mainstreamed classroom in Long Island, New York. She currently serves as a graduate assistant for Dr. Florence Denmark and is a member of Psi Chi and the American Psychological Association.

John Burgess is professor at the University of Newcastle, New South Wales, where he is the coordinator of the Work and Organisation Group in the Centre for Institutional and Organisational Studies. He has published extensively with Glenda Strachan in the areas of EEO in Australia, and women and work. His current research includes HR practices of multinational corporations, workplace change in call centers, and public policy and industry cluster development. Recent books include *Industrial Relations in Australia* (with Richard Sappey, Michael Lyons, and Jeremy Buultjens); *New Employment Actors: The Case of Australia* (with Grant Michelson and Susanne Jamieson); *International Perspectives on Temporary Agency Work* (with Julia Connell); and *Managing Diversity in Australia: Theory and Practice* (with Glenda Strachan and Erica French).

Breena E. Coates, PhD, has been chair of the Department of Management, College of Business and Public Administration, California State University, San Bernadino. She has been a professor strategic management, planning, and organizational behavior in the Department of Command, Leadership, and Management at the U.S. Army War College. Dr. Coates has also served as interim associate dean and divisional chairperson at San Diego State University. Her research includes market controls on corporate social responsibility, women in the military, culture and cognition in a complex mega organization, and an understanding of stress on social systems in dynamic organizational environment. Dr. Coates's current teaching interests include organizational behavior, strategic management, planning and leadership, and the impact of public management, policy, and law on organizations. In 2009 she received the Commandant's Award for Outstanding Teaching and Service, U.S. Army War College. She also received the Outstanding Professor Award from San Diego State University's Imperial Valley Campus in 2005.

Jo Coldwell is associate professor and associate head of school (teaching and learning) in the School of Information Technology at Deakin University. Before becoming an academic Coldwell had extensive industrial experience in the United Kingdom and Australia as a programmer, business analyst, and project leader. Her teaching revolves around foundation skills in IT and professional practice. Coldwell's research expertise is in e-learning in general but focuses on the use of educational technologies to support, and the impact of them on, learning and teaching. Coldwell also has an interest in factors that impact on, and developing strategies to support, students-at-risk; and exploring the gender imbalance in the IT sector and developing, implementing, and evaluating strategies to encourage females to participate in IT education and training.

Annemieke Craig is associate professor and associate head (international) of the School of Information Systems in the Faculty of Business and Law, Deakin University. Craig researches in the field of Information Systems with particular emphasis on trying to increase the involvement and representation of women in the computing professions. Craig has contributed to building the Women in Computing community that focuses on the attraction, retention, and progression of women in the field of ICT, nationally and internationally. She established VicWic and was a founding board member of AWISE. She has been co-chair of the Australian Women in Computing Conference in 2006 and 2009 as well as on the program or organizing committee of at least three other Aus Wit conferences. On an international scale Craig is currently a council member of ACM-W, was the first Australian ambassador for the ACM's Committee for Women from 2000 to 2004. She then led this program involving ambassadors in nine countries from 2005 to 2009. She has chaired the Global Advisory Committee for the past two Grace Hopper Conferences (2009 and 2010) as well as organized international panels at three Grace Hopper Conferences. Craig has published and presented numerous articles in leading journals and conferences on her research activities related to gender and ICT. She is a chief investigator in the ARC-funded research project Digital Divas.

Sara Deitrick completed her BS in hospitality and tourism management from Virginia Tech in 2003. After that, she worked in the hotel industry in Washington, D.C., and New York City before attending the University of Texas at Tyler to work on her MS in clinical psychology, specializing in neuropsychology. Currently, she works as a research assistant investigating literacy issues in local middle schools, and also as a psychometrist for a local psychological private practice where she assesses both children and adults with cognitive, emotional, and/or behavioral concerns. She plans on pursuing her PhD in clinical psychology, with research interests related to neuroplasticity and recovery of function following a brain injury.

Florence L. Denmark is an internationally recognized scholar, researcher, and policy maker. She received her PhD from the University of Pennsylvania in social psychology and has five honorary degrees. Denmark is the Robert Scott Pace Distinguished Research Professor of Psychology at Pace University in New York. A past president of the American Psychological Association (APA) and the International Council of Psychologists (ICP), Denmark holds fellowship status in the APA and the Association for Psychological Science. She is also a member of the Society for Experimental Social Psychology and a Fellow of the New York Academy of Sciences. She has received numerous national and international awards for her contributions to psychology. She received the 2004 American Psychological Foundation Gold Medal for Lifetime Achievement for Psychology in the Public Interest. In 2005, she received the Ernest R. Hilgard Award for her Career Contribution to General Psychology. She is the recipient in 2007 of the Raymond Fowler Award for Outstanding Service to APA. Also in 2007, Denmark was elected to the National Academies of Practice as a distinguished scholar member. She received the Elder Award at the APA National Multicultural Conference in 2009. Denmark's most significant research and extensive publications have emphasized women's leadership and leadership styles, the interaction of status and gender, aging women in cross-cultural perspective, and the history of women in psychology. Denmark is the main nongovernmental organization (NGO) representative to the United Nations for the American Psychological Association and is also the main NGO representative for the International Council of Psychologists. She is currently chair of the New York NGO Committee on Ageing and serves on the Executive Committee of the NGO Committee on Mental Health.

Lukas Droege earned his bachelor of science degree in business engineering from the Karlsruhe Institute of Technology in 2010. After his second academic stay in the United States, he graduated from Union Graduate College with a master of business administration in 2011. He is currently completing his master of science in Karlsruhe and is working for Audi China Strategy in Beijing.

Julie Fisher is professor and associate dean research in the Faculty of Information Technology at Monash University Australia. Fisher has a strong background having been involved with, researched and published in the area of gender and information technology for 20 years. Julie has worked with industry exploring how to address the gender imbalance in IT. She was a member of the inaugural board of the Victorian ICT for Women Network, a government and business initiative. Her research achievements in this area include co-editor of a special issue of the *Journal of Information Systems* focusing on gender, IT and intervention strategies, editor of a special issue on gender and IT published in the *Australasian Journal of Information Systems,* and conference chair for three women and IT conferences run over the last 16 years. A current research project Fisher is the lead chief investigator for is the Digital Divas project where a girls' only elective has been implemented a number of Victorian secondary schools. The project team has designed specific materials to excite girls' interests in IT. Fisher has published in leading information systems journals such as *European Journal of Information Systems* and *Journal of the American Society for Information Science and Technology.*

Erica L. French is associate professor, management, QUT Business School, Queensland University of Technology, and currently researches and teaches in the areas of equity and diversity management, organizational studies, and project management. French has been a consultant in the private and public sectors particularly in the area of equity management. She has also designed and delivered equity management training to management boards and work teams at a variety of organizations in the private, public, and nonprofit sectors. French has published her research on women in management, strategic change, and equal employment opportunity both nationally and internationally in academic journals such as the *British Journal of Management, Women in Management Review, Equal Opportunity International*, and *Transportation Research Part A: Policy and Practice.* French has been the president of the Equal Opportunity Practitioners Association Queensland for 10 years, a nonprofit organization for practitioners, where she has been responsible for developing seminar and conference programs for equity practitioners. She is also a board member and founding member of the Equal Employment Opportunity Network Australasia. She has recently published *Managing Diversity in Australia: Theory and Practice* with Glenda Strachan and John Burgess.

Jeanine M. Galusha is a graduate student in the MS clinical neuropsychology program at the University of Texas at Tyler. Her academic goals include earning a doctorate in psychology and continuing research in dementia. She is a 2010 graduate of the University of Texas at Tyler, where she earned a BS in psychology and graduated magna cum laude. While an undergraduate, she was accepted as a member of Psi Chi, the national honor society in psychology, and worked with several professors on various research projects.

Shanna T. German is a doctoral student in the School-Clinical Child Psychology graduate program at Pace University. Shanna graduated with a bachelor of arts with honors in psychology and a minor in English from the University at Albany. There she was elected and served as vice president of Psi Chi–Albany Chapter. German received her master of arts degree from Yeshiva University in applied psychology and holds a Certificate in Group Therapy from the Eastern Group Psychotherapy Society. After receiving her MA, she worked for 2 years as a research assistant at the New York University, Child Study Center, Department of Child and Adolescent Psychiatry, on an NIMH-funded intervention project working with at-risk pre-kindergarten children and their families. There she coauthored a poster on predictors of parent involvement in school in a culturally diverse sample, as well as a paper symposium on overweight and elementary school functioning among white, African American, Latino, and Asian children in the United States. German currently serves as a graduate assistant to Dr. Florence Denmark.

Katie Halpin graduated summa cum laude from Bentley University in 2008 with a BS in marketing and is expected to graduate from Union Graduate College with her MBA (concentrating in human resources and management) in 2012. Halpin currently works as a human resources generalist for Time Warner Cable's News & Local Programming division. Prior to her experience with Time Warner Cable, Halpin was employed by Harvard University at the Harvard Kennedy School as a human resources coordinator.

Motoko Honda-Howard is lecturer at Showa Women's University, Department of Psychology. She received her PhD in psychology from Japan Women's University. Her research interests include collective deviance, group-individual relationship change, and occupational socialization. She is coauthor of "Mega-holism" (Hankyu Communications, 2010) and "Whistle-Blowing" (Shin-Yo-Sha, 2006). Her research has appeared in journals such as the *Asian Journal of Social Psychology* and the *Japanese Association of Industrial/Organizational Psychology Journal*.

Betty A. Hulse received her master of science degree from the Physician Assistant Studies Program at the University of South Dakota, Vermillion. She is currently an assistant professor and clinical coordinator for the Physician Assistant Studies Program at the University of South Dakota in the School of Health Sciences. She practices as a PA-C part-time at the Keystone Treatment Center in Canton, South Dakota.

Holly Kearl is a leading expert and writer on gender-based street harassment. She is the founder of www.StopStreetHarassment.org and International Anti-Street Harassment Day. In 2010 she authored *Stop Street Harassment: Making Public Places Safe and Welcoming for Women* (Praeger) and since then she has written numerous articles and given more than 40 talks on the topic. Kearl's work has been cited by the United Nations, New York City Council, BBC, CNN, *New York Times, Washington Post, Feministing,* and *Jezebel.* She also works at the American Association of University Women, where she manages programs relating to workplace discrimination, student leadership, and Title IX. She is the coauthor of the AAUW's 2011 report on sexual harassment in grades 7–12. Kearl is a gender reviewer for UN-HABITAT's 2012 Global Reports on Human Settlements, and she serves on the board for Holla Back DC!, an antistreet harassment organization in Washington, D.C.

Janet L. Kottke is a professor of psychology at California State University, San Bernardino (CSUSB), where she founded the master's program in industrial-organizational psychology. Her research interests include diversity, diversity management, measurement, and pedagogy. She has published book chapters, journal articles, and has presented at regional and national conferences. She was named the Outstanding Professor at CSUSB for 2008–2009.

Catherine Lang is associate professor has been researching the underrepresentation of women in IT since 1996 and completed her PhD at the University of Melbourne in 2008. She currently holds an ARC Linkage Grant with colleagues from Monash and Deakin Universities developing and implementing a curriculum initiative for secondary schools called Digital Divas. Her other research interests are student transition to higher education and ICT education pedagogies. Catherine was ACM-W Australian Ambassador from 2005 to 2011 and is active in the Women in Computing community in Australia and internationally.

Miriam Liss is an associate professor of psychology at the University of Mary Washington. She received her PhD in clinical psychology from the University of Connecticut in 2001. Her research on gender issues includes feminist identity, sexualization and objectification, expectations regarding the division of household labor, and ideologies about motherhood. She has also published on psychoanalysis, self-injury, sensory processing sensitivity, and autism.

Paula K. Lundberg-Love is a professor of psychology at the University of Texas at Tyler (UTT) and the Ben R. Fisch Endowed Professor in Humanitarian Affairs for 2001–2004. Her undergraduate degree was in chemistry and she worked as a chemist at a pharmaceutical company for 5 years prior to earning her doctorate in physiological psychology with an emphasis in psychopharmacology. After a 3-year postdoctoral fellowship in nutrition and behavior in the Department of Preventive Medicine at Washington University School of Medicine in St. Louis, she assumed her academic position at UTT, where she teaches classes in psychopharmacology, behavioral neuroscience, physiological psychology, sexual victimization, and family violence. Subsequent to her academic appointment, Dr. Lundberg-Love pursued postgraduate training and is a licensed professional counselor in Texas. She is a member of Tyler Counseling and Assessment Center, where she provides therapeutic services for victims of sexual assault, child sexual abuse, and domestic violence. She has conducted a long-term research study on women who were victims of childhood incestuous abuse, constructed a therapeutic program for their recovery, and documented its effectiveness upon their recovery. She is the author of nearly 100 publications and presentations and is co-editor of *Violence and Sexual Abuse at Home: Current Issues in Spousal Battering and Child Maltreatment, Intimate Violence Against Women: When Spouses, Partners, or Lovers Attack,* and *Women and Mental Disorders.* As a result of her training in psychopharmacology and child maltreatment, her expertise has been sought as a consultant on various death penalty appellate cases in the state of Texas.

Jennifer L. Martin, PhD, is an assistant professor of education at Mount Union University. Prior to working in higher education, Dr. Martin worked in public education for 16 years, 14 of those as the department head of English at an alternative high school for at-risk students. She has served as a mentor to high school, undergraduate, and graduate students, as well as to new teachers in a variety of areas such as writing and publishing, career and leadership development, and advocacy. Dr. Martin is the editor of the two-volume *Women as Leaders in Education* (Praeger, 2011). She has conducted research, published numerous peer-reviewed articles and book chapters on bullying and harassment, peer sexual harassment, educational equity, mentoring, issues of social justice, service-learning, and teaching at-risk students.

Natasha S. Mauthner is a reader at the University of Aberdeen Business School, where she teaches courses on gender, work and organization, as well as research methods. She trained as an undergraduate natural scientist, and postgraduate social scientist, at the University of Cambridge. She then spent a year on a postdoctoral fellowship at Harvard University funded by an International Fellowship from the American Association of University Women, a Fulbright Scholarship, and a Wingate Scholarship. She has held research and lecturing posts at the Universities of Edinburgh and Aberdeen. Her research interests include health and well-being; gender, work and family; and knowledge-making in the academy (including interpretive, collaborative, and data-sharing practices). She has written about the politics of feminist research management in higher education.

Vanessa Meterko earned her master's degree in forensic psychology from John Jay College of Criminal Justice in New York City. In addition to her education in psychology, she has a background in health care research and experience with crisis counseling. Her current research interests include wrongful convictions, bias crime, and subtle discrimination.

Wendy J. Murphy, JD, is an adjunct professor at New England Law/Boston, where she teaches a seminar on sexual violence and directs two projects she developed in conjunction with the school's Center for Law and Social Responsibility. The Sexual Violence Legal News project is an Internet-based alert service that distributes appellate cases of interest, with editorial comment, related to interpersonal violence. The Judicial Language Project uses sociolinguistic research to critique the language used in law and society to describe interpersonal violence. She was a visiting scholar at Harvard Law School from 2002 to 2003, where her work focused on the status of women in their capacity as victims in the criminal justice system. She previously taught "Reproductive Rights and Technologies" at the Massachusetts Institute of Technology and in 2002 served as the Mary Joe Frug Visiting Assistant Professor of Law at New England Law/Boston, where she has taught courses on sexual violence, reproductive rights and technologies, and constitutional criminal procedure.

Murphy is a trial and appellate attorney specializing in the representation of crime victims, women, children, and victim service providers and is the founder and director of the Victim Advocacy and Research Group, a volunteer legal advocacy organization that has provided free legal services to victims and other third parties in the criminal justice system since 1992.

Kevin L. Nadal, PhD, is an associate professor of psychology and mental health counseling at John Jay College of Criminal Justice-City University of

New York, who earned his doctorate in counseling psychology from Columbia University. He has published several works focusing on Filipino American, ethnic minority, and LGBTQ issues in the fields of psychology and education. He is a fellow of the Robert Wood Johnson Foundation and is the author of the books *Filipino American Psychology: A Handbook of Theory, Research, and Clinical Practice* and *Filipino American Psychology: A Collection of Personal Narratives.*

Wesley S. Parks completed a master of science in clinical psychology at the University of Texas in Tyler, with a specialization in neuropsychology. His undergraduate degree also was in psychology. For the past 7 years, he has worked at a private forensic and clinical psychology practice in the Dallas-Fort Worth Metroplex, where he has been involved in wide-ranging, and often high-profile, forensic psychology and legal cases. Prior to that, his career involved product- and service-oriented retail management, corporate training, and consulting. His research interests include effects of exposure to traumatic events, business and organizational psychology, the role of psychology in shaping public policy, outcome assessment, and jury.

Kathie L. Pelletier is an assistant professor in the Department of Management at California State University, San Bernardino. Her publications include the topics of toxic and ethical leadership, organizational corruption, ethics program effectiveness, and women's issues in the workplace. Dr. Pelletier has also held leadership positions for 26 years, in both private and public sectors. She worked with a major freight carrier for 16 years, and has 10 years of leadership experience in county and city government.

Catherine H. Raycroft has been an advocate on behalf of employed women for several years. She has served as president of the Schenectady, New York, chapter of the Business and Professional Women Organization. She also served as the president of the New York State Business and Professional Women's Organization. She served as director of the Human Services Planning Council in Schenectady, New York. She has served on numerous task forces and boards, including the YWCA, Habitat for Humanity, and the League of Women Voters.

Jenny K. Rodriguez is a lecturer in human resource management at Newcastle University Business School in Newcastle upon Tyne. Dr. Rodriguez's research interests include gender and organizations, women in management, public sector management, gender and public policy, and organizational culture and human resource management.

William E. Schweinle received his doctorate in quantitative and social psychology at the University of Texas at Arlington under William Ickes.

He received postdoctoral education in quantitative psychology at the University of Missouri-Columbia. He has studied men's maltreatment of women, including partner abuse and sexual harassment, for 15 years and has published several original articles and book chapters on these subjects. He is currently an assistant professor of biostatistics in the University of South Dakota School of Health Sciences.

Glenda Strachan is professor in the Department of Employment Relations in Griffith Business School, Griffith University Queensland. She has developed a body of research on contemporary and historical workplace change, especially issues that relate to equity and diversity and women's working experiences. She has published extensively with John Burgess and Erica French in the area of equal employment opportunity in journals including the *British Journal of Industrial Relations, Equal Opportunities International, Women in Management Review,* and *Asia Pacific Journal of Human Resources and Managing Diversity in Australia: Theory and Practice.* Her published historical work appears in journals such as *Labour History* and *Continuity and Change* as well as book chapters. Before becoming an academic, she worked with trade unions.

Josephine C. H. Tan is an associate professor with the Department of Psychology, Lakehead University, which is located in Thunder Bay, Ontario, Canada. She is involved with the graduate collaborative Women's Studies program and is a part of the multi-institutional research Centre for Biological Timing and Cognition. She is active in service to the profession, having been elected and served on the council and various committees of the Ontario provincial professional psychology regulatory board, and is the currently the past president of the Canadian Council of Professional Psychology Programs (CCPPP). She received the CCPPP Award of Excellence in Professional Training (Academic) in 2008 for her work and mentoring as the director of clinical training in her program and was elected to fellow status by the American Psychological Association in 2009.

Vivian M. Vargas received her master's degree in forensic psychology from John Jay College of Criminal Justice. Her career goals are to work with juveniles within the criminal justice system. She currently resides in New Jersey and continues to research microaggressions toward various minority groups.

Michelle Wideman attained a master's degree in forensic mental health counseling from John Jay College of Criminal Justice, City University of New York. She currently lives in Virginia and has research interests in microaggressions toward special identity groups.

Index